Race, Empire, and the Crisis of the Subprime

Race, Empire, and the Crisis of the Subprime

Edited by Paula Chakravartty
and Denise Ferreira da Silva

The Johns Hopkins University Press, Baltimore

The Johns Hopkins University Press
2715 North Charles Street
Baltimore, Maryland 21218-4363
www.press.jhu.edu

ISBN 13: 978-1-4214-1001-2
ISBN 10: 1-4214-1001-X

Library of Congress Control Number: 2012949786

A catalog record for this book is available from the British Library.

These articles were originally published in the September 2012 issue of *American Quarterly*.

Front cover: "SL House 2" © Bernard J. Kleina; back cover: "Equality Richville" © Bernard J. Kleina.

Special discounts are available for bulk purchases of this book. For more information, please contact Special Sales at 410-516-6936 or specialsales@press.jhu.edu.

The Johns Hopkins University Press uses environmentally friendly book materials, including recycled text paper that is composed of at least 30 percent post-consumer waste, whenever possible.

Contents

The Postracial Urban: Security, Space, and Resistance

Preface

This special issue, *Race, Empire, and the Crisis of the Subprime*, interjects into the discourse and conditions of an ongoing global economic and racial crisis. That is, it is not a "coda" to the crisis, signaling a conclusion, or a kind of retrospective on the ravages of global and racial capitalism. Neither does it serve to locate the "origins" of what has come to be known as the "subprime crisis." Rather, it is a necessary intervention in the *midst* of crisis, a recognition of the historical legacies that envelop and frame the 2008 global economic crisis, as well as a call to critically acknowledge the varied spaces and homes worldwide that this latest crisis has shaped, destroyed, or irrevocably changed. As such, this special issue is an excellent example of the efforts by American studies scholars, as well as those in other disciplines, to imagine and theorize an "American" studies that is deeply, and inevitably, transnational and transhemispheric. Above all else, it is a reminder that global racial capitalism cannot be understood within the frame of economics alone; rather, it needs to be theorized and imagined as a set of cultural, political, and geographic practices on and within persons and places.

As is clear from the volume of scholarship on the current global economic crisis, including the essays presented in this special issue, there are complex, multilayered, and deeply interrelated reasons for, and effects of, the global economic crisis of 2008. During the years 2007–8, around the world, stock markets fell, large financial institutions collapsed or were bought out, and governments in even the wealthiest nations scrambled to develop rescue packages to bail out their financial systems. The collapse of the U.S. subprime mortgage market and the reversal of the housing boom in other industrialized economies had a ripple effect in other nations. The failure of the national economies of Spain and Greece (to name just two) has had resounding impacts on the European Union (EU) experiencing the disciplinary power of debt. Importantly, however, as the authors in this volume persuasively point out, the current crisis has important precedents in other crises in Africa, Asia, and Latin America in the 1980s and 1990s. Relatedly, and most urgently for the contributors to this volume, the 2008 global crisis was triggered by what the volume's coeditors call "unpayable debts" by "high-risk borrowers," namely (in the United States), black and Latino/a borrowers and communities.

The culture of the current economy has generated a variety of impulses and reactions to the financial crisis of the early twenty-first century: there have been financial responses in the form of government corporate subsidies; subversive challenges to capitalism in terms of alternative lifestyles; ideological proclamations about what capitalism is and should be; recuperative answers that privilege a new, "leaner," global market; and so on.

While there has been a range of reactions, for the most part state responses have not called attention to larger infrastructural failures that contributed to the global economic crisis, such as mortgage fraud, corporate greed, racism, and colonial histories. Rather, the global crisis has often been staged as a sort of "media event," where there are contrived debates between pundits on television, conservative radio hosts on talk radio, and corporate "citizens," who carelessly and dangerously point to what the coeditors of this special issue recognize as the stylized "high-risk borrower," the working class and people of color, who become the literal iteration of the "subprime" as a way to place blame on particular persons while exonerating others, particularly those at the "top of the guilt [profit] hierarchy." Indeed, the 2008 global economic crisis has been skillfully shape-shifted into an *opportunity* for some corporate players, where there are efforts to *brand* the crisis, as a way to frame it as an opportunity for—indeed, a moral obligation of—the *individual* worker to address. In turn, this focus on particular individuals as recuperative players in a global crisis renders invisible the "high-risk borrower" and the ravages of capitalism on racialized communities.

Importantly, the coeditors of this volume pose a different set of questions to both understand the politics of economic crisis and to figure how to situate the current moment historically and transnationally. In their introduction, and throughout each of the eleven essays in the volume, the authors ask: how do we theorize racial/ postcolonial subjugation and economic exploitation in relation to the current financial crisis? This volume insists the "subprime" be read through the "dual lens of race and empire": indeed, as explicit referents to these modernizing practices, but to also delve into the intersections and contradictions within these globalizing historical processes.

Global racial capitalism forged, and was forged by, the nation-state form and its modes of governance. In a time of global crisis, it is surely the case that the nation is more important than ever; fluid economic boundaries and cultural hybridity do not make the nation obsolete, but rather center its importance even more, as the nation mounts its response to threat. It is imperative we measure the flux of the nation as well as how it is stabilized, and the essays in this volume work efficiently to do just that.

As with every issue, this special issue wouldn't be possible without the tireless energies of the *AQ* managing editor, Jih-Fei Cheng. He has greatly assisted not only in the timely production of the volume but also in gathering media materials for the print edition and accompanying webpage for special issues, "Beyond the Page" (found on the *AQ* website, americanquarterly.org). We were also fortunate to have the help of two volunteer editorial assistants each semester provided by the M.A. program in American Studies at the California State University, Fullerton. In the past few years, they have included Jamal Batts, Keith G. Kottenbach, Patrick Covert, Monica Duboski, Yvonne L. England, Melissa Hoon, Nathan Kuntz, John Carlos Marquez, Joseph B. Meyer, Casey Ratto, Marley Rosner, Diann Rozsa, George Gregory Rozsa, Rahima Schwenkbeck, Corrigan Vaughan, and Jason Ward. Paula Dragosh, the copy editor for *AQ*, remained patient and attentive throughout, even when pressed for time. Our gratitude also goes to Kristopher Zgorski and Brian Shea at the Johns Hopkins University Press for the time and care they have invested in the production of the journal issue and the management of our website. We appreciate greatly the support of others at the Press, including Suzanne Flinchbaugh, Greg Nicholl, Michele Callaghan, and the interns who helped transition this issue into its book form.

Sarah Banet-Weiser
Editor
American Quarterly

Race, Empire, and the Crisis of the Subprime

Accumulation, Dispossession, and Debt: The Racial Logic of Global Capitalism—An Introduction

Paula Chakravartty and Denise Ferreira da Silva

I could feel the knife in my hand, still slippery with perspiration. A Slave was a slave. Anything could be done to her. And Rufus was Rufus—erratic, alternately generous and vicious. I could accept him as my ancestor, my younger brother, my friend, but not as my master, and not as my lover . . .

. . .

I pulled the knife free of him somehow, raised it, and brought it down again into his back.

This time he only grunted. He collapsed across me, somehow still alive, still holding my arm.

. . .

Something harder and stronger than Rufus's hand clamped down on my arm, squeezing it, stiffening it, pressing into it—painlessly, at first—melting into it, meshing with it as though somehow my arm were being absorbed into something. Something cold and nonliving.

Something . . . paint, plaster, wood—a wall. The wall of my living room. I was back home—in my own house, in my own time. But I was still caught somehow, joined to the wall as though my arm were growing out of it—or growing into it. . . . I looked at the spot where flesh joined with plaster, stared at it uncomprehending. I was the exact spot Rufus's finger had grasped.

I pulled my arm toward me, pulled hard.

And suddenly, there was an avalanche of pain, red impossible agony! And I screamed and screamed.

—Octavia Butler, *Kindred*

Houses are unsettling hybrid structures. A house is, in all its figurings, always *thing*, *domain*, and *meaning*—home, dwelling, and *property*; shelter, lodging, and *equity*; roof, protection, and *aspiration*—*oikos*, that is, house, household, and home. A house is a juridical-economic-moral entity that, as *property*, has material (as asset), political (as dominium), and symbolic (as shelter) value. Houses, as such, refer to the three main axes of modern thought: the economic, the juridical, and the ethical, which are, as one would expect, the registers of the modern subject. It is, in fact, impossible to exaggerate the significance of individual (private) property in representations of modernity.[1] No wonder, in *Kindred*, Octavia Butler chose to signal the end of Dana's incomprehensible task—her travels to antebellum Maryland to save her white ancestor, Rufus, whenever his life was in danger—with her losing part of her arm (at the "exact spot Rufus's fingers had grasped") stuck in the wall of her house. A "red impossible agony" marked the end of her forced journeys, reminding Dana that whenever summoned by Rufus she could either kill him or let him die. Since her charge was to keep him alive, the only choice she ever had was never hers to make. Having made the choice, she finally realized that, as his descendant, she had a *debt* to Rufus, expressed as the *obligation* to keep him alive. Failing to meet this obligation, killing him or letting him die, tantamount to refusing the *debt*, and with it the *relationship*, as it did, would result in punishment of the worst kind for Dana.

Failing to pay a mortgage, the notorious subprime loan, charged interest rates far in excess of those offered to "prime borrowers," "high-risk borrowers," like Dana, also owe a *debt* that exceeds the legitimacy of both the law (contract) and morality (obligation). References to law and morality, expectedly, prevail in condemnations of those served with "subprime" loans, who are construed as intellectually (illiterate) and morally (greedy) unfit if measured against any existing descriptors of the modern economic subject: the (liberal) rational self-interested, the (historical-materialist) productive-creative laborer, and the (neoliberal) obligation-bound debtor/creditor. The "immanent risk of foreclosure" and ultimately loss of home for millions in the United States overwhelmingly affected Black and Latino/a borrowers and communities. Lacking property and stocks passed down through generations and burdened by greater reliance on consumer credit, Black and Latino/a borrowers were less able to weather the sudden decline in home values.[2] Foregrounding their predicament, the incomprehensible task of affording the consequences of not-paying what the lenders knew were unpayable debts allows questions that challenge the assumption that the failure to meet an obligation should necessarily lead to punishment when the lender's profits are secured by betting and spreading the risk globally, *against* the "high-risk" borrower.[3]

In considering the unpayable debts as a trigger for the current financial crisis, this special issue highlights the racial and colonial logic of global capitalism. Since the late 1980s and early 1990s, Ulrich Beck, Anthony Giddens, Roland Robertson, and other early theorists of globalization have called attention to the significance of risk.[4] Few of these scholars, however, anticipated that racial/cultural difference, as an element of representation, would enter into risk calculations in the ways it did during the boom phase of the housing market. Moreover, subsequent research on the "circulation of risk," shifting the analytic focus away from the postindustrial North, revealed that "unregulated flows of capital are engendering a turbulence that is undermining the lives of even peoples who inhabit territories incomparably distant and different from the landscapes of metropolitan capital."[5] Nor did this scholarship anticipate that the state—the nation-state most theorists saw disappearing, engulfed by a global political entity to come—would play such a pivotal role in creating the institutional conditions to test these risk calculations.

Given the public outrage against the unjust "socialization of loss" extracted by investment banks, it is difficult to see the bailout of Wall Street as anything other than a massive debt forgiveness scheme for those at the "top of the guilt [profit] hierarchy" for the current crisis.[6] Why then should the holders of the "subprime mortgage" pay the exorbitant interest rates attached to their loans? Why should the economically dispossessed be expected to take on the risk assumed by those who, enabled by the privatization of public housing and the deregulation of financial markets, bet against them? Why should they pay for those who bet on the "truth" of prevailing constructions of Blacks' and Latino/as' racial (moral and intellectual) traits, on the certainty that they lack in "creditworthiness" and are "untrustworthy" debtors? Questioning and challenging the moral grammar of neoliberal debt management can be traced back to civil disobedience and calls for a "debt jubilee" for structurally adjusted Africa a decade before the current crisis, and were foreshadowed in Argentina's unprecedented sovereign default in 2001 paving the way for the "unthinkable" possible exit of Greece from the eurozone in 2012.[7] "Millennial capitalism," where wealth is generated "purely through exchange . . . as if entirely independent of human manufacture," has unleashed debtors' revolts in many forms.[8] In the global South, the last three decades have seen an upsurge of what the anthropologist Janet Roitman has called "fiscal disobedience," from food and price riots, tax revolts, boycotts, farmer suicides and protests, organized and spontaneous opposition to high-interest microfinance loans—which set powerful precedents for the kinds of anti-austerity uprisings and movements that we see in Europe and North America today.[9] This special issue reads the subprime crisis as a "relative" of crises that transformed the political economic horizons of Africa, Asia, and Latin America in the 1980s and 1990s. We hope to highlight these resonances approximating national and global responses to the logic of neoliberalism to profit from calculated "mistakes" (like lending money to persons and nations precisely because they would *not* be able to pay it back) and read the subprime crisis through a dual lens of race and empire.

American studies as a field has housed scholars interested in the relationship between the architectures of U.S. Empire and the apparatuses of social (racial-ethnic, class, and gender-sexual) subjugation.[10] The global financial crisis cannot but compel us to further this exploration. In putting together this special issue, we posed the following question: How could the predatory targeting of economically dispossessed communities and the subsequent bailout of the nation's largest investment banks, instantly and volubly, be recast as a problem *caused* by the racial other ("illegal immigrants" and "state-dependent minorities")?[11] Beyond the immediate politics of blame, our interest is in situating the *racial* moment of the financial crisis in the last three decades of neoliberal backlash waged across the *postcolonial* (global) South. As a starting point for our discussion we assume that these recent histories are themselves embedded in the colonial and racial matrix of capitalist accumulation of land (conquest and settlement), exploitation of labor (slavery, indentured labor, forced migration), appropriation of resources, and ultimately the very meaning of debt in what Walter Mignolo calls the "modern/colonial world system."[12]

We begin to frame an answer to our question by considering how this unpayable debt marks the particular operation of postcolonial/racial subjugation, one that shows how the state continues to play a crucial role ensuring the health of global capitalism. In this sense, we argue that the term *subprime mortgage* has become a racial signifier in the current debate about the causes and fixes for a capitalism in crisis. Here, our argument resonates with Ananya Roy's compelling point that microfinance loans "targeting" poor women in remote villages and urban peripheries are the "new subprime frontier of millennial capitalism." As with high-risk mortgages, these are "instruments of financial inclusion and instances of exploitative, even predatory, lending." For Roy, the contradictory premise is that the "subprime marks the limits of the democratization of capital," in this case the tenuous promise of a "pro-market pro-poor" fix to the problem of unequal neoliberal development.[13] Similarly, we read the "subprime" as a racial/postcolonial, moral and economic referent, which resolves past and present modalities and moments of economic expropriation into *natural* attributes of the "others of Europe." With this, we seek to dissolve the subprime signifier of 2008 as the latest in a succession of historic processes of what David Harvey identifies as "accumulation by dispossession."[14]

Naming the global crisis the "subprime crisis," the dominant voices across the U.S. media did more than merely reproduce the conservative mantra that blames Blacks and Latino/a immigrants for all the evils that befall the nation. In the remainder of the introduction, we highlight how the subprime crisis facilitated this exacting of profits from *places* and *persons* produced as unsuitable economic subjects. We do so by shifting the focus on to how conquest and slavery, along with the postcolonial apparatus of raciality, produce places and persons marked by a debt that—like Dana's to her slave-owner ancestor—cannot be settled even with death.

In the next section, we foreground a racial/postcolonial analysis of the crisis in relation to a brief overview of the works of two critical scholars: David Harvey and David Graeber. Framing the discussion of the subprime crisis in terms of how it represents a moment of racial/colonial—that is, postcolonial—subjugation characteristic of a new configuration of the state/empire and market axis, the second section of the introduction provides a historical overview of the current moment of crisis. In the final section, we show how the essays assembled in the special issue interrogate the "official story" of the crisis across three interrelated dimensions. The first set of essays locates the current moment of crisis both temporally and spatially, drawing connections to previous moments of debt, austerity, and resistance in response to U.S.-led neoliberal transformations both at "home" and abroad. Reading literary and media texts, the second set of essays targets more directly the political-symbolic (discursive, ideological, and cultural) realms, and describes how the naming of the crisis "subprime" refigures old and new mechanisms of writing of the racial subaltern as *naturally* (morally and intellectually) unable to thrive in the modern capitalist configurations built by Europeans and their descendants everywhere. Finally, the third set of essays focuses on how economically dispossessed Blacks and Latino/as, living in urban United States, now exist in a racial architecture in which postracial discourse and neoliberal practices combine to exact even more profit from the very penury resulting from the expropriation unleashed in previous moments and modalities of racial and colonial subjugation.

Dispossession and Debt: The Racial Logic of Global Financial Capitalism

In his account of the global financial crisis, *The Enigma of Capital,* David Harvey recalls that the early wave of foreclosures did not cause much alarm because "the people affected were low income, mainly African American and immigrant (Hispanics) or women single-headed households."[15] Panic began to spread when foreclosures hit "white middle-class" households in 2007, and it was only in September 2008 when Lehman Brothers declared bankruptcy that the crisis became official, its demise caused by "the mountain of 'toxic' mortgage-backed securities held by banks or marketed to unsuspecting investors all around the world. Everyone had acted as if property prices could rise forever."[16] Many of the essays assembled in this special issue draw from Harvey's generative concept of "accumulation by dispossession" to describe the workings of contemporary U.S. capitalist empire. Here we are engaging with Harvey's arguments because of its significance in current critiques of race and empire. However, when designing this introduction, and considering the contributions as a unified intervention in both American studies and critical racial and ethnic studies, we were left with a question: if, as scholars in these fields recognize, colonial, racial and imperial modalities of power include very efficient mechanisms of expropriation (of land, resources, and labor) what is left to be dispossessed in this new moment of (accumulation by) dispossession? How is it that they are rendered expropriatable anew?

In *The New Imperialism* Harvey provides a gripping analysis of the world after 9/11, where the combined wars in Afghanistan and Iraq, he argues, mark a new phase of U.S. imperial domination. For Harvey, "accumulation by dispossession" describes this new imperial moment, where primitive accumulation (forced extraction and privatization of the commons) has become a more dominant feature of neoliberal globalization as opposed to expanded reproduction (economic growth where workers are incorporated as consumers). He argues that in addition to the "appropriation and cooptation of pre-existing cultural and social achievements as well as confrontation of supersession,"[17] "primitive accumulation" and its new guise "accumulation by dispossession" are contingent on the (state-sanctioned) use of force with the effect of reconstituting the power of global elites against the diminished capacity of organized labor worldwide. Drawing on Hannah Arendt's liberal critique of imperialism, Harvey argues that the very constitution of neoliberal globalization can be seen as a process of acquisition of "new territories"—either through national or regional financial crises. Explaining the current crisis in *The Enigma of Capital*, Harvey points to the squeezing of variable capital (wages) for the vast majority of U.S. workers: "Household debt skyrocketed, but this required that financial institutions both support and promote the debts of working people whose earnings were not increasing. This started with the steadily employed population. [By the late 1990s, the] market had to be extended to those with lower incomes. . . . Financial institutions, awash with credit, began to debt-finance people who had no steady income."[18] Returning once again to Dana's predicament, the essays in this issue ask the question that Harvey does not even consider, one that he also seems to see as already asked and answered by the subprime mortgages themselves and their securitization, which is: what is it about blackness and Latinidad that turns one's house (roof, protection, and aspiration) and shelter into a death trap?

A brief discussion of the anarchist anthropologist David Graeber's alternative history, *Debt: The First 5,000 Years*, can unpack this question. In this much-lauded book, Graeber offers an alternative account of economic history, returning exchange to the core of the critique of capitalism.[19] Having a historical trajectory that precedes the advent of money, he argues that three "modalities of behavior" have existed to different degrees in all societies across time: communism, exchange, and hierarchy. In Graeber's reading, Blacks and Latino/as might have been so "naturally" blamed for the crisis because of their unrootedness, by the fact that as racial subalterns they are but strangers. Regarding prevailing accounts of human collectives and human relationships, Graeber's argument extends familiar accounts of human relationships—including Robert E. Park's definition of "race relations" as the kind that develop between strangers.[20] What he does add to these discussions is an argument that ties violence and monetization; only with the advent of money do all earlier forms of obligation become quantifiably precise debt. Graeber's argument is relevant here because this assemblage of essays and Graeber's book have something to contribute to one another. That something seems crucial to the subprime enigma. For the colonial, following his logic, marks Blacks and Latino/as as unrooted—they exist in an impersonal social context from which they originate and from which their very presence produces. Instead of taking this fact for granted, we see the authors in our volume engaging the following question: How could anyone expect to profit from unpayable loans *without* debtors who were already marked by their racial/cultural difference ensuring that at least some among them would not be able to pay? This is precisely what makes "high-risk" securities profitable. The Black and Latino/a holders of subprime loans, like Dana, owe incomprehensible and unpayable monetary debts precisely because they are not constructed as referents of either the *relationship* between persons presumed in commerce (which Graeber states precedes all other economic circumstances) or the *capacity* that according to Karl Marx ultimately determines their value of exchange (the productivity which John Locke, David Ricardo, and Marx agreed elevated the human thing). Here raciality, the onto-epistemological toolbox that has transmutated the spatial "others of Europe" into historical "others of whiteness," seizes and undermines any possible *relationship* by establishing that the white/European alone is superior because he alone knows transcendentality.[21] Raciality, as it places the "others of Europe" before the horizon of death,[22] disappears with the very possibility of a relationship that would make a debt/credit situation comprehensible and hence the debt something that could be eventually paid precisely because of how it makes the colonial (African and Indigenous) other and their descendants as lacking the moral attributes (self-determination, self-transparency, and self-productivity) characteristic of persons and places (the ones they originate from) that truly embody the traits that distinguish the proper economic subject.[23]

What we suggest is missing in the preceding discussions of accumulation/dispossession and debt is the consideration of how these "new territories" of consumption and investment have been mapped onto previous racial and colonial (imperial) discourses and practices. If we go back to C. L. R. James's *Black Jacobins,* Cedric Robinson's *Black Marxism*, and Frantz Fanon's *The Wretched of the Earth,* to name only three classic anticolonial, racial, and global interrogations of historical materialism, we are reminded of how historical materialism alone cannot account for the ways in which capitalism has lived off—always backed by the colonial and national state's means of death—of colonial/racial expropriation.[24] As Manu Goswami writes in her critique of *both* historical materialism and the "excision" of "socioeconomic coordinates from colonialism" in postmodern theory, we must look at the "tangled causal relationships" of the lived experiences of the colonial space and the "expansive logic of capital."[25] Contesting the "evolutionary assumptions" that guide Harvey's theories ("Flexible accumulation follows Fordist production as barbarism follows savagery"), Anna Tsing proposes instead the notion of "spectacular accumulation," which "occurs when investors speculate on a product that may or not exist."[26] This could mean biotechnology or real estate, but her point is that it could also take us back to the "South Sea bubble and every gold rush in history."[27] Returning to how the subprime crisis allows us to highlight links otherwise missed by prevailing accounts of racial subjugation, we draw on Roy's argument that microfinance (subprime) loans targeting poor women in the global South are part of a "frontier of empire." Roy traces the travel of microfinance mediated by a "kinder and gentler World Bank" from Bangladesh to Afghanistan and throughout the Middle East: "As microfinance is a preferred weapon of mass salvation, so the Middle East is the site at which the war on terror and the war on poverty are conjoined."[28] This evokes a kind of space of death Achille Mbembe describes as distinctive of the postcolony.[29] In short, the essays in this issue add to the library of postcolonial and critical racial theories of the state that establish how neoliberal architectures and discourses of dispossession act on earlier forms of racial and colonial subjugation.

Building on this challenge, we come back to the question of how to theorize racial/ postcolonial subjugation and economic exploitation in the context of the current financial crisis.[30] The concept of differential inclusion seeks to attend to the degrees in which the various racial subaltern collectives enter into the U.S. racial configuration,[31] but cannot help explain why Blacks and Latino/as figure as highly profitable as aberrant economic subjects in the very articulation of postracial claims of achieved equality. Race in the *naturalized* ways U.S. Americans deploy the term cannot be the privileged and sole critical descriptor of the variety of ways in which the racial/colonial logic of displacement, dispossession, debt, and death have visited the "others of Europe," as conquered/ colonized natives, enslaved Africans, Asian indentured laborers, and so on. The common usage of the term assumes that race as a social operator enables and protects white privilege against every other nonwhite collective. In the case of the subprime crisis, this might mean that because Asian home owners were more protected than their Black and Latino/a counterparts, one could make the case that class inequalities as opposed to race offer more explanatory insight. In fact, scholarly and popular writing about inequality in the United States today and its social consequences by both liberal scholars like Theda Skocpol and neoconservative provocateurs like Charles Murray of *Bell Curve* infamy make exactly this argument.[32] As with other improper economic subjects, the excess value the Black and Latino/a subprime mortgage holder refers to their ontological deficiency, or as G. W. F. Hegel describes Africa, for being a thing.[33]

How raciality disappears with that *relationship* and the *capacity* that substantiates it can be understood only if one attends to two other aspects of the modern subject—which both raciality and historicity attribute to *persons* and *places* to determine their legitimacy as juridical, economic, and ethical entities. Raciality thus produces the "other of Europe" as a being without self-determination. Both natural history and science of life take geographic and bodily traits as signifiers of mental (moral and intellectual) characteristics, which register how universal reason has deployed its productive powers. For natural history, these correspondences were welcome as a moment of the very cataloguing that was knowledge itself, a knowledge that reiterated European/ white superiority but had no concern with the "others of Europe" because it also established that they would not be able to thrive or survive outside their *original* environs. For the science of life the stakes were higher. In the post-Enlightenment era, once universality and historicity became ethical descriptors of the properly human, then the task of justifying how rights such as life (security) and freedom had not been ensured for all human beings required that human difference—which could be registered only as mental difference—become irresolvable.[34] Expropriating or killing the native or the slave would not be morally tenable if they could claim the same self-productive (mental) capacity as conquerors, settlers, and masters. As Sylvia Wynter has described in her groundbreaking work, two major epistemological and cosmological transmutations corresponding to Michel Foucault's chronology of modern thought very effectively reconciled the foundational ethical turn within colonial history: from the secular (terrestrial) human that characterized the Renaissance to the scientific (global) mapping of humanity in the nineteenth century. Raciality skillfully located the modern subject within the confines of Western Europe and its North American outpost.[35]

In turn, the proximity that is eradicated by monetization as assumed in Graeber's account of the emergence of debt/credit does not hold. As Wynter describes, the first question asked about the inhabitants of "discovered lands" was whether these were divine creatures, whether their nakedness marked the innocence of proper subjects of the divine ruler or the wickedness of those who do not fear his name. After the "first encounter," the recurrent question left to those with a scientific itch led to the following question: Given the fact that their heads (and other body parts) clearly indicated their mental (intellectual and moral) inferiority, would their inferior traits contaminate the mixed offspring? And in the case of Brazil, whether they would aid the task of civilization by accelerating their (in this case the Blacks') demise?

Focusing on the productive effects of the analytics of raciality allows us to shift the question from a consideration of how exclusion and differentiation contradict the modern ethical embrace of the universal. This allows us to see how racial and cultural differences have instead been deployed to reconcile a conception of the universal (as encapsulated by the notion of humanity) with a notion of the particular (of difference as marked in bodies and spaces). This discussion is meant to show how incomprehensible (moral) obligations and unpayable (monetary) debts—such as Dana's and those offered subprime loans—expose a political-economic architecture that has always thrived on the construction of modern subjects who lack mental (moral and intellectual) capacities. In other words, the analytics of raciality allow us to see how, since the last third of the nineteenth century at least, modern political-economic architectures—in Europe and in its colonies—have been accompanied by a moral text, in which the principles of universality and historicity also sustain the writing of the "others of Europe" (both a colonial and racial other) as entities facing certain and necessary (self-inflicted) obliteration. Just like this time around in the global financial capitalist casino, the house (the cozy state-financial capital home) cannot but always win because when betting on the other's (Black and Latino/a) inability to pay back its debts, it is betting on something it has itself brought into being.

Debt, Neoliberalism, and Crises

In The *Darker Nations*, Vijay Prashad makes a polemic and persuasive case that debt played a central role in the "assassination of the Third World"; in fact, its "obituary" was written in New Delhi in 1983, at the meeting of the Seventh Non-Aligned Movement (NAM) meeting. Prime Minister Indira Gandhi mediated between Fidel Castro's address to delegates "about how the unfolding debt crisis portended the end of the Third World" and the promise of a technocratic neoliberal future spelled out by S. Rajaratnam, Deputy Prime Minister of Singapore. Prashad writes of the growing consensus among "the more influential" NAM elites to resolve the debt crisis engulfing Latin America and Africa, who argued that "individual contracts between the indebted state and its debtor should be the approach, rather than the totality of the Third World against their creditors."[36] We feel that it is useful to revisit the trajectory of neoliberalism beginning with the "assassination" of the anticolonial utopian project, fully aware of its many internal flaws.

Fields like American studies and cultural studies are well versed in critical research that has tracked how neoliberalism as a mode of government and a political rationality became hegemonic in the United States and the United Kingdom in the 1980s and 1990s.[37] It is, however, sometimes forgotten that it was Latin America—the Southern Cone countries including General Augusto Pinochet's Chile in the 1970s—that became a "laboratory experiment" for Friedrich von Hayek, Milton Friedman, and the "Chicago Boys" to carry out the first iterations of austerity that were adopted by the World Bank in the 1980s.[38] By the early 1990s and under the presidency of George Walker Bush, the neoliberal program seemed well on its way to institute its own worldwide version of Pax Americana in the guise of what Timothy Mitchell has termed "McJihad."[39] That peace could not begin to materialize, as the Cold War was followed by two simultaneous shifts that rendered the human a global (racial) signifier: first, the elevation of the human rights framework into the new global ethical program, and second, the emergence of a new principle for international relations, which allowed for the use of force to stop humanitarian crisis.[40] Leading both efforts, the United States, with its economic and military might, became the sole ruling power advancing the cause of hegemony of financial capitalism. We can look back at this period as one where scholarly attention turned to much more optimistic accounts of globalization, when very few would challenge the description of the U.S. performance in the global context as that of an empire.[41]

During President Bill Clinton's two terms, the U.S. postracial moment was established with the systematic and effective dismantling of welfare provisions, investments in the carceral system, the growing precarity in labor markets, and the attacks on affirmative action and other race-conscious policies. Clearly, this was not because the goals of the civil rights movement had been achieved. Rather, the few existing mechanisms for redress had been eliminated, and it was time to announce that they were officially obsolete. Already a significant portion of the library of critical racial and ethnic studies is composed by scholarship examining the discursive strategies—replete with tropes like the "welfare queen," the "gang banger," and the non-tax-paying dependent "illegal" immigrant—deployed to justify the gutting of welfare programs and the design and implementation of extreme crime and immigration policies.

Less attention, however, has been given to the temporal discursive continuities—between the "welfare queen" and the prototypical subprime borrower as the "single African American woman"—or to the accumulation of the effects of the corresponding policy changes. Even more dramatically, the succession of a "war on drugs" by a "war on terror" also registers a spatial discursive continuity, and the ways in which the main tools of raciality (racial and cultural difference) effectively produce the kind of necessary subaltern subjects. In the context of the U.S.-led occupation and ongoing wars in Afghanistan and Iraq, there is now recognition that in contrast to prevailing counts of globalization in the 1990s, "Empire is back," as Randy Martin asserts in the opening lines of *An Empire of Indifference: American War and the Financial Logic of Risk Management*. Martin argues that "preemption or bringing the future into the present" through military strategies based on logics of securitization and arbitrage have structured a "pre-emptive approach to foreign policy." As revelations about the Obama administration's "exponential expansion" of targeted assassinations and reliance on drone strikes make apparent,[42] a decade plus of pre-emptive warfare has indeed led to indifference for much of the American public steeped in discourses of self-management and an "ethos of responsibility," ready to blame Afghanis, Iraqis, and now Pakistanis for their *own* descent to violence, chaos, and corruption. Martin argues that the war on terror "is modeled on earlier wars against crime and drugs and various populations (youth, the poor, the underperforming) considered at 'risk of social failure.'" In Afghanistan and

Iraq "the urge to cut and run from an investment gone bad while proclaiming victory . . . becomes obligatory to formulate yet impossible to execute," while in the process, "a debt is amassed that circulates but can never be closed or cancelled."[43] How effectively the neoliberal translates the harmful aftereffects of its economic technologies and strategies and the negative side effects of its own remedies can be comprehended only if one acknowledges that the success of this discursive technique rests on what the tools of raciality already offers it, the appropriate *persons* and *places* to attribute moral failures.

Unquestionably the latest financial crisis, its historical roots and sociopoliti- cal cultural aftermath, is already and will remain the subject of a broad range of academic inquiry.[44] This issue was organized by a very explicit formulation plac- ing the workings of race and empire at the center of inquiry. From beginning to end, the essays in this issue embraced this question, rearranging it according to a given disciplinary, theoretical-methodological, and thematic preference. In a sense, the essays in the first section of the issue, under the heading "Debt, Discipline, and Empire," provide a reading of the current crisis against the backdrop of the "assassination of the Third World." In "Debt, Power, and Crisis: Social Stratification and the Inequitable Governance of Financial Mar- kets," James Heintz and Radhika Balakrishnan introduce an account of credit markets that exposes all that Adam Smith's invisible hand conveniently hides. The essay describes the empirics of "debt-fueled economic distress" highlight- ing the continuities among the Latin American debt crisis, capital flight from Africa, and the more recent subprime crisis and the European sovereign debt crisis. The authors show how power in credit markets refers to a relationship that links the present to the future: the creditor gives funds now expecting access to revenue later. Because inequality is presupposed in this relationship, in moments of distress, any remedial intervention should attend to and redress the debtors, not the creditors. Needless to say the very opposite has happened in all four cases they discuss: those already in a subaltern position—as social or global (postcolonial) subjects—have paid for fixing or keeping the system intact, while those who have profited from the inequality/vulnerability of debtors have been rescued either by a particular government or a multilateral juridico-economic body (the European Union or the International Monetary Fund [IMF]). The essay ends by offering an "alternative approach to govern- ing credit markets," one foregrounding economic and social rights that can be seen as potentially subverting the dominant human rights framework by (re)introducing a redistributive mandate.

Turning to the Asian crisis, in "The Uses of Asianization: Figuring Crises, 1997–98 and 2007–?," Laura Hyun Yi Kang examines how race and empire work very productively when deployed to describe and justify assessments of the trajectory of an economic subject, in this case a *place*, namely, Asia. Refusing the view that strangeness alone would account for how some debtors are treated more "impersonally"—hence less amicably—than others, Kang assesses the limitations of the discourse of modular *Asian* developmental nation-states in East and Southeast Asia and their subsequent fall from grace in 1997. She exposes how the practices and interpretations of the "Asian miracle," the "Asian crisis," and the "Asian recovery" were the joint production of a juridico-economic assemblage made up of the U.S. government (Treasury), financial capital (Wall Street), and the World Bank/IMF. Further, she reads and guides us through the workings of the figuring (as a productive strategy) of "Asia" as a unified economic subject and place. Here Kang tackles the critical task, namely, to de-Asianize the 1997–8 Asian Financial Crisis—namely, *denaturalize* the expert discourse that both creates the Asian miracle and sets the terms for the Asian recovery aftermath of the Asian crisis. Kang's essay effortlessly ties together the critique of empire and of race when it traces how these three moments of "Asianization" of financial troubles are deeply gendered in their consequences for workers and citizens in Asia.

In "The Tale of Two Gulfs: Life, Death, and Dispossession along Two Oil Frontiers," Michael Watts takes us on a surreal geo-economic-politico-historical trip to the Niger delta and the Gulf of Mexico. Expanding on Harvey, he deploys the construct "oil frontier" to describe two "local pockets of disorder and catastrophe in the oil assemblage" that point to the "deep pathologies and vulnerabilities within the operations of imperial oil." Watts's analysis reads like a recurring nightmare that cannot but make us think of economic affairs in terms of Graeber's formulation of debt and credit. Along with the previous two essays, Watts asks us to engage the subprime by considering today's disaster capitalism through its legacies of colonial expropriation: "The petroleum frontier followed the slave and palm oil frontiers." Watts invites us to consider how financial capital—calling attention to the significance of "paper oil" in this process—benefits from existing political structures, including practices such as corruption introduced through the colonial encounter. Perhaps more importantly, his essay also shows how the "material" referent (paper oil) is a natural resource capable of the same kind of total—ideologically unmediated—violence Fanon states prevails in the colonial context and will remain sine qua non for profit. Naming the "oil frontier" the place of dispossession, Watts's essay invites the question of whether it matters that the crises of global financial capitalism are temporal (happening once and then again) or spatial (happening here and there).

The last essay in this first section reminds us that power, if it is a concept relevant to critical scholarship, needs to be reworked at every significant juncture. In "Debt and Discipline," Tayyab Mahmud asks us to rework the concept of power in very dramatic ways, combining critical political economy with the "conceptual tool kit of Michel Foucault." In this essay, power is returned to the account of the economic both in its productive and in its restrictive guises—as *poesis* and *nomos*. As Mahmud writes, "In the neoliberal era the hidden hand of the market and the iron fist of the law worked in concert to forge governmentalities that suture debt with discipline." Mahmud provides a detailed overview of the internal U.S. neoliberal counterrevolution, emphasizing the state's "radical use of monetary policy and smashing the power of organized labor" in favor of precarious labor markets. The essay takes us through the state's active role in the "creation of aggregate demand through private debt," which ultimately leads to what Mahmud calls "the entrapment of working classes and racial minorities into a circuit of debt" while investing in the "penalization of poverty." Mahmud astutely observes that it is the "self-discipline" of debtors in the neoliberal era that marks the present moment as distinct from previous historical and colonial forms of debt. It is all the more disturbing when we are reminded of how strategies to bring about freedom—such as individual responsibility, entrepreneurship, and so forth—lead to worship and hope but become means through which we are but well-functioning cogs in the neoliberal financial machine. The essay concludes on a more hopeful note, pointing to the wave of global opposition movements in the wake of the Arab Spring, Occupy Wall Street, and resistance to austerity measures in Europe, and in this sense links back to Heintz and Balakrishnan's alternative proposal, what Mahmud calls the "popular democratization of finance."

The three essays in the second section, titled "Cultures of Neoliberalism: Contesting the Pathologies of Debt," invite us to raise more direct questions about the prevailing representations of the causes and solutions for the global financial crisis. All three essays focus on the United States. However, each one questions how economic subjects—both victims and perpetrators of the crisis—are invariably misrepresented. And in doing so, these essays offer critical insight in terms of reconsidering the logics of blame that structure the global crisis of the "subprime." In "Gambling with Debt: Lessons from the Illiterate," Sarita See draws inspiration from Fred Moten's provocation and begins her essay by asking "what debt do we owe the subprime debtor?" What if the house that was bought but could never be paid for was a referent to a wholly distinct conception of existence, one that might not be resolved by any of the instantiations of the economic (the thing, the dominium, the meaning).

Responding to the pedagogic tendency among both liberals and progressives for financial literacy of the economically dispossessed, See wants us to reverse the "direction of learning and edification. Let us for once consider the lessons that the illiterate offer to the literate rather than the other way around." Her thoughtful essay focuses on the short story and stage adaption of Carlos Bulosan's "Romance of Magno Rubio" published in the 1940s, but "staged in Filipino America for years preceding and succeeding the 2008 financial crisis." Reading Magno Rubio's calculations that resolved words in an economy of love, See's essay at once signals and brackets the power differentials charactering the kinds of exchanges, the debt/creditor relationships, named subprime.

In "Realty Reality: HGTV and the Subprime Crisis," Shawn Shimpach also invites us to follow him on a trip through text and context, one that provides us with a popular cultural "literacy" necessary to respond to the dominant views of the causes of the "crisis of the subprime" circulating among the Tea Party digerati. Shimpach begins his essay by stating the obvious, which bears repetition: "The current financial crisis was not caused by duped viewers of basic cable television." What follows is a discussion of the successful television network HGTV (Home and Garden Television) to show the "complexity of the processes by which political economies become textualized." Successfully avoiding the dominant Manichaean take on popular culture and reality television in particular, Shimpach analyzes how HGTV was able to carve its niche, with low-budgets and subcontracted staged programs that fulfilled many of the needs of neoliberal governmentality. This includes serving one of the most effective elements in the production of subjects, which is the mere satisfaction of aspirational desire for, let us say, peering into someone's else process of choosing a home. Reading this essay and its account of the "staging of the economy" after having been called to reconsider power in financial relationships by Mahmud's essay is particularly effective. As Shimpach argues, "In the context of increasingly global, increasingly abstract, highly financialized ways of being in the world, this textual staging offers much more than lessons in the mundanities of middle-class life: it also offers a way to imagine participation and proximity to others. It effaces the reality of a continuing legacy of significant racial disparities in access to this middle-class life by staging the way to imagine it as accessible to all."

Precisely the possibility, the need, the history, of counterproduction is the subject matter of the last essay in this section, by Catherine Squires, "Coloring in the Bubble: Perspectives from Black-Oriented Media on the (Latest) Economic Disaster." Following through the trust of the critical racial analytic program, Squires analyzes Black U.S. news media as potential sites of "counterdiscourse" in their coverage of causes and responses to the subprime crisis. Squires first examines how postracial and neoliberal discourses are "intertwined, promoting a view of empowered, multicultural individuals now unhindered by racism" and "free" to consume or fail. Squires compares the historical role of the "black public sphere" and its association with critiques of capitalism and consumer culture with its modern digitally transformed niche-marketed counterpart. She then focuses on three "black-oriented news outlets" to "provide some coordinates for where neoliberal logics have been incorporated into black media vehicles set up ostensibly to provide information and opinions not widely circulated in dominant media." While there are surely signs of hope with online publications like *Colorlines*, Squires concludes her essay along the lines of Heintz and Balakrishnan, and Mahmud above, by pointing to the urgent need for public engagement in media-based activism to propose meaningful political alternatives.

In the final section of this issue, "The Postracial Urban: Security, Space, and Resistance," we turn to four essays that focus on the subprime crisis as a reflection of a discursive and institutional shift in the contemporary U.S. racial panorama. Each delves deeper into the confluence of the neoliberal juridico-economic regime to map how racial inclusion (postracial) and security discourses combine to support the range of state- and market-based strategies that assembled the financial architecture responsible for the crisis of the subprime. In "New Racial Meanings of Housing in America," Elvin Wyly and his coauthors take us on a whirlwind, data-filled journey to show us how and why Blacks and Latino/as would bear the bulk of the burden (monetary and moral) of financial deregulation coupled with the effects of de jure racial discrimination and segregation. Fleshing out the empirics of power differentials highlighted by Heintz and Balakrishnan and Mahmud, this essay examines the postracial move toward the predatory incorporation of previously excluded populations. As with Watts's essay highlighting the disjunctive spatial dimensions of such crises, this piece is also written by critical geographers and focuses on the crucial spatial dimensions of the crisis: "The predatory exploitation of the urban core has gone mainstream, altering the spatial relations of privilege on the expanding frontiers of Sun Belt suburbia." Neither racial exclusion nor differential inclusion can account for the fact that despite the fact that non-Hispanic whites numerically held more subprime loans, Blacks and Latino/as account for the overwhelming majority of foreclosures. Against the prevailing argument that attributes this outcome to greed and illiteracy, this essay shows how the global financial crisis resulted from regulatory changes that facilitated the consolidation of the current financial regime and artfully mapped the effects of past and present racial subjugation (accumulated expropriation) onto the new global financial web of risk.

In "Welcome to My Cell: Housing and Race in the Mirror of American Democracy," Ofelia O. Cuevas turns our attention to another necessary discursive dimension: the discourse of security that connects U.S. racial and imperial practices that emerge under the George W. Bush administration in the wake of 9/11. Cuevas identifies three distinct and interconnected features of this discourse: the costly deployment of the military in Iraq, Afghanistan, and Pakistan to protect U.S. Americans "at home"; the weakening of constitutional protections "at home" to facilitate legal practices necessary to secure the homeland; and policies to increase the rate of home ownership to ensure economic security. Importantly, Cuevas brings to the fore an often unremarked aspect of the debate on housing in the United States: "What was elided in this revamped discourse of security and its emphasis on home . . . was the fact . . . that the state has pursued its own 'ontological security' by undertaking one of the most massive public housing projects in the history of the world: the incarceration of millions and millions of its citizens." Exploring the discursive, institutional, and juridical contradictions inherent to the notion of security, Cuevas argues that "the relationship of the racial subject to property and home is one that exists in the violent abstraction of the future which they will pay for in the form of debt." She shows how raciality, as in every time security refers to property, immediately positions Blacks and Latino/as in an ontologically distinct place. Cuevas's essay insightfully unpacks how the subprime crisis found a fertile terrain already prepared by the workings of the U.S. state in the last three decades and the cultivation of the postracial discourse that built (and later exported) the carceral system.

At this point, it might be productive to ask what it might take for an organized political response to emerge, given the "evidence" presented in the essays summarized thus far, to finally bring the postracial neoliberal bandwagon to a halt? In "The Black Mohicans: Representations of Everyday Violence in Postracial Urban America," John D. Márquez reads the conditions of production of the very "evidence" that both justifies the assemblage of the U.S. carceral system and the Obama administration's decision not to help the "greedy and illiterate" *ghetto* (Black and Latino/a) borrowers. Márquez introduces a notion of "ghetto violence" to unsettle the deployment of racial and colonial difference that *naturalizes* violence, which is an effect of strategies of "total violence" and symbolic violence characteristic of colonial domination and racial subjugation. To situate a decolonial approach that both rejects and undoes this naturalizing effect, characteristic of existing social-scientific tools, this essay deploys two analytic strategies, which move the racial critique against the grain of available socio-scientific "truths" and the postracial discourse. First, it examines media representations of the deaths of victims of "ghetto violence" in Chicago, which were crucial to justify the implementation of the policies and structures of the U.S. carceral system. Second, he deploys a historical analysis that shows leaders of Black and Latino gangs register the role of anticolonial theorizing and practice in the design of their organizations. Márquez's essay ultimately turns our attention to the most pressing and difficult task before those building political movements of opposition and the necessity to resist the homogenization of the 99%.

In "Blues Geographies and the Security Turn: Interpreting the Housing Crisis in Los Angeles," Jordan T. Camp takes up the above challenge and reflects on the "racial, spatial and class dynamics" of the activist politics and ethics of housing in Los Angeles. Camp highlights another often missed dimension of the transformed housing market—the coincidence between urban renewal programs that are gentrifying downtown Los Angeles as the foreclosures caused by the subprime crisis increases the number of homeless Black individuals and families moving to Skid Row. Once again in this essay, security more immediately expresses how the crisis reflects the workings of the state-market axis through the criminalization of homelessness, experiments in new policing technologies, and mass incarceration. In tracing the genealogy of radical Black organizing for social justice and racial equality, Camp draws on the legacy of Clyde Woods and writes of the "pressing need for scholars of neoliberalism to analyze its historical and geographical roots in the racist counterrevolution against the Second Reconstruction." Further exposing the *naturalizations* that sustain the "subprime" logic, Camp situates today's protests against housing injustice in a genealogy of post–civil rights organizing for social justice and racial equality. Our last essay, like the first essay in this collection, calls for a radical rethinking of the human rights framework. Building on this historical trajectory for social justice in LA, similar to the trajectory described by Márquez above, allows us to imagine possibilities for the politics of opposition against both neoliberalism and *postcolonial* empire.

Conclusion

Let us close with two provocations by way of the question that now more than ever hovers over our work intellectual and political: What is to be done? In her presidential address to the American Studies Association in 2011, Ruth Wilson Gilmore made a passionate plea to better understand—and to formulate a plan of action for dissolving—the relationship between race, economy, and empire, not simply as an academic exercise but as a political act essential in an age of growing militarization and inequality.[45] Her picture of the neoliberal drawing board highlights three sites: namely, "structure adjustments," "security enhancement," and "the anti-state state." For Gilmore the first task before those of us who find this drawing deeply violent—those of us who attend to and respond to the fact that it both deploys and reproduces the arsenal of racial/knowledge power, which renders so many, as she puts it, vulnerable to "premature death"—is to organize. "Policy," she teases, "is to politics what method is to research."[46] Policy and politics have framed this special issue because the papers collected here, as they engage the state-market axis, or the political and economic moments of violence, deploy conceptual, analytic, and methodological tools that signal the relevance of both. These conversations and debates about the subprime crisis demonstrate the point highlighted in the first part of this introduction, that *debt* allows morality to encompass the *relationship*, thus foreshadowing how Dana's relationship with her master is also fundamentally political in character.

Any program that takes up Gilmore's challenge would have to begin by undoing the separation between the ethical and the political at the core of liberal (and neoliberal) thinking. This would release us from the burden of representation, to dissipate what David Lloyd describes in his discussion of "what is to be done," after Gayatri Spivak's "Can the Subaltern Speak?": "Discussion of the essay seems to lead inevitably to a sense of ontological consternation, in that it gets read over and again as posing to the reader not merely the pragmatic question as to 'what is to be done?' in relation to the subaltern, but the question, 'by what right are you here assuming any relation to the subaltern?'"[47] Because the violence of racial and colonial subjugation works so effectively at the level of representation, we need to refuse "ethical consternation" and recuperate the relationship as a descriptor of difference, and *not* commonality.[48] This also allows us to avoid the equally paralyzing and more common obverse effect of "ethical oblivion": "We have no relation to the subaltern, so why should we care?"[49] More importantly, moments and movements of resistance might be better understood by methods heeding Avery Gordon's call to engage the ghosts or Fred Moten's invitation to ask what subprime debtors might teach us, offering a wholly distinct ethical program, as suggested by Nahum Chandler.[50]

In a book published a year before the transformative events of the Arab Spring, Asef Bayat wrote of "the non-movement of the urban dispossessed" in the Middle East: "the collective actions of non-collective actors . . . that have come to represent the mobilizations of millions of the subaltern, chiefly the urban poor, Muslim women, and youth." Bayat's description of how the "quiet encroachment of the ordinary" impinging on the propertied and the powerful through the "unlawful acquisitions of land and shelter" resonate with everyday forms of resistance across much of the global South after three long decades of neoliberal reform. Bayat, among other observers of Middle Eastern history and politics, has argued that it was the "middle class poor"—educated but unemployed and "subsisting at the margins of the neoliberal economy"— who sparked the events in Tunisia and Egypt and who would inspire a new global politics of protest in 2011.[51] A nonmovement movement sparked by the indignation of Arab "street vendors, sales-persons, boss-boys, or taxi drivers" found unity in the ousting of U.S.-backed autocratic leaders like Hosni Mubarak.[52] While it is beyond the scope of this introduction to delve into a meaningful discussion of the lessons from the (ongoing) uprisings in the Middle East and North Africa, this detour is meant simply to signal the need to better understand the logic of solidarities forged out of difference.

Similarly, those in the global North who celebrate the resurgence of a universalist oppositional politics with audible sighs of relief that the "era of identity politics is behind us" might be reminded by the essays in this collection that neoliberal dispossession and debt are not lived in the same way by everyone.[53] Recognizing the significant political success of the OWS movement in shifting the debate on the economy away from the populist Tea Party narratives, Rinku Sen of the Applied Research Center called for organizing "that challenges segregation, not only that of the 1% from everyone else, but also that which divides the 99% from within."[54] This cannot simply be accomplished, as some researchers have suggested, with "occupiers reaching out to working class people and people of color" engendering "trust and solidarity" by "occupying the hood and barrio."[55] Once again, as many of the essays in this collection remind us, this paternalistic approach—because it begins from the assumption of the absence of a *relationship*—to the targeting of "othered" populations can hardly bring about radical social or global justice.

The crises of neoliberalism at the heart of empire and the vast oppositional energies it has mobilized make Gilmore's provocation for a politics of organization based on an alternative ethic and for a method that will take us beyond structures of racial/postcolonial subjugation all the more pressing. For as indicated by the essays in this issue, these politics and policies would assume a negative answer to the question: Why should economically dispossessed Blacks and Latino/as pay for those who bet on and profited from their inability to pay the unpayable debts? In each of the financial crises discussed in this issue, we find that the blame has been placed on *persons* and *places* that, like Dana, have been produced by racial power/knowledge as marked by mental traits that render them unable to inhabit the economic, legal, and moral positions unique to the modern subject. An alternative ethics, the essays in this issue suggest, would have to necessarily focus on the very *relationship* and *capacity* arrested and denied by the tools of raciality—in particular by racial and cultural difference. From there, politics that acknowledges temporal and spatial differences, historical and geographic specificities could emerge, without "oblivion" or "consternation," while recognizing the unpayability of such debt. Without such attention to the productive yet violent effects of raciality, and the kind of comprehension of social and global difference it enables, it will be difficult to realize the kinds of solidarities necessary to sustain the organizing that Ruth Wilson Gilmore reminds us oppositional movements cannot do without.

Notes

We would like to thank Sarah Banet-Weiser for being a truly supportive and generous editor throughout this rather lengthy process; Jih-Fei Cheng (*AQ*'s managing editor) and Paula Dragosh (copy editor) for being extremely patient and accommodating; and last but not least we wish to express our gratitude to the anonymous reviewers whose comments and feedback helped structure and improve the essays in this collection. It goes without saying that we are grateful and, indeed, *indebted*, to all of the authors of these essays.

1. For John Locke (*Two Treatises on Government* [Cambridge: Cambridge University Press, 1988]), for instance, the household remains the last domain of patriarchal rule, where the patriarch enjoys full freedom, where both as master and as husband, the citizen obeys but has the obligation to protect and punish his own, namely, wife, children, and servants (or slaves). Indeed, neither Locke's system of reward and punishment (the law) nor Thomas Hobbes's artificial body (the state)—the juridico-political figures manufactured by the social contractors—would intrude in the household in such a way.

2. According to a number of studies on racial and ethnic disparities in the aftermath of the subprime crisis, it is a relatively uncontested fact that while non-Hispanic whites made up the majority of at-risk borrowers, African Americans and Latina/o borrowers were much more likely to experience foreclosure (one study found this rate to be 76 percent and 71 percent, respectively, compared with non-Hispanic whites). For more detailed discussion of this point, see James Carr, Katrin B. Anakar, and Michelle L. Mulcahy, "The Foreclosure Crisis and Its Impact on Communities of Color: Research and Solutions," White Paper, National Community Reinvestment Coalition, 2011, www.ncrc.org/resources/reports-and-research/item/665-white-paper-the-foreclosure-crisis-and-its-impact-on-communities-of-coloras, well as Wyly et al., this issue.

3. These include, among other strategies, financial "innovations" like the infamous "no income no jobs no assets" (NINJA) loans targeting women and communities of color. Karen Ho's rich ethnographic study of Wall Street sheds light on the specifics of such practices and the ways in which investment bankers claimed that "their ingenuity was finally breaking down barriers of race and class, which the traditional 'redlining' commercial was unable to do with his simple, 'vanilla' toolkit of conventional loans that lacked the advantage of global securitization." See Karen Ho, *Liquidated: An Ethnography of Wall Street* (Durham, N.C.: Duke University Press, 2009), 298–302.

4. Among other titles, see Roland Robertson, *Globalization: Social Theory and Global Culture* (London: Sage, 1992); Ulrich Beck, *Risk Society: Towards a New Modernity* (London: Sage, 1992); Anthony

Giddens, *The Consequences of Modernity* (Oxford. Polity, 1990); and the collection edited by Mike Featherstone, *Global Culture: Nationalism, Globalization, and Modernity* (London: Sage, 1990).

5. Edward Li Puma and Benjamin Lee, *Financial Derivatives and the Globalization of Risk* (Durham, N.C.: Duke University Press, 2004), 5.

6. Paula Chakravartty and Dan Schiller write about the dominant media's framing of the bank's logic, which continues to demand the privatization of profit and the socialization of loss. See Paula Chakravartty and Dan Schiller, "Neo-Liberal Newspeak and Digital Capitalism," *International Journal of Communication* 4, http://ijoc.org/ojs/index.php/ijoc. Dennis Kelleher, a financial reform activist, states that investment banks aggressively opposing regulatory intervention are quick to forget that they are "at the top . . . of the hierarchy of guilt" for the crisis (quoted in Annie Lowrey, "Facing Down the Bankers," *New York Times*, May 30, 2012, www.nytimes.com/2012/05/31/business/kelleher-leads-a-nonprofit-better-markets-in-fight-for-stricter-banking-rules.html?pagewanted=all).

7. Janet Roitman, *Fiscal Disobedience: An Anthropology of Economic Regulation in Central Africa* (Princeton, N.J.: Princeton University Press, 2005); Eric Helleiner, "The Strange Story of the Bush Administration and the Argentine Debt Crisis," *Third World Quarterly* 26.6 (2005): 951–69.

8. Millennial or "messianic" capitalism as discussed in Jean Comaroff and John Comaroff, "Millennial Capitalism: First Thoughts on a Second Coming," *Public Culture* 12.92 (2000): 301.

9. For more on the politics of debt revolts in response to microcredit lending schemes, see Ananya Roy, *Poverty Capital: Microfinance and the Making of Development* (New York: Routledge, 2010), chap. 5; and Julie Elyachar, *Markets of Dispossession: NGOs, Economic Development, and the State in Cairo* (Durham, N.C.: Duke University Press, 2005).

10. See, for instance, Lisa Lowe, *Immigrant Acts: On Asian American Cultural Politics* (Durham, N.C.: Duke University Press, 1996); Vicente Rafael, *White Love and Other Events in Filipino History* (Durham, N.C.: Duke University Press, 2000); and the collections: Lisa Lowe and David Lloyd, *The Politics of Culture in the Shadow of Capital* (Durham, N.C.: Duke University Press, 1997); Amy Kaplan and Donald Pease, *Cultures of United States Imperialism* (Durham, N.C.: Duke University Press, 1993).

11. As early as September 2007, Glen Beck on Fox was placing the blame on "illegal immigrant" home owners and pointing fingers at federal programs introduced in the Clinton administration promoting home ownership for minority communities, echoed across Fox News, Rush Limbaugh, the financial press, and across much of the online discussions. For more on dominant media discourse on the financial crisis, see Catherine Squires, "Bursting the Bubble: A Case Study of Counter-Framing in the Editorial Pages," *Critical Studies in Media and Communications* 28.1 (2011): 28–47.

12. Walter Mignolo, *Local Histories/Global Designs* (Princeton, N.J.: Princeton University Press, 2000).

13. Ananya Roy, *Poverty Capital: Microfinance and the Making of Development* (New York: Routledge, 2010), 218–19.

14. See David Harvey, *The New Imperialism* (Oxford: Oxford University Press, 2005).

15. David Harvey, *The Enigma of Capital* (London: Profile Books, 2010), 1.

16. Ibid., 4.

17. See Harvey, *New Imperialism*, 146.

18. Harvey, *Enigma of Capital*, 17.

19. David Graber, *Debt: The First 5,000 Years* (Brooklyn: Melville House, 2011).

20. Robert Ezra Park, *Race and Culture* (New York: Free Press, 1950). To be sure, old and recent accounts of the political also rehearse this view that, in the absence of moral ties, violence rules human relationships; this is the case in Carl Schmitt's definition of the political in terms of a distinction between friend and enemies, in Jacques Derrida's elaboration of hospitality as a choice in face of the arrival of the stranger, and even in Giorgio Agamben's description of "bare life" as one stripped of a moral claim (the one that can be killed but not sacrificed). See Carl Schmitt, *The Concept of the Political* (Chicago: University of Chicago Press, 2007); Jacques Derrida and Ann Dufourmantelle, *Of Hospitality* (Stanford, Calif.: Stanford University Press, 2000); and Giorgio Agamben, *Homo Sacer: Sovereign Power and Bare Life* (Stanford, Calif.: Stanford University Press, 1998).

21. For an elaboration of the view of how the racial transmutates the colonial, see Denise Ferreira da Silva, "Before Man: Sylvia Wynter's Rewriting of the Modern Episteme," in *The Realization of Living: Sylvia Wynter and Being Human*, ed. Katherine McKittrick (Durham, N.C.: Duke University Press, forthcoming).

22. For an elaboration of how the analytics of raciality produces the racial subaltern subject as an onto-epistemological figure defined by the logic of obliteration, how transcendentality (and its principles of

universality and historicity) and self-determination are deployed to describe the post-Enlightenment European/white *persons* and *places*, see Denise Ferreira da Silva, *Toward a Global Idea of Race* (Minneapolis: University of Minnesota Press, 2007).

23. Such an effect is also reproduced in what Barnor Hesse sees as modern philosophers' refusal to recognize the deep racial (because referents of the colonial) character of modernity's favored self-description ("Racialized Modernity: An Analytics of White Mythologies," *Ethnic and Racial Studies* 30.4 [2007]: 643–63).

24. C. L. R. James, *The Black Jacobins* (New York: Vintage Books, 1989); Frantz Fanon, *The Wretched of the Earth* (New York: Penguin Classics, 2001); and Cedric Robinson, *Black Marxism: The Making of the Black Radical Tradition* (London: Zed Books, 1983).

25. Manu Gowswami, *Producing India: From Colonial Economy to National Space* (Chicago: University of Chicago Press, 2004). Relevant to our argument here, see the introduction and chapter 1.

26. Tsing is responding to Harvey's previous writings, but her point is no less relevant in terms of pointing out "the heterogeneity of capitalism at every moment of time." See Anna Lopenhaupt Tsing, *Friction: An Ethnography of Global Connection* (Princeton, N.J.: Princeton University Press, 2005), 75–77.

27. Ibid. This brings to mind Arjun Appadurai's essay on the layers of history that shape the "spectral" quality of real estate speculation in ethno-linguistically and class-fractured globalized cities like Mumbai. Describing a more complex and contested process of no less violent a process of accumulation, Appadurai writes: "To speak of spectrality in Bombay's housing scene moves us beyond the empirics of inequality into the experience of shortage, speculation, crowding and public improvisation. It makes the space of speculation and specularities, empty scenes of dissolved industry, fantasies of urban planning, rumors of real estate transfers, consumption patterns that violate their spatial preconditions, and bodies that are their own housing ("Spectral Housing and Urban Cleansing: Notes on Millennial Mumbai," *Public Culture* 12.3 [2001]: 635).

28. Roy, *Poverty Capital*, 114–15.

29. Achille Mbembe, "Necropolitics," *Public Culture* 15.1 (2003): 11–40.

30. We recognize the explanatory advantages of concepts such as racism, race consciousness, and even coloniality of power. See Anibal Quijano, "Coloniality of Power, Eurocentrism, and Latin America," *Nepantla: Views from the South* 1.3 (2000): 533–80. All of these concepts attempt to show how colonialism and (its attendant) slavery have performed a crucial work of power—in particular economic but also political—for a political (juridical, economic, and symbolic) configuration that defines itself by the opposite principles. What this framing of raciality does, however, is to show that exclusion and unfreedom have been more than necessary (for primitive or "spectacular" accumulation) or expedient aspects subcontracted to the others of Europe/whiteness. Raciality, as the naming of a productive assemblage enables the ethical demand that these "others of Europe" be done away with so that reason and freedom—embodied in the European/white being—can flourish in the stage of world history.

31. For an example of the effects of deployment of differential inclusion, see Yen Le Espiritu, *Home Bound: Filipino American Lives across Culture, Communities, and Countries* (Berkeley: University of California Press, 2003).

32. Charles Murray, *Coming Apart: The State of White America (1960–2010)* (New York: Crown Forum, 2012); Theda Skocpol and Vanessa Williams, *The Tea Party and the Remaking of Republican Conservatism* (Oxford: Oxford University Press, 2012).

33. G. W. F. Hegel, *The Philosophy of History* (New York: Wiley Book, 1899), 96.

34. This argument is developed in Silva, *Toward a Global Idea of Race*; and Denise Ferreira da Silva, "No-Bodies: Law, Raciality, Violence," *Griffith Law Review* 18.2 (2009): 212–36.

35. Sylvia Wynter, "Unsettling the Coloniality of Being/Power/Truth/Freedom: Toward the Human, After Man, Its Overrepresentation—an Argument," *CR: The New Centennial Review* 3.3 (2003): 257–337.

36. Vijay Prashad, *The Darker Nations: A People's History of the Third World* (New York: New Press, 2008), 210–14.

37. Lisa Duggan, *The Twilight of Equality? Neoliberalism, Cultural Politics, and the Attack on Democracy* (Boston: Beacon, 2004); Nicholas Rose and Peter Miller, *Governing the Present: Administering Economic, Social, and Personal Life* (New York: Polity, 2008).

38. Greg Gradin, *Empire's Workshop: Latin America, the United States, and the Rise of the New Imperialism* (New York: Holt, 2010), 171–73.

39. Mitchell's term is useful in shedding light on the false distinction that was made even by critics of U.S. Empire in this period, that contrasted the globalizing power of capitalism with the "tribal particular-

isms" that opposed the homogenizing force of capital. That "McWorld" and "Jihad" were actually co-constitutive of U.S. Empire in the Middle East is meant to show the "lack of contradiction between the logic of capitalism and other forces and ideas it encounters." See Timothy Mitchell, "McJihad: Islam in the US Global Order," *Social Text*, no. 73 (2002): 1–19.

40. This argument has been advanced by several recent works including Roy, "Poverty Capital"; and James Peck, *Ideal Illusions: How the US Government Co-opted Human Rights* (New York: Metropolitan Books, 2011). For an especially sharp analysis of humanitarianism and U.S. Empire, see Mahmood Mamdani, *Saviors and Survivors: Darfur, Politics, and the War on Terror* (New York: Three Rivers, 2010).

41. For an elaboration of this point, see Paula Chakravartty and Yuezhi Zhao, *Global Communications: Toward a Transcultural Political Economy* (Boulder, Colo.: Rowman and Littlefield, 2008), 11–16.

42. www.salon.com/2012/06/07/probing_obamas_secrecy_games/singleton/.

43. Randy Martin, *An Empire of Indifference: American War and the Financial Logic of Risk Management* (Durham, N.C.: Duke University Press, 2007), 9–12.

44. For example, Craig Calhoun and Georgi Derlugian have recently published a three-volume series titled *Possible Futures* on the history, governance regimes, and possible aftermath of the financial crisis that provides a useful comparative overview by prominent scholars of globalization: Craig Calhoun and Giorgi Delurgian, *Business as Usual: The Roots of the Global Financial Meltdown* (New York: New York University Press, 2011); Calhoun and Delurgian, *The Deepening of the Crisis: Governance Challenges after Neoliberalism* (New York: New York University Press, 2011); Calhoun and Delurgian, *Aftermath: A New Global Economic Order?* (New York: New York University Press, 2011).

45. Ruth Wilson Gilmore, "What Is to Be Done?" *American Quarterly* 63.2 (2011): 245–65.

46. Ibid., 264.

47. David Lloyd, "Representation's Coup," *Interventions* (forthcoming): 2.

48. This goes against Graeber's formulation of strangers bound by "moral ties" as discussed in the first section of this introduction. Graeber has, of course, risen to great prominence as the media-appointed "antileader" of the Occupy Wall Street movement.

49. For an articulation of ethical oblivion as an effect of the workings of raciality, see Silva, "Before Man."

50. Avery Gordon, *Ghostly Matters* (Minneapolis: University of Minnesota Press, 1997); Fred Moten, *In the Break* (Minneapolis: University of Minnesota Press, 2003).

51. Asaf Bayat, *Life as Politics: How Ordinary People Change the Middle East* (Palo Alto, Calif.: Stanford University Press, 2010).

52. Asaf Bayat, "A New Arab Street in Post-Islamist Times," *Foreign Policy–Middle East Channel* (2011), http://mideast.foreignpolicy.com/posts/2011/01/26/a_new_arab_street.

53. The following statement by Todd Gitlin, author of a new book titled *Occupy Nation*, is representative of this kind of commonsense argument: "I hadn't realized this until I checked off the movements of my recollection, that they had started as minority uprisings—at least expressions of dissidence—in comparison to the population as a whole. So the Civil Rights Movement, which obviously was popular with black people but not with Americans overall, certainly not in the South, when it broke out. The anti-Vietnam War movement represented a small minority, maybe a little more than 10%, when it erupted. The women's movement, it's hard to say—possible exception there. The gay movement was certainly not a popular movement over all. I see this more as the rule than the exception (www.3quarksdaily.com/3quarksdaily/2011/10/todd-gitlin-on-why-ows-is-different-from-all-other-social-movements.html).

54. Rinku Sen, "Race and Occupy Wall Street," *Nation* (2011): www.thenation.com/article/164212/race-and-occupy-wall-street.

55. Jeff Juris, "Reflections of Occupy Everywhere: Social Media, Public Space, and Emerging Logics of Aggregation," *American Ethnologist* 39.2 (2012): 259–79.

Debt, Power, and Crisis: Social Stratification and the Inequitable Governance of Financial Markets

James Heintz and Radhika Balakrishnan

T he human costs of the recent global economic crisis, the true extent of which first became evident in 2008, have been enormous. In the United States alone, the financial meltdown sent shock waves throughout the economy, causing record levels of sustained joblessness, home foreclosures, cutbacks to government services, and rising levels of poverty. The toll has also been substantial at the international level, and the austerity budgets adopted by many countries indicate that the repercussions of the crisis will be with us for decades. Although it is widely recognized that the behavior of global financial institutions led to the crisis, the narratives in the wake of the meltdown have assigned responsibility to the reckless behavior of borrowers—including those holding subprime mortgages and governments in peripheral countries. Financial firms enjoyed sizable bailouts, while others were left to shoulder the burden of adjustment.

This essay explores the role of credit markets in the financial crisis. Both financial fragility, which made the crisis possible, and the trajectory of policy responses postcrisis have been shaped by power dynamics in credit markets that interact with existing structures of stratification along the lines of race, gender, nationality, and other group differences. These dynamics are not unique to the 2008 global economic catastrophe and have been evident in other episodes of debt-fueled economic distress. Despite the centrality of credit markets in a range of financial crises and their contribution to perpetuating structural inequalities, controls on financial institutions have been loosened in recent years rather than tightened, suggesting that the concentration of power in these markets has grown.

Indeed, the influence of financial institutions and interests has expanded significantly in the decades since the 1980s, a time of far-reaching changes to the regulatory environment that has altered the landscape of global economic governance. Existing national and global institutions have failed to redress the unequal balance of power in credit markets and the distributive consequences of financial crises. This raises important questions of which frameworks are appropriate for developing an alternative approach to governing financial and credit markets. We suggest that ongoing developments with regard to economic and social rights have the potential to provide the basis for an alternative approach, with significant implications for the regulation and governance of financial institutions.

We begin by considering the power dynamics embodied in debt relationships, the reasons for the propensity of credit markets to create conditions of economic fragility, and how financial markets interact and reinforce existing patterns of social stratification. With this theoretical background, we then examine concrete examples of the relationships between credit markets and economic crisis, beginning with the racialized lending in the subprime mortgage markets. We demonstrate the parallels between the subprime market and the dynamics of credit markets in other situations: the European sovereign debt crisis, the Latin American debt crisis, and capital flight out of sub-Saharan African countries. The essay concludes with a consideration of how the framework of economic and social rights can provide an alternative approach to macroeconomic governance.

Debt, Power, and Economic Stratification

Over the past four decades, countries around the world have experienced a process of financialization—the growing dominance of finance in the economy and in people's lives. There are various approaches to conceptualizing financialization. Some define financialization as a specific regime of capitalist accumulation in which financial activities play a central role.[1] The role of financialization in the accumulation process is frequently contradictory. Certain aspects of financialization support capitalist accumulation associated with productive activities involving capital and labor, while others undermine traditional forms of production and accumulation, focusing instead on purely financial transactions. One measurement of the extent to which financialization dominates the accumulation process is the extent to which profits are generated through financial activities rather than trade and production.[2]

Other scholars take a slightly different approach and analyze financialization with a primary focus on the shifts in the objectives of capital itself, involving new forms of corporate governance. They identify a movement away from long-run profitability supported by productive activities and toward the maximization of shareholder value through financial manipulations.[3] Maximizing shareholder value involves strategies unconnected to capitalist production, such as a corporation buying back its own stock to increase its scarcity value and raise share prices.

Financialization has also been seen as a broader phenomenon that has transformed the economic situation of households in addition to the strategies of capital. This is particularly evident in the case of the U.S. economy. One observation commonly made is that the debt burden of U.S. households has grown significantly during the period of financialization. This is certainly true, but the influence of financialization runs much deeper than debt. Over the past several decades, household net worth—the wealth of households less what they owe—has increased faster than income for the broad middle of the income distribution in the United States.[4] Rising asset values in homes and pension funds help explain these trends. Those at the bottom of the income distribution did not experience similar improvements in net worth. Those at the top enjoyed the largest increases in both income and wealth. Nevertheless, over this period, the economic interests of the "middle class" have become more closely tied to asset markets than incomes, mirroring the same shift in priorities observed in corporate America during financialization. Robert Reich notes that these changes have transformed a broad swath of the U.S. population from "citizens," potentially concerned with the social problems generated by a capitalist economy, into "investors" who see their economic interests tied to asset prices and shareholder value.[5]

For the purposes of this essay, we follow Gerald Epstein in adopting a broad interpretation of financialization,[6] defining it in terms of the increasing dominance of financial motives, financial institutions (including financial markets), and financial interests. Critically, financialization has been associated with far-reaching changes to the regulatory environment that has limited the scope for government intervention in financial markets. Therefore institutions, both nationally and globally, are weak and currently do not meaningfully mitigate the unequal balance of power between financial institutions, the state, nongovernment institutions, and the nonfinancial segments of the economy. Financial institutions exert a strong influence over economic governance and the direction of policy during economic crises. This raises important questions of what can be done to change how finance is regulated to avoid the serious negative consequences of debt-driven crises. We return to this question in the conclusion when we consider economic and social rights as an alternative framework for economic governance.

Profits earned from financial activities are referred to as rents—income secured by controlling scarce resources. Unlike other scarce resources that earn rents, such as natural resources, modern financial assets are not backed by a physical commodity, and as a result their scarcity is socially constructed—based on monetary policy decisions, the structure of financial institutions, and the regulatory environment. Rentiers, those who control scarce financial resources, are able to stake a claim on the income produced in the rest of the economy. The dominance of rentier interests is a central feature of financialized economies.

Credit markets lay at the heart of the various crises that we explore in this essay. Credit markets represent a particularly critical subset of financial activities in which lenders provide borrowers with access to current funds in exchange for a claim on future streams of income or revenues. The power relationship in credit markets is derived from these claims on future income combined with the ability of those on the short-side of the credit market to sanction the other party in exchanges.[7] In credit markets, lenders represent the short-side of the market, since they control access to scarce financial resources in a context in which demand for loans frequently exceeds supply. The threat of withholding access to credit, and the ability to demand repayment on specified terms, serves as an effective sanction and gives lenders power over borrowers. Debt becomes a disciplinary device that can be used to control individual behavior, shape government policy, reinforce global dependencies, and restructure economies (see Tayyab Mahmud, this issue).

These power relationships exist even when both lenders and borrowers have freely chosen to enter into an agreement.[8] The fact that borrowers are perceived to have voluntarily entered into credit agreements is often used to argue that they are responsible for any negative consequences arising from the loan. After all, they could have chosen not to have taken out the loan in the first place. However, this line of reasoning ignores the creditor's role and the existence of unequal power dynamics, even when borrowers freely choose to take on debt. Moreover, the choice to enter into a credit agreement may not be freely chosen if, for example, the refusal to borrow would be associated with more dire consequences (i.e., the effective bankruptcy of a country). If we consider the case of the subprime mortgage crisis, the meaning of "free choice" becomes questionable when loans were made in the context of incomplete information and, in many cases, outright fraud.[9]

It is not always profitable for creditors to withhold credit as a way of exercising power and the availability of credit ebbs and flows. Lenders, in an effort to boost profitability, create new markets, often extending loans to economically marginalized borrowers or groups previously excluded from credit markets, although on less favorable terms. The search for greater profits can result in a shift from economic exclusion to unfavorable inclusion (see Elvin Wyly et al., this issue). The expansion of credit and the creation of new markets are mutually reinforcing processes, as has been theorized by post-Keynesian economists such as Hyman Minsky.[10] Post-Keynesian theories of financial instability provide important insights into the financial causes of crises in capitalist economies, particularly those undergoing financialization. The expansion of credit during good times helps keep the economy humming, leading to strong profits, higher levels of spending, and rising asset values—all of which encourage the extension of still more credit. However, these dynamics lead to a buildup of debt, which eventually produces conditions of economic fragility.

Fragility arises from the growing claims of creditors in terms of interest and loan repayments relative to the income available to borrowers. In a highly indebted, fragile economy, a shock to incomes and revenue streams can quickly precipitate a crisis.[11] Borrowers who are no longer able to meet their obligations default on their loans. Moreover, when a crisis occurs, credit dries up and creates a situation in which lenders are able to exercise a significant degree of power over borrowers. Financial institutions are able to protect their interests by this exercise of power, thereby shifting the burden of adjusting to a crisis onto less powerful groups in ways that reinforce existing social stratifications. In this process, the responsibility for the crisis is assigned to the borrowers—often portrayed as reckless, profligate, naive, or irresponsible.

Neoclassical economists and economic policymakers primarily see credit and financial markets as aspects of the economy that operate at the aggregate, or macroeconomic, level and therefore have little to do with distributive outcomes. In reality, these markets interact with institutions and structures that embody distributive dynamics and power inequalities along the lines of race, gender, class, nation, in addition to other forms of stratification. Changes at the macroeconomic level—such as a credit boom or a financial crisis—produce outcomes that reflect existing social stratifications. Feminist economists have put a great deal of effort in demonstrating that policies considered "gender blind" are not always "gender neutral," since women occupy distinct positions in the economy relative to men.[12] For similar reasons, macroeconomic dynamics play out in ways that reinforce racial inequalities. Economic shocks frequently have long-run consequences, which suggests that, when the costs of adjusting to changes in the macroeconomic environment are unevenly distributed, economic crises contribute to the persistence of patterns of stratification.[13]

For instance, as Elvin Wyly et al. (this issue) argue, the aggregate expansion of credit and liquidity in the U.S. economy during financialization has produced distinct racialized outcomes because of various structural factors: the segregated spatial organization of cities, the dysfunctional regulatory system, and discriminatory lending practices. Similarly, an empirical study by Stephanie Seguino and James Heintz found that policy decisions taken by the U.S. Federal Reserve to raise interest rates have a disproportionately negative effect on the unemployment rate of blacks relative to that of white males and on the unemployment rate of women relative to white males.[14] Moreover, these racial and gender distinctions in the response to macroeconomic policies vary from state to state, with the relative importance of the race effect and the gender effect sensitive to the racial composition of each state's population. This suggests that variations in the nature of social stratification shape the distributive consequences of macroeconomic policy.

Collective action among dominant groups secures their material advantages and facilitates the reproduction of social stratification over time.[15] The construction of identities of "whiteness," masculinity, and nationality facilitate such collective action. Scholars have theorized that the emergence and persistence of race and gender identities are sensitive to the economic benefits of maintaining those identities.[16] During an economic downturn, when jobs become scarce and household resources come under pressure, the relative benefits of maintaining identities associated with dominant, privileged groups may increase, leading to more pronounced racist, masculinist, and/or nationalist practices. At the same time, narratives of individual choice and responsibility often erase the role of collective action and the importance of constructed identities. These discourses provide alternative explanations of the existence of intergroup disparities, locating the reasons for persistent inequalities in personal failings, a lack of individual responsibility, insufficient human capital, genetics, or behaviors linked to cultural differences.[17]

Similar dynamics are evident at the global level. Powerful nations secure their material advantages in the global economy in ways that replicate international inequalities and construct national collective identities that reward those able to adopt these identities (i.e., citizens) with concrete benefits, while excluding others. Outside the countries that dominate the global economy, economic crises are often explained by an inability of governments to manage their economies effectively and such characterizations are often racialized. For example, Laura Hyun Yi Kang (this issue) analyzes the discourses that emerged after the 1997–98 "Asian crisis," showing how the causes of the crisis, although global in scope and tied to the neoliberal policies of the Washington Consensus, were blamed on Asian "cronyism" and mismanagement.

The global financial architecture exhibits structural inequalities that reinforce the international distribution of income and power. The dollar remains the global reserve currency, giving the United States a sizable advantage in international transactions. When other countries face balance of payments problems—for example, difficulties in paying for imported goods and servicing foreign debt—access to an international currency, primarily the dollar, becomes critical. In the absence of any other source of foreign exchange, countries must borrow, often from the IMF, thereby subjecting themselves to the power dynamics associated with debt. The United States does not face these constraints, having access to an abundant source of dollars.

However, there are limits to even the supply of dollars available to the United States. Someone must be willing to hold dollars, and, most recently, countries such as China and Korea, with large foreign exchange reserves, have taken on this role. This produces a particular balance of power in the global economy between large debtors (e.g., the United States) and large creditors (e.g., China). Stephen S. Cohen and J. Bradford DeLong stress this point regarding the global balance of financial power with the Wall Street quip: "If you owe the bank $1 million, the bank has you; if you owe $1 billion, you have the bank."[18] For those outside this select circle of financial goliaths, the existing structure of global financial markets can impose significant constraints on what can and cannot be done.

In summary, we have argued that the operation of credit markets—with their power dynamics discussed above—interact with existing stratifications and thereby produce distinct distributive outcomes that reinforce the economic positions of financial interests while shifting the cost of adjustment onto economically subordinate populations. To see how these dynamics have played out in detail and to provide some empirical support to these theoretical arguments, we begin with an exploration of the recent subprime mortgage and the sovereign debt crises.

Debt and Crisis: Subprime Mortgages and the European Sovereign Debt Crisis

The full extent of the recent global financial crisis first became clear in the second half of 2008, and, at the time of writing, the full ramifications of the crisis remain unclear. Although it is common to speak of "the global crisis," in reality the financial crisis has been composed of several subsidiary, interrelated crises. Here we look at two of these component crises that have been shaped by dynamics within credit markets: the U.S. subprime mortgage crisis and the European sovereign debt crisis. What we discover when making this comparison is that there are striking parallels in the relationships among credit markets, crisis, and the consequences of crisis in these two cases.

Over the past three decades, credit has been made readily available in the U.S. economy, through mortgage loans to buy property, credit cards to buy consumer goods and services, and other forms of credit, such as home equity loans, to finance a range of expenditures. Availability of credit and household indebtedness have increased significantly since the early 1980s. According to the Flow of Funds accounts released by the Federal Reserve Board of Governors, household debt averaged 65 percent of personal disposable income from 1960 to 1979.[19] Since the 1980s, household indebtedness began to increase and grew to 132 percent of disposable income in 2007—the year before the unfolding of the recent global crisis, which drew attention to how serious the financial crisis had become.

Despite this expansion in the availability of credit at the aggregate level over recent decades, access to credit had been circumscribed by race and gender. Specifically, discriminatory lending practices marginalized racialized groups in credit and housing markets.[20] With the expansion of subprime mortgages, that is, mortgages that required lower up-front cash and lower incomes than standard mortgages, these patterns of exclusion from credit markets began to shift. Credit was extended to previously excluded populations, although on unfavorable terms. Women and people of color were targeted by providers of subprime mortgages. This allowed marginalized groups access to housing markets, although at the cost of higher interest and fee payments than for standard mortgages. An ongoing expansion of credit requires the generation of new markets for loans, and subprime lending to the previously excluded represented a profitable new market opportunity.

Two studies for the Consumer Federation of America examined the race and gender dimensions of subprime mortgage lending.[21] The studies found that about 24 percent of male borrowers received subprime mortgages compared with about 32 percent of female borrowers. They also found discrimination between different racial and ethnic groups: about 20 percent of white borrowers and 13.5 percent of Asian borrowers received subprime loans in 2005, compared with almost 40 percent of Latino borrowers and over 50 percent of African American borrowers. African American women were 5.7 percent more likely to receive a subprime mortgage than African American men, and 256 percent more likely to receive one than white men. The costs of a subprime mortgage relative to a standard mortgage were substantial. Subprime borrowers were estimated to pay between $85,000 and $186,000 more in interest than average borrowers over the period of a typical mortgage.

Through the growth of credit, people in the United States appeared to be experiencing an expansion in access to economic goods and services. Average hourly wages, adjusted for inflation, had been stagnant in the United States for decades. According to data from the U.S. Bureau of Labor Statistics, the hourly wage of production, nonsupervisory workers, measured in 2007 dollars, was $18.08/hour in 1970 and $17.81/hour in 2007—the year before the major effects of the financial crisis became known.[22] Household incomes increased, even taking into account inflation, but this was due to longer hours work by all household members, explained in large part by women's increased labor force participation. Income inequality between households grew significantly during this period, but growth of consumer demand of low-income households was sustained by a rapid growth in household indebtedness, which helped lay the foundation for the economic crisis.[23]

Debts have to be repaid at some point, but the rising prices of houses led many to feel secure, because rising prices made individuals wealthier, given prevailing asset values. These wealth effects help explain expansions in the general demand for credit. Higher asset prices meant that households found their wealth was increasing without having to save, allowing for more borrowing without diminishing their net worth—the total value of assets owned less what is owed.

The subprime mortgage crisis—and the broader financial crisis—was triggered by an abrupt change in this economic environment interacting with the fragile situation created by large amounts of debt. The U.S. Federal Reserve provided an impetus for the collapse of the housing bubble by dramatically raising its key interest rate, the Federal Funds rate, from a low of 1.1 percent in 2003 to 5 percent by 2006. Interest rates had been lowered during the 2001 recession and were later raised due to concerns over modest increases in inflation. The subprime mortgages were not fixed-rate mortgages. Instead, monthly payments were tied to market interest rates. When the Federal Reserve raised its interest rate by a multiple of over four times the low rates that prevailed during the height of the boom, monthly payments on subprime loans quickly became unaffordable. Defaults became commonplace, and the housing market collapsed.

The collapse of the housing market created ripple effects throughout the global financial sector. Financial institutions had been investing in various financial instruments whose ultimate value was linked to the mortgage markets. Mortgages were bundled in a process called "securitization" and then repackaged to produce new, innovative financial products.[24] The complexities of these products prevented any accurate assessment of risk. However, they did create an environment of economic fragility that was much more substantial than that associated with the subprime mortgage market alone. Nevertheless, the financial crisis had its roots in the racialized lending associated with subprime mortgages.

The previously marginalized borrowers who were disproportionately represented in the subprime mortgage markets also suffered disproportionately from the negative fallout from the collapse of the housing market. According to a report from the Center for Responsible Lending, approximately one-quarter of African American and Latino borrowers who took out loans from 2004 to 2008 lost their homes to foreclosure or were seriously delinquent by February 2011, compared with just under 12 percent of white borrowers.[25]

In contrast, financial institutions were bailed out, in part through the federal budget and the Trouble Asset Relief Program (TARP), and much more significantly through the actions of the Federal Reserve, which bought up questionable assets linked to the subprime mortgage market.[26] While the original federal rescue package (TARP) was meant to include provisions for preserving home ownership and providing mortgage debt relief, in reality the funds were only distributed to help financial institutions.[27] The bailouts were justified on the grounds that failures of large financial institutions posed a serious threat to the U.S. economy. The implication was that mortgage defaults by African Americans, Latinos, and women in low-income households represented an isolated risk with few implications for those not directly involved.

Stepping back from the details of the rise and fall of the subprime mortgage market, we find that the policy response appears to have treated the large financial players as if they were "blameless victims"—deserving of government intervention and not held responsible for decisions made. In contrast, subprime borrowers received far less support—consistent with the perspective that they were responsible for the defaults and foreclosures, having made unwise, unsustainable, and risky choices. The contrast in the image of the systemically important investment banker (white, mostly male, privileged, shrewd) and the "typical" subprime mortgage borrower (nonwhite, poor, female, and reckless) is mirrored in the policy response.[28] The role of credit in the crisis is fundamental as is the ways in which power is distributed through credit markets. In the midst of the crisis, both subprime borrowers and major investment banks were holding large amounts of debts and assets with questionable value, but the relative vulnerability of the two groups was dramatically different.

We see similar dynamics for debt, power, and marginalization playing out internationally with the sovereign debt crisis in Europe. The European sovereign debt crisis was a result of the inability of smaller eurozone countries to continue to finance their public debt—specifically, Greece, Ireland, and Portugal.[29] The sovereign debt crisis shares many similar features to the subprime mortgage crisis. The global financial meltdown that began in U.S. financial markets triggered the sovereign debt crisis in Europe. Just as higher lending rates led to default in the U.S. subprime mortgage market, rising debt-servicing costs created a situation in which public debt in the European crisis countries was no longer sustainable.[30] In the wake of the global financial crisis, credit ratings agencies downgraded their risk assessments for the sovereign debt in the affected countries, contributing to higher costs of borrowing. In some cases, notably Ireland, the origins of the crisis were primarily in the banking sector and the government's assumption of private debts when the financial crisis hit.[31] In Greece and Portugal the causes of the crisis were primarily fiscal—that is, high levels of debt that had built up before the crisis were not sustainable after the crisis unfolded because of rising costs.

The sovereign debt crisis introduced systemic risks to the European Union and the eurozone economies. In other words, the costs of the crisis spread well beyond the countries initially affected. The European financial sector held large amounts of this sovereign debt, and the sector's stability was directly threatened by the possibility of default. For these reasons, rescue packages were organized to stabilize the situation.[32] The rescue packages included emergency loans and agreements to restructure the debts to make the debt-servicing payments affordable. Unlike the U.S. situation, in which the Federal Reserve orchestrated bailouts of the financial sector, the European Central Bank (ECB) limited its role in addressing the sovereign debt crisis. The ECB could have played "lender of last resort" by buying significant amounts of sovereign debt, just as the Federal Reserve bought mortgage-backed securities.[33] However, the ECB has not followed this course, arguing that such actions violate a principle not to finance government borrowing. Instead, the ECB has primarily focused on providing emergency loans to banks and financial interests in Europe.

The rescue packages included conditionalities requiring large cuts to government spending. The cost of adjusting to the financial crisis is therefore being borne by the populations of the countries introducing austerity programs. There is a parallel to the subprime mortgage crisis. In both cases, the bailouts focused primarily on stabilizing the financial sector while the burden of adjusting to consequences of the crisis fell on populations whose supposedly reckless actions, or those of their governments, were primarily responsible for the harsh fallout from the crisis. In the case of the sovereign debt crisis, the eurozone has been characterized by two distinct parts, a "core" (including Germany, France, and the United Kingdom) whose stability is being threatened by the "periphery" (i.e., Greece, Portugal, and Ireland).

Blaming the "other Europe" for the sovereign debt crisis provides a justification for the harsh conditionalities attached to the rescue programs. In a relatively short time period, the focus has shifted from the root cause of the financial crisis—tied to the behavior of global financial institutions—to the supposed profligacy of a few small countries. The shift has occurred despite the fact that a portion of the increase in debt was linked to the bailouts of the financial sector itself. In some cases (e.g., Greece) much of the buildup of the debt happened before 2008. However, even here the charge of fiscal recklessness needs to be unpacked. Creditors were willing to lend to countries like Greece prior to the crisis and did not deem such lending to involve excessive risks. Like the subprime mortgage market, sovereign debt represented a profitable market in a global economy awash with available credit. This is not to say that the government of Greece was a passive player as the public debt increased. Rather, the point is that credit markets involve *both* borrowers and lenders and are structured by distinct power dynamics that create asymmetries in the response to economic crises.

Latin America's Debt Crisis and Capital Flight from Africa

Subprime mortgages and sovereign debt are both closely tied to the 2008 global financial crisis. However, the economic and power dynamics associated with credit markets and debt have been evident elsewhere. In many respects, the subprime mortgage and sovereign debt crises are typical, rather than exceptional, with regard to how these scenarios play out. To see this, it is worth taking a look at some additional examples not tied to this recent financial crisis: the Latin American debt crisis of the 1980s and capital flight from sub-Saharan Africa.

The parallels between the Latin American debt crisis, leading to the region's so-called lost decade in the 1980s, and the sovereign debt crisis are remarkable. The oil shocks of the 1970s had significant negative consequences for the global economy and for many countries in Latin America. At the same time, credit was readily available—that is, there was excess liquidity in global markets, meaning that there was an abundant supply of credit looking for markets.[34] Borrowing by Latin American governments increased significantly in the 1970s and the very early 1980s. However, changes in global credit markets, partly because of dramatic shifts in monetary policies in countries like the United States, meant that easy credit was no longer available beginning in the early 1980s. Just as in the European sovereign debt crisis, many Latin American countries found that they could no longer finance their public debts. High global interest rates added to this problem. Many large Latin American countries, including Brazil, Argentina, and Mexico, faced a sovereign debt crisis of their own.

The Latin American debt crisis raised the specter of contagion and serious systemic risks for global markets and financial interests outside the region.[35] For these reasons, stabilization packages were initiated by the International Monetary Fund (IMF) and the United States in an attempt to rescue Latin American financial institutions. For instance, the U.S. Brady Plan involved the issuance of bonds, backed by guarantees, that would replace bank loans made to Latin American countries and thereby relieve some of the pressures created by the large debts.[36] Loans from the IMF were subject to conditionalities that involved spending cuts, significant devaluation of currencies, and limits on wages in an attempt to control inflation.[37] As with the European sovereign debt crisis, the burden of adjustment primarily fell on the borrowers. Moreover, the Latin American debt crisis represented a watershed in the history of the IMF, in the sense that it gave the IMF significant power over the governance of economies in Latin America.

As with the subprime mortgage crisis and the European sovereign debt crisis, the mainstream narrative that emerged out of the Latin American debt crisis was one of overborrowing, policy mistakes, and macroeconomic mismanagement on the part of the Latin American countries.[38] The question of overlending and financial institutions' responsibility for the crisis were not reflected in the policy response. Once again, in this narrative, the banks effectively became the victims of the irresponsible behavior of reckless borrowers. The negative consequences of the debt crisis and the policy conditionalities were substantial—declining per capita incomes, high rates of unemployment, falling wages, and a collapse of investment.[39]

The second example of these kinds of credit market dynamics is that of debt-financed capital flight from sub-Saharan Africa. Léonce Ndikumana and James Boyce have documented the extent of capital flight and its relationship to debt in a large number of sub-Saharan African countries.[40] In their work, capital flight is defined as unrecorded financial flows out of a country—that is, flows not related to trade, foreign investment, interest payments, or external borrowing. Political and economic elites in many African countries have moved large amounts of money out of their countries, converting this money into personal assets, such as bank accounts or other investments. These outflows of finance are unrecorded—and therefore constitute a sizable share of what Ndikumana and Boyce refer to as capital flight. They show that many sub-Saharan African countries are net creditors to the rest of the world. In other words, taking capital flight into account, financial flows out of African countries to the rest of the world have exceeded inflows.

Ndikumana and Boyce find a relationship between external borrowing and capital flight in many sub-Saharan African countries. This suggests that borrowing facilitates capital flight, and the resources that enter a country in the form of loans can leave the country in the form of capital flight. Political and economic elites become richer, while debt burdens grow. This debt must be serviced, placing pressures on government expenditures and generating real human costs in terms of lack of basic medical care, curtailed access to education, and lower levels of public services.[41]

Like the other examples of debt and credit markets, the debt burden of African countries is often said to be the result of macroeconomic mismanagement and excessive borrowing. In some respects this is true. Given the existence of capital flight and considering the ultimate destination of the funds, borrowing could certainly be said to have been excessive. The African political and economic elites who benefited from capital flight are portrayed as corrupt, enriching themselves at the expense of the rest of the population. These narratives are based on the actual experiences of many countries.[42] However, what is often missing from the story is the role of the international banks and financial institutions, usually based in the global North, whose cooperation was essential in order for capital flight to take place. These financial institutions facilitate capital flight because it is profitable to do so. In addition, they protect the assets and the identities of the elites in African countries who are responsible for capital flight. Yet the role of these institutions is often ignored and the responsibility for the debt burden racialized—that is, portrayed only in terms of corrupt and uncivilized behavior that is assumed to be characteristic of underdevelopment in Africa.

As the debt of sub-Saharan African countries became unsustainable, they were often subject to similar rescue packages with similar conditionalities to those imposed on Latin America and the European countries affected by the sovereign debt crisis. The debt situation in these sub-Saharan African countries was deemed dire enough to create a new label for them: "heavily indebted poor countries," or HIPCs. Again—the burden of adjustment fell on the borrowers. In the case of capital flight from the sub-Saharan African countries, the requirement that the borrowing country bear the primary burden is particularly unjust—the consequences of debt are borne by the general population, while collaboration between political elites and overseas financial institutions yielded large benefits for those directly involved in moving money out of the countries.

Economic and Social Rights: An Alternative Approach for Governing Credit Markets

The contribution of credit markets to these economic crises raises serious concerns over how these markets are currently governed. Finance does not operate in a vacuum, independent of the rest of society and the economy. The financial crises and related phenomena highlighted here come at a high cost, the costs are unequally distributed, and they are intricately linked to how credit markets operate. In this concluding section, we look at specific principles from one framework that could be used to justify an alternative approach to regulating finance: that of economic and social rights. There has been relatively little dialogue between those working within the framework of economic and social rights and those analyzing various aspects of macroeconomic governance.[43] Our aim is to show how certain concepts coming from the human rights framework with the specific attention to economic and social rights have potentially far-reaching implications for the way in which credit markets operate.

Human rights-based approaches to social justice have been subject to numerous critiques, and the potential limitations of the framework should be kept in mind.[44] Some have argued that the current construction of human rights is culturally biased, is therefore not universal in nature, and should not be used to assess social justice.[45] In the mainstream discourse on human rights, economic and social rights are often pushed aside in favor of civil and political rights, with a specific emphasis on individual liberty. In some cases, interpretations of civil rights directly undermine the realization of economic and social rights. For instance, the decision of the U.S. Supreme Court with regard to *Citizens United v. the Federal Election Commission*, which eliminated restrictions on corporate donations to electoral campaigns, represents the latest in a series of U.S. judicial decisions in which justification for protecting a civil right ("free speech") leads to outcomes that could undermine economic and social rights. Similarly, the discourse of human rights may be co-opted and used to reinforce the exercise of power at a global level, such as military interventions justified on the basis of the need to protect rights.[46] The economic and social rights framework also has a particular institutional focus. It sees the state as the primary duty bearer, potentially disregarding the role of other institutions, community-based traditions, or diverse forms of collective action.

These limitations should be kept in mind. However, we have specific reasons for choosing to look at elements of the economic and social rights framework in the wake of the 2008 global financial crisis. First, as mentioned above, some of the principles have potentially important implications for governance of financial institutions and markets, yet these possibilities have been underexplored. Second, economic and social rights have a concrete institutional and legal grounding. Global declarations, international treaties, covenants, and, in a number of cases, national constitutions have incorporated aspects of the economic and social rights framework—providing an institutional infrastructure in national and international law. Some have suggested that a consideration of global justice may not be a useful pursuit because of the institutional complexities involved.[47] However, this does not get around that fact that global institutions already have an impact on social justice, both positive and negative. We feel that it is useful to tease out the implications that elements of alternative frameworks have for economic governance, specifically those supported by existing institutions. Economic and social rights represent one such concrete framework. Finally, the framework is an evolving one, and ongoing discussion and deliberation is necessary to address underdeveloped areas and potential deficiencies.

It is useful to compare the elements of economic and social rights framework to other approaches to social justice. Economic and social rights focus on outcomes or realizations as the primary entry point—for example, health, jobs, education, or housing.[48] An alternative approach would be to begin with institutions—for example, if a particular economic system is considered unjust, then an institutionalist approach would define a different set of institutions that, if put into place, would constitute a just economic system. Focusing on realizations in the first instance does not imply that institutions are unimportant to economic and social rights, rather that the identification of appropriate institutions is based on desired outcomes. A second characteristic of the economic and social rights framework is that rights are progressively achieved, allowing for engagement with existing social arrangements, even if all injustices are not addressed at once. This differs from transcendental approaches to social justice, which emphasize the definition and achievement of a perfectly just world.[49] The concept of progressive realization is therefore central to economic and social rights.

The set of economic and social rights considered here were initially set out in the Universal Declaration of Human Rights. Examples of key economic and social rights include the right to food, the right to housing, the right to work, the right to health, and the right to an adequate standard of living, among others. The principles undergirding these specific rights and the obligations of states with respect to economic and social rights have been elaborated in subsequent international agreements.[50] Here we focus on a select group of these obligations and principles. The reason for focusing on these obligations and principles, rather than the specific economic and social rights (e.g., food, housing, work), is that they provide a basis for an alternative approach to financial governance ultimately linked to the realization of basic rights.

In doing so, we argue that the role of economic and social rights should shift from simply providing a safety net or a core set of basic goods and services to changing the rules under which the economy operates. Consider social assistance and social protection programs, such as "employer of last resort schemes," which are meant to provide emergency employment for poor households, and conditional cash transfers, which provide cash grants to families meeting specific criteria.[51] Such interventions frequently assume that broad economic parameters are fixed and implement social programs taking these constraints as given. However, the availability of resources to administer these social programs is determined by macroeconomic dynamics, which are themselves the outcome of deliberate policy choices. Taking this broader context as untouchable does little to address the power dynamics in financial markets, which limit the resources available to fund social assistance programs. In addition, social assistance programs operate through direct government provisioning of jobs, cash payments, or social services. A comprehensive approach to economic and social rights accommodates a wider range of institutions, in which the realization of rights is not limited to state provisioning but also considers the state's role in providing the appropriate legislative, budgetary, and judicial environment conducive to the realization of rights.[52] This introduces larger ideas of economic governance into the discussion of basic economic rights.

The obligations and principles considered here include the following:

- The obligation to protect—requires the state to take steps in order to protect economic and social rights from actions by third parties that interfere with the enjoyment of those rights.
- The principles of progressive realization and nonretrogression—the state must take steps to progressively realize economic and social rights over time and to prevent an erosion of those rights.
- The principle of maximum available resources—requires the state to undertake steps to use the maximum of available resources to progressively realize economic and social rights.[53]
- The principle of nondiscrimination and equality—the state must ensure the equal enjoyment of rights in terms of both its conduct and the outcomes of its policies. Because of the focus on substantive outcomes, "race blind" or "gender blind" policies are not sufficient for compliance with this principle. Nondiscrimination also implies that positive steps must be taken to reduce already existing inequalities.

• The principle of accountability, participation and, transparency—governments are obliged to provide mechanisms through which people can hold the state accountable, can participate in policymaking, and can access the information required to do so.

Compliance with these obligations and principles imply a very different way of regulating credit markets and responding to financial crises than the dominant approach over the past several decades. For instance, deregulation of financial markets allowed global investors to take decisions that led to the 2008 global financial crisis. The outcome of the crisis in many countries has been a retrogression of economic and social rights, as the consequences of the European sovereign debt crisis illustrate. This represents a failure of the obligation to protect. The lack of any systematic mortgage regulation in the U.S. markets, which allowed predatory lending to flourish, also represents a failure with regard to the obligation to protect and, given the demographics of those caught up in the subprime mortgage crisis, a violation of the principle of nondiscrimination and equality. Similarly, the use of resources by governments and central banks to bail out financial institutions and the subsequent imposition of austerity budgets without demanding greater accountability of the rescued banks and investment firms could be said to violate the principle of maximum available resources as well as the principle of accountability, participation, and transparency.

Moreover, the principle of maximum available resources could be used to justify reform that requires financial institutions to support the progressive realization of economic rights, since the "available resources" include the credit and monetary system. This could be achieved, for example, by requiring banks to provide credit to populations shut out of financial services on favorable terms or by regulating the extension of credit so that a portion of loans support affordable housing, health care facilities, or investments that generate jobs in areas of high unemployment. A recognition of economic and social rights as entitlements that the state must defend, and that extend well beyond property rights which provide the current institutional foundation for market economies, would alter the power dynamics in credit markets. We have argued that the asymmetries of power in credit and financial markets have been responsible for the kind of financial crises we have witnessed and the dramatically uneven consequences of those crises. The economic and social rights framework suggests a fundamentally different approach to financial governance that begins to address these concerns.

Of course, the actual implementation of the principles and obligations associated with economic and social rights is far more difficult. Not all states are party to the various agreements that constitute the existing framework, and even among signatories the enforcement of government obligations is frequently limited. International institutions, like the International Monetary Fund, claim that they cannot be held accountable for economic and social rights because the IMF is not a state and is not bound by the agreements. Since the state is the prime duty bearer in the economic and social rights framework, the global dimensions of financial regulation need much further elaboration. These barriers are not trivial and present real challenges for applying the economic and social rights framework to the question of financial and credit markets.

In particular, there is a tension between the capacity of individual states to take steps to support the realization of economic and social rights and the dynamics of an integrated global economy in which financial interests have significant power. Under these conditions, coordinated action by states, including government agencies like central banks, will be needed to fully support the core principles and obligations discussed here. To give a concrete example: how financial markets in the United States are regulated has implications for realizing economic and social rights elsewhere. If this framework is to move beyond a focus on the nation-state and to recognize the need for action globally, a number of conditions must be met. Countries should not be able to opt out of their obligations with respect to economic and social rights—that is, such rights must truly be universal. Global and international institutions must be accountable to the same set of human rights obligations as individual governments. The obligations that states have with regard to other countries need to be much better defined, explicitly recognizing power differentials in the global economy. Effective mechanisms for coordination across countries must be developed, including the creation of a common set of rules for regulating transnational businesses and financial players.

Clearly, the institutional requirements for a truly global approach to economic and social rights do not currently exist. We are not suggesting that the economic and social rights framework, as it currently stands, is a fully conceptualized approach to global justice backed by a complete set of effective institutions. Instead, we are suggesting that the concept of economic and social rights, including the current principles and obligations associated with this framework, implies a fundamentally different approach to macroeconomic governance, including reform of the role of financial institutions in the economy. There has been very little exploration of these issues, and this is unfortunate. The human rights framework is often dismissed as being too narrowly focused on individual liberties and political freedoms. In practice, this is often true, but it is a result of the marginalization of economic and social rights in the broad human rights discourse. This can result in the rejection of economic and social rights without fully understanding the potential of this approach for advancing social justice. We suggest that this is a mistake and that the constructive development of the economic and social rights approach, and the institutions that back it, would lead to a fundamentally different kind of global economy demanding a transformation of how financial markets and institutions operate.

Conclusion

In many respects, debt and credit markets lie at the core of the agglomeration of financial markets and institutions that have become increasingly influential in recent decades: directly influencing the paths that economies take, determining—to a large extent—the policies adopted, and limiting the scope for advancements in social justice. We have argued that the operation of these markets reflect inherent power relationships that interact with existing patterns of stratification, producing mainstream discourses that hide unequal racial and gender dynamics and reshape policy responses. These features of credit markets are not unique to the 2008 collapse and can be found in numerous other economic debacles that have occurred in this era of global financialization, in which policy decisions have exacerbated, rather than curtailed, the growing power of finance.

We feel that the economic and social rights approach has significant potential to turn this situation around, yet, in considering this alternative, we must recognize that it is still early days. The field of economic and social rights is quite young and, in many ways, underdeveloped. Perhaps the biggest challenge with regard to applying this approach to global finance is the need to flesh out how best to coordinate action among states at the global level in ways that take into account unequal power dynamics and support the realization of basic economic and social rights. Clearly, the institutional infrastructure is not currently in place to make this happen. Nevertheless, steps can be taken to build on what currently exists and to push out the frontiers of economic governance. In the meantime, much can still be done at the national and subnational level. For example, revisiting the U.S. subprime mortgage crisis through the lens of economic and social rights reveals a fundamentally different approach to economic governance when compared with the recent dominance of neoliberal policies. There is a long way to go before these alternatives are realized, and it will not happen overnight. If the aim is to progressively realize a new approach to finance, we suggest that much can be gained through ongoing explorations of the potency, and possible limitations, of the economic and social rights framework.

Notes

The authors would like to thank the anonymous reviewer, Paula Chakravartty, and Denise Ferreira da Silva for their numerous helpful comments and suggestions in preparing this essay.

1. David Harvey, *The Enigma of Capital* (Oxford: Oxford University Press, 2010); John Belemy Foster, "The Financialization of Accumulation," *Monthly Review* 62.5 (2010): 1–17; Greta Krippner, "The Financialization of the American Economy," *Socio-Economic Review* 3 (2005): 173–208; Giovanni Arrighi, *The Long Twentieth Century: Money, Power and the Origins of Our Times* (New York: Verso, 1994).
2. Krippner, "Financialization of the American Economy."
3. William Lazonick, "How Shareholder Value Ideology Is Destroying the U.S. Economy," in *The Oxford Handbook on the Political Economy of Financial Crises*, ed. Gerald Epstein and Martin Wolfson (Oxford: Oxford University Press, forthcoming); James Crotty, "The Neoliberal Paradox: The Impact of Destructive Product Market Competition and 'Modern' Financial Markets on Nonfinancial Corporation Performance in the Neoliberal Era," in *Financialization and the World Economy*, ed. Gerald Epstein (Northampton, Mass.: Elgar, 2005), 77–110.
4. Arthur B. Kennickell, "Ponds and Streams: Wealth and Income in the U.S., 1989 to 2007," Finance and Economic Discussion Paper 2009-13 (Washington, D.C.: Federal Reserve Board, 2009).
5. Robert Reich, *Supercapitalism: The Transformation of Business, Democracy, and Everyday Life* (New York: Knopf, 2007).
6. Gerald Epstein, "Introduction: Financialization and the World Economy," in Epstein, *Financialization and the World Economy*, 3–16.
7. Samuel Bowles and Herbert Gintis, "The Revenge of Homo Economicus: Contested Exchange and the Revival of Political Economy," *Journal of Economic Perspectives* 7.1 (1993): 83–102.
8. Ibid.
9. The U.S. Federal Bureau of Investigation recognized the existence of widespread mortgage fraud in the United States during the period in which the subprime mortgage market was expanding rapidly. See http://www.fbi.gov/news/stories/2008/january/fin_fradu013108.
10. Hyman Minsky, *Stabilizing an Unstable Economy* (New Haven, Conn.: Yale University Press, 1986).
11. Ibid.
12. Lourdes Benería, "Towards a Greater Integration of Gender in Economics," *World Development* 23.11 (1995): 1839–50; Diane Elson, "Gender Aware Analysis and Development Economics," *Journal of International Development* 5.2 (1993): 237–47; Stephanie Seguino, "The Global Economic Crisis, Its Gender and Ethnic Implications, and Policy Responses," *Gender and Development* 18.2 (2010): 179–99.
13. This can happen when the shocks associated with a crisis period have long-run consequences. For example, episodes of unemployment have been shown to negatively affect future earnings (Wiji Arulampalam, "Is Unemployment Really Scarring? Effects of Unemployment Experiences on Wages," *Economic Journal* 111 [November 2001]: F585–F606). Similarly, transitions into the labor market during bad economic times appear to have long-run effects on career paths (Lisa Kahn, "The Long-Term Labor Consequences of Graduating from College in a Bad Economy," *Labour Economics* 17.2 [2010]: 303–16).
14. Stephanie Seguino and James Heintz, "Contractionary Monetary Policy and the Dynamics of U.S. Race and Gender Stratification," *American Journal of Economics and Sociology* 71.3 (forthcoming).

15. Charles W. Mills, *The Racial Contract* (Ithaca, N.Y.: Cornell University Press, 1999); and William Darity, "Stratification Economics: The Role of Intergroup Inequality," *Journal of Economics and Finance* 29.2 (2005): 144–53. Mills uses the concept of a "racial contract," in contrast to the "social contract" construct of contractarian social theory and ethics, to describe forms of collective action among whites that promote their collective interests and subordinate those who are not white.

16. William Darity, Patrick L. Mason, and J. Stewart, "The Economics of Identity: The Origin and Persistence of Racial Norms," *Journal of Economic Behavior and Organizations* 60.3 (2006): 283–305.

17. Darity, "Stratification Economics"; Rhonda Williams and William Spriggs, "How Does It Feel to Be Free? Reflections on Black-White Economic Inequality in the Era of 'Color-Blind' Law," *Review of Black Political Economy* 27.1 (1999): 9–21.

18. Stephen S. Cohen and J. Bradford DeLong, *The End of Influence: What Happens When Other Countries Have the Money* (New York: Basic Books, 2010), 5.

19. The Flow of Funds Accounts are produced by the U.S. Federal Reserve and contain estimates of financial assets and liabilities for various sectors of the U.S. economy. For more details, see http://www.federalreserve.gov/apps/fof/.

20. Gary Dymski, "Discrimination in the Credit and Housing Markets: Findings and Challenges," in *Handbook on the Economics of Discrimination*, ed. William M. Rodgers (Cheltenham, U.K.: Elgar, 2006), 215–59.

21. A. J. Fishbein and P. Woodall, *Subprime Locations: Patterns of Geographic Disparity in Subprime Lending* (Washington, D.C.: Consumer Federation of America, 2006); Fishbein and Woodall, *Women Are Prime Targets for Subprime Lending: Women Are Disproportionately Represented in High-Cost Mortgage Market* (Washington, D.C.: Consumer Federation of America, 2006).

22. See www.bls.gov. Hourly wages were inflation-adjusted using the consumer price index for all urban consumers. Estimates of hourly wages came from the Bureau of Labor Statistic's Current Employment Survey program.

23. Robert Reich, *Aftershock: The Next Economy and America's Future* (New York: Vintage, 2011); Branko Milanovic, *Two Views on the Cause of the Global Crisis* (Washington, D.C.: Carnegie Endowment for Peace, 2009), www.carnegieendowment.org/publications/index.cfm?fa=view&id=23053; Seguino, "Global Economic Crisis."

24. Financial products directly linked to mortgages were called "mortgage-backed securities" or "asset-backed securities." The "collateralized debt obligations," or CDOs, represented one form of mortgage-backed security. Other financial products, such as "credit default swaps," effectively acted as insurance policies in the event of a default on debt.

25. Debbie Gruenstein Bocian, Wei Li, Carolina Reid, and Roberto G. Quercia, *Lost Ground 2011: Disparities in Mortgage Lending and Foreclosures* (Durham, N.C.: Center for Responsible Lending, 2011).

26. General Accountability Office, "Troubled Federal Reserve System: Opportunities Exist to Strengthen Policies and Processes for Managing Emergency Assistance," GAO-11-696 (Washington, D.C.: General Accountability Office, July 2011); General Accountability Office, "Troubled Asset Relief Program: Status of Efforts to Address Transparency and Accountability Issues," GAO-09-296 (Washington, D.C.: General Accountability Office, January 2009). According to a story published by Bloomberg Market Magazine on November 27, 2011, based on the analysis of documents obtained through a freedom of information request, the Federal Reserve had committed $7.7 trillion to bail out the financial system by March 2009, http://www.bloomberg.com/news/2011-11-28/secret-fed-loans-undisclosed-to-congress-gave-banks-13-billion-in-income.html.

27. See the op-ed by Neil M. Barofsky, who was the special inspector general for the Troubled Asset Relief Program, "Where the Bailout Went Wrong," *New York Times*, March 29, 2011.

28. In reality, white borrowers accounted for a significantly larger absolute number of foreclosures and delinquencies than African American or Latino borrowers (Bocian et al., "Lost Ground 2011").

29. Spain and Italy are sometimes included in discussions of the sovereign debt crisis.

30. Adrian Blundell-Wignall and Patrick Slovik, "A Market Perspective on the European Sovereign Debt and Banking Crisis," *Financial Market Trends*, February 2011, 1–28.

31. Ibid.

32. Deborah Zandstra, "The European Sovereign Debt Crisis and Its Evolving Resolution," *Capital Markets Law Journal* 6.3 (2011): 285–316. Two stability mechanisms were used to administer the rescue programs: the European Financial Stability Mechanism and, when more substantial interventions were required, the European Financial Stability Facility.

33. Blundell-Wignall and Slovik, "Market Perspective."

34. Manuel Pastor, "Latin America: The Debt Crisis and the International Monetary Fund," *Latin American Perspectives* 16.1 (1989): 79–109.

35. David Felix, "Latin America's Debt Crisis," *World Policy Journal* 7.4 (1990): 733–71.

36. Ibid.; Pastor, "Latin America."

37. Pastor, "Latin America."

38. Ibid.

39. Felix, "Latin America's Debt Crisis."

40. Léonce Ndikumana and James Boyce, *Africa's Odious Debts: How Foreign Loans and Capital Flight Bled a Continent* (London: Zed Books, 2011).

41. Ibid.

42. Ibid.

43. For a much more detailed examination of the relationship between economic and social rights and macroeconomic policy, see Radhika Balakrishnan and Diane Elson, eds., *Economic Policy and Human Rights: Holding Governments to Account* (London: Zed Press, 2011).

44. We do not consider here the question of whether human rights can be said to exist prior to the legislation or legal institutions that define those rights. For a fuller discussion of these issues, see Amartya Sen, "Elements of a Theory of Human Rights," *Philosophy and Public Affairs* 32.4 (2004): 315–56; Sen, *The Idea of Justice* (Cambridge, Mass.: Harvard University Press, 2010).

45. See, for example, M. W. Mutua, "Savages, Victims, and Saviors: The Metaphor of Human Rights," *Harvard International Law Journal* 42.1 (2001): 201–45. Mutua argues that traditional human rights discourse creates "savages," "victims," and "saviors," which reinforce existing global stratifications (e.g., the saviors are represented by governments and human rights organizations in the global North that attempt to rescue victims from savages in the global South).

46. David Kennedy, *The Dark Side of Virtue: Reassessing International Humanitarianism* (Princeton, N.J.: Princeton University Press, 2005).

47. Thomas Nagel, "The Problem of Global Justice," *Philosophy and Public Affairs* 33.2 (2005): 113–47.

48. Sen, *Idea of Justice*.

49. Ibid.

50. Key international agreements that elaborate the details of the economic and social rights framework include the Convention on the Elimination of All Forms of Racial Discrimination, the International Covenant on Economic, Social and Cultural Rights, the Convention on the Elimination of All Forms of Discrimination Against Women, and the Convention on the Rights of the Child. The obligations implied by international human rights instruments have been spelled out more fully though a number of mechanisms, including General Comments and General Recommendations issued from time to time by UN treaty monitoring bodies, such as the Committee on Economic, Social and Cultural Rights, and by experts in international law, such as the groups of experts who produced the Limburg Principles on the Implementation of the International Covenant on Economic, Social and Cultural Rights and the Maastricht Guidelines on Violations of Economic, Social and Cultural Rights.

51. India's National Rural Employment Guarantee Act is an example of an "employer of last resort" program. Brazil's *bolsa família* is an example of a conditional cash transfer program.

52. In the economic and social rights framework, this is referred to as the obligation of the state to fulfill rights and does not necessarily imply direct provisioning by the government.

53. Some of these principles do not apply to civil and political rights. For example, civil and political rights are often deemed to be immediate rights. Therefore the principles of progressive realization and maximum available resources are not applied.

The Uses of Asianization: Figuring Crises, 1997–98 and 2007–?

Laura Hyun Yi Kang

If we do not learn from history, we are unlikely to fully recover from it.
—Financial Crisis Inquiry Commission, 2011

In this jumbled and humbled reformulation of George Santayana's dictum, "Those who do not learn from history are condemned to repeat it," the collective future is enchained to a past that continues to afflict even as this event sounds as if it happened to someone else. What began in 2007 with a rash of defaults on U.S. home mortgages exposed a much larger circuit of unruly capital speculation involving banks, Wall Street firms, and foreign investors. Even after widespread bankruptcies, massive bailouts, and ongoing sovereign debt crises have exposed the deep dysfunctions of neoliberal deregulation on a global scale, many still attribute the origin of the ongoing crisis to the racialized figure of undeserving and undisciplined "subprime" *borrowers* in the U.S. housing market.

Crises are also archives of figuration, which demand critical reading, disfiguration, and reframing. Through conjuring particular subjects as knowing perpetrators or unwitting casualties, accounts of crises delineate particular axes of intelligibility while obscuring and precluding others. Certain components and arc of the narration of the "subprime crisis" have striking parallels to the earlier "Asian crisis" of 1997–98. Then, too, an unprecedented availability of credit and transnational mobility of speculative capital created a scene of unserviceable debt by banks and firms in South Korea, Thailand, and Indonesia. Regarding these Asian countries as a bigger incarnation of subprime borrowers generates several parallels. Both had been excluded from proper accreditation and the attendant access to the funds that would merit meaningful global and national citizenship. That entire nations are assigned a fluctuating and often punitive "credit rating" in the global marketplace affirms this cofiguration. These countries were attempting to move up from "developing" to "developed" and from "newly industrializing countries" (NICs) to "advanced" status, signaled by open capital markets. In both scenarios, the measure of economic ascent

51

is greater indebtedness and exposure to the vagaries of capital markets rather than self-sufficiency and solvency. When both sets of debtors became unable to make timely payments, "Asian" and "subprime" came to signify a deficient mutation of capitalist development and fiscal maturity. In this sense, subprime suggests both subordination and temporal-historical lag.

The rendering of a crisis produces contending diagnoses of cause but also differentially motivated prognoses about the future, with warnings and recommendations for its rightful shaping by current interventions. By attributing the 1997–98 crisis to an untenable Asian permutation of an original and righteous "Western capitalism," the International Monetary Fund (IMF) and the U.S. Treasury Department compelled restructurings, which further buttressed the rightness of a specifically U.S.-dictated neoliberal program of deregulation, privatization, and financial liberalization. The possible lessons to be learned in 1997–98 about the dangers of unfettered capital mobility and the outsized market in arcane financial instruments were foreclosed by the "Asianization" of the crisis.

The dominant figurations of a crisis also delineate the proper disciplinary and interdisciplinary boundaries of study. While the racialization of the subprime crisis renders it the commonsense and even urgent object of American studies and critical ethnic studies, the location of the 1997–98 crisis in Asia pushes it beyond a shared frame of analysis. The temporal bracketing of crises with a definite beginning and ending additionally elides important preconditions, lingering effects, continuities, and reversals. Thinking through the "crisis of the subprime" entails discerning the enmeshed actors, events, and processes that connect the Asian crisis to the subprime crisis. This article attempts to bring the Asian crisis within the necessary purview of a transnational, interdisciplinary American studies by connecting the histories of U.S. empire in Asia with the dismantling of the U.S. domestic manufacturing base, the rise of U.S. foreign debt to the expansion of domestic consumer credit, and the dispossession of those who must borrow to the financialized abstraction of risk. To that end, I recite and juxtapose several dispersed archives in Asian studies, feminist political economy, and development economics. I also cite newspaper and journal articles as well as reports by the World Bank and the International Monetary Fund. Most were written and published in the immediate aftermath of the 1997–98 crises and consequently provide instructive demonstrations of the analytic work that confronts us in the ongoing crisis.

This article is organized into several linked arguments. First, I problematize the temporal enclosure of the 1997–98 crisis by recalling three interconnected Asianizations in the 1990s, from "Asian miracle" to "Asian crisis" to "Asian recovery." The Asianization of crisis was preceded by the more sanguine figuration of an Asian miracle, which touted the prodigious economic growth of first Japan and later the "Four Dragons" (South Korea, Taiwan, Hong Kong, and Singapore). Even though certain enabling conditions of their growth were part and parcel of the history of the U.S. Cold War empire in Asia, the Asian miracle insinuated a mystifying aura to this distinguished formation. When it became increasingly evident that their economic ascent was significantly accomplished by distinct departures from neoclassical laissez-faire economics, the Asian miracle took on increasingly dubious connotations. By the 1990s Asian miracle and its variant of East Asian miracle became highly charged and contested designations in a debate about two contrasting models of development, an "Asian model" distinguished by strategic state planning and intervention and a "Washington Consensus" paradigm of a greatly reduced state that mainly facilitates the international flow of goods and capital. The 1997–98 crisis was figured as the inevitable outcome and confirmation of this Asian model, further confirming this bifurcation of "Asian" and "American" capitalisms.

Second, I attempt to *de-Asianize* the 1997–98 crisis by contextualizing it in terms of three other interconnected "stories" about the 1990s. The first regards the global drive toward privatization, deregulation, and financial liberalization, which began in the 1970s. The greatly accelerated internationalization of capital markets in the 1990s unleashed a series of interlinked financial crises; the 1997–98 crisis was preceded by the 1994 Mexican crisis and was followed closely by the Russian crisis of 1998 and the Brazilian crisis of 1998–99, ending with the bailout of Long-Term Capital Management, which threatened to destabilize the U.S. financial system. A second "story" highlights shifts across two stages and modalities of U.S. empire in Asia, from Cold War hegemony to the Wall Street–Treasury–IMF complex. In the early 1990s the United States actively promoted financial liberalization of Asian markets and then played a leading role in the figuration and the management of the Asian crisis in ways that clearly protected the interests of Wall Street and other private investors. This political-economic repositioning of the United States is closely interrelated with a complementary shift in the mission and actions of the Bretton Woods institutions, especially the IMF, which forms the third "story" in this broadened narration of the 1997–98 crisis. To be sure, my aim in thus de-Asianizing the 1997–98 crisis is not to erase or minimize the errors and complicities of various political and economic actors in Asia. Rather, it demonstrates how global financial liberalization through the fortification of the Wall Street–Treasury–IMF complex in the 1990s was an important episode in the history of U.S. empire in Asia.

Third, I point to important connections and missed connections between the 1997–98 crisis and the subprime crisis of 2007–8. As the mortgage defaults and bankruptcies expanded into a financial crisis involving major Wall Street, and later British, firms, there was a fresh round of "Asian triumphalism," which excoriated the hubris of neoliberal orthodoxy and further reinforced a bifurcation of Asia and the United States. Against these uses of Asianization, which elide significant heterogeneities and inequalities, I end with a de-Asianization by drawing attention to the multiple uneven effects of development, globalization, and financialization on women in Asia, which also contests the progressive emplotment of miracle-crisis-recovery-triumph.

"Asian Miracle" and U.S. Cold War Hegemony

An earlier Asianization of the miraculous economic development of several countries preconditioned the Asianization of the 1997–98 crisis. The term *miracle* was first deployed to distinguish Japan's impressive recovery and unprecedented economic growth after the devastations of World War II.[1] As a strategic Pacific base for the U.S. military, the miraculous figuration of Japanese economic growth affirmed U.S. geopolitical interests during the initial bipolar years of the Cold War. As Chalmers Johnson summed up, "From approximately 1950 to 1975, the United States treated Japan as a beloved ward, indulging its every economic need and proudly patronizing it as a star capitalist pupil," whereby Japan could be held up as "a capitalist alternative to mainland China, a model and a showcase of what Asians might expect if they threw in their lot with the Americans."[2] To that end, the United States also facilitated the entry of Japan into the United Nations and the Organisation for Economic Co-operation and Development (OECD). Even as the Cold War framework called for Japan to adopt certain political and economic components of free market capitalism, Japan pursued a "third way," which integrated state controls of certain industries, banking, and finance. The United States would later support the state-guided, export-driven industrialization of South Korea to showcase both countries as "paragons of non-communist development."[3] That such tolerance and support did not extend to other countries and regions underscores the unevenness of U.S. empire during the Cold War era.

The broadened terms *East Asian miracle* and *Asian miracle* were later applied to the rapid economic growth of South Korea, Taiwan, Hong Kong, and Singapore throughout the 1970s. These "first-generation NICs" were held up as models of export-oriented development for other countries in Asia, Latin America, and Africa. The economic rise of virulently anticommunist South

Korea and Taiwan further displaced Japan as the "star capitalist pupil" of the United States. Then, in the 1980s, Thailand, Indonesia, Malaysia, and the Philippines emerged as second-generation NICs, further expanding the geographic boundaries and political-economic variations of the Asian miracle. Walden Bello has usefully distinguished the "fast-track capitalism" of these Southeast Asian economies as "sustained not principally by domestic savings and investment but by foreign investment."[4] With its earlier economic ascendance and expanding reserves, Japan became an important source of both bilateral aid and direct investment, as Japanese firms began to transfer production offshore to these NICs. Japan's status in Asia was also shifting as the memories of its imperial violence and the Asia-Pacific war meshed with this new role as investor, lender, and donor. This brief summary merely touches on a few details to demonstrate the intra-Asian heterogeneities, which repudiate a singular Asian miracle.

Amid the widespread invocation and scholarly analyses of the Asian miracle in the late 1980s and 1990s, the World Bank published *The East Asian Miracle: Economic Growth and Public Policy*, which included Thailand, Indonesia, and Malaysia, along with Japan, South Korea, Taiwan, Hong Kong, and Singapore.[5] *The East Asian Miracle* demonstrates how the Asianization of miracle that preceded the Asianization of crisis must be understood as a discursive and ideological struggle. It was a muddled product of an escalating struggle within the World Bank between Japan and the United States about the role of state guidance and interventions in economic development. Since the early 1980s the World Bank had been imposing structural adjustment programs, composed of deregulation, cuts in public spending, privatization of state resources, and openness to foreign investments, as a condition of lending. By the end of the decade the World Bank turned its attention to the financial sector, convening a bank task force on financial sector operations that endorsed extensive liberalization. The 1980s also marked the growing financial contributions of Japan to the World Bank and to development efforts worldwide.[6] Given its enhanced international standing and regional leadership, Japan began to articulate criticisms of the reigning neoliberal orthodoxy along with a more assured advocacy of its own distinctive path to economic growth and stability. In 1991, in response to pressure from the Japanese Ministry of Finance, the World Bank commissioned a multicountry examination of the role of state guidance. In return Japan agreed that it would not oppose what eventually became operational directive 8.30, financial sector operations (February 1992), which championed thorough financial deregulation.[7] Even though the final *East Asian Miracle* report acknowledged the effectiveness of state planning and strategic intervention in certain instances, it largely affirmed the free market Washington Consensus, which was toned down slightly as a "market-friendly" approach.

The positive outlook of these "miracle" economies attracted unprecedented international investments, which had been redirected from the United States where interest rates remained low through the early 1990s. The naming of the Asian miracle, however, elided an important distinction between industrial productivity and macroeconomic performance versus foreign capital flows into these countries, which accelerated in the 1990s. Unlike foreign direct investments in machinery, plants, and other infrastructure, portfolio investments in stocks, bonds, currencies, and derivatives are much easier to take out quickly if the terms become unfavorable. After the Mexican crisis of 1994, investors increasingly turned toward Asia. By raising their interest rates above the U.S. rates and pegging the value of their currencies to the U.S. dollar, these countries provided a lucrative and safe alternative for investors. Between 1994 and 1996 over $220 billion were pumped into South Korea, Thailand, Indonesia, Malaysia, and the Philippines.[8] Just in 1996 there was a net capital inflow of $93 billion into these economies. Such massive influx of foreign capital increases the value of local currencies; this makes imports cheaper, fueling a consumption boom, and exports more expensive, leading to an account deficit. The suddenly bloated foreign debt soon exceeded each country's foreign currency reserves. More consequential still was the fact that much of this foreign debt was mostly short-term loans, with 62 percent set to mature in one year or less, and a sizable number of those with a repayment window of ninety days or less.[9]

The specific trajectory of South Korea from miracle to crisis complicates both its Asianization and its clear temporal demarcation. The country had been able to weather earlier external shocks in the 1970s and 1980s because of strict government oversight of and intervention into banking and finance, including restricting borrowing by Korean firms only for productive investments rather than speculation and increasing government spending to enable firms to generate needed revenue. In 1993 the U.S. Department of Treasury successfully convinced the Clinton administration to pressure South Korea into greater financial liberalization *against* the opposition of its own Council of Economic Advisers.[10] In response to pressure from the United States and in order to join the OECD—dubbed the "club of rich nations"—the government abolished its Economic Planning Board in 1994, loosening restrictions on both foreign borrowing by Korean banks and the movement of foreign capital investments into and out of the country.[11] By 1997 Korean banks and corporations had incurred $160 billion in foreign debt.[12] Many of these loans were short-term, so that repayment was due in twelve months or less in some cases. Several Korean banks, flush with this new capital, began to make speculative investments in "junk" bonds in Russia and Latin America.[13]

Two other events further contest the Asianization of miracle and crisis. A significant development in the 1990s was the emergence of China as the leading export manufacturer *without* financial liberalization. China devalued its yuan in 1990 and again in 1994, raising the value of exports from other Asian countries.[14] Then in 1995 Japan and the United States struck an accord whereby the yen depreciated 60 percent against the dollar by April 1997, thereby lowering the prices of Japanese exports to the United States and stimulating demand.[15] These two devaluations hurt the export competitiveness of Thailand and Indonesia, whose currencies were pegged to the dollar, and further compromised their ability to meet foreign debt obligations.

The collective rush to invest in Asia turned to a panicked retreat after July 2, 1997, when Thailand became the first country to fail to meet its foreign loan payments and floated its baht. Investors realized that many firms were carrying high debt loads, and several countries did not have enough foreign currency reserves to cover a massive flight of capital. The earlier competitive dash to invest in Asian markets and economies reversed into a rush to get out quickly before others could do so. Foreign lenders called in their loans and stopped extending new credit.[16] Indonesia, Malaysia, and the Philippines floated their currencies shortly thereafter.

"Asian Crisis" and the Wall Street–Treasury–IMF Complex

In the immediate aftermath of the 1997–98 crisis, many Western commentators were quick to blame the "meltdown" on a specifically Asian pathology of "crony capitalism," characterized by excessive government involvement in industrial growth, nepotism, and favored protection of specific firms, and a lack of transparency.[17] As the concerned editors of a special issue of the *Cambridge Journal of Economics* explained: "We were, we felt, witnessing a revival of Orientalism, in which all manner of fantasies and prejudices are projected onto Asia, with no concern for their veracity. . . . 'cronyism,' for example, was becoming the modern substitute for 'Oriental despotism' or 'Asiatic absolutism.'"[18] Indeed, it was a distinctly *American* moment of triumph and self-congratulation. In an article in the February 13, 1998, edition of the *New York Times* bearing the blunt title, "Greenspan Sees Asian Crisis Moving World to Western Capitalism," the chairman of the Federal Reserve is quoted as testifying before the

Senate Foreign Relations Committee: "What we have here is a very dramatic event towards a consensus of the type of market system which we have in this country."[19] As Johnson critically noted ten days later, "With East Asia's economic troubles in mind, many Americans have entered the last years of the twentieth century in a mood of truly obscene jingoism, or what the Germans call *Schadenfreude*, the malicious pleasure of gloating over the misfortunes of others."[20] Quoting an array of commentators from Greenspan to the financier George Soros to then IMF deputy managing director Stanley Fisher, Robert Wade articulated an especially lively depiction of these dynamics:

> The tone of voice ranges from gloating, to sanctimonious, to schoolmasterly. It is not hard to imagine the offense of Japanese, Korean, and other Asian policy-makers at the triumphalism of Westerners who picture the Asian political economy as a system whose movement toward America-without-the-ghettoes the current crisis has simply accelerated.[21]

Wade does not explicate what he means by "America-without-the-ghettoes" here, but it does portend a striking figurative link to the subprime crisis of 2007 yet to come.

The 1997–98 crisis created the occasion for a further bifurcation of the so-called Asian model from the Washington Consensus in what Johnson characterized as "the clash of capitalisms."[22] Such hyperbolic divisions confound a more sober account of several interrelated political economic processes conditioning the crisis. The first broad context is the crises-ridden globalization of finance capitalism, which began in the 1960s with the massive U.S. military spending (through borrowing) during the Vietnam War. Then the OPEC oil boom of the 1970s made an even larger pool of money available for circulation. In the 1980s the invention and proliferation of new financial instruments such as derivatives, intended to manage the growing risks such as currency fluctuations in international markets, also created new channels of investment. These new financial instruments also came to function increasingly as vehicles of speculation and outsized bets, generating large commissions and profits for some but also intensifying volatility and uncertainty. Contrary to the prevalent figuration of Asian capital markets as overly protected and underdeveloped in the 1990s, many Asian firms were very much actively integrated into this transnational circuit of speculative capital and offshore finance.

The oversupply of money circulating in an unevenly integrated circuit of established and emerging markets created a hazardous scene well before 1997–98. Gabriel Palma has argued that the primary cause of the Asian crisis as well as the earlier 1982 crisis and the Mexican crisis of 1994 was "excess international liquidity," which leads to two mutually constitutive "market failures": first, "the propensity to 'over-lend,'" and second, "the propensity to 'over-borrow.'" The first excess in lending is attributed to how "competitive pressures to recycle funds impair international financial operators' capacity to assess and price risks properly and to allocate resources effectively—i.e., they inexorably move . . . from lending to those who do not need to borrow to those who will not be able to pay."[23] The potential risks of default are offset by the profits to be made through higher interest payments and shorter repayment periods. The intermediaries who receive commissions and charge transactional fees are also motivated to "recycle funds" quickly and often. The bloated availability of capital created by this overlending, in turn, produces and encourages overborrowing. Palma explains this as "a closely interrelated process with a clear direction of causality": "Access to lending fuels expectations regarding the performance of the economy—performance which is improved, at least initially, by the additional expenditure brought about by the extra borrowing and availability of foreign exchange."[24]

Another related global shift was toward more private lending. Framing the 700 percent rise in "net private capital inflows" including portfolio investments (bonds and equities) into developing countries in the 1990s against a decrease of "net official capital inflows" from foreign governments and international financial institutions (IFIs) such as the IMF and the World Bank, Diane Elson has usefully summarized this conjuncture as a "delinking of social goals and international finance."[25] Whereas the IFIs were at least nominally committed to alleviating poverty or restoring national economic soundness, private investors were motivated by quick returns and easy entry and exit from these emerging markets. Volatility is exploited and capitalized on by foreign investors who have no ties or commitments to the specific countries that are adversely affected by these decisions.

The perils of this delinking were made clear in the 1994 Mexican crisis, which was a telling precursor to the 1997–98 crisis. Widely touted as a model of economic reform and potential, Mexico was the second most-favored destination of international private investment, behind China, in the early 1990s. Much of this was in short-term loans or highly liquid financial instruments. As Moises Náim pointed out in 1995, two years before the Thailand crash, "Mexico's crisis is as much a story about the new international financial system as it is a story about Mexico."[26] In that case, too, the localization and ethnicization of crisis as "a story about Mexico" worked to obscure the role of private investors set loose in a greatly expanded, unruly circuit of speculation. The demotion and pathologization of Mexico were reinforced by the counterexample of the Asian miracle. Pointing to such clear contrasts as that between the low domestic savings of Mexico and the high savings rates in the Asian countries deflected attention from the volatility of international capital flows that connect the two crises.

Several commentators have attributed the massive private capital infusion into Asia in the 1990s to the capriciousness and "herd mentality" of bankers and investors.[27] Another important development that fed the frenzy was the regional proliferation and later transnational consolidation of business and finance news. As Bello recalled, "Among the more momentous deals was the purchase of the famous *Far Eastern Economic Review* by Dow Jones, of *Asia Week* by Time-Warner, and of Star Television in Hong Kong by Rupert Murdoch. CNN, another Time-Warner subsidiary, and CNBC also moved in, with much of their programming devoted to business news." Often working on spotty knowledge of local contexts, these news analysts "highlighted the boom, glorified the high growth rates, and reported uncritically on so-called success stories, mainly because their own success as publications was tied to the perpetuation of the psychology of boom."[28] Characterizing the international banks and investors as "much more worried about what the other investors were doing" rather than any substantive understanding of the still fairly sound fundamentals, Jeffrey Sachs noted that "each creditor started to rush for the doors precisely because the other creditors were doing the same thing," thus creating a "self-fulfilling stampede."[29] According to Wade, the debt crises in Thailand and Indonesia came to be figured as a more-encompassing "Asian financial crisis" in October 1997 when Taiwan, which had large foreign exchange reserves, devalued its currency partly to discourage such a panicked withdrawal. Although Taiwan did not become one of the countries later subject to the IMF bailouts, the devaluation activated a *conceptual* shift on the part of international investors: "After Taiwan, the conceptual category of 'Asian financial crisis' came into being. Capitalists began to sell the Hong Kong dollar and the Korean won."[30] The Asianization of the crisis as a localized structural problem of crony capitalism misses how investors were fueled by such blunt mappings of "Asian" sameness, with little or no regard to substantive differences in economic fundamentals among these countries. The figurations of financial "contagion" as the "tequila effect" of the 1994 Mexican crisis and the "yellow fever" of the 1997–98 crisis implicate the enduring force of racialization under finance capitalism.[31]

Another connecting thread across these crises was the moral hazard created by their management and rescue by governments and the IMF. Rather than formulate necessary limits and rules to discourage such overexposure to risk, they repeatedly bailed out private lenders and investors and shifted the costs onto the public, which encouraged further risky investments and lax lending practices. Palma points to the Thai government's 1996 bailout of the Bangkok Bank of Commerce in Thailand and the World Bank loan of $307 million to Indonesia in 1992 to bail out its state-run banks as local precedents that created the expectation that the Asian governments and IFIs would again come to the rescue.[32]

The Asian crisis was and is also a "story about the United States" and significant political and economic shifts conditioning the ascent of Wall Street in Washington. First, investment practices shifted from individual savings and domestic stocks and bonds to international markets: "In 1993 alone, U.S. investors bought more foreign equities—about $68 billion—than in the whole decade of the 1980s."[33] The United States also led the innovation of new vehicles of securitization such as derivatives. The deregulation drive was accelerated and internationalized under the Clinton administration, which actively championed free trade and financial liberalization. Most consequential was the political ascendance of Wall Street. In addition to supplying campaign contributions, fund-raising for specific politicians, and direct lobbying, Wall Street significantly enhanced its political power by placing its top executives in important positions in the Department of the Treasury and other agencies charged with monitoring and regulating the financial industry and the broader economy. Robert Rubin went from Goldman Sachs to serve as Clinton's first director of the National Economic Council and later treasury secretary. This transmigration of a small pool of individuals from Wall Street investment banks to the Department of the Treasury and other government agencies has been dubbed the "Wall Street–Treasury Complex" and the "Wall Street–Washington Corridor."[34]

The United States took an active role in promoting free trade and financial liberalization throughout the Asia-Pacific region. In the early 1990s American mutual funds alone invested $4 billion to $5 billion per year in Asian markets. President Bill Clinton convened the first APEC (Asia-Pacific Economic Cooperation) Economic Leaders' Meeting in November 1993 in Blake Island. According to Johnson, "At annual meetings in different Pacific Rim countries, [the United States] insistently propagandized that the Asian 'tiger economies' open up to global market forces" and committed the participants in the 1994 APEC meeting in Bogor, Indonesia, to "free trade and investment in the Pacific."[35] This tireless cheerleading continued through the November 1997 meeting in Vancouver when the "Asian financial crisis was already underway." In a series of speeches and publications in the immediate aftermath of the crisis, Rubin and especially Lawrence Summers repeatedly pointed to weak domestic institutional structures and a lack of "transparency" across all the affected countries, thereby associating certain features of the Asian model with the more dubious and closed crony capitalism.

The Asianization of the 1997–98 crisis also obscures a third story about the changing mission and role of the IMF in the post–Bretton Woods era. Elson lucidly contextualizes the "Asian financial crisis" within "a surreal financial architecture" of a reoriented IMF and World Bank, from promoting important "social goals" to mandating "sound finance" through open markets on the part of debtor nations. I have already discussed the neoclassical orthodoxy reigning at the World Bank throughout the 1980s and fortified through its "market-friendly" neutralization of the challenge from Japan in the early 1990s. Since the 1970s, the IMF has increasingly imposed certain conditions on borrowing countries, which included privatizing public enterprises, lifting trade restrictions, opening up capital markets, and cutting public expenditures. Rather than stabilize and ensure the solvency of developing economies, it has increasingly become an auditor for private capital. Even as the IMF has intensified surveillance of certain developing countries and imperiled economies, demanding that they demonstrate greater *transparency*, as Elson pointedly clarifies, "the emphasis is mainly on transparency towards international investors, rather than towards their citizens."[36] I would even argue that the IMF's conditioned demand for accountability and transparency props up the fiction that there is a supranational agency, which could and indeed does account for a definite standard of sound finance and foolproof measure of transparency.

The Asian crisis could be reframed as a story about the damaging force and expanding repertoire of IMF interventions. Several analysts have pointedly accused the IMF of creating the crisis by championing what Bello characterizes as "indiscriminate capital account liberalization" and holding up Indonesia and Thailand as models for rapidly opening up to foreign investments in the 1990s.[37] Then, the IMF's blanket diagnoses of "immature institutions" and "lack of transparency" prodded and amplified investors' panic. Others accused the IMF of worsening the crisis through its blunt macroeconomic restructurings that combined cutting public expenditures and raising taxes and interest rates. In January 1998, in a rare public disagreement between the Bretton Woods institutions, Joseph Stiglitz, the chief economist at the World Bank, openly criticized the IMF's approach as contradictory to both its prior advice to Japan to widen its deficits and the U.S. government rescue of the savings and loan industry.[38]

The 1997–98 crisis also proved to be the occasion wherein the IMF asserted its overarching commitment to protecting the owners of capital. Several Asian governments, including Thailand and Malaysia, that had opposed liberalizing financial services during the WTO negotiations of 1996–97, were compelled to approve the agreement in December 1997: "either they signed or their receipt of IMF bail-out funds would be complicated."[39] In turn, the IMF, World Bank, and WTO were able to strengthen their standing in the eyes of "the owners and managers of capital" through these actions "both as organizations that can get them out of the crisis without serious losses and as organizations that can cajole Asian governments to reshape their domestic economies in line with Western models."[40] In his examination of IMF actions in Korea, Ha-Joon Chang pointed to a "mission creep" whereby the IMF has extended its reach beyond its original purpose of dealing with problems in maintaining current account balances to dictating domestic budgetary and monetary policies, "including hitherto-untouched areas such as corporate governance system and labour law . . . issues that it has neither the mandate nor the expertise to deal with."[41]

The active role of U.S. officials in dictating the terms of the "bailouts" affirmed both American influence in the IMF and Wall Street's influence on U.S. economic and foreign policy. Robert Wade and Frank Veneroso offered the expanded term, "Wall Street–Treasury–IMF Complex," to identify this newly fortified political-economic bloc. Early on in the crisis at a G7 meeting in September 1997, Japan, with the backing of several other Asian countries, proposed creating a $100 billion Asian Monetary Fund (AMF), with a $50 billion contribution from Japan and the rest from the other still healthy economies of the region, Taiwan and Singapore. This was roundly rejected by the IMF and the United States, represented by Deputy Treasury Secretary Summers:

> Concern about the US reliance on East Asian holdings of Treasuries may have been equally important. If regional central banks led by the Bank of Japan had sold out from their huge holdings of Treasuries to finance this costly operation, the interest rates on Treasuries and US long-term interest rates would probably have soared and halted the US economic upturn.[42]

Back in the United States, in arguing for additional contributions to the IMF before the Senate Foreign Relations Committee on February 13, 1998, Alan Greenspan, along with Summers and Treasury Secretary Rubin, testified that "the IMF had succeeded in using its bailouts to force nations to open their markets and transform their economies."[43] Bruce Cumings painted a more coercive picture: "Sources in Washington acknowledged that several reforms had been specifically demanded by US Treasury officials, in keeping with former US Trade Representative Mickey Kanter's view that the IMF could be a 'battering ram' for American interests."[44] But here, we should be mindful that only particular American interests—namely, Wall Street and weapons sales—were being protected and promoted.[45] Pointing to how $2 billion of J.P. Morgan's exposure to Korea involved derivative contracts, J. A. Kregel noted, "This perhaps explains why Morgan was at the forefront of the move to convert Korean banks' short-term debt into sovereign debt."[46] Such unabashed expressions of a Wall Street–Treasury–IMF complex also announced the attenuation of the protector-sponsor status of the United States in Asia.[47] Clarifying that the bailout funds would go to the foreign banks who made "shaky and imprudent loans" and not the people or domestic firms, Johnson flatly declared, "The ultimate in crony capitalism is actually the U.S. dominated International Monetary Fund (the IMF)."[48]

Several observers have repeatedly used the term *fire sale* to refer to how investors rushed back in to buy up the devalued Asian firms and assets in the aftermath of the IMF interventions.[49] Commentators in Asia thus dubbed these intrusions a "Second Opium War." Asking whether these actions manifest a "surging U.S. imperialism," Joseph Medley pointed to how even though the IMF had prevented the South Korean government from saving or protecting its firms, the U.S. government was working to bail out Long-Term Capital Management: "Greenspan said the intervention was necessary to avoid a 'fire sale' of U.S. assets that might trigger a slowdown of the U.S. economy in 1999."[50] I would argue that the coercive terms, select beneficiaries, and detrimental effects of the IMF reforms also starkly illustrated that economic and financial globalization is crucially organized by "discriminatory inclusion and segmentation" rather than horizontal inclusion and multilateral cooperation.

"Asian Recovery" and the "Subprime Crisis"

Several analyses published in the immediate aftermath of the 1997–98 crisis presented lessons and warnings that could have been instructive in anticipating, if not avoiding, the current crisis. "The great lesson of the Asian crisis," Wade and Veneroso argued, "is that the desirability of free movements of short-term capital has to be put in question."[51] Many called for greater auditing of international banks and financial institutions. The IMF's demand for transparency from the Asian countries and firms provoked and energized calls for greater transparency on the part of the IMF itself. Sachs criticized the IMF for lack of "transparency" about its own decisions and programs, even as it imposes this as a normative standard for the recipient countries.[52] Arguing that "bad economics was only a symptom of the real problem: secrecy," Stiglitz extended his criticism to the Treasury for its flouting of "democratic accountability."[53]

Another lesson of the 1997–98 crisis involved the proliferation of new instruments of securitization and speculation in the 1990s. Wade was especially prescient when he questioned the destabilizing potential of the growth of derivative markets that "escape established methods of bank regulation."[54] Granted, these new "over-the-counter" financial instruments have functioned to manage risk and to generate new capital, which can be used for material and productive investments. However, their mathematical intricacy, private exchange involving intermediaries, and shortened time frame can obfuscate the extent of exposure to risk and liabilities, which sometimes far exceed assets and revenue streams. Indeed, there was a concerted effort in the U.S. government to monitor and regulate these financial instruments in 1998. In early 1998 Brooksley Born, then head of the Commodities Futures Trading Commission, proposed that these new over-the-counter derivatives be monitored and regulated, which was roundly rejected by Fed Chairman Greenspan, Treasury Secretary Rubin, Deputy Treasury Secretary Summers, and Arthur Levitt, head of the Securities and Exchanges Commission (SEC).[55] I would argue that the self-satisfied American "triumphalism" about the then unfolding "Asian crisis" precluded a sober and serious consideration of Born's proposal.

In 1999, when several of these Asian economies demonstrated faster-than-expected signs of economic upturn, the "recovery" was interpreted as affirmation of the IMF reforms and financial liberalization. In contesting this heralding of recovery, Ha-Joon Chang made several linked observations, which may be instructive for the present. First, he argued that the expansion was partly produced by the severely contractionary effects of the IMF-mandated policies, and the signs of recovery manifested themselves only after some of these policies were revised and even reversed. Second, he notes that while there was an increase in output, "the country's performance in unemployment and equality has been poor." Perhaps the most important observation was that the rise in stock prices was fueled by the frenzy of foreign investors "snap(ping) up bargain-price blue-chip stocks following the post-crisis asset price collapse" and the opening up of stock trading to a larger pool of Koreans; this growth in portfolio investments occurred "in the face of a dramatic collapse in real investments."[56]

This "recovery" would revise the temporal framing of the earlier crisis, but not its Asianization. C. P. Chandrasekhar and Jayati Ghosh have argued that upholding Asian economies as a model success and dismissing the 1997–98 crisis as a temporary "aberration" were "ideologically important since neoliberal policies were fast losing their credibility in Latin America and Africa."[57] The recovery of certain Asian economies had much to do with their breaking away from the IMF-mandated program of financial liberalization and social disinvestment. In 1998 both South Korea and Thailand reinstated some state interventions such as extending low-interest loans to at-risk businesses.

The preferred reading of the Asian recovery as confirmation of the IMF-mandated liberalizations supported the further ascendance of the Wall Street–Treasury–IMF complex in the following decade. The unending "war on terror" inaugurated in the aftermath of September 11, 2001, entailed massive military spending and government borrowing. There was a dramatic growth in the U.S. financial sector, whose debt increased to $36 billion (double the GDP) by 2007.[58] The shadow economy of over-the-counter derivatives rapidly expanded throughout the 2000s. By 2008 the notional value of derivatives was estimated at $596 *trillion*, far exceeding the $167 trillion value of "*the world's* financial assets—including all stock, bonds, and bank deposits."[59] This was a delinking of international finance not just from laudable "social goals" but from its measures of asset valuation! The "revolving door" of leadership between Wall Street and Washington dominated both the U.S. economy and domestic and foreign policy, fortified by aggressive lobbying and electoral financing.[60]

Although several accounts date the beginning of the subprime crisis to February 2007, when HSBC became the first major bank to disclose losses from default of subprime loans, there are several important connections and missed connections to the earlier Asian crisis. Since the other articles in this special issue elucidate the specific details of the U.S. mortgage crisis, I restrict my discussion to a few points. First, the Cold War trade of U.S. military bases for Japanese and Korean exports to the United States, which contributed to the decline of the U.S. manufacturing base, is an important prehistory to the stagnant wages of the 1970s and 1980s.[61] After the series of crises in emerging markets throughout the 1990s, Asian and other foreign investors, firms, and governments expanded their investments in the United States, especially in safe Treasury bills: "You had a huge inflow of liquidity. A very unique kind of situation where poor countries like China were shipping money to advanced countries like the United States rather than keeping it in their own countries."[62] The Federal Reserve's lowering of interest rates also fueled a surge of refinancing in the 2000s. While this extraction increased Americans' spending power, it also increased their debt: "The mortgage debt of American households rose almost as much in the six years from 2001 to 2007 as it had over the course of the country's more than 200-year history."[63]

Second, this expansion of debt was enabled by the triumphant fortification of the Wall Street–Treasury–IMF complex in the aftermath of the earlier 1997–98 crisis. The exponential growth of securitization was partly conditioned by the thorough deregulation of U.S. banking and finance. The oversupply of capital generated certain moral hazards. Since the loans would be "offloaded" almost immediately to a Wall Street bank that sold them in turn to other investors, securitization relieved the initial lender from the risks of default, and lenders made more and more "nontraditional loans" that were easy to obtain but on perilous terms.

Third, the extension of short-term, usurious credit exploited intractable categories of ethnic, cultural, and racialized difference. According to one study, African Americans, regardless of income, were more likely to receive loans from nonregulated and often corrupt lenders.[64] Another illuminating study by a team of geographers, completed in 2005, drew attention to the "discriminatory *inclusion* and segmentation" of subprime lending, which distinguished it from the earlier discriminatory exclusion of African Americans from home loans and purchases.[65] Therefore it may be more accurate to attach the degraded and demoting force of "subprime" to these predatory lending practices, lenders, and investors.[66] To say that is not to exonerate the borrowers as uniformly innocent and unwitting victims whose "propensity to over-borrow" was fueled by the "propensity to over-lend" in this setting of "excess international liquidity." We should keep in mind that racial-ethnic categories do not map neatly onto the striated positions of borrower, broker, lender, banker, and investor. Thus, rather than a moral condemnation or vindication, we could frame it in terms of the conjuncture of an unprecedented availability of credit in a context of racist exclusion and growing income inequality. As I alluded to earlier, the phrase "discriminatory inclusion and segmentation" also bears a striking resonance to the coercive and unequal integration of emerging economies into the "surreal financial architecture" of the Wall Street–Treasury–IMF complex.

When the subprime crisis exposed billions of dollars of uncollateralized exposures by Wall Street investment banks, the broadened spotlight on the U.S. financial system expanded it into a "global financial crisis" in 2008. The revelations of the high debts being carried by several European countries provoked yet another racializing figuration. The unsavory and demeaning acronyms of PIGS or PIIGs were widely deployed to refer to Portugal, Ireland, Greece, and Spain and later also Italy. On August 31, 2008, the *Financial Times* featured an article titled "Pigs in Muck," which began by noting that PIGS "is a pejorative moniker but one with much truth."[67] The largely German-funded bailout of these ailing economies, in turn, was received with ethnocentric contempt and revived racist figurations mapped onto fiscal behavior: "Thrifty, hard-working Germans in May bailed out dissolute, corrupt, feckless, spendthrift and lazy Greeks, Spaniards, Italians and Portuguese. That, at least, is how it appears to the German public."[68] Once again, such clear demarcations functioned to eclipse a much more complex web of international speculation and profit-chasing. The *New York Times* reported in February 2010 that Wall Street firms, led by Goldman Sachs, had contributed to the making of the crisis by helping the Greek government borrow billions in 2001 through the use of derivatives, which allowed these liabilities to be hidden from EU regulators and investors.[69] Also in 2010, an expanded acronym, STUPID, began circulating in the financial press and cybersphere, which included several more countries with large capital account deficits—Spain, Turkey, United Kingdom, Portugal, Italy, and Dubai.[70]

These American and European crises provoked another round of Asianiza-tion. But this time it would be marked by the return of what others have noted as an "Asian triumphalism." Strikingly, certain financial practices became not so much racialized but regionalized as a distinctively *Asian* subject-position. One 2008 commentary in the *Financial Times* pointed out:

> Amazingly, in the thousands of words spun in the incestuous western discourse on this crisis, little attention has been paid to Asian views, even though the calm and steady responses of China, India and Japan, the three anchor Asian economies, provide hope that there may be some pillars of stability in the swirling storm.[71]

The naming of the "three anchor Asian economies" attests to a significant shift with the dramatic economic ascendance of China and India in the years since the 1997–98 crisis, which significantly revised the meaning of "Asian" as a signifier of global economic power and futurity. Asserting that "Asian minds have never been captured by the strange ideological belief that markets know best and government should step aside," Kishore Mahbubani chides the now discredited *American* faith in deregulated, unfettered markets, specifically nam-ing Ronald Reagan and Greenspan: "By contrast, virtually all Asian govern-ments believe that the virtues of the 'invisible hand' in the market have to be balanced by the 'visible hand' of good governance." While the United States is the most prominent figure of neoliberal hubris, this narrative of non-Asian misjudgment and downfall extends to a "European banker" who was chas-tised by the officer of the Reserve Bank of India: "After subprime, we are not sure of US regulation; after Northern Rock, British regulation; after Société Générale, French regulation and after UBS, Swiss regulation." This recoding of subprime as a distinctively American laissez-faire folly offers a provocative, albeit problematic, alternative to its more common and persistent racialization. In contrast to an earlier culturalist discourse of "Asian values," the concerted

Asian minds here is a historical achievement, borne of an earlier abjection with their own hard lesson with neoliberal globalization. However, it is crucial to note that this rebuke of European and American regulatory failure is emphatically distinguished from a resolutely sanguine stance toward *globalization*. Against the potential that the United States and European countries might "retreat into protectionism," Mahbubani notes that "Asian societies also know they are becoming the biggest beneficiaries of globalisation and must assume greater responsibility in stabilising the economic system." The rousing ending of Mahbubani's comment clarifies that these Asian minds are distinguished by their resolutely *confident* futurity: "The really good news is that few Asians have lost their optimism about the future. They have no illusions about the crisis but are confident that they remain on the right trajectory to deliver the Asian century. This is why the key Asian economies will react calmly in this storm. Confidence in the future is a great asset in such times."[72]

Against Asianization and Crisis Enclosure

Another way to contest the Asianization of the 1997–98 crisis and to connect it to the present crisis is to focus on the unevenly detrimental social impact of the earlier crisis. The linear enfolding of miracle-crisis-recovery-triumph is revealed as wishful when we pay attention to gender and class differences. The interlinked and mutually reinforcing regionalization, culturalization, and racialization of these Asianizations can be broken up by focusing on particular and *differentiated* effects on women in Asia. The export-led industrialization of many Asian economies was crucially powered by low-paid and often harshly disciplined female labor in the free trade zones and special economic zones throughout Asia. Although the female factory workers in garment, shoe, and electronics assembly are most commonly conjured in relation to globalization and Asian economic development, women's labor has been important to the growth of clerical sectors and service economies linked to the global expansion of finance. Uhn Cho usefully recalls that foreign investment in Korean capital markets, which began as early as 1981, led to increasing numbers of female workers, especially young unmarried women, in clerical jobs.[73] In the 1990s, when foreign direct investment was channeled toward the service sector, there was an especially marked increase in women's employment in the new global chain and department stores. Married women were preferred by these global retail chains because they could influence their neighbors and also were less prone to unionization.[74]

In the immediate aftermath of the 1997–98 crisis, a range of journalists, NGOs (nongovernmental organizations) and INGOs (international nongovernmental organizations), and scholars issued reports and studies that focused attention on the special impact of the crisis on Asian women. On June 11, 1998, the *New York Times* carried an article titled "With Asia's Economies Shrinking, Women Are Being Squeezed Out," which pointed to the disproportionate retrenchment of women workers, increased domestic violence, taking daughters out of school, and the rise in female prostitution and sex trafficking.[75] According to a report commissioned by the Asian Development Bank, the deleterious effects of the crisis on women included a decrease in support for education, medical care, family planning, and reproductive health along with an increase in crime, violence, and environmental degradation.[76] The occasion of a specific crisis can make women visible in particular ways, but the newly urgent figurations of gendered vulnerability can effect another order of Asianization, which elides diverse effects on different groups of women in each country and across international borders. I highlight just a few examples below.

The naming of a crisis as such works to necessitate and justify more disciplining of workers and citizens, which proceeds unevenly across gender and class differences. In South Korea the IMF-mandated restructurings led to massive layoffs. More women than men were laid off, especially in the service sectors. One out of five female white-collar workers was laid off. Married women were targeted for layoffs by a refortified patriarchal logic of the male head of household as the primary breadwinner. But, as Cho pointed out, "in reality, women were pushed into the labour market at lower wages on behalf of unemployed husbands."[77] At the same time, this gender-specific response to crisis also produced new gendered figures such as the "IMF *chonyo*" (IMF maiden), referring to the predicament of single women who delayed marriage plans because married women would be the first targeted for layoffs. In the Philippines the "women-specific impact" of the crisis included higher rates of unemployment and more income generation in the informal economy; cuts in health care further increased women's burden of caring for sick family members.[78] Women made up the majority of the workers in two of the three most negatively affected industries, garment manufacturing and electronics. In addition, the agricultural sector, which also employed more women than men, cut two hundred thousand jobs in the first quarter of 1998. Finally, the austerity measures entailed large job cuts in the public sector, the largest employer of women.[79]

The 1997–98 crisis also accelerated the migration of women workers. This regional and international migration of labor has had a differentially marked impact on specific countries, which further contest the Asianization of the crisis. The case of Filipina migrant workers in Hong Kong offers an illustrative case of the complexity and dynamic shifts. The number of Filipina domestics in Hong Kong increased more than twofold over the 1990s, from 66,000 in 1991 to 140,000 by 1999. Although there had long been ethnocentric biases against these Filipina domestic workers, Kimberley Chang and Julian McAllister Groves noted how antipathy toward these women was further "fueled by the Asian economic crisis."[80] Rising local unemployment provoked calls for cutting the minimum wage for domestic workers and instituted new measures of surveillance and deportation. A new immigration policy dubbed "Operation Hoover" went into effect whereby young foreign women suspected of prostitution were detained and interrogated, a measure intended to thwart these migrant women workers from extending their stays in Hong Kong.

To sum up, the 1997–98 financial crisis had the compounded effect of contesting the geographic bounding of Asian women within Asia and the very categorical designation of "Asian women" or "Asian women workers" as similarly affected by globalization. The Asianization of recovery in an orderly succession of miracle-crisis-recovery-triumph glossed over the multiply detrimental effects of the crisis, which lingered well past 1998. It also eclipsed the differentially gendered casualties *and* beneficiaries of the IMF "bailout." As Diane Elson and Nilufer Cagatay stressed: "The macroeconomic policies insisted upon by the IMF did not simply have a negative social impact; they were designed embodying a profoundly unjust social content, prioritizing the financial rights of creditors over the human rights of the peoples of East Asia, with particularly low priority accorded to poor women."[81]

Thanh-Dam Truong's postcrisis analyses were especially suggestive in utilizing a focus on women to *broaden* the temporal and geographic frame of analysis. She suggested that rather than an anomaly or localized failure, "The trends characterizing women's experiences in crisis situations are manifestations of a deeper problem that had emerged in times of economic growth, i.e. the gendered logic of industrial organization in East and South East Asia."[82] The much-touted "flexibility" of the regional workforce was made possible by a concomitant hardening of gendered ideologies that further feminized "caring work" and reproductive labor while upholding male sexual privilege and male workers' need for "sexual comfort," which, in turn, rationalized the proliferation of sex work and female sexual exploitation. Truong concluded, "If a gender analysis had been part of the evaluation of ANICs' industrial transformation, the outcomes of this transformation would not have received the label of a miracle, and the crisis might possibly have been anticipated."[83] In another essay from 2000, Truong further asserted that rather than disprove the moniker, as Greenspan and others declared, the 1997–98 crisis posed a challenge as to "whether the miracle can stand as a miracle of social transformation rather than merely industrial transformation."[84] If this challenge had been taken up, as she suggested, by reopening "the discussion on the relationship between polity and economy, economic performance and governance," the Asian crisis and subprime crisis could have been connected very differently.

In the wake of the more recent financial crisis, several scholars and researchers with INGOs have again pointed to its detrimental effects on workers and women in Asia, which contradict the triumphalist pronouncements of Mahbubani quoted earlier. In March 2009 Amelita King Dejardin, a senior adviser to the International Labor Office, published an op-ed titled "Economic Meltdown Has a Woman's Face," further noting a "gender bias" to the crisis: "Here in Asia, working women will be affected more severely, and differently, from their male counterparts."[85] She supports this prognosis by recalling these statistics from the 1997–98 crisis: "In Thailand, 95 percent of those laid off from the garment sector were women; in the toys' sector, it was 88 percent. In South Korea, 86 percent of those who lost their financial services and banking jobs were female." Dejardin ends by urging the inclusion of women in the "social dialogue" about the proper response to the current crisis, which did not happen in the deliberations of 1997–98. If each new crisis produces an opening for making particular casualties visible, these figures are also tethered to the spatiotemporal bracketing of the crisis. The categorical incarnation of Asian women's vulnerability also risks affirming persistent Asianizations of patriarchy and gender inequality. Then, too, even the most spectacular figures of suffering and sturdy empirical details could be revised, rationalized, and effaced at the onset of a declared recovery. What is needed then is an interdisciplinary and transnational analysis that is attentive to local specificities but resists the enclosure of crises. The extensive manifestation and unending repercussions of the "Wall Street meltdown" of 2008, the U.S. "debt ceiling crisis" of 2011, and the vividly unfolding eurozone sovereign debt crises have forced many commentators to concede that the unfettered and much privileged drive of global financial liberalization has reached a terminus. If, as I have argued, the Asianization of the 1997–98 crisis worked to vindicate and further propel this neoliberal capitalist trajectory, the more recent *global* qualification of financial crisis demands a recalibration of who should be enjoined in this pressing social dialogue. Its participants will need to resist the wish for and faith in a full recovery, which risks misreading partial recoveries and ongoing dispossessions.

Notes

1. Chalmers Johnson traces the origin of the "miracle" to 1962 when the Japanese first became aware of this status when the *Economist* published a two-part essay "Consider Japan" in September 1962, which was translated and published in Japan as "Amazing Japan" (Johnson, *MITI and the Japanese Economic Miracle: The Growth of Industrial Policy, 1925–1975* [Palo Alto, Calif.: Stanford University Press, 1982], 1).

2. Chalmers Johnson, *Blowback: The Costs and Consequences of American Empire* (New York: Henry Holt, 2000), 177.

3. Bruce Cumings, "The Korean Crisis and the End of 'Late' Development," *New Left Review* 231 (September–October 1998): 46.

4. Walden Bello, "The Asian Financial Crisis: Causes, Dynamics, Prospects," *Journal of the Asia Pacific Economy* 4.1 (1999): 36. Bello deploys the alternate regional terms *Southeast Asian collapse* and *Southeast Asian "miracle."*

5. World Bank, *The East Asian Miracle: Economic Growth and Public Policy* (Oxford: Oxford University Press, 1991).

6. Robert Wade, "Japan, the World Bank, and the Art of Paradigm Maintenance: The East Asian Miracle in Political Perspective," *New Left Review* 217 (May–June 1996): 6–7.

7. Ibid., 18. This essay offers a fascinating, detailed account of the political economy underwriting this textual production, including its highly strategic and negotiated conceptualization, writing, revision, and editing by an international, but largely American-dominated, team. Wade discloses that Japan endorsed the naming of an "East Asian miracle" as signaling a distinctive alternative to the reigning Washington Consensus, but which also steered clear of "the dangerous idea of Japanese uniqueness" by "presenting them as general principles confirmed by other East Asian experiences."

8. Gabriel Palma, "Three and a Half Cycles of 'Mania, Panic, and [Asymmetric] Crash': East Asia and Latin America Compared," *Cambridge Journal of Economics* 22 (1998): 792. The total foreign debt of these five countries doubled in a three-year period to $275 billion by June 1997.

9. Ibid.

10. Joseph Stiglitz, "What I Learned at the World Economic Crisis," *New Republic,* April 17, 2000, 56.

11. Chalmers Johnson, "Cold War Economics Melt Asia," *Nation,* February 23, 1998, 17.

12. Robert Wade and Frank Veneroso, "The Asian Crisis: The High Debt Model versus the Wall Street–Treasury–IMF Complex,'" *New Left Review* 228 (March–April 1998): 10.

13. As Wade emphasizes, they did so under the assumption that the Korean won–U.S. dollar exchange rate would stay stable: "As the won fell, the banks began to sell foreign securities in order to boost liquidity. Their sell-off helped to spread the financial contagion" (Wade, "The Asian Debt-and-Development Crisis of 1997–?" *World Development* 26.8 [1998]: 1544).

14. Wade and Veneroso, "Asian Crisis," 10. See also Johnson, "Cold War Economics Melt Asia," 17.

15. Johnson framed this as a "deal intended to help re-elect President Clinton the following year . . . [by keeping] U.S. interest rates at politically desirable levels." In return, Johnson continues, "The Clinton Administration also agreed to take a dive on the auto talks, abandoning its efforts to impose duties on Japanese luxury cars; the Administration shut up about America's billion-dollar-a-week trade deficit with Japan" ("Cold War Economics Melt Asia," 17).

16. Wade and Veneroso, "Asian Crisis," 10.

17. Paul Krugman, "What Happened to Asia?" January 1998, http://web.mit.edu/krugman/www/DIS-INTER.html.

18. Ha-Joon Chang, Gabriel Palma, and D. Hugh Whittaker, "The Asian Crisis: Introduction," *Cambridge Journal of Economics* 22 (1999): 649.

19. David Sanger, "Greenspan Sees Asian Crisis Moving World to Western Capitalism," *New York Times,* February 13, 1998, quoted in Wade, "Asian Debt-and-Development Crisis."

20. Johnson, "Cold War Economics Melt Asia," 16. Johnson continues with this prescient warning: "But we, of all people, should be extremely cautious in preaching deregulation, the superfluousness of government and the suitability of open markets for all seasons. These are more or less the same things Herbert Hoover prescribed for dealing with the financial panic of 1929—and they produced the structural collapse of demand known as the Great Depression."

21. Wade, "Asian Debt-and-Development Crisis," 1536.

22. Chalmers Johnson, "Economic Crisis in East Asia: The Clash of Capitalisms," *Cambridge Journal of Economics* 22 (1998): 653–61.

23. Palma, "Three and a Half Cycles," 790.
24. Ibid., 793.
25. Diane Elson, "International Financial Architecture: A View from the Kitchen," 1, http://www.net-workideas.org/featart/jan2004/fa13_Diane_Elson.htm (accessed May 1, 2009).
26. Moises Náim, "Mexico's Larger Story," *Foreign Policy* 99 (Summer 1995): 114. Náim then outlines "several lessons of macroeconomic management" for other governments, which bear a striking relevance to the crises to come in 1997–98.
27. Wade and Veneroso, "Asian Crisis," 9.
28. Walden Bello, "Asian Financial Crisis: The Movie," in *The Future in the Balance: Essays on Globalization and Resistance*, ed. Anuradha Mittal (Oakland, Calif.: Food First Books, 2001), 71.
29. Jeffrey Sachs, "The IMF and the Asian Flu," *American Prospect* 37 (March–April 1998): 16–21.
30. Wade, "Asian Debt-and-Development Crisis," 1542.
31. I have seen many references to the so-called tequila effect. The first, and I think the only, time I have seen the reference to the so-called yellow fever is in a published lecture by Lawrence Summers, "International Financial Crises: Causes, Prevention, and Cures," *AEA Paper and Proceedings*, May 2000, 6.
32. Palma, "Three and a Half Cycles," 797.
33. Moisés Naím, "Latin America the Morning After," *Foreign Affairs* 74.4 (1995): 50.
34. Jagdish N. Bhagwati, "The Capital Myth: The Difference between Trade in Widgets and Dollars," *Foreign Affairs*, May 1, 1998. See also Simon Johnson and John Kwak, *Thirteen Bankers: The Wall Street Takeover and the Next Financial Meltdown* (New York: Pantheon, 2010), 113.
35. Johnson, *Blowback*, 208.
36. Elson, "International Financial Architecture," 10.
37. Bello, "Asian Financial Crisis," 41.
38. Bob Davis and David Wessel, "World Bank, IMF at Odds over Asian Austerity—Some Economists Contend That Harsh Measures Could Worsen the Crisis," *Wall Street Journal*, January 8, 1998.
39. Wade and Veneroso, "Asian Crisis," 19.
40. Wade, "Asian Debt-and-Development Crisis," 1547.
41. Ha-Joon Chang, "The 1997 Korean Crisis: Causes and Consequences," in *Brazil and South Korea: Economic Crisis and Restructuring*, ed. Edmund Amann and Ha-Joon Chang (London: Institute of Latin American Studies, 2004), 119.
42. Kristen Nordhaug, "Asian Monetary Fund Revival?" *Focus on Trade*, no. 51 (June 2000), http://www.focusweb.org/publications/2000/Asian%20Monetary%20Fund%20revival.htm.
43. Sanger, "Greenspan Sees Asian Crisis Moving World."
44. Cumings, "Korean Crisis and the End of 'Late' Development," 53.
45. Pointing out that "the thing our government most seemed to fear was that contracts to buy our weapons might now not be honored," Johnson recounts how then Secretary of Defense William Perry traveled to the Asian countries to secure these payments (*Blowback*, 5–6). In light of this, we might consider the alternately expanded name of the Wall Street–Treasury–Defense–IMF complex.
46. J. A. Kregel, "Derivatives and Global Capital Flows: Applications to Asia," *Cambridge Journal of Economics* 22 (1998): 688.
47. Cumings characterized it more definitively as follows: "The deep meaning and intent of the American and IMF response to the Asian liquidity crisis is to close the historical chapter in which the sheltered 'developmental states' have prospered" ("Korean Crisis and the End of 'Late' Development," 51–52).
48. Johnson, "Economic Crisis in East Asia," 654.
49. Wade, "Asian Debt-and-Development Crisis," 1544.
50. Joseph Medley, "The East Asian Economic Crisis: Surging U.S. Imperialism?" *Review of Radical Political Economics* 32.3 (2000): 385.
51. Wade and Veneroso, "Asian Crisis," 21.
52. Jeffrey Sachs, "The IMF Is a Power unto Itself," *Financial Times*, December 11, 1997.
53. Stiglitz, "What I Learned."
54. Wade, "Asian Debt-and-Development Crisis," 1550.
55. See Michael Hirsch, "The Reeducation of Larry Summers," *Newsweek*, February 20, 2009. See also the illuminating PBS *Frontline* documentary "The Warning." This is another crucial thread connecting the 1997–98 crisis with the subprime crisis of 2007–8 and the ongoing financial crisis. I examine this in another essay titled "Money, Gender, and Power: A Feminist Genealogy of Brooksley Born and Larry Summers" (forthcoming).

56. Chang, "1997 Korean Crisis," 119.

57. See C. P. Chandrasekhar and Jayati Ghosh, "The Asian Face of the Global Recession," *Monthly Review,* February 26, 2009, http://www.monthlyreview.org/mrzine/cg260209.html.

58. Financial Crisis Inquiry Commission (FCIC), *Financial Crisis Inquiry Report* (Washington, D.C.: U.S. Government Printing Office, 2011), xvii.

59. Jacon Leibenluft, "$596 Trillion!" Slate.com, October 15, 2008, http://www.slate.com/articles/news_and_politics/explainer/2008/10/596_trillion.html.

60. "From 1999 to 2008, the financial sector expended $2.7 billion in reported federal lobbying expenses; individuals and political action committees in the sector made more than $1 billion in campaign contributions" (FCIC, *Financial Crisis Inquiry Report*, xviii).

61. Johnson, *Blowback*, 30.

62. Former Fed governor Frederic Mishkin, quoted in FCIC, *Financial Crisis Inquiry Report*, 104.

63. FCIC, *Financial Crisis Inquiry Report*, 7.

64. Angie Beeman, Davita Silfen Glasberg, and Colleen Casey, "Whiteness as Property: Predatory Lending and the Reproduction of Racialized Inequality," *Critical Sociology* 37.1 (2011): 27–45.

65. Elvin K. Wyly, Mona Atia, Elizabeth Lee, and Pablo Mendez, "Race, Gender, and Statistical Representation: Predatory Mortgage Lending and the U.S. Community Reinvestment Movement," *Environment and Planning A* 39 (2007): 2139. The brilliance of their methodology was to examine the large numbers of subprime loans marked by the *nondisclosure* of the borrower's racial and ethnic identity. In 2002 revisions to the 1975 Home Mortgage Disclosure Act were finalized, which required lenders to collect and submit data on the "race," "sex," and "ethnicity" (the two boxes were "Hispanic or Latino" and "Not Hispanic or Latino") of loan applicants. As soon as the data were made publicly available in spring of 2005, consumer groups were able to discern the rough profile of the recipients of these "high-cost loans." The group Fair Finance Watch found that "African-American borrowers at Citigroup and its subsidiaries were more than four times as likely to receive high-cost 'rate-spread' loans compared with non-Hispanic Whites" (2141). Against this data, they conclude that the growing "disappearance" and invisibility of race-ethnicity in subprime loans reflected a concerted effort by mortgage brokers or originators to disguise their targeting of specific racial-ethnic groups to receive these predatory loans.

66. The FCIC report cites various practices that were allowed to proliferate in a deregulated environment, for example, "lenders had opened subsidiaries to perform appraisals, allowing them to extract extra fees from 'unknowing' consumers and making it easier to inflate home values" (18).

67. The article actually opened by endorsing a more sanguine moniker: "Exciting countries get exciting acronyms, at least in financial circles. Fast-growing Brazil, Russia, India and China, for example, are called Brics, the very initials implying solid growth. Other countries are less fortunate" ("Pigs in Muck," *Financial Times*, September 1, 2008, http://www.ft.com/intl/cms/s/3/5faf0b0a-778a-11dd-be24-0000779fd18c.html#axzz1t4vTdQPB). Protests of the derogatory cast of the term compelled the *Financial Times* to ban its use.

68. Spengler, "PIIGS to the Slaughter," *Asia Times Online*, July 21, 2010, http://www.atimes.com/atimes/Global_Economy/LG21Dj03.html.

69. Louise Story, Landon Thomas Jr., and Nelson D. Schwartz, "Wall St. Helped to Mask Debt Fueling Europe's Crisis," *New York Times*, February 14, 2010. Characterizing these "tactics [as] akin to the ones that fostered subprime mortgages in America," the article discloses that Goldman Sachs was paid $300 million for arranging this deal.

70. Katie Allen, "Acronym Acrimony: The Problem with Pigs," *Guardian*, February 10, 2010, http://www.guardian.co.uk/business/2010/feb/12/pigs-piigs-debted-eu-countries (accessed April 11, 2012).

71. Kishore Mahbubani, "Why Asia Stays Calm in the Storm," *Financial Times*, October 28, 2008. At the time of publication, Mahbubani was dean of the Lee Kuan Yew School of Public Policy of the National University of Singapore.

72. The IMF has also contributed to this positive Asianization in the wake of the ongoing crisis (http://www.imf.org/external/np/exr/facts/asia.htm). Under the subheading "Lessons from the Asian Crisis," the report claims, "The large amounts of financing provided by the IMF and others during the crisis provided the breathing room needed for many of their governments to undertake deep and painful reforms. Many of these same economies have performed remarkably well since then." The Asianization of the 1997–98 crisis is reinforced by contrasting it to the truly "global" nature of the 2007–8 crisis. This distinction is sustained in a brief videotape posted on the IMF website in February 2009, titled

"Dominique Strauss-Kahn thanks Japan for $100 billion loan." See http://www.imf.org/external/mmedia/view.aspx?vid=79187341001.

73. Uhn Cho, "Global Capital and Local Patriarchy: The Financial Crisis and Women Workers in South Korea," in *Women and Work in Globalising Asia*, ed. Dong-Sook S. Gils and Nicola Piper (London: Routledge, 2002), 57.

74. Ibid., 59.

75. Nicholas D. Kristof, "With Asia's Economies Shrinking, Women Are Being Squeezed Out," *New York Times*, June 11, 1998. See also Teena Amrit Gill, "Asian Crisis Hits Women Hardest," *Asia Times Online*, June 6, 2000, http://www.atimes.com/asia-crisis/BF06Db01.html.

76. Ernesto M. Pernia and James C. Knowles, "Assessing the Social Impact of the Financial Crisis in Asia," Economics and Development Resource Centre, Asian Development Bank, November 1998.

77. Uhn Cho, "Global Capital and Local Patriarchy," 62.

78. Jenina Joy Chavez, *The Asian Financial Crisis and Filipino Households: Impact on Women and Children* ([U.K.]: Focus on the Global South and Save the Children, 2001), 27–28.

79. Lori J. Pennay, "The Disproportionate Effect of the Asian Economic Crisis on Women: The Filipina Experience," *University of Pennsylvania Journal of International Economy* 21 (2000): 443, 447–48, 450.

80. Kimberley Chang and Julian McAllister Groves, "Neither 'Saints' nor 'Prostitutes': Sexual Discourse in the Filipina Domestic Worker Community in Hong Kong," *Women's Studies International Forum* 23.1 (2000): 73.

81. Diane Nelson and Nilufer Cagatay, "The Social Content of Macroeconomic Policies," *World Development* 28 (2000): 1355.

82. Thanh-Dam Truong, "A Feminist Perspective on the Asian Miracle and Crisis: Enlarging the Conceptual Map of Human Development," *Journal of Human Development* 1.1 (2000): 159–64.

83. Ibid., 161.

84. Thanh-Dam Truong, "The Underbelly of the Tiger: Gender and the Demystification of the Asian Miracle," *Review of International Political Economy* 6.2 (1999): 146.

85. Amelita King Dejardin, "Economic Meltdown Has a Woman's Face," *Japan Times*, March 8, 2009, http://search.japantimes.co.jp/cgi-bin/eo20090308a1.html.

A Tale of Two Gulfs: Life, Death, and Dispossession along Two Oil Frontiers

Michael J. Watts

> When the drill bored down toward the stony fissures
> and plunged its implacable intestine
> into the subterranean estates,
> and dead years, eyes of the ages,
> imprisoned plants' roots
> and scaly systems
> became strata of water,
> fire shot up through the tubes
> transformed into cold liquid,
> in the customs house of the heights,
> issuing from its world of sinister depth,
> it encountered a pale engineer
> and a title deed.
> —Pablo Neruda, "Standard Oil Co.," *Canto General*

Oil's relation to modernity has been construed in three broad sorts of ways with very little intellectual traffic between them. One focuses on oil-producing states and, to quote the title of Michael Ross's new book (2012), on "how petroleum wealth shapes the development of nations." In Ross's dystopian account it is the scale, source, instability, and secrecy of oil and the attendant rise of the so-called new seven sisters—the massive national oil companies of petrostates like Nigeria, Russia, Saudi Arabia, and Iran—which explain the so-called paradox of plenty, namely, the state pathologies and human developmental failures of oil-rich states (the "resource curse"). In his influential book *The Bottom Billion*, the Oxford economist Paul Collier offers a version of this thesis in which oil revenues are captured by rapacious political elites ("the survival of the fattest") thereby contributing to autocratic rule, and those revenues are also predated or looted by rebels for whom oil finances not so much emancipatory politics (social justice, self-determination) but organized crime conducted as insurgency and war (in Collier's account, greater oil dependency produces an increased likelihood of civil war and violence). An "oil curse" appears, in analytic terms, rather like hydrocarbon determinism; or at the very least the causal powers attributed to oil are given particular sorts of meanings and valencies. Oil here means oil *money* and oil politics means *rents* captured by state agencies and the political class. The agency of oil corporations, or the oil service industries or financial institutions, for example, is almost entirely nonexistent. Put differently, in the universe of the resource curse an Exxon or a Shell is an agent that in conceptual terms is only present as an entity to be predated by rebels who have figured out how to make oil a profitable business (in effect, violent accumulation through a protection racket).

Another line of reasoning—Michael Klare's new book *The Race for What's Left* (2011) is a good exemplar—is almost entirely focused on "Big Oil" and global geopolitics (from the vantage point of American empire, what he has called the U.S. global oil acquisition strategy). Here the driving logic resembles another form of commodity determinism, this time emitting a robust Malthusian signal. Resources like oil are finite; industrial capitalism's enormous appetite for oil and gas is now spurred on by extraordinary capitalist dynamism in South and East Asian economies—more than half of the oil consumed between 1860 and the present was accounted for in the three decades after 1980. Peak Oil in now upon us, which necessarily amplifies the geopolitical pressures and struggles precipitated by tight oil markets, slower rates of discovery, and challenging operating environments (the "end of cheap and easy oil," as the oil industry puts it). Precisely because of its strategic qualities, oil exploration and development has a praetorian cast, a frontier of violent accumulation working hand in hand with militarism and empire. Haunted by the specter of depletion, states and corporations embark on a desperate scramble for oil (and other natural resources, as the new McKinsey report on the "resource revolution" emphasizes),[1] which is leading inexorably to a tooth and nail struggle for both conventional and unconventional hydrocarbons (e.g., the tar sands, shale gas, deepwater oil and gas). In this account we are about to enter a new "thirty-years" war for resources characterized by market volatility, ruthless resource grabs, and a sort of military neoliberalism.[2] Here it is less oil as money than oil as post–Cold War power politics (or oil as national security in the contemporary argot). What is on offer is a Big Oil–Big Military–Big Imperial State triumvirate. The invasion of Iraq in 2003 is, in this account, a sort of paradigmatic case.[3]

Finally, there is oil as an item of mass consumption, or more properly the relations between oil and modern forms of life, most especially the post-1945 American way of life defined, one might say, through petrochemistry. Here the language—theoretical and empirical—is of a rather different register. Oil is capacious, central to virtually every aspect of our lives; as the *New York Times* put it, oil "oozes through your life," showing up in everything from asphalt to milk shakes to drugs to plastics to fertilizers.[4] Oil is capacious, the lifeblood of just about everything including, it turns out, the sorts of civic freedoms and political liberties that most Americans have come to take for granted: unlimited personal mobility, cheap food, the prospect of property ownership in the suburbs.[5] Oil underwrites modern life, but the social cost is addiction ("Drill, baby, drill"), the terrible costs of which are now clear: carbon emissions and global warming, the assumption of new technological and environmental risks as unconventional sources are exploited, and continued political dependency on parts of the world that, as Dick Cheney famously noted, do not have U.S. interests at heart. Not only is the era of easy oil a thing of the past, but the burdens of oil exploitation will increasingly be felt on the domestic front in Alaska, in the Gulf of Mexico, and across the Marcellus and Barnett shales in the mid-Atlantic and southern states. In this rendering, oil is a form of bio-power,[6] a resource central to the life of populations and to the management of populations.[7] To deploy the language of Stephen Collier and Andrew Lakoff, oil actively constitutes a particular "regime of living"—but also, as I show, a regime of death, of bare life.[8]

In much of this writing, oil has been invested with Olympian powers. Oil distorts the organic, natural course of development; oil wealth ushers in a bloated economy of hyperconsumption and spectacular excess: decadent shopping malls in Dubai or flagrantly corrupt Russian "oilygarchs." The danger in all this sort of oil talk is that there is a slippage between oil as a commodity of indisputable political, economic, and cultural significance and what one might call commodity determinism. Oil, says Imre Szeman, is hardly incidental to capital or to modernity, but "that is not the same as saying it is a prime mover of all decision making."[9] Oil rarely escapes the long shadow of Malthusian scarcity—peak oil thinking, after all, saturates much of the thinking on the political right and left. But hugely inflated powers are vested in the thing itself: petroleum undermines or promotes particular forms of democracy, it causes war and rebellion, it retards economic growth, it captures political office. To see oil in this way not only exaggerates the powers of the thing itself (as opposed to thinking about oil capital and oil markets) but also provides too blunt, and curiously too truncated, an accounting of the political economy of what I call the oil assemblage.

Many of those who write about oil typically, and rather curiously, have little to say about the materiality of oil and the political economy of what falls within the circumference of a vast, complex industry.[10] Timothy Mitchell properly notes that most explanations of oil "have little to do with the ways oil is extracted, processed, shipped and consumed,"[11] or the apparatuses by which oil is converted into forms of affluence and influence. Often, he says, oil is an affliction of governments that deploy petrodollars, "not of the processes by which a wider world obtains the energy that drives its materials and technical life."[12] I want to explore these apparatuses of oil—the oil assemblage—to address the questions of this special issue, namely, empire, dispossession, race, and the insecurities of neoliberal life.

To do so, I read two experiences against each other: first, the onshore oil world in the global South (the Niger delta in Nigeria as part of the wider Gulf of Guinea), and the offshore world of deepwater oil and gas exploration and production in the United States (specifically, the Gulf of Mexico and the Deepwater Horizon blowout). Both arenas can be seen as oil frontiers—frontiers of accumulation and dispossession—rooted in the operations of specific oil assemblages. I hope to do justice both to the relations between the deep infrastructures of the oil world—pipelines, rigs, flowstations, tankers, financiers, engineering firms, security forces, and so on—and to the regimes of life and death in the postcolonial South and the advanced capitalist North. Mitchell claims that the structure of the oil industry is ignored at great cost precisely because it becomes a sort of abstraction—it can be copied or deposited from place to place in a modular fashion—in contradistinction to the notion that political, economic, and social relations are in fact "engineered out of the flows of energy."[13] This fabrication is place and time specific because oil is always "discovered" in space-time (say, Spindletop, Texas, January 10, 1901), and subsequently inserted into a very specific localized (if more or less globalized) political economy even if the properties of the wider oil assemblage are in some sense generic or normalized. This insertion process is never just a reflection of a political or economic order developed de novo by Big Oil but the outcome of complex accommodations, compromises, complicities, oppositions, and violence. As Mitchell puts it in regard to the Middle East, the oil industry was "obliged to collaborate with other political forces, social energies, forms of violence and powers of attachment."[14] As Pablo Neruda's great poem says, the trail of oil leads to the engineer, the title deed, and the customhouse.

Opening up these frontiers—whether in Angolan or Brazilian deepwater, Russian Siberia or increasingly now the frozen frontiers of the Arctic—necessitates engagements with place-specific social and political forces,[15] none of which necessarily or easily are compatible with some presumed set of desires of corporate oil capital (political stability, surplus management, price control) or indeed of imperialist oil-consuming states. In one case the terminal point is an insurgency and combustible politics threatening the very operations of the oil industry and the petrostate itself; in the other it is the violence of a blowout, the loss of human and environmental life and livelihoods—and of the deadly consequences of substituting technical and financial over political risks. But my story has to start elsewhere, with the prosaics of the oil apparatuses themselves.

The Oil Assemblage

A key starting point is to see oil and gas as a global production network with particular properties, actors, networks, governance structures, institutions, and organizations (a global value chain in the industry argot) but what is, in effect, a regime of accumulation and a mode of regulation.[16] Seen in this way, oil and gas is gargantuan on all counts. The value of the recoverable oil and gas globally is perhaps $160 trillion (more than the value of all equity markets and equal to the total value of all tradable financial assets); the value of the oil and gas market alone is over US$3 trillion. Assets of the entire industry now total over US$40 trillion. Close to 70 percent of all oil produced is traded (over 50 million barrels per day), accounting for the largest component in world trade. Not unusually, over 1 billion barrels of oil can be traded in a day on the New York Mercantile Exchange and the InterContinental Exchange, much of this being "paper oil" (never delivered physically as oil), which is to say part of the booming commodities futures market. By way of comparison, if Exxon were a country it would be twice as large as the GDP of Nigeria (a major oil producer and home to 150 million people) and comparable to Sweden; the largest five oil companies' collective revenues exceed the GDP of all of Africa.[17]

The production network is held together materially by a global oil infrastructure with its own particular geography. Close to 5 million producing oil wells puncture the surface of the earth (77,000 were drilled last year, 4,000 offshore); 3,300 are subsea, puncturing the earth's crust on the continental shelf in some cases thousands of meters below the sea's surface. There are by some estimations over 40,000 oil fields in operation. More than 2 million kilometers of pipelines blanket the globe in a massive trunk-network (another 180,000 kilometers will be built at a capital cost of over $265 billion over the next four years); another 75,000 kilometers of lines transport oil and gas along the sea floor. There are 6,000 fixed platforms, and 635 offshore drillings rigs (the international rig total for June 2011 is over 1,158, according to Baker Hughes).[18] Over four thousand oil tankers move 2.42 billion tons of oil and oil products every year—one-third of global seaborne trade; over eighty massive, floating production and storage vessels have been installed in the last five years. This petro-infrastructure also accounts for almost 40 percent of global CO_2 emissions. All in all, there is nothing quite like it.

A seemingly unstoppable rush to discover and refine more of a resource that everyone agrees is finite feeds this oil hardware, literally and figuratively. Gavin Bridge calls this the technological imperative that manifests itself in the aggressive pursuit of economies of scale in production and refining, and in transportation.[19] There is a dialectical interaction, as he sees it, between efforts to reduce unit costs (by scaling up production) and the scaling up of transportation (to handle increased product volumes). This imperative drives the oil frontier to the ends of the earth, or more properly a mad gallop to the bottom of the ocean. Deepwater exploration is the new mantra (deepwater offshore production grew by 78 percent between 2007 and 2011). On August 2, 2007, a Russian submarine with two parliamentarians on board planted a titanium flag two miles below the North Pole. At stake were the lucrative new oil and gas fields—by some estimations 10 billion tons of oil equivalent—on the Arctic seafloor. What is on offer is a great deepwater land grab, which requires a vast floating and submersible infrastructure: very large crude carriers; the floating, production, storage, and offloading vehicles; massive submersible technologies linking umbilicals, risers, wellheads to floating production and storage devices; high-capacity production rigs and refineries capable of turning overnight 250,000 barrels of oil into 10 million gallons of gasoline, diesel, and jet fuel.

Overlaid on the oil and gas network is an astonishing patchwork quilt of territorial concessions. Spatial technologies and spatial representations are foundational to the oil industry: seismic devices to map the contours of reservoirs, geographic information systems to monitor and meter the flows of products within pipeline, and of course the map to determine subterranean property rights. Hard rock geology is a science of the vertical, but when harnessed to the marketplace and profitability it is the map that becomes the instrument of surveillance, control, and rule. The oil and gas industry is a cartographer's dream-space: a landscape of lines, axes, hubs, spokes, nodes, points, blocks, and flows. As a space of flows and connectivity, these spatial oil networks are unevenly visible (subsurface, virtual) in their operations.[20]

Mitchell's exhortation to "closely follow the oil" means tracing the links between pipelines and pumping stations, refineries and shipping routes, road systems and automobile cultures, that is, across the infrastructural networks, across the worlds of engineering and title deeds, into the charnel houses of finance and the military and thereby to discover "how a set of relations was engineered among oil, violence, finance, expertise and democracy."[21]

In seeing oil as an assemblage and as a zone of political and economic calculation, I want to emphasize the variety of actors, agents, and processes that give shape to our contemporary iteration of hydrocarbon capitalism: this is obviously the supermajors, the national oil companies (NOCs) and the service companies (Halliburton, Schlumberger) and the massive oil critical infrastructures, but also the apparatuses of the petrostates themselves, the massive engineering companies and financial groups, the shadow economies (theft, money laundering, drugs, organized crime), the rafts of nongovernmental organizations (human rights organizations, monitoring agencies, corporate social responsibility groups, voluntary regulatory agencies), the research institutes and lobbying groups, the landscape of oil consumption (from SUVs to pharmaceuticals), and not least the oil communities, the military and paramilitary groups, and the social movements that surround the operations of, and shape the functioning of, the oil industry narrowly construed. But this is only a start. The financial sector is key both in terms of project financing but also as oil itself becomes a financialized asset reflecting a radical change in the oil market itself in the last decade or so. This opens the door to securitization, speculation, and the question of regulatory agencies and the lack thereof. These governance institutions include the commodity exchanges but also the newly emerging global governance mechanisms such as the International Energy Forum. And not least for every barrel of oil produced, moved, refined, and consumed there are carbon emissions (and thereby carbon trading, carbon credits, offsets, and carbon markets), which is itself a complex market with its own politics and dynamics. The connectivities between oil, finance, the military and defense industries, petrochemicals, and the new life science industries only hints at the circumference of this vast assemblage.

The oil assemblage resembles, in some respects, what Andrew Barry has called a "technological zone," a space within which "differences between technical practices, procedures or forms have been reduced, or common standards have been established."[22] Barry sees such a zone as containing or producing different and multiple spaces (some of which have no boundaries as such) through the operations of metrological (measurement), infrastructural (connection), and qualificatory (assessment) standards. To pursue the analogy, an oil assemblage is what Mitchell calls a coordinated but dispersed set of regulations, calculative arrangements, infrastructural and technical procedures that render certain objects or flows governable.[23] An oil assemblage is a sort of vast governable, and occasionally very ungovernable, space.[24] If the oil assemblage is a space of standardization, its operations, however, are always temporally and geographically contingent. One of the assemblage's structuring forces, always constituted locally, is what I call the permanent frontier.

Frontiers of Dispossession: A Tale of Two Gulfs

At roughly 10 p.m. on April 20, 2010, mud and water shot up and out of the derrick of BP's drilling rig Deepwater Horizon, located in deepwater in the Gulf of Mexico (GOM), and was followed shortly by a massive explosion instantly converting the rig into a raging inferno. Located almost fifty miles off the coast of southern Louisiana, Deepwater Horizon sank two days later to the ocean floor, resting one mile below the sea's surface. As the rig sank, it ruptured the risers (the marine drilling riser connects the floating rig to the subsea wellhead), and a mixture of oil and gas, under extreme pressure, was released into the warm and biologically rich waters of the Gulf. By mid-May 2010, the Macondo well discharge was hemorrhaging at a rate of over 200,000 gallons per day; surface oil covered 3,850 square miles. When it was all over almost 5 million barrels had been released and 35 percent of the Gulf Coast affected. Rarely noted during the crisis was the long and deep history of spills and blowouts in the Gulf, and the systematic destruction of the Gulf coastline, especially in the Mississippi delta, over the previous century.[25]

In the midst of the Deepwater Horizon catastrophe, Royal Dutch Shell released a report on its activities in Nigeria, the jewel in the crown of the West African Gulf of Guinea, an oil-producing region of global significance and a major supplier of high quality "sweet and light" crude to U.S. markets.[26] During 2009 Shell confirmed that it had spilled roughly 14,000 tons of crude oil into the creeks of the Niger delta, the heart of Nigeria's oil economy. In other words, in *one* year, a *single* oil company (Shell, incidentally, currently accounts for roughly one-third of Nigerian national output) was responsible for 4.2 million gallons of spilled oil; in 2008 the figure was close to 3 million gallons. In related figures released in April 2010, the Federal Ministry of the Environment released a tally sheet of 2,045 recorded spill sites between 2006 and 2009. Since the late 1950s when oil became commercially viable, over seven thousand oil spills have occurred across the Niger delta oil fields. Cumulatively over a fifty-year period, 1.5 million tons (4 billion gallons) of crude oil has been discharged in an area roughly one-tenth the size of the federal waters of the GOM. As an Amnesty International report put it, this spillage is "on par with [an] Exxon Valdez [spill] every year."[27] Since 1960, to put it more concretely, each acre of the Niger delta has been the recipient of 40 gallons of spilled crude oil.

These two instances of petrocalamity—each centered on exploration and production at different points in the global value chain but with common points of reference in the history of the Black Atlantic—provide an opportunity to explore the instabilities and contradictions in the oil assemblage. Both are oil frontiers, understood not simply as a territory peripheral to, or at the margins of the state in some way, but as a particular space—at once political, economic, cultural, and social—in which the conditions for a new phase of (extractive) accumulation are being put in place (the establishment, in short, of the conditions of possibility for a new phase of capital accumulation).

In the world of big oil, a frontier has a specific set of connotations. A geological province, a large area often of several thousand square kilometers with a common geological history, becomes a petroleum province when a "working petroleum system" has been discovered.[28] A commercial petroleum system (or "play") consists of several core features: a source rock with rich carbon content and a geological depth capable of converting organic carbon to petroleum; a sedimentary reservoir rock with sufficient pore space to hold significant volumes of petroleum and permeability to permit petroleum to flow to a well bore; a nonporous sedimentary rock as effective barrier to petroleum migration; and a structural trapping mechanism to capture and retain petroleum. Once these preconditions are met, the oil frontier comes to life in the play.

The discovery of a petroleum field—a play with commercial potential—triggers a process of appraisal and development, namely, drilling many new wells to confirm the extent and properties of the reservoirs and fluids and to determine whether the configuration warrants further investment. The development of the initial fields in a new province is replete with technical uncertainties that collectively shape the ultimate volume of oil that can be recovered. The properties of reservoir rock, the fluids it contains, and the fluid dynamics in the rock are key, but so too are the fluids that vary in their composition, specific gravity, and viscosity. As Peter Nolan and Mark Thurber point out,[29] uncertainties around each of these field variables translate into uncertainty in ultimate recovery volumes, peak production, the life of the field, and so on.

The frontier, in sum, refers to the spatiotemporal dynamics in which fields, in a petroleum province, are discovered, developed, and recovered; the process from so-called primary reserve creation to tertiary recovery from existing "mature" reservoirs. With the development of one or more commercial fields, a frontier becomes "proven" and some uncertainties are reduced, which often induces an influx of new entrant companies that were deterred when entry barriers were high, which includes state companies and smaller independents. Another frontier emerges—a function of new technologies and aging reservoirs—as aging oil fields attract investments through tertiary recovery. But the idea of the frontier captures something else, namely, a process, covering many decades, through which the industry has seen the continual discovery, exploitation, and extension of the oil frontier from onshore sedimentary basins through shallow offshore basins and into the deep and ultradeepwater basins. Recent and emergent frontiers include the challenges of very deep Arctic water and the commercialization of vast resources of unconventional oil and gas like Canadian tar sands and the U.S. oil and gas shales. The frontier within and between provinces is thus permanent and dynamic, both geographically expansionary and, as it were, involutionary. Frontiers are customarily seen as spaces "beyond the sphere of the routine action of centrally located violence-producing enterprises," in which typically land and property rights are contested, the rule of law is in question, and frontier populations (often racialized and excluded because of the coercive forms of capital accumulation in train) inhabit a zone in which "violence and political negotiation [are] . . . at the center of social and economic life."[30] Frontiers, as I deploy the term for oil, possess all of these qualities rather than be confined to the technical relations of resource exploitation (as the industry understands frontiers). The permanent frontier marks the ongoing recursive construction of new spaces of accumulation (whether the discovery of first oil in the 1950s in Nigeria or the explosion of offshore oil development off coastal Louisiana after 1938) and the creation of the conditions of possibility for the local operation of the oil assemblage.[31]

Oil frontiers have their own temporalities and spatialities—shaped naturally by technological considerations unique to oil—but like frontiers everywhere, questions of access to and control of land, property, the state as a prerequisite for accumulation is key. As a territorial resource, oil is constantly in the business of creating new—and refiguring old—frontiers; complex processes of dispossession, compromise, violence, and engagement mark them. As a technologically dynamic industry, the frontiers so created are "deep, shifting, fragmented and elastic territories."[32] Eyal Weizman's extraordinary account of the Israeli occupation of Palestine comes close to what I have in mind:

> The dynamic morphology of the frontier resembles an incessant sea dotted with multiplying archipelagoes of externally alienated and internally homogenous . . . enclaves. . . . [It is] a unique territorial ecosystem (in which) various other zones—political piracy, barbaric violence, . . . of weak citizenship—exist adjacent to, within or over each other.[33]

These oil frontiers are textbook cases of what Henri Lefebvre calls the "hyper-complexity" of global space in which social space fissions and fragments, producing multiple, overlapping, and intertwined subnational spaces with their own complex internal boundaries and frontiers.[34]

Figure 1.
An oil spill from an abandoned Shell Petroleum Development Company well in Oloibiri, Niger Delta. Wellhead 14 was closed in 1977 but has been leaking for years, and in June of 2004 it finally released an oil spill of over 20,000 barrels of crude. Workers subcontracted by Shell Oil Company cleaned it up without adequate protection. Photo by Ed Kashi.

Frontier Dispossession and Insurgent Oil: The Niger Delta

Nigeria, the eleventh-largest producer and the eighth-largest exporter of crude oil in the world, typically produces over 2.4 million barrels per day (b/d) of oil and natural gas liquids. The oil-producing Niger delta in the southeast of the country has provided "sweet" (low sulphur) oil to the world market for over half a century, during which time the Nigerian state has captured close to $1 trillion. Nigeria's petrofuture is very much in question. The vertiginous descent of the Niger delta oil fields into a strange and terrifying underworld of armed insurgency, organized crime, state violence, mercenaries and shady politicians, and massive oil theft casts a long shadow over Nigeria's purportedly rosy oil future. A powerful insurgent group called the Movement for the Emancipation of the Niger Delta (MEND) emerged from the creeks in 2006, an insurgency that reflected a much deeper history of growing militancy since the 1980s. Within two years of taking office in 2007 the new President saw oil revenues fall by 40 percent because of audacious and well-organized attacks on the oil sector; Shell, the largest operator and accounting for almost half of all oil output, had alone lost US$10.6 billion since late 2005. In the Port Harcourt and Warri regions—the two hubs of the oil industry—there were over five thousand pipeline breaks and ruptures in 2007 and 2008 perpetrated by insurgents and self-proclaimed militants. An article in the *International Herald Tribune* captures vividly the brave new world ushered in by the violent struggle over oil: "[Oil] companies now confine employees to heavily fortified compounds, allowing them to travel only by armored car or helicopter. . . . One company has outfitted bathrooms with steel bolts to turn them into 'panic' rooms . . . another has coated the pylons of a giant oil-production platform 130 kilometers, or 80 miles, offshore with waterproof grease to prevent attackers from climbing the rig. . . . Larry Johnson, a former U.S. Army officer who was recently hired . . . by Eni, said 'Even Angola during the civil war wasn't as bad.'"[35] According to a report released in late 2008, in the first nine months of 2008 the Nigerian government lost a staggering $23.7 billion in oil revenues because of militant attacks and sabotage. By the summer of 2009 Shell's western operations were in effect closed down, and more than 1 million barrels of oil were shut in. Ken Saro-Wiwa's desolate prediction in 1990 of a "coming war" had seemingly come to pass.[36]

Nigeria is a petrostate with a vast shadow economy and shadow political apparatuses in which the lines between public and the private, state and market, government and organized crime are blurred and porous. The delta's coastal waters are, according to the International Maritime Bureau, a pirate haven, comparable to the lawless seas of Somalia and the Moluccas. A new study, *Transnational Trafficking and the Rule of Law in West Africa* by the UN Office for Drugs and Crime, estimates that 55 million barrels of oil are stolen each year from the Niger delta, a shadow economy in which high-ranking military officials and politicians are deeply involved. Amnesty International's report *Petroleum, Pollution, and Poverty in the Niger Delta*, released in June 2009, grimly inventories the massive environmental despoliation caused by 1.5 million tons of spilled oil, describing the record of the slick alliance of the international oil companies and the Nigerian state as a "human rights tragedy." A United Nations study of Ogoniland—a small four-hundred-square-mile area within the oil fields—discovered systematic contamination by the oil firms and estimated that it will take thirty years and $1 billion to clean up.[37] Nigeria's oil complex is a vast and increasingly ungovernable space, a frontier of primitive accumulation, what Mike Rogin, describing Jacksonian America, called the "heroic age of capitalism."[38] Nigeria's spectacular petrocapitalism combines the most brutal forms of capitalist dispossession and racialized accumulation with the ecological wreckage of a modern high-tech global oil and gas industry. Corrupt politicians, wealthy contractors, corporate executives, and the feared security forces stand, cheek by jowl, with poor fisherfolk, uneducated and sick children, angry youths, and the massive detritus of the industry itself. Inevitably, it is a world that is combustible and explosive.

Nigeria is a relative latecomer as an "oil-state" and delivered its first oil exports to the world market in 1958. Now, the enormity of the oil presence in the Niger delta is hard to fully appreciate. Virtually every inch of the region has been touched by the industry directly through its operations or indirectly through neglect. Over six thousand wells have been sunk, roughly one well for every ten-square-kilometer quadrant in the core oil states. There are 606 oil fields (355 on shore) and 1,500 "host communities" with some sort of oil or gas facility or infrastructure. There are seven thousand kilometers of pipelines, 275 flow stations, ten gas plants, fourteen exports terminals, four refineries, and a massive gas supply complex. The national oil company (Nigerian National Petroleum Company) and its joint-venture partners (Shell, Exxon, Mobil, Agip, and TOTAL) directly employ an estimated one hundred thousand people.

A half century of oil wealth has propelled Nigeria into the ranks of the oil rich at the same time as much of the petrowealth has been squandered, stolen, and channeled to largely political, as opposed to productive, ends. Nigeria has long had its 1% versus 99% politics (85 percent of oil revenues accrue to 1 percent of the population). According to former World Bank president Paul Wolfowitz, around $300 billion of oil revenues accrued since 1960 have simply "gone missing." Nigerian anticorruption czar Nuhu Ribadu claimed that in 2003, 70 percent of the country's oil wealth was stolen or wasted; by 2005 it was "only" 40 percent. The state, he said, was organized crime. The Wikileaks U.S. Department of State cables released in November 2010 revealed extraordinary corruption, including a $20 million payment for basic contract signatures and oil-lifting decisions made by politicians and cronies within the presidency; all in all, a model felonious state. Between 1970 and 2000 the number of income poor grew 19 million to a staggering 90 million. Over the last decade GDP per capita and life expectancy have, according to World Bank estimates, both fallen. According to the United Nations Development Program (UNDP),[39] Nigeria ranks in terms of the human development index below Haiti and Congo. It is not a pretty picture.

Nowhere are the failures more profound and visible than across the oil fields of the Niger delta, an impoverished and politically marginalized multi-ethnic region (now encompassing nine states of the thirty-six state federation) composed of what are euphemistically referred to as "minorities." The current population of the oil-producing states is 28 million (of the total population of 160 million Nigerians), but for the vast majority, oil has brought only misery, violence, and a dying ecosystem. A United Nations report concluded that the vast resources from an international industry have barely touched pervasive local poverty.[40] The majority of the oil wealth is captured by the federal state and allocated to the so-called ethnic majorities in the politically dominant northern and western states. By almost any measure of social achievement, the core oil states are a calamity. Between 1996 and 2002 the human development indexes actually *fell* in the delta states.[41] Literacy rates are barely 40 percent, the proportion of primary school children enrolled is, according to a Niger Delta Environmental Survey, 39 percent. There is one secondary health care facility for every 131,000 people serving an area of 583 square kilometers. The number of persons per hospital bed is three times higher than the already appalling national average. Electricity is a running joke. Canalization dredging, gas flaring, large-scale effluent release, mangrove clearance, massive pollution of surface and groundwater, these are the hallmarks of a half century of oil and gas extraction. The region's delicate ecosystems now constitute one of the most polluted places on the face of the earth.

Nigeria's oil frontier began in 1956 when the first helicopters landed in Oloibiri in Bayelsa State near St Michael's Church to the astonishment of local residents. A camp was quickly built for workers; prefabricated houses, electricity, water and a new road followed. Shell-BP (as it then was) sunk seventeen more wells in Oloibiri, and the field came to yield, during its lifetime, over 20 million barrels of crude oil before oil operations came to a close twenty years after the first discovery. Misery, scorched earth, and capped wellheads are all that remain now. In the decade that followed, the Nigerian oil industry grew quickly in scale and complexity. A giant field was quickly discovered at Bomu in Ogoniland, west of Port Harcourt in 1958, and Shell-BP, which had acquired forty-six oil mining leases covering fifteen thousand square miles, rapidly expanded its operations across the oil basin. Ten years of feverish activity saw the opening of the Bonny tanker terminal in April 1961 and the extension of the pipeline system including the completion of the Trans Niger Pipeline in 1965. Oil tankers lined the Cawthorne Channel like participants in a local regatta, plying the same waterways that, in the distant past, housed slave ships in the sixteenth century and the palm oil hulks in the nineteenth. The petroleum frontier followed the slave and palm oil frontiers.

The onshore oil frontier—the offshore frontier began much later and the first deepwater oil production only commenced in 2005—operated in a distinctive fashion. Oil-bearing lands were in effect nationalized, and leases and licenses awarded (typically with little or no transparency) to oil companies that were compelled to participate in joint ventures with a Nigerian state. A memorandum of understanding determined, among other things, the very substantial government take on every barrel of oil produced. Local communities across the delta lost access to their lands. They were typically compensated (in an ad hoc and disorganized fashion) for loss of land rights and for the cost of spillage. Communities—there are over 1,500—deemed "host communities" by virtue of having oil in their customary territories or being directly affected by oil infrastructure were to receive "community benefits" from the oil companies that, in the absence of an effective local state, came to be seen as local government. Oil companies built alliances with local political powers, which in effect meant dealing directly with powerful chiefs and chieftaincy systems marked by the exercise of lineage-based gerontocratic powers. For the better part of three decades the companies could operate with impunity, cutting deals with chiefs and elders who through direct cash payments and community funds acquired considerable wealth. Meaningful community development was nonexistent, and locals benefited only minimally from employment, since the oil industry is labor intensive only in its construction phase. With the 1980s came the first protests from the oil-field communities—women groups protesting lost of livelihoods, youth protesting lack of employment—and then the electrifying impact of Saro-Wiwa and the Ogoni movement during the 1990s.

The history of oil development in Nigeria is largely the history of the vicious political struggles surrounding the distribution of oil revenues. Since 1960 the shifting geometry of the politics of revenue allocation has a clear trend-line. A process of radical fiscal centralism by the state, which now controls all oil revenues through various statutory monopolies, diverts oil to powerful regional constituencies in the thirty-six-state Nigerian federation (dominated by so-called ethnic majorities). As a consequence, the oil-producing states (populated by so-called ethnic minorities) have lost, and the non–oil producing ethnic majority states and the federal government have gained. Currently, roughly half of all the oil wealth is captured by the federal government through about fifty oil laws that allow the state to establish a statutory monopoly over oil and dispossess local communities; roughly one-third is devoted to the states, but until the late 1990s a disproportionately high share of this revenue allocation ended up in non–oil producing states. In 1960 the oil-producing states, through a principle of "derivation," took at least half of all the oil revenues produced in their state; by the 1980s this had fallen to 1 percent. Driven by the popular pressures for "resource control," Niger delta states were able to roll back the secular decline in derivation income. As oil prices rose after 2001, enhanced derivation inserted a vast quantum of monies (driven by high oil prices and the increase in derivation from 1 to 13 percent) into the oil-producing states through the machinery of state and local government.

This fiscal system since the return to civilian rule in 1999 has produced new political alignments on the ground. First, corruption has flowed downward—in effect, it has been decentralized—with the vast local takings to be had as more oil revenues flowed to the major oil-producing states, especially Delta, Bayelsa, and Rivers States. Second, there has been something like a democratization of the means of violence, as militants of various political and criminal stripes, often armed by politicians and a porous military, now control large swaths of territory in the creeks and disrupt the operations of the oil and gas industry at will. And third, expanded increased derivation income has fueled the rise of a hugely powerful political class—"godfathers," as they are called—that is not only a counterweight to the federal center but also has its own machine politicians. It from this trio of forces that the current wave of violence since the return to civilian rule in 1999 has emerged.[42] The reservoir of political rage and alienation is deep in Niger delta communities. A large survey of Niger delta oil communities by the World Bank in 2007 discovered that an astonishing 36.23 percent of youth interviewed revealed a "willingness or propensity to take up arms against the state"[43]

The current crisis extends beyond a guerrilla struggle against the alliance of the state and the oil companies. According to a UNDP report, there are currently 120–150 "high risk and active violent conflicts" in the three core oil-producing states.[44] The field of violence operates at a number of levels. Insurgent groups like MEND are engaged in armed struggle against the state and the oil companies. There are also intercommunity (both interethnic and intra-ethnic) conflicts often driven by land and jurisdictional disputes over oil-bearing lands (and correspondingly over access to cash payments and rents from the oil companies). There is also urban interethnic warfare—most dramatically seen in the decade-long battles between Ijaw, Urhobo, and Itsekeri ethnic communities in Warri over "who owns Warri." Central to these struggles in which perhaps 700,000 people have been displaced and thousands killed is the ethnic delineation of electoral wards and local government councils (undertaken by the states but with federal backing), which are the means for urban ethnic communities to access oil wealth, either as rents paid by oil companies for land used for oil infrastructure (such as pipelines, refineries, and flowstations) or as part of the revenue allocation process that now ensures that local government coffers are awash with so-called excess oil profits. Other communities are torn apart by intracommunity youth violence—the famed city-state of Nembe is a case in point—in which armed youth groups battle one another and their chiefs to provide protection services to the oil companies and get access to various sorts of standby (a salary for doing nothing) and cash payments doled out in the name of "community development."

By the summer of 2009 the oil frontier had become a space of extraordinary violence and political turbulence. According to a report released in late 2008—prepared by a forty-three person government commission and titled *The Report of the Technical Committee of the Niger Delta*—in the first nine months of 2008 the Nigerian government lost a staggering $23.7 billion in oil revenues because of militant attacks and sabotage. As oil production plummeted still further in 2009, on May 13, 2009, federal troops launched a full-scale counterinsurgency against what the government saw as violent organized criminals who have crippled the oil and gas industry. The militants in return launched ferocious reprisal attacks, gutting Chevon's Okan manifold, which controls 80 percent of the company' shipments of oil. Over two months, from mid-May to mid-July, twelve attacks were launched against Nigeria's $120 billion oil infrastructure, and 124 of the Nigeria's 300 operating oil fields were shut by mid-July. Then late in the night of July 12, fifteen MEND gunboats launched an audacious and devastating assault on Atlas Cove, a major oil facility in Lagos, the economic heart of the country, three hundred miles from the Niger delta oil fields (a year earlier, to accentuate both their strike capability and the ineptitude of the naval security forces, MEND overran and compromised the large floating production and storage on the massive Shell-owned Bonga field seventy miles offshore). Overall the oil and gas industry, on- and off-shore, has been crippled. By late 2009 Shell has closed its western operations completely, and the eastern region is barely producing 100,000 b/d. Many of the engineering, construction, and oil service companies have withdrawn core personnel and in some cases withdrawn completely. In three years the oil industry in effect came to a standstill.

As the situation deteriorated, the oil companies, which had in effect attempted to keep the oil flowing by cutting local deals with corrupt chiefs, now discovered that a generation of youth—many armed and all without job prospects of any kind—challenged the corrupt oil-fueled chieftaincy system itself, which by the 1990s was in deep crisis. The effects of dispossession in short were turned inward into the heart of customary rule. Armed youth groups in some cases rejected chiefly rule violently and in other cases asserted themselves as middlemen and brokers providing protection services to the companies and interposing themselves between the local oil operations and the chiefs.

Along the oil frontier three processes were at work. The first is what one might call local petronationalisms—the process by which the ethnic minorities of the delta became "oil minorities" with a political project for resource control. Over the last decade this has been most visible in the deepening of Ijaw nationalism and a popular mobilization of youth, especially in the wake of the state repression of the Ogoni during the 1990s. The Ijaw are the largest ethnic oil minority in the delta and are distributed across the heart of the oil fields, especially in Rivers and Bayelsa states. Their exclusion from the oil wealth (and the federal revenue allocation process), to say nothing of their bearing the costs of oil operations across the oil fields, became central to the emergence of a new sort of youth politics (in effect, a disenfranchised generation). Kathryn Nwajiaku has traced the origins of Ijaw nationalism to the 1920s and 1930s,[45] but it was overtaken during the 1990s by youth politics and the rise of the Ijaw Youth Council in 1998 and its radical founding document, the Kaiama Declaration,[46] which marked a watershed in the growth of popular mobilization from below and in the gradual turn to direct actions against both the federal state and the international oil companies. Control of oil in relation to what local peoples saw as a deep history of theft, appropriation, and unjust exploitation provided a powerful idiom to mobilize Ijaw claims and a discourse of rights (including legal, constitutional, and fiscal reforms). Ijaw nationalism proved to be a complicated category because of the internal heterogeneity of so-called Ijaw peoples (differing clan and community structures, differing language and cultural histories). Oil, as Nwajiaku points out, provided a way to draw Ijaw together but also generated other local forms of identity at the clan, village, or local territorial levels. What was true for the Ijaw was as true for every oil minority.

Second, the militant groups themselves were often the *products*, if not the creation, of state-supported electoral thuggery. A welter of so-called militias, cults, organized criminals were bankrolled and in many cases armed by ambitious corrupt politicians and local political godfathers, especially during the electoral cycles of 1999 and 2003. Two important militias, which arose before MEND, namely, the Niger Delta Vigilante and the Niger Delta People's Vigilante Force, were both funded by machine politicians and the local state. After a decade of deepening militancy, the boundaries between states and militants was blurred, and the reality on the ground is one of a dizzying and bewildering array of militant groups, militias, and so-called cults—the Niger Delta Militant Force Squad, Niger Delta Coastal Guerillas, South-South Liberation Movement, Movement for the Sovereign State of the Niger Delta, the Meinbutus, the November 1895 Movement, the Arogbo Freedom Fighters, Iduwini Volunteer Force, the Niger Delta People's Salvation Front, COMA (Coalition for Military Action), the Greenlanders, Deebam, Bush Boys, KKK, Black Braziers, Icelanders, and a raft of others. Nonstate armed groups often got their start as a way of doing violent oil politics for the Nigerian oil elites and then took on a life of their own, redeployed into other pursuits as the oil frontier advanced.

And finally, the proliferation of a massive oil theft business ("bunkering," as it is dubbed locally) in which insurgent groups were able to insert themselves (typically as underlings beneath high-ranking military officials and politicians). Local illegal refineries in the creeks produced refined fuel from oil tapped from pipelines, but the serious money lay elsewhere, in the larger quantities of oil moved offshore in barges and sold internationally. It is, and remains, a massive business (Wikileaks revelations again pointed to high-ranking military, politicians, and business people as central to the operations of what in 2011 was estimated to be a bunkering trade of $20 billion, perhaps running at 250,000 barrels per day) that nevertheless enabled youth groups and local criminal operatives to acquire arms and embolden their military offensive (and their popular appeal to a generation of enraged youth). Of course, the line between crime and politics here is murky and difficult to determine. Some bunkerers may have articulated the rhetoric of "popular appropriation" but were clearly part of criminal syndicates, which included the military, businessmen, and politicians. In others, the bunkering business was indeed a way in which insurgency could be financed. In both cases it produced a class of violent entrepreneurs—the militias resembled the mafias of mid-nineteenth-century Sicily who stood between a weak state and deep class struggles surrounding the latifundia—and a ferocious battle over bunkering territories.[47]

Oil wealth in Nigeria has helped produced a multiplicity of overlapping spaces of oil, from the new states and local government areas bankrolled by the oil revenue process to reconfigured spaces of chieftainship and ethnicity in which a panoply of political movements (youth groups, ethnic militias, oil thieves) struggles for control of different sorts of territory, to the violent spaces of the creeks controlled by insurgents and federal military forces. These spaces, often unruly, and deeply conflicted, represent a ferocious struggle over how nation building—in this case fueled by the centralized control over oil wealth—is to proceed and in whose name and interests. These political struggles over who has access to oil and by what means reflect the complex politics—what Mitchell called engineering political relations for energy flows—that attends the movement of the onshore oil frontier across the Niger delta. On its face, the oil assemblage in Nigeria appears to be in question: supermajors like Shell are selling assets and acreage, others move offshore in the vain hope of avoiding the militants, while the prospects of a military conflagration unsettles the oil markets. At the same time, with prices at $100 a barrel, the entire rickety structure can stagger on: the Nigerian government, the rebels, the supermajors, the oil bunkerers, and the political godfathers can all get their cut despite, and because of, the ungovernability of the entire system. Violent racialized accumulation in the oil assemblage can, paradoxically, be self-producing as an economy of violence.

Deepwater Horizon: Finance Capital, Neoliberalized Risk, and the Louisiana–Gulf of Mexico Frontier

The outer continental shelf (OCS) in the GOM is the largest U.S. oil-producing region. Not unexpectedly, the Gulf's oil complex—the assemblage of firms, the state, and communities that shape the character of oil and gas extraction—is massive by any accounting. With over four thousand currently operating wells, the Gulf accounts for one-third of U.S. crude oil production and over 40 percent of U.S. refining capacity. Over the past century, companies have drilled over fifty thousand wells in the Gulf (twenty-seven thousand have been plugged), almost four thousand of them in deepwater (more than one thousand feet). In the last fifteen years more than sixty wells have been drilled in the ultradeepwater zones—in more than five thousand feet of water—deploying dynamic positioning systems that use computers and satellites to keep rigs and supply vessels steady in rough seas and high winds. By 2001 deepwater oil production surpassed the shallow-water shelf extraction. There are 3,020 platforms currently operating, but they represent only a small part of the Gulf's oil and gas infrastructure: thirty-three thousand miles of pipeline on- and offshore connected with a network of terminals, as well as a huge capital investment of refineries, storage facilities, shipyards, and construction facilities stringing the coast from Mississippi to Texas. It is a massive industrial cluster directly employing more than four hundred thousand people in Louisiana, Texas, Alabama, and Mississippi, generating $70 billion annually in economic value and $20 billion annually in tax revenue and royalty payments to local, state, and federal government. The total fixed capital in the Gulf oil complex is now valued at an estimated $2 trillion.[48]

Louisiana's section of the Gulf, which contains many of the nation's largest oil fields, holds more than nine-tenths of the crude-oil reserves in that region. As of 2011, Louisiana was the fifth-largest producer of crude oil and the fourth-largest producer of natural gas in the United States. More than 228,000 wells have been drilled searching for oil and gas in the state since the first commercial oil well was drilled in 1901 in Jennings. The Louisiana OCS oil and gas production is greater than any other federally regulated offshore area in the United States. Including federal reserves, Louisiana has nearly one-fifth of total U.S. oil reserves, one-tenth of natural gas reserves, and historically has produced about 88 percent of the 17.9 billion barrels of oil and 80 percent of the 170 trillion cubic feet of natural gas extracted from all federal OCS territories. The industry's history in the state is synonymous with the history of U.S. offshore frontier development. While the first onshore well was drilled in the state in 1901, much of the subsequent developments were in shallow water along the coast. Since 1938 the state inner and outer continental shelf has become the driving force for the development of deepwater and ultradeepwater oil and gas production.

Louisiana's deep connection to oil means it is also America's very own petrostate, a living testimony to the petropopulism and oil-based human and ecological development failures that have typically afflicted oil-producing states in the global South.[49] Petrocorruption and the shady politics of oil development were there from the beginning, as the oil industry emerged on the backs of an extractive economy (timber, sulfur, rice, salt, furs). Local businessmen snapped up land and threw themselves into a chaotic land grab backed by Texas drillers and operators with little regard for the law. Wildcatting sprung up with no regulation; leases, especially along the coast wetlands, were allocated behind closed doors. Huey P. Long famously launched his career with an attack on Standard Oil and then proceeded to build his own subterranean oil empire.[50] While senator, Long and his political cronies established the Win or Lose Corporation, which acquired cut-rate mineral leases through the government and resold them at a healthy profit. At the same time he used oil severance taxes to begin a populist program of public service provision, which integrated a white working class (and subsequently African American petrochemical workers) into a program of economic modernization.[51]

In the 1920s and 1930s the wetlands leases opened up a new frontier as companies built a sprawling network of roads, canals, platforms, and wells, all of which left an indelible mark on the wetlands. By the 1970s, when oil was providing 40 percent of state revenues, Louisiana ranked at the very bottom of the heap in terms of basic development indicators. According to the *Measure of America Report* on Louisiana,[52] currently the state ranks forty-eighth (only Mississippi and West Virginia are lower) in terms of human development indexes. Massive inequalities between white and black populations mark all measures of human well-being; infant mortality and homicide rates are comparable to parts of Central America and sub-Saharan Africa. In some parishes well-being is roughly at the average level of the United States in 1950. The report points out that 80 percent of wetland losses in the United States over the last century have been in Louisiana. As the Tulane law professor Oliver Houck put it: "What oil and gas did is replace the agricultural plantation culture with an oil and gas plantation culture."[53]

The history of the oil industry is a textbook case of frontier dispossession and reckless accumulation running far in advance of state oversight and effective regulation.[54] Off-shore drilling technology was in effect born and nurtured in Louisiana with an assist from Venezuela—the former along the shallow coastal waters, the latter on Lake Maracaibo. Technology quickly developed from oil derricks on piers to stationary, mobile, and, by the 1930s, submersible drilling barges. All of this was propelled by new seismic technologies, which uncovered numerous salt domes across the coast and offshore region. Between 1937 and 1977 almost twenty-seven thousand wells were drilled in the coastal parishes including shallow offshore. It was the first wave of leases and backroom petropopulism that unleashed a torrent of canal construction, dredging, and pipeline corridor construction (to say nothing of the emerging petrochemical complex in what became "Cancer Alley") and permitted large-scale salt intrusion and rapid coastal degradation.

Off-shore development is customarily dated to 1905 in Louisiana but began in earnest in 1938 with a Brown and Root–constructed freestanding structure 1.5 miles from shore in fourteen feet of water, the so-called Creole Field. In 1945 Louisiana offered the first lease sale, and one year later a platform was built five miles out in shallow water and, in a move repeated many times over, drew on the local fishing industry to assist in construction and ferrying workers to the "floating hotels."[55] By 1947 Kerr-McGhee had drilled the first well "out of sight of land" using war-surplus barges and other equipment to house drilling and workers, thereby reducing the size and cost of the self-contained drilling and production platform. These first, tentative developments precipitated, however, a titanic seven-year struggle over jurisdiction of the outer continental shelf in which the oil companies supported states rights (to continue the lax, or rather nonexistent, regulation) over federal claims. Finally resolved in 1953 through two key pieces of legislation—the Submerged Lands Act and the Outer Continental Shelf Lands Act—which authorized the secretary of the interior to offer leases for competitive bidding beyond the three-mile limit. By 1957 there were 446 platforms in federal and state waters, and the rush was on.[56]

In practice, the moving offshore frontier was transformed through four giant waves of frontier development, a quartet of land grabs and dispossession. The first was almost wholly unregulated during the late 1940s and 1950s prior to and immediately after the resolution of the state jurisdiction question. A second occurred in the wake of the oil import quotas of 1959, which unleashed another round of major leasing; 2 million acres were leased in 1962, in water depths up to 125 feet, more than all previous sales combined. Oil production almost tripled between 1962 and 1968, and deepwater operations had by this time reached 300 feet. The first subsea well was drilled in 1966. As the National Commission on the BP Deepwater Horizon Oil Spill noted,[57] this period was associated with massive hurricane damage and serial accidents including blowouts, injuries, and helicopter crashes. A 1973 National Science Foundation report noted what was clear to everyone, namely, widespread collusion between industry and government and very light government oversight. The U.S. Geological Service freely granted waivers from complying with the limited regulations and inspection demands while the regulatory agencies were hopelessly underfunded and understaffed (twelve people in the lease management office oversaw 1,500 platforms).

In the wake of the Santa Barbara spill in 1969, OCS development nationally was stymied, but the Gulf of Mexico proved to be a striking exception to the larger national trend. Exploration proceeded apace with the first deepwater (one thousand feet and more) play made by Shell in 1975 in the Mississippi Canyon. The landmark 1978 National Energy Act and the OCS Lands Act Amendments in the same year fundamentally transformed offshore leasing by vesting expanded power in the secretary of the interior, developing an exploration and production planning process expressly requiring the secretary to demand environmental and safety studies, a requirement, however, that the secretary could override if "incremental costs" were deemed high.[58] In short, the good news was that finally—three decades after the beginning of the offshore boom—there was something like an effort to provide serious government regulatory oversight (though the Oil Pollution Act was not passed until 1990); the bad news was that the Gulf of Mexico was granted an exemption from all of the review and oversight legislation. The 1978 Lands Act Amendments expressly identifies the GOM "for less rigorous environmental oversight under NEPA";[59] three years later in 1981 the Interior Department categorically excluded from NEPA review applications to drill wells in the central and western Gulf. The 1980s provided in a sense an ideological resolution to the issue: the environmental enforcement capacities were eviscerated, and what emerged was a "culture of revenue maximization," as the National Commission on the BP Deepwater Horizon Oil Spill put it.[60]

The election of Ronald Reagan in 1981 marked not just the third round of leasing but an assault on the Carter reforms, and a full-fledged neoliberalization of the Gulf deploying the now-expanded powers of Interior Department. Under the leadership of Secretary of the Interior James Watt came a promise to open up the OCS to areawide leasing; he placed 1 *billion* acres on the block. He began by establishing a new agency in 1982—the Minerals Management Service (MMS)—which created eighteen large planning areas rather than the traditional three-mile-square blocks. While Watts subsequently resigned amid controversy and congressional opposition to OCS development on the east and west coasts, the Gulf was exempt, and the result was a land rush and massive exploration and production that constituted the third deepwater frontier wave (the record lease sale prior to 1982 was 2.8 million acres; the first areawide lease in the Gulf produced a sale of 37 million acres!). Seven sales between 1983 and 1985 leased more acreages than all previous leases combined since 1962; 25 percent were located in deepwater, and the lion's share was captured by Shell, the leading innovator and player in offshore technology and production. At the same time, the reforms provided for radically reduced royalties and federal bonus bids, with the consequence that companies paid 30 percent less despite a sixfold acreage expansion (average lease prices per acre fell from $2,224 to $263). In 1987 the MMS reduced the minimum bid for deepwater tracts (from $900,000 to $150,000), enabling a few companies to lock up entire basins for ten years for almost nothing. The fruits of this frontier expansion were visible a decade later: in that period deepwater (one thousand feet and more) wells grew from 4 to over 45 percent of all Gulf production.[61]

The 1990s proved to be nothing short of a "stampede."[62] Seismic innovations, a new generation of drilling vessels capable of drilling in ten thousand feet of water and through thirty thousand feet of sediments (tension-leg, SPAR, and semisubmersible platforms), and new drilling techniques ("downhole steerable motors") pushed the deepwater frontier to the so-called subsalt plays. Ten years later the Gingrich revolution ushered in another reform to lay the basis for another round of accumulation by dispossession: the OCS Deep Water Royalty Relief Act of 1995 suspended all royalties to be paid by the companies for five years. In turn, this produced another land grab in which 2,840 leases were sold in three years. By 2000 deepwater production topped shallow-water output for the first time. At the same time, the ascendant BP was increasingly displacing Shell's hegemony in the Gulf. By using new 3-D seismic technologies, BP had made a series of remarkable discoveries and by 2002 was the largest acreage holder in deepwater (accounting for over one-third of all deepwater reserves). The MMS budget reached its budgetary nadir precisely during this boom (a record number of wells were drilled in 1997). The *Houston Chronicle* reported that over the 1990s there was an 81 percent increase in offshore fires, explosions, and blowouts. In the following decade it increased fourfold.

The final wave of frontier accumulation was triggered by the election of George Bush in 2001 and the events of September 11. On May 18, two days after Cheney's Energy Task Force report was delivered, Bush issued Executive

Order 13212 (titled Actions to Expedite Energy Related Projects) the purpose of which was to "expedite [the] review of permits or other actions necessary to complete the completion of such projects."[63] The language was, as a number of commentators pointed out, almost identical to that of a memorandum on the "streamlining" of development in the OCS submitted by the American Gas Association to the Cheney Task Force. The MMS was already laboring under a congressionally mandated rule to limit permit review to an impossibly confining thirty days, but the new order pushed things much farther: in its wake four hundred waivers were granted every year for offshore development. As offshore exploration and production stepped into historically unprecedented ultradeepwater, the permitting process and enforcement were laughable. MMS was not simply toothless and staffed by the sorts of oilmen it was designed to regulate but, according to a 2008 inspector general report, was a hothouse of among other things a culture of substance abuse and promiscuity. To round out the abandonment of anything like supervision, in June 2008 Bush removed the ban on offshore drilling. Oversight deteriorated to the point where NOAA was publicly accusing MMS of purposefully understating the likelihood and consequences of major offshore spills and blowouts. Watt's new system was nothing more than "tossing a few darts at a huge map of the Gulf."[64]

Shell announced the birth the new "neoliberal frontier" in 2009. The Perdido platform, located two hundred miles offshore in water two miles deep, is nearly as tall as the Empire State Building, drawing in oil from thirty-five wells in three fields over twenty-seven square miles of ocean.[65] Sitting atop an "elephant" field rumored to contain as much as 600 billion gallons of oil, the scramble was on. In similar fashion BP pushed forward on a hugely ambitious program to develop multiple fields in the most demanding and unforgiving of environments, pushing deeper into old Paleogene and Lower Tertiary strata. The likes of Thunder Horse—BP's massive semisubmersible production facility almost destroyed by Hurricane Dennis in 2005—located in the Mississippi Canyon 252 Lease and the Macondo well (forty miles distant) represented, as the National Commission on the BP Deepwater Horizon Oil Spill put it, "formidable tests."[66]

Viewed on the larger canvas of the *longue durée* of offshore development, Perdido and Macondo were the expressions of what one might call the accumulation of insecurity, and the neoliberal production of systemic risks in the Gulf of Mexico—each rooted in the politics of substituting technological and financial for political risk. BP and Shell were drilling in five to ten thousand feet of water fifty miles offshore to produce deepwater oil close to the U.S. market offering a regulatory framework that can best be characterized as producer friendly, which, especially in the wake of September 11, produced a much better risk audit than dealing with the Russians in Siberia or the Angolans in the Gulf of Guinea.

The Deepwater Horizon catastrophe was overdetermined by the vast accumulation of risks fabricated along the shifting frontier of offshore accumulation. The Macondo well—named after Gabriel García Márquez's famous fictional town in *One Hundred Years of Solitude*—was drilled from a semisubmersible mobile rig owned by Transocean, while BP as the field operator (as is often the case in the Gulf) shared the field with Anadarko Petroleum and Mitsui Oil Exploration. Halliburton completed the cementing of the well, but on the day of the explosion there were indications of flow into the well. A large blowout of methane gas traveled up the drilling pipe and ignited the platform, leading to an explosion and a fire, which sank the rig. The disaster happened on the same day that BP executives visited the rig to congratulate management on a job well done. It was coincidentally the fortieth anniversary of Earth Day.[67]

Nowhere are the links between deregulation and neoliberal capitalism clearer than in the 2011 report by the Deepwater Horizon Study Group.[68] In its devastating assessment, the catastrophic failure resulted from multiple violations of the laws of public resource development, and its proper regulatory oversight, by a BP safety culture compromised by management's desire to "close the competitive gap" and to save time and money—and make money—by making trade-offs for the certainty of production. Because there were perceived to be no downsides, BP's corporate culture embedded in risk taking and cost cutting, and not least the histories and cultures of the offshore oil and gas industry and the governance provided by the associated public regulatory agencies.

The Deepwater Horizon disaster has more than a family resemblance to the 2008 financial crisis. And it is financialization, in fact, that adds yet another dimension to the oil frontier. At the time of the disaster, BP was one of the largest traders in the emerging oil futures and securitization markets. Standing at the heart of this financialization is the shift to oil as an asset class.[69] Oil prices have not always depended on the futures markets. In the 1970s and 1980s, before the advent of active crude-oil futures trading in the New York and London markets, most of the oil produced was traded via long-term contracts.[70] In the last twenty years oil has broken its relation to "market fundamentals" and is dominated by the flow of money and by the investment banks, as seen in unprecedented price volatility. Behind this newfound volatility and the speculative role of paper oil was the fact that "innovations in the financial industry made it possible for paper oil to be a financial asset in a very complete way. Once that was accomplished, a speculative bubble became possible. Oil is no different from equities or housing in this regard."[71] The volume of unregulated over-the-counter commodity transactions had grown enormously since 2000, a development made possible largely by the Commodity Futures Modernization Act of December 2000. These changes and what Dan Dicker calls assetization (the rise of commodity index funds and exchange traded funds), financialization (new and mostly over-the-counter customized energy products similar to the derivative markets), and electronic access to oil markets collectively not only made oil into an asset class similar to equities and bonds but also gave the commodities market a massive boost.[72] As a result, it was not so much minor speculators as large institutional investors who sought exposure to the commodities market. They regarded commodities as an alternative investment category in their portfolio allocations and invested a significant proportion of their assets accordingly. The new actors in the oil trade have produced a situation in which, according to Kent Moors,[73] 60 percent of the oil futures market is coming from speculators. Oil has become a source or store of liquidity sometimes preferable to the dollar because the oil market allows a better hedge against the loss in dollar value in foreign exchange. The movement into crude oil and oil product futures contracts as a flight to liquidity, which is a barely a decade old, has decisive implications for oil volatility. This is the heart of the so-called oil vega problem: the increasing inability to determine the genuine value of crude oil based on its market price. The inability to plan, predict, and compensate indicates that "we have a developing market (dis) order—a pervasive and endemic disequilibrium masquerading as the 'new order' in the oil market."[74]

An assemblage generating massive new systemic risks of financial and market volatility is one new expression that throws the "formidable tests" of deepwater oil into sharp relief. Others risks are biophysical and would include of course the potentially catastrophic costs of hurricane damage, which are endemic to the region but seemingly now are rendered even more devastating by the products of the oil industry itself (carbon emissions, global warming, and extreme climatic events). The 2005 hurricane season crippled the Gulf energy sector and left $120 billion in losses. Of course this is what the insurance and reinsurance industries are, in theory, in the business of protecting. But the 2005 season consumed the entirety of global premiums insurers had collected from energy underwriting.[75] The Gulf "wind market"—major underwriters already have high rates and have capped coverage—is a big question mark. Gulf oil seems to combine the worst of Wall Street, the worst of corporate rapaciousness, and the worst of technological hubris all running headlong into the global climate crisis. A perfect storm of catastrophic risk: the unrelenting accumulation of insecurity.

The dynamics along these two oil frontiers—one onshore, one offshore—have family resemblances, but each also highlights quite different, and often contradictory, dynamics in the local operations of the oil assemblage. Both produce a sort of ecological slow death,[76] but each also manufactures radical turbulence (one political and military, the other financial and economic) that threaten the very operations of the industry itself. Accumulation by dispossession along the oil frontier is key to both. If the Niger delta frontier reveals one explosive dynamic in the oil assemblage that resembles a combination of violent accumulation with fragmented sovereignties, the Deepwater Horizon suggests another. The Macondo well disaster reveals the deadly intersection of the aggressive enclosure of a new technologically risky resource frontier (the deepwater continental shelf in the Gulf), with the operations of what one can call neoliberalized risk, a lethal product of cutthroat corporate cost cutting, the collapse of government oversight and regulatory authority, and the deepening financialization and securitization of the oil market. These two local pockets of disorder and catastrophe in the oil assemblage point to, and are expressions of, the deep pathologies and vulnerabilities in the operations of imperial oil. If the onshore frontier in Nigeria ends in insurgency, in Louisiana and the Gulf the political story ends with class action suits, a reorganization of the regulatory but ultimately the abandonment of President Obama's moratorium and the gradual resumption of deepwater drilling. In both Gulfs, the oil assemblage lurches forward, simultaneously advancing the frontier and multiplying—and amplifying—the production of profit and risk.

Notes

1. Richard Dobbs, Jeremy Oppenheim, Fraser Thompson, Marcel Brinkman, and Marc Zornes, *Revolution in Resources* (London: McKinsey, 2011), www.mckinsey.com/Features/Resource_revolution.
2. Michael Klare, *The Race for What's Left* (New York: Metropolitan Books, 2012).
3. For an argument against the "blood for oil" thesis, see RETORT, *Afflicted Powers* (London: Verso, 2005).
4. Stephanie Clifford, "Oil Oozes through Your Life," *New York Times*, June 25, 2011.
5. Matt Huber, "Enforcing Scarcity: Oil, Violence, and the Making of the Market," *Annals of the Association of American Geographers* 101.4 (2011): 816–26 (special issue on energy); Peter Hitchcock, "Oil in the American Imaginary," *New Formations* 10 (2009): 810–97.
6. Michel Foucault, *Society Must Be Defended* (London: Allen Lane, 2003).
7. David Campbell, "The Biopolitics of Security," *American Quarterly* (2005): 943–71; Huber, "Enforcing Scarcity."
8. Stephen Collier and Andrew Lakoff, "On Regimes of Living," in Global Assemblages, ed. Aihwa Ong and Stephen Collier (Oxford: Wiley, 2004), 22.
9. Imre Szeman, "System Failure: Oil, Futurity, and the Anticipation of Disaster," *South Atlantic Quarterly* 106.4 (2007): 819.

10. See Gavin Bridge, "Global Production Networks and the Extractive Sector," *Journal of Economic Geography* 8 (2008): 389–419.

11. Timothy Mitchell, *Carbon Democracy* (London: Verso, 2012), 2.

12. Ibid.

13. Ibid., 2, 5.

14. Ibid., 230.

15. See John Broder and Clifford Kraus, "Offshore Oil Drilling's New and Frozen Frontier," *New York Times*, May 24, 2012.

16. See Oystein Noreng, *Crude Power* (London: Taurus, 2006); Paul Roberts, *The End of Oil* (London: Taurus, 2005).

17. Steve Coll, *Private Empire: ExxonMobil and American Power* (New York: Penguin, 2012).

18. More than 478 offshore platforms and 7,888 wells will require decommissioning in the period to 2041 that involves the removal of some 4 million tons of steel and other materials; the lowest cost estimate for this decommissioning, according to Douglas-Westwood Associates, is a staggering $65 billion.

19. Bridge, "Global Production Networks."

20. Andrew Barry, "Visible Invisibility," *New Geographies* 2 (2009): 67–74.

21. Timothy Mitchell, "Carbon Democracy," *Economy and Society* 38.3 (2009): 399–432.

22. Andrew Barry, "Technological Zones," *European Journal of Social Theory* 9.2 (2006): 239.

23. Mitchell, "Carbon Democracy."

24. Nikolas Rose, *Powers of Freedom* (London: Cambridge University Press, 1999).

25. National Commission on the BP Deepwater Horizon Oil Spill and Offshore Drilling, *Deep Water: the Gulf Disaster and the Future of Offshore Drilling* (Washington, D.C.: Oil Spill Commission, U.S. Congress, 2011), www.oilspillcommission.gov/final-report; James Theriot, "America's First Energy Corridor" (PhD diss., University of Houston, 2011).

26. Ricardo de Oliveira, Oil and Politics in the Gulf of Guinea (London: Hurst, 2007).

27. Amnesty International, *Petroleum, Pollution, and Poverty in the Niger Delta* (London: Amnesty International, 2009), 16.

28. Peter Nolan and Mark Thurber, *On the State's Choice of Oil Company*, Working Paper No. 99 (Stanford, Calif.: Stanford Program on Energy and Sustainable Development, Stanford University, 2010).

29. Ibid.

30. Silvio Beretta and John Markoff, "Civilization and Barbarism," in *States of Violence*, ed. Fernando Coronil and Julie Skurski (Ann Arbor: University of Michigan Press, 2006), 36.

31. Ibid., 38.

32. Gavin Wright and Jesse Czelusta see this moving frontier as compelling evidence for innovation and economic growth rather than the oil curse. They have absolutely nothing to say about the political and human developmental costs of the process ("The Myth of the Resource Curse," *Challenge* 47 [March–April 2004]: 6–38).

33. Eyal Weizman, *Hollow Land* (London: Verso, 2007), 4.

34. Henri Lefebvre, *The Production of Space* (Oxford: Blackwell, 1978); Manu Goswami, *Producing India* (Chicago: University of Chicago Press, 2004).

35. Jad Mouawad, "Oil Companies in the Niger Delta Face a Growing List of Dangers," *New York Times*, April 22, 2007, www.nytimes.com/2007/04/22/business/worldbusiness/22iht-oil.1.5388689.html.

36. On May 19, 2009, the government launched a counterinsurgency against MEND in the region around Gbaramatu, southwest of the oil city of Warri in Delta State, an area known to harbor a number of militant encampments. The militants in return launched ferocious reprisal attacks. A state-brokered amnesty was struck in late 2009—over twenty thousand militants and their commanders signed up—but the situation remains utterly precarious, marked by the dramatic car bombing in the capital of Abuja in October 2010 attributed to delta militants.

37. United Nations Environment Program (UNEP), *Environmental Assessment of Ogoniland* (Nairobi: UNEP, 2011).

38. Mike Rogin, *Fathers and Children* (Trenton, N.J.: Transaction, 1991).

39. United Nations Development Project (UNDP), *Niger Delta, Situation Assessment and Opportunities for Engagement* (Port Harcourt/Abuja: UNDP, 2007).

40. United Nations Development Project (UNDP), *Niger Delta Human Development Report* (Abuja: UNDP, 2005).

41. Human Rights Watch, *Chop Fine* (New York: Human Rights Watch, 2007); International Crisis Group, *Swamps of Insurgency*, Report No. 115 (Dakar: International Crisis Group, 2006).

42. Human Rights Watch, *Rivers and Blood* (New York: Human Rights Watch, 2005); Human Rights Watch, *Chop Fine*.

43. Aderoju Oyefusi, "Oil and the Propensity for Armed Struggle in Niger Delta Region of Nigeria," Post Conflict Transitions Papers No. 8 (WPS4194) (Washington, D.C.: World Bank, 2007).

44. UNDP, *Niger Delta, Situation Assessment*.

45. Kathryn Nwajiaku, "Oil Politics and Identity Transformation in Nigeria" (PhD diss., Oxford University, 2005).

46. Ike Okonta and Oronto Douglas, *Where Vultures Feast* (London: Verso, 2002).

47. Ellis Goldberg, Erik Wibbels, and Eric Mvukiyehe, "Lessons from Strange Cases: Democracy, Development, and the Resource Curse in the US," *Comparative Politics* 41.4 (2008): 477–514.

48. For new research on the Gulf petrochemical industry, race and organized labor, and landscapes of risk, see the June 2012 special issue of the *Journal of American History*, especially Craig Colten, "An Incomplete Solution," *Journal of American History* 99 (2012): 91–99; and Tyler Priest and Michael Botson, "Bucking the Odds," *Journal of American History* 99 (2012): 100–110.

49. Allan Sindler, *Huey Long's Louisiana: State Politics, 1920–1952* (Baltimore, Md.: Johns Hopkins Press, 1956); Adam Fairclough, *Race and Democracy: The Civil Rights Struggle in Louisiana, 1915–1972* (Athens: University of Georgia Press, 1999).

50. Anton Blok, Violent Entrepreneurs (New York: Harper, 1974).

51. Brady Banta, "Money, Resources, and Gentlemen: Petroleum Severance Taxation, 1910–1925," in *Louisiana Politics and the Paradoxes of Reaction and Reform, 1877–1928*, ed. Matthew Schott, vol. 7 of Louisiana Purchase Bicentennial Series in Louisiana History (Lafayette: Center for Louisiana Studies, 2000), 624–45; Roman Heleniak, "Local Reaction to the Great Depression in New Orleans, 1929–1933," in *The Age of the Longs: Louisiana, 1928–1960*, ed. Edward Haas, vol. 8 of Louisiana Purchase Bicentennial Series in Louisiana History (Lafayette: Center for Louisiana Studies, 2001).

52. Sarah Lewis Burd-Sharp, Kristin Lewis, and Eduardo Martins, *A Portrait of Louisiana*, American Human Development Project (New York: Social Science Research Council, 2009).

53. Cited in Steve Mufson, "Oil Spills, Poverty, Corruption: Why Louisiana Is America's Petrostate," *Washington Post*, July 18, 2010, www.washingtonpost.com/wp-dyn/content/article/2010/07/16/AR2010071602721.html?hpid=opinionsbox10.

54. Robert Cavnar, *Disaster on the Horizon* (White River Junction, Vt.: Chelsea Green, 2011).

55 William Freudenburg and Robert Gramling, *Blowout in the Gulf* (Cambridge, Mass: MIT Press, 2011).

56. Diane Auston, Bob Carriker, Tom McQuire, Joseph Pratt, Tyler Priest, and Allan Pulsipher, *History of the Offshore Oil and Gas Industry in Southern Louisiana*, vol. 1 (Baton Rouge: Center for Energy Studies, Louisiana State University, 2001); Robert Gramling, *Oil on the Edge* (Albany: State University of New York Press, 1996).

57. Freudenburg and Gramling, *Blowout in the Gulf*, 28.

58. National Commission, *Deep Water*, 62.

59. Ibid., 80.

60. Ibid., 76.

61. Peter Lehner, *In Deep Water* (New York: OR Books, 2010), 88.

62. National Commission, *Deep Water*, 39.

63. Cavnar, *Disaster on the Horizon*, 156.

64. Freudenberg and Gramling, *Blowout in the Gulf*, 148.

65. Lehner, *In Deep Water*, 92.

66. National Commission, *Deep Water*.

67. See John Konrad and Tom Shroder, *Fire on the Horizon* (New York: Harper Collins, 2011); Lauren Steffy, *Drowning in Oil* (New York: McGraw Hill, 2011).

68. Deepwater Horizon Study Group, *Final Report on the Macondo Well Blowout* (Berkeley: University of California, 2011), 510.

69. Kent Moors, *Oil Vega* (New York: Wiley, 2011); D. O'Sullivan, *Petromania* (Petersfield, N.H.: Harriman House, 2009); Leah Goodman, *The Asylum* (New York: Morrow, 2011).

70. Dan Dicker, Oil's Endless Bid (Hoboken, N.J.: John Wiley, 2011).

71. John Parsons, "Black Gold and Fools Gold," *Economia* 10.2 (2010): 82.

72. Dicker, *Oil's Endless Bid*.

73. Moors, *Oil Vega*, 98.

74. Ibid., 6.

75. Rob Nixon, *Slow Violence and the Environmentalism of the Poor* (Cambridge, Mass: Harvard University Press, 2011).

76. Leigh Johnson, "Financializing Energy and Climate Risks" (unpublished manuscript, Geography Department, University of Zurich, 2012), 3.

Debt and Discipline

Tayyab Mahmud

Neoliberalism is a reorganization of capitalism where hegemony of finance capital displaces Keynesian compromise. This transformation entails a rollback of the welfare state, breaking the power of organized labor, precarization of labor markets, financialization of the economy, and exponential expansion of debt. In this ensemble, debt sustains aggregate demand, fuels liquidity to lubricate financialization, and facilitates assemblage of entrepreneurial subjects responsible for their own economic security. Public welfare is replaced by self-care, and working classes are obliged to fund their private welfare through private debt while calibrating their conduct with demands of precarious labor markets. Subprime mortgages that engulfed dispossessed and subjugated communities are emblematic of the symbiosis of debt and discipline forged by neoliberal public policies and the market working in concert.

Political Economy Meets Foucault

In this essay I combine insights of critical political economy with the conceptual tool kit of Michel Foucault to unpack the connection between debt and discipline. While critical political economy helps uncover macro-level neoliberal economic transformations, Foucault's constructs train on the attendant micro-level processes of market-mediated subject formation. Of particular utility are Foucault's constructs of governmentality, biopower, and assemblage of self-caring subjects through "modes of subjectification . . . in which people are invited to recognize their moral obligations."[1]

The construct of governmentality concerns the proper arrangement of the dynamic field of exchange of "individuals, goods, and wealth."[2] It focuses on the practice of "economic government," where the economy designates "a field of intervention for government."[3] While at a general level it refers to "any manner in which people think about, and put into practice, calculated plans for governing themselves and others," more specifically, it refers to the ensemble of technologies of governance that aim at "the care and maximization of the potential of the *population*."[4] Biopower emerges in the shift from "a complete and unitary policing project . . . to a neutral area, which is the economy."[5] In this frame, *Homo economicus* reappears under neoliberalism not only as a "partner of exchange" but as "an entrepreneur, an entrepreneur of himself."[6] This entrepreneur of herself/himself is "eminently governable" through the technologies of the self fashioned by the market's incentive structure.[7]

An obstacle to fruitful use of Foucault to analyze the debt-discipline combine is that he underestimates the role of law and the state in the exercise of power. He posits that techniques of normalization "develop from and below a system of law, in its margins and maybe even against it."[8] He insists that "disciplines will define not a code of law, but a code of normalization."[9] He sees liberal political economy as driving "a formidable wedge" between the powers of the state and the sphere of daily human life.[10] Contrary to Foucault's designation of capitalist economy as a "neutral area," my position is that capitalism should be conceived not as a depoliticized and desubjectified market economy governed by "economic laws" but as a set of politically contested social relations under the hegemony of capital. Capitalism is a relation of power where the state and the market remain intertwined. I argue that the confluence of debt and discipline demonstrates that neoliberalism has transformed the state rather than driving it back—"the outcome [is] not implosion but reconstitution."[11] Consequently, rather than directly determine subjectivities, governmentality forms a "habitat of subjectification,"[12] within fields of operation demarcated by law. Foucault comes closer to this position when he acknowledges that operations of power constitute "a triangle: sovereignty, discipline, and governmental management, which has population as its main target."[13] Moreover, those modalities of power are "deployed conterminously, and in complex amalgams."[14] Accordingly, I argue that in the neoliberal era the hidden hand of the market and the iron fist of the law worked in concert to forge governmentalities that suture debt with discipline.

To substantiate this argument, this essay first examines the radical use of monetary policy in the United States to trigger the transition from Keynesian welfare to the hegemony of finance. It then focuses on the role of law and public policy in forging a link between financialization of the economy and entrapment of the working classes and racial minorities in relationships of debt including subprime mortgages. It then brings into relief the increasingly precarious labor markets that add to the pressure on working classes to turn to debt. Finally, it explores neoliberal governmentalities that assemble compliant subjects disciplined to conform to the logic of the financialized market.

From Keynesian Compromise to Neoliberal Counterrevolution

It is often claimed that neoliberalism is "more an ethos or an ethical ideal, than a set of completed or established institutions."[15] I discern, instead, a "programmatic coherence"[16] in the neoliberal socioeconomic transition in the United States that can be seen, following Karl Polanyi, as historical alternation of stages of desocialization, resocialization, and a new desocialization.[17]

Born amid the carnage of the Great Depression, Keynesian economics rests on the premise that capitalism is "a flawed system in that, if its development is not constrained, it will lead to periodic depressions and the perpetuation of poverty."[18] The linchpin of Keynesian economic theory is that aggregate demand systematically fails in capitalist economies.[19] Consequently, capitalism can be stuck periodically, even permanently, in a condition of slow growth, high unemployment, and excess capacity.[20] The post-Depression policy response was the so-called Keynesian compromise between capital and labor, with national fiscal and monetary policies calibrated to aim at full employment. With this turn the welfare state was born. The chronic aggregate demand problem of capitalism was to be resolved through full employment and enhanced purchasing power of the working classes.

Containment of finance capital was a critical component of this compromise. While John Maynard Keynes's desire for "euthanasia of the rentier,"[21] and the stated policy goal to "driv[e] the usurious money lenders out of the temple of international finance,"[22] remained elusive, elaborate national and international regulatory regimes were set in place to make finance capital subservient to production and national priorities. The result was a prolonged era of growth, rising wages, and mass consumption often termed "the golden age" of capitalism.

By the early 1970s the Keynesian welfare state appeared exhausted. The costs of accelerating demands from below for expanded economic and social rights, imperial wars, and declining balance of payments created a crisis for wealth-owning classes. Rates of profit fell, and the share of income of wealth-owning classes shrank. This led to "the worst bond bear market not just in memory but in history."[23] While some predicted "the death of equities,"[24] the Bank of International Settlements raised the alarm of "a genuine Dollar crisis."[25] Wealth-owning classes desired a fundamental break with the Keynesian compromise about welfare state and full employment.[26] Breaking the power of the working classes was an essential step toward that. This is when the neoliberal counterrevolution was launched.

Neoliberalism is a strategy of wealth-owning classes to reverse the setbacks to their wealth and privilege and to expand their reach globally under the hegemony of the United States. Neoliberalism did not displace the state as much as it reformulated it, turning the "nation-state" into a "market-state."[27] Neoliberalism was first road-tested in Chile after General Augusto Pinochet's coup d'état,[28] then in New York City by the 1975 "*coup d'etat* by financial institutions against the democratically elected government,"[29] and finally in the U.K. by the International Monetary Fund to reverse the course of Keynesian policies.[30] These trial runs "established a principle that, in the event of a conflict between the integrity of financial institutions and bondholders on the one hand and the well-being of the citizens on the other, the former would be given preference."[31] Finally, a decisive "financial coup"[32] was launched in 1979 by way of the "Volcker Shock," characterized by Paul Volcker himself as a "triumph of central banking."[33] This involved radically limiting the money supply and allowing interest rates to rise exponentially to ostensibly break the back of inflation, the enemy of finance capital. Note that "monetary policy involves a tradeoff between inflation and unemployment. Bondholders worry about inflation; workers, about jobs."[34] High interest rates induced an inflow of capital, U.S. government securities became an investment of choice, and the U.S. dollar again became secure as the global currency. The attraction of highly liquid U.S. Treasury bills induced a massive secondary market in bonds and allowed the United States to rely on global savings to run up deficits. Volcker Shock thus "represented a convergence of imperial and domestic responsibilities."[35] Bondholders were now the "disciplinarians of U.S. policy makers."[36]

To be able to institute a new global capitalist discipline, the United States had to, in Volcker's words, "discipline ourselves."[37] The "induced recession" triggered by the Volcker Shock was intended to emasculate organized labor.[38] While the specter of inflation was invoked, what guided the Federal Reserve was "a baseless fear of full employment."[39] It "wanted wages to fall, the faster the better. In crude terms, the Fed was determined to break labor."[40] The timing of the series of rate hikes substantiates this. Repeatedly, the Fed voted to raise interest rates just before major union contract renegotiations, forcing employers to be cautious about wages.[41] To establish its credibility with finance capital, the Fed "had to demonstrate its willingness to spill blood, other people's blood."[42] Volcker knew that there would be "blood all over the floor, and "there was blood indeed."[43]

The scorecard of distribution of gains and costs of neoliberalism testifies to its success as a strategy of the wealth-owning classes. The rate of profit, which was 7.8 percent in 1952–71, and fell to 6.4 percent during the 1970s, rose to

8.3 between 1995 and 2005.[44] The share of total income received by the top 1 percent of the income bracket rose from 9 percent in 1980 to 23 percent in 2007.[45] After three decades of neoliberalism, the average person earns less per hour worked.[46] Incomes of the bottom 90 percent fell by 9 percent, while incomes for the top 1 percent increased by 101 percent, and those of the top 0.1 percent rose 227 percent.[47]

Along with unemployment induced by high interest rates, the power of organized labor was crushed by direct coercive action. The opening salvo was smashing of the air traffic controllers' strike in 1981 by President Ronald Reagan, termed by Volcker as "the most important single action of the administration in helping the anti-inflation fight."[48] Alan Greenspan called this blow to organized labor "a paradigm shift" and a "political turning point."[49] In its demonstration effect on corporate behavior, this state action "recast the crimes of union busting as acts of patriotism."[50] Henceforth there was "a capitalist offensive that involved both political mobilization and relentless hostility to unions."[51] As neoliberal globalization buttressed by ideologies of market fundamentalism took hold, union power further weakened.[52] Liberalization of international trade and capital movements induced investments to flow to regions where prevailing political and social conditions kept wages depressed and allowed higher returns on investments. Wage pressure from countries with low labor costs was transmitted to the United States. With workers in different parts of the world in direct competition, labor's efforts at international solidarity fragmented. The end result was the near collapse of American unions.[53]

In 2010, 11.9 percent of workers belonged to a union; in 1983 this figure was 20.1 percent.[54] In the private sector, the union membership rate fell from 25 percent in 1975 to 6.9 percent in 2010[55]—the lowest level since 1901.[56] Decline in union membership was accompanied by a loss of union efficacy. From 1969 to 1979, strikes involved around 950,000 workers every year; from 1987 to 1996, by contrast, strikes involved less than half a million workers.[57] The number of work stoppages slowly declined from 3,517 in 1950–60, to 2,829 in 1960–70, 2,888 in 1970–80, 831 in 1980–90, 347 in 1990–2000, 201 in 2000–2010, and 11 since 2010.[58] Wages were directly affected by the decline of unions. In 2007 the union wage premium was 14.1 percent (17.1 percent for men and 10.7 percent for women).[59] Unionized workers are 28.2 percent more likely to be covered by employer-provided health insurance, and 24.4 percent more likely to receive health insurance coverage in their retirement.[60] The union wage premium is larger for those with low wages, in lower-paid occupations, and with less education.[61] Racial minorities were particularly hard hit by the decline of unions because the union wage premium is significantly larger for them; 17.4 percent for Asians, 18.3 percent for blacks, 21.9 percent for Hispanics, and 12.4 percent for whites.[62] The decline of unions was accompanied a 29.9 percent decline in minimum wage's value between 1979 and 1989; even after subsequent legislated raises, in 2009, it was 6.8 percent less than its peak value in the late 1960s.[63] Furthermore, between 1989 and 2000, annual working hours for the bottom fifth of wage earners increased by 7.3 percent, while those for the top fifth decreased by 0.5 percent.[64] Average yearly hours worked for all workers increased from 1,703 in 1979 to 1,883 in 2006.[65]

Anemic growth, high systemic unemployment, and a decrease in the rate of accumulation despite a rise in profits, enduring features of the neoliberal era, exerted added pressure on the working classes. Real GDP grew at an average annual rate of 5.9 percent in the 1940s, 4.2 percent in the 1950s and 1960s, 3.4 percent in the 1970s, 3.2 percent in the 1980s and 1990s, and 1.9 percent in the 2000s.[66] During the 1950s and 1960s, for about 40 percent of the time, the unemployment rate was below 4 percent; from the 1970s through 2010, unemployment was less than 4 percent for less than 1 percent of the time, and higher than 6 percent over half the time.[67] In the neoliberal era, the paradigm of shareholder value maximization became the "zeitgeist" of corporate governance.[68] The emphasis on shareholder value necessitated squeezing out other stakeholders; job cuts, lower wages, and fewer benefits were a natural corollary. The share of after-tax profits paid out as dividends rose from 51 percent in the 1960s and 1970s to 74 percent in the 1980s and 1990s, and peaked above 100 percent after 2000.[69] Share buybacks that were less than 5 percent of U.S. corporate profits until the early 1980s reached 90 percent in 2007 and 280 percent in 2008.[70] Besides reducing the wage bill, capital expenditures were reduced by cutting back investment. Investment as a share of U.S. national output declined from 20.5 percent in the 1980s to 18.7 percent during 1990–2009.[71] Today the number of unemployed and underemployed stands at 28.4 million.[72] A prolonged sluggish economy with high rates of unemployment is the "new normal,"[73] with prospects of a steep and lasting drop in wages.[74]

In sum, the radical use of monetary policy and smashing the power of organized labor inaugurated the neoliberal era. These systemic changes decisively transformed the grounds of aggregate demand from full employment to consumer debt. Financialization of the economy operationalized this historic shift.

Financialization, Subprime Mortgages, and Private Deficit Spending

Financialization refers to a marked increase in the significance of financial markets and institutions in the economy and a dramatic increase in the volume, velocity, complexity, and connectedness of financial flows.[75] It entails a "set of transformations through which relations between capitals and between capital and wage-labor have been increasingly financialized—that is, increasingly embedded in interest-paying financial transactions."[76] Financialization of the economy furnished the prerequisites for the dramatic growth of household debt and the connection between debt and discipline.

Mythologies of neoliberal deregulation notwithstanding, elaborate new regulations were fashioned to pave the way for the ascendency of finance capital. After over three decades of the neoliberal era, the United States still has a regulatory regime with over one hundred authorities overseeing different segments of the financial market.[77] After the much-heralded neoliberal deregulation, the financial sector remains "among the most heavily regulated sectors of the American economy."[78] The new legal regime that enabled neoliberal financialization included the Depository Institutions Deregulation and Monetary Control Act of 1980, which eliminated interest rate caps; the addition of the 401K provision to the tax code in 1980, which channeled incomes into private pension plans; the Garn-St. Germain Depository Institutions Act of 1982, which allowed S&Ls to engage in commercial lending and corporate bonds; the Secondary Mortgage Market Enhancement Act of 1984, which permitted investment banks to buy, pool, and resell mortgages; the Tax Reform Act of 1986, which created the Real Estate Mortgage Investment Conduit, making mortgage-backed securities more attractive; the Financial Institutions Reform, Recovery, and Enhancement Act of 1989, which rearranged the government-sponsored mortgage-facilitating entities; the Interstate Banking and Branching Act of 1994, which allowed banks to operate across state lines; the Community Reinvestment Act of 1977, which directed financial institutions to expand their market base; the Financial Services Modernization Act of 1999, that permitted comingling of commercial and investment banking; the Commodities Futures Modernization Act of 2000, which left derivatives out of regulatory oversight; and the Bankruptcy Abuse Prevention and Consumer Protection Act of 2005, which made it difficult for consumers to seek bankruptcy protection. The courts and regulatory agencies played a supportive role in interpreting and enforcing these legislations. The resulting new legal terrain was indispensable for financializing the U.S. economy and consolidating debt as a primary source of aggregate demand.

Financialization of the U.S. economy also facilitated Americanization of global finance and helped embed the imperial role of the United States into global financial flows. In particular, the deepening and the global expansion of financial markets made it possible for global savings to flow to the United States at an unprecedented scale.[79] These capital flows secured by a deficit-ridden military power are "an imperial tithe."[80] For U.S. policymakers, the current account became a "meaningless concept,"[81] and the imperial hegemon become "the superpower of borrowing."[82] The escalating U.S. current-account deficit and debt-driven consumer spending allowed the U.S. economy to function as "the 'Keynesian engine' of the global economy."[83] Financialization, then, was "paradoxical financial Keynesianism" whereby demand was stimulated by asset bubbles, and these bubbles together with the reserve currency status of the U.S. dollar made the United States "catalyst of world effective demand."[84]

It was the financialized economy facilitated by the new legal regimes that turned debt, rather than full employment, as the propellant of aggregate demand. Consumption, which from 1952 to 1980, as a percentage of GDP, was around 62 percent, rose steadily to about 70 percent since 2001,[85] making the U.S. consumer "by far the most important consumer in the world."[86] Between 1980 and 2008 the size of debt of all U.S. sectors as a percentage of GDP rose from 155 percent to 353 percent by 2008.[87] Gross debt of households rose from 50 percent of GDP in 1980 to 98 percent of GDP in 2007.[88] Outstanding consumer debt as a percentage of disposable income grew from 62 percent in 1975 to 127.2 percent in 2005.[89] The flow of interest paid by households that was 4.4 percent of GDP in 1979 rose to 5.7 percent in 2007.[90]

From 1996 to 2000 all debt increased by an average of $1.6 trillion per year, with household debt alone averaging over $400 billion per year, at a time when the GDP grew at an average rate of about $500 billion per year.[91] From 2001 through 2007 all debt increased by $3 trillion per year, with household debt increasing by $900 billion per year, while the GDP increased by less than $600 billion per year.[92] At the end of 2008, 70 percent of U.S. families held credit cards, with the total credit card debt reaching $972.73 trillion.[93] The turn to debt is linked with the decline in savings triggered by the decline in wages. While between 1965 and 1980 savings amounted to 9.3 percent of disposable income, by 2005 savings declined to 1.2 percent (–3.7 if residential investment is treated as consumption).[94]

Liquidity is the lifeblood of financialization. One crucial step in this search for liquidity was siphoning of workers' savings by privatizing and securitizing pension funds. Tapping this colossal reservoir of liquidity served three related functions: it fed the ever-growing indebtedness of firms and households, it gave workers a stake in the health of the financial markets, and it augmented the ideology of "ownership society" and "shareholder nation" by a discourse of workers-as-shareholders.[95] Pension securitization intensified, and the proportion of pension funds channeled into stocks grew from 35.1 percent ($871 billion) in 1980 to 49.5 percent ($8.6 trillion) in 2008.[96] The other crucial step in liquidity generation was expansion and securitization of debt. In this context, "the purpose of making loans, mortgages and offering credit cards is, increasingly, the generation of tradable financial assets on the cycle of monthly payments."[97] This, in turn, propelled "artificial liquidity," "liquidity black holes," "liquidity illusion," and "ponzi finance," the ubiquitous characterizations of the financial boom that rested substantially on derivatives based on bundled and securitized subprime mortgages.[98] Securitization of mortgage debt was a considered policy pursued since the 1980s to boost property demand and liquidity for financial markets. At the end of the 1980s Greenspan acknowledged that an important objective of U.S. foreign economic policy was "diversifying international securities portfolios . . . disproportionately in dollars."[99] Subprime mortgages and their securitization stepped in to help siphon off global savings and maintain hegemony of the U.S. dollar.

Far from being "democratization of finance,"[100] subprime mortgages testify to the enduring grammar of modern power's engagement with alterity as one of engulfment/subordination and not of exclusion.[101] The subprime lending boom was "reverse redlining"—racial minorities traditionally denied credit were now targeted with high-risk credit.[102] It demonstrated that, to grow and increase profits without engaging the sphere of production, finance needed to spread its reach beyond the middle class to the poor and to bring racial minorities within circuits of credit.[103] With the neoliberal turn, equity markets began to rise, propelled by inflow of funds from newly created funded pension schemes, and big companies increasingly relied on equity markets for finance.[104] In response, banks pushed lending into more marginal markets, developed new financial instruments, and invented new ways to make mortgage loans to lower-income workers and racial minorities whom lenders had previously avoided.[105] The scope of the financial market was expanded by hunting out economically marginal groups for mortgage and consumer credit. In this process, "economically marginal people constituted, in effect, a 'developing country' within the United States."[106] African Americans, who historically had limited access to credit markets on account of racial prejudice and discrimination, now became "the most profitable group to lend to."[107]

For low-income workers and racial minorities, the subprime mortgages boom was "asset-based welfare"[108] that emerged as a "welfare trade-off" between housing as a social right to be satisfied by public resources and home ownership as a mode to store and accumulate wealth.[109] Neoliberal reduction of the redistributive function of the welfare state was complemented by "privatization of deficit spending"—creation of aggregate demand through private debt.[110] Demand for credit and complex financial products did not naturally flow from their supply; it had "to be created and liquidity relied critically on demand being whipped up."[111] Financial markets cultivated expectations of growing and infinite increases in asset prices and the resulting wealth effect—an inflationary increase without which it would be impossible to co-opt the have-nots. Concurrently, financial markets relied on the Fed to keep the system awash with liquidity to sustain the wealth effect procreated by credit-driven financialization. Particularly in response to the dot.com crash of early 2000s, the Fed lowered interest rates and kept them low, incessantly creating liquidity and a credit-fueled boom. After adjusting for inflation, negative rates prevailed for almost three years.[112] Housing demand and prices soured, and the supply of asset-backed securities doubled between 2003 and 2004, and doubled again between 2004 and 2005.[113]

Legal regimes played a pivotal role in the expansion and securitization of subprime loans, and their channeling into global financial markets. New Deal legislations designed to support the housing market created FHA to provide lenders with protection against losses and established Fannie May to buy mortgage loans of banks, thus providing them liquidity to expand mortgage lending.[114] For over four decades, such public backing facilitated expansion of home ownership by high-wage earners—the so-called middle class. As wages started to stagnate in the 1970s, and this market was saturated, public policy promoted a broadening of the mortgage market by inducing the financial sector to reach new borrowers, particularly racial minorities, and to develop new financial instruments. Often discourses of civil rights and equal opportunity were deployed to effectuate these changes. It was Ginnie Mae, created to cater particularly to low-income workers and racial minorities, that invented mortgage-backed securities.[115] Freddie Mac was created with the specific purpose of securitizing mortgage loans and selling those in secondary markets.[116] Subsequent legislations explicitly forbade redlining practices and required Fannie Mae and Freddie Mac to concentrate more on the lower income and minority groups.[117] Soon, Wall Street became "addicted to mortgage-backed securities," and demand from investors and banks "for subprime loans outstripped supply."[118]

By modifying Keynesian-era legal regimes and fashioning new ones, neoliberal policies had ignited the subprime mortgage frenzy. Hailed at the time as instruments of progressive expansion of home ownership, the expanded borrower-base and mortgage-backed securitization had three interlinked effects: ever larger sections of the working classes and racial minorities were brought within the fold of housing debt, the secondary markets for these securities helped siphon global savings to the United States, and the size and profits of finance exploded.

In 1994, 32 percent of subprime loans were securitized for a value of US$11 billion; in 2003 the figures rose to 61 percent and US$203 billion.[119] By the end of the1990s the value of outstanding mortgage-backed securities was US$1 trillion, with the share of Fannie Mae and Freddie Mac at 90 percent.[120] With foreign investors holding one-third of the debt of the two agencies, compared with 13 percent of the U.S. mortgage-backed securities market in general, Fannie Mae and Freddie Mac served as the key link between global finance and the U.S. mortgage market.[121]

The subprime mortgage saga and the entrapment of the working classes and racial minorities into circuits of credit, then, resulted from the financial sector's search for depth and liquidity, as debt became the primary instrument to sustain aggregate demand. Redesigned legal regimes and public agencies were critical to this transformation.

New Economy and Precarious Labor

The turn to debt by the working classes and racial minorities was also propelled by precarization of labor markets. Besides the demise of unions and compression of wages, compelling changes in the employment landscape include the reduction of socially necessary labor, flexible contingent labor, and ever vaster pools of free labor. The contingent workforce includes independent contractors, contracted workers, leased employees, part-time employees, and temporary employees.[122] Estimates of the numbers of contingent workers range between 20 and 30 percent.[123] This "crisis of work"[124] and "contingency explosion"[125] issue from firms' drive to maximize labor market flexibility, changes in information technologies, work relationships in forms that avoid employee status and its accompanying legal strictures and responsibilities, and as a union avoidance tool.

The "just-in-time" inventory management, a hallmark of cost-effective flexible production, has led to "just-in-time labor."[126] Besides flexible labor markets and flexible wages, flexible production produces flexible individuals, who change jobs frequently and whose social relations are increasingly transitory and flexible.[127] A growing number of workers "are living neither inside nor outside the world of work, but along its margins. . . . a new netherworld, the vocational purgatory of the 'unjob.'"[128] In the financialized economy, profits, like rent, "increasingly depend on mechanisms of value appropriation that proceed from a position of exteriority in respect of the organization of production."[129] Labor practices made possible by new information technologies

Figure 1.
Photo by Helen Liggett.

expand the scope of immaterial labor, helping blur the line between work and nonwork. As a result, increasingly "the factory spreads throughout the whole of society."[130]

The new speculative profit-making rests in part on the value-making capabilities of "common work."[131] The new order becomes one of externalization of the production process, of "crowdsourcing"[132] and "unpaid labor"[133] of the crowd. Here we see deployment of biolabor—"life put to work, outside the times officially certified by private law."[134] The consumer-as-producer phenomenon is part of this complex. Bagging one's own groceries and IKEA may be the emblematic example of externalizing fixed and variable costs by assigning tasks to the consumer. Similarly, costs of labor are shifted to consumers through mechanisms like externalization of program evaluation, beta-testing, technical assistance by users, and open-source program development.[135]

The information/communication revolution has resulted in the centrality of cognitive/nonmaterial labor, the loss of strategic importance of fixed capital, and the transfer of a series of productive-instrumental functions to the living body of labor-power. This is a rapidly unfolding phenomenon, evocatively labeled "cognitive capitalism."[136] Armed with new technologies, immaterial organizational systems now "pursu[e] workers in every moment of their lives . . . [and] the work day, the time of living labor, is extended and intensified."[137] Modalities of value production move "from factory to the *social* factory."[138] The information revolution procreated a new labor culture that absorbed the need for liberty and informality born of preceding cycle of social struggles, imported the dissolution of the borders between work-time and life-time from academic labor, and promoted the ideology of entrepreneurship.[139] It has produced a new economic model capable of generating value by mass use of the Internet.[140] In this realm, ubiquitous activities such as using a search engine, visiting a Web site, even carrying a cell phone that transmits the carrier's location, generate opportunities for enterprises to target advertising and harvest value.

Knowledge-based innovation and value-production by highly skilled precarious labor is a distinct sign of cognitive capitalism. In this context, higher education and incessant skills-development play an increasingly critical role in establishing an individual's ranking in the hierarchy of employability.[141] At the same time, public education faces disinvestment, and the cost of education has soared.[142] The average tuition at a four-year nonprofit college in 2009–10 was $21,324, while at public colleges it was $10,747.[143] From 1999 to 2009 tuition at public two-year colleges increased 71 percent, while the median family income, adjusted for inflation, declined 4.9 percent.[144] Unsurprisingly, reliance on debt for education and retraining soared. Surging above $1 trillion, student loans now exceed credit card and auto loan debt.[145] In this context of a financialized economy, precarization of labor, and demands for enhanced skills, increasing reliance on debt to retrain, indeed to live, became the only available option for the working classes and racial minorities.

Discipline of Debt

In the perennial search of social orders for effective modes to contain and control the dispossessed, debt surfaced on the agenda of American ruling classes as early as the early 1900s. In particular, home mortgage was advocated as an effective tool of social control, indeed, a "prophylactic against mob mind."[146] As organized labor took root, captains of industry recommended that workers be induced to "invest their savings in their homes and own them. Then they won't leave and they won't strike. It ties them down so they have a stake in *our* prosperity."[147] While a beginning was made along this agenda during the Keynesian era, neoliberal financialization dramatically expanded the scope and reach of credit in general and mortgage-driven home ownership in particular. Concurrently, neoliberalism opened up new frontiers for the disciplinary operations of debt: self-discipline by indebted masses engulfed by the financialized economy and refashioned governmentalities.

Before there was money, there was debt.[148] Throughout history, debt both lubricated circuits of value extraction and acted as a disciplinary device. From Athenian debt-bondage to contemporary labor trafficking, debt-peonage has been part of labor management regimes of a variety of modes of production. The historical role of debt in moral discipline is evidenced by the fact that in all Indo-European languages, words for debt are synonymous with those for sin or guilt.[149] Debt has also played a foundational role in modern imperial domination. During the colonial era, colonial powers often intervened militarily to enforce debt contracts.[150] After decolonization, conditions accompanying international credits were deployed to control public policies of postcolonial formations.[151] The recurrent international debt crises of the last three decades were used to enforce neoliberal restructuring of economies of debtor states.[152] Debt levels of corporations unavoidably tend to discipline the employment relationship, as firms with higher debt reduce their payrolls, use more part-time employees, pay lower wages, and have anemic pension plans.[153] The disciplinary impact of debt in all these instances issued from direct coercion and/or express provisions of debt contracts. What is distinctive about the neoliberal era is the self-discipline of debtors procreated by governmentalities unencumbered by direct coercion or express undertakings in a contract.

Neoliberal rationality aims at congruence between a responsible and moral individual and an economic-rational actor—prudent subjects whose moral quality rests on rationally assessing economic costs and benefits of their actions. The prescription of subjectivity to obtain interiorization of the market's goal in the context of precarization of labor is accomplished through generalization of debt. The objective is assemblage of subjectivity that "accepts" itself as a *homo economicus*.[154] The result is "a dependent subjectivity, a subjectivity conforming to capital, and in which the rationality of *homo economicus*, of *human capital*, replaces the idea of social rights and common goods."[155] This ensures self-discipline whereby time and life outside the bounds of any specific site of production or contract remain subjected to value appropriation.

Economic policies and an attending discourse of responsibility furnished the grounds for the symbiosis between debt and discipline. Neoliberalism fashioned "workfare regimes" intended to "throw a long shadow, shaping the norms, values, and behavior of the wider populations, and *maintaining a form of order*."[156] Evocatively styled, the Personal Responsibility and Work Opportunity Act of 1996 ended "welfare as we know it" and instituted workfare—forced deskilled wage labor as the sole means of support on the pretext of setting the indigent on the road to "independence."[157] Similarly, the Quality Housing and Work Responsibility Act of 1998 ended public housing and turned the indigent toward private rental market. Hailed by the U.S. Chamber of Commerce as an affirmation of "America's work ethic,"[158] workfare underscored the imperative of wage labor by issuing "a warning to all Americans who are working more and earning less, if they are working at all. There is a fate worse, and a status lower, than hard and unrewarding work."[159] The new behavior-related rules of workfare aim to build "habits of responsible behavior."[160] "Stripped down to its labor-regulatory essence," workfare seeks "'docile bodies' for the new economy: flexible, self-reliant, and self-disciplining."[161]

Responsibilization joined obligation and prescription as dominant registers of subject-formation. Responsibilization turns on the ubiquitous neoliberal construct of "human capital."[162] Through the lens of human capital, wage is not the selling of labor power but an income from a special type of capital. This capital is integral to the person who possesses it and consists of both physical predispositions and the skills acquired as a result of "investment" in education, training, and improvements in physical capacity. A human being, thus, is deemed a "machine-stream ensemble," even a "capital-ability."[163] This actively responsible agent is a subject of the market and is obliged to enhance her quality of life through her own decisions. In this schema, everyone is an expert on herself, responsible for managing her own human capital to maximal effect. A politics of the self emerges wherein we are all induced to "work on ourselves" outside the purview of the social.[164] This biopolitical governmentality produces a subject to represent herself as enough for herself, complete, self-sufficient, without acknowledging the necessary and unavoidable social connections—a "narcissistic separation of *living labor* from the public sphere . . . [where] labor *becomes individual business* and/or *human capital*."[165]

As welfare safety nets are removed, workers are asked to think of themselves as freestanding businesses that shield themselves, much as corporations do by measuring and apportioning risks and by diversifying operations and investments. Risk, which was deemed harmful and needed careful calculation and management by actuarial experts,[166] is now represented as an opportunity to be negotiated, cultivated, and exploited by the entrepreneurial financial subject.[167] Ideologues of neoliberalism warn against "diffusing, equalizing, concealing, shuffling, smoothing, evading, relegating, and collectivizing, the real risks," and argue that "with more of the risks borne by individual citizens . . . the overall system may be more stable."[168]

Everyday life is increasingly framed as a space of investment, and the individual is positioned as an investor in a life project to continuously pursue opportunities and negotiate risks in the expectation of rewards. With the neoliberal call for individuals to secure their freedom, autonomy, and security through financial markets and not the state, practices of investment, calculation, and speculation become signs of initiative, self-management, and enterprise. Eliding the fact that much of human behavior is irrational,[169] neoliberalism expects individuals to rationally evaluate risk. Indeed, in the neoliberal ensemble, "risk is itself being more positively evaluated,"[170] with the result that "investment appears as the most rational form of saving."[171] In the assemblage of investor/entrepreneur subjectivity, "without significant capital, people are being asked to think like capitalists."[172] The consolidation of finance as a way of life introduces "a new set of signals . . . as to how life is to be lived and what it is for."[173] In this context, finance becomes "a way of working money over, and ultimately, a way of working over oneself."[174] Tying everyday practices to global financial networks—retirement plans, pensions, purchase of goods, payment of bills, credit cards, student loans, and mortgages—induces the self-fashioning of financial subject positions and identities. Finance, then, by constituting a primary frame of interpellation of subjectivity, becomes a primary "technology of the self."[175] This assemblage of the risk-taking entrepreneur is facilitated by attendant discourses of rational economic actors, efficient and self-correcting markets, and the tamed business cycle.

The Keynesian productivity-wage and production–mass consumption connections are substituted by a debt-consumption connection driven by the wealth effect. The wealth effect is tied to the emergence of "an asset economy," which, in turn, results in a "patrimonialization of behaviors."[176] The so-called wealth effect is an evocative instrument of this mode of control and discipline. The wealth effect, "a sort of illusory social insurance for the crumbling Fordist social security,"[177] induced by increases in asset value, particular stocks, and housing, "affects consumption behaviors more than the expected wealth due to increase in wages."[178] In the wake of the displacement of the welfare state with neoliberal reordering of the economy, personal well-being and financial security have become increasingly bound up with the fortunes of the international financial markets through pensions, mortgages, and stocks.[179] The result is inescapability of finance, as everyday life becomes increasingly financialized.[180] This ensemble of production and consumption of financial products and services constitutes and calls forth a particular subjectivity by demanding that the individuals increasingly act as entrepreneurial investor subjects as part of a wider individualization of risk.[181] It leads individuals to believe that their well-being depends more on financial markets than on demands for wages or other claims on public resources. Indeed, debtors often harvested the wealth effect, further fueling aggregate demand—cash-out volumes for all prime conventional loans amounted to $26 billion in 2000 and reached $318 billion in 2006.[182]

In this context, for the risk-taking entrepreneurial subject, taking and living with debt appear both essential and rational. Living with debt, however, is living in a "credit panoptican,"[183] with disciplining effects both at the inception of debt and through its career. The marketing of credit is built around time- and space-specific concepts of the "normal" consumer held in financial institutions. These normative expectations inform profiles of consumers including embedded understandings of normalcy and deviance.[184] Therefore, to qualify for debt a borrower has to demonstrate subscription to such standards of normalcy. Once indebted, debtors become subjected to normalization by debt and are less likely to claim nonconformist views or indulge in nonconformist conduct.[185] Indeed, Alan Greenspan, who presided over the subprime mortgage boom, expressed confidence that the more debts workers have, the less inclined they will be to strike.[186] In sum, conformity with rules of the new financial and labor markets renders the debtor a responsible subject called forth by neoliberalism. Thus disciplined, the atomized and self-sufficient subject of the market becomes incompatible with projects of solidarity, collective rights, and antisubordination.

Just in Case . . .

To be on the safe side, the neoliberal order did not leave the project of disciplining the working classes entirely to debt. It complemented the "invisible hand" of the precarious labor market and burdens of debt with the "iron fist" of the penal state.[187]

Betraying an "an eerie similarity" between criminal justice and welfare reform,[188] the neoliberal era is marked by a "culture of control,"[189] "penalization of poverty,"[190] and an "*enlargement and exaltation of the penal sector*" of the state.[191] A renewed deployment of the penal apparatus "increase[es] the costs of exit into the informal economy of the street" and "neutralizes and warehouses" its most disruptive factions or those "rendered wholly superfluous" by the new economy.[192] Today, in the United States, over seven million adults are subjected to the correctional system, including 2.3 million incarcerated, and 4.9 million under criminal justice supervision outside prisons.[193] Racial minorities and the economically marginalized constitute disproportionate parts of this population.[194] While between 1950 and 1970, the imprisonment rate declined, it saw an exponential boom after 1975.[195] Between 1975 and 2000 the total incarcerated population increased by 500 percent.[196] Since 1975, "corrections" posted the fastest expansion in public expenditures and has become the third-largest employer in the United States.[197] At a time when public housing was dismantled as part of welfare reform, prisons have "*effectively became the country's main public housing program.*"[198] In tune with the neoliberal agenda of turning the state into a market-state, the penal system has been increasingly privatized. For-profit private prisons, reinstituted in 1983 after having been outlawed in 1925, saw an exponential growth, yielding handsome profits for the burgeoning industry.[199] In line with replacing taxes with user fees, federal and state governments increasingly adopted "carceral taxation" to have inmates pay for cost of their own incarceration.[200]

For the working classes, the expanded deployment of the penal arm of the state increases the cost of not participating in the flexible labor markets. The prospect of falling off the treadmill of the financialized debt-driven becomes more frightening than ever. This further substantiates the position that law and the state remain critical enablers of subject-forming governmentalities.

Conclusion

Assemblage of self-caring subjects through a symbiosis of debt and discipline is a defining feature of the neoliberal era. Strategic use of monetary policy and radical rearrangement of legal regimes facilitated financialization of the economy, broke the power of organized labor, and expanded debt to sustain aggregate demand. Financial markets extended their reach by bringing ever-increasing sections of the working classes and racial minorities within the ambit of the credit economy. Faced with shrinking welfare, wage pressures, and precarious labor markets, working classes and racial minorities increasingly turned to debt for their economic survival. Neoliberal rationalities procreated constructs of individual responsibility and human capital and facilitated assemblage of subjects who were coaxed to engage the financialized economy as risk-taking entrepreneurs. Engulfment in relationships of debt induced self-discipline and conformity with the logic of the financialized economy and precarious labor markets.

For three decades, neoliberal financialization combined with globalization contained the crisis of profitability and produced debt-encumbered self-disciplined working classes. In the process, however, it sowed the seeds of a larger crisis. Siphoning savings from the periphery to sustain demand in the core and securitizing subprime mortgages to generate liquidity had its limits. Pushed beyond the frontiers of sustainability, this empire of debt collapsed. Securitization of debt, designed to spread risk, now spread contagion. The result was the 2008 global financial meltdown and the resulting Great Recession. This trajectory underscores that throughout its history capitalism never solves its foundational contradictions and tendencies to crisis; it only transforms them.

The magnitude of the ongoing crisis procreated by neoliberal financialization is alarming. The global losses of the financial sector exceed $3.4 trillion, and the bill for public rescue of financial institution exceeds $20 trillion.[201] Worldwide, over 60 million jobs were lost, 200 million working people slipped below the poverty line, and high unemployment has become the "new normal."[202] Value of derivatives at $596 trillion dwarfs the entire world output of $47 trillion.[203] By 2014 government debt of G20 countries is projected to be 120 percent of GDP.[204] The credit worthiness of the United States stands questioned, and the status of the dollar as the dominant global currency is in jeopardy.[205] The policy responses to the crisis thus far are consistent with the track record of the last three decades: using crises to reinforce the priority of financial institutions and bondholders over well-being of working classes. The myriad policy responses have stubbornly refused to ease the debt burdens of consumers and sovereigns, lest the disciplinary role of debt falters. The policy responses to the crisis thus far appear to fall broadly in five categories: one, massive injections of liquidity into the financial system and bailouts of major financial institutions; two, imposition of fiscal discipline through austerity measures, turning governments into collection agencies for the bond markets; three, accelerated hollowing out of welfare systems and further pressure on wages; four, activation of racist xenophobia to recalibrate of the boundaries of legitimate membership in society; five, acceleration of militarization and use of direct violence both locally and globally.

The crisis and the policy responses have also triggered resistance from below. From the Arab spring to Greek general strikes and from the Occupy Movement in the United States to mass demonstrations in London, new spaces and modes of resistance are being forged. However, the disciplinary function of debt is yet to find priority in the agendas of these movements. It is imperative that theory and praxis aimed at emancipatory transformation and global justice take account of the nature and magnitude of the contemporary crisis and the implications of policy responses on the offer. In particular, we must focus on new and refurbished disciplinary regimes that are reinforcing the discipline of debt on national policies to transfer all costs of the crisis to the working classes and the marginalized. Popular democratization of finance by managing finance as a public utility must be high on the agenda of popular movements. An urgent challenge is to explore agendas, coalitions, and organizational forms of resistive social movements suitable to pursue popular democratization of finance. Also needed are designs of political and economic governance conducive to organizing banking and finance as public utilities. The current crisis has opened up the possibility of alternative social orders and modes of life. What shape the future will take in no small measure depends on how contending social forces will face the perennial question of finance and the relationship between debt and discipline.

Notes

1. Michel Foucault, *Ethics: Essential Works of Michel Foucault, 1954–1984* (New York: Penguin, 1998), 264.
2. Michel Foucault, *Security, Territory, Population: Lectures at the College de France, 1977–1978* (New York: Picador, 2009), 94.
3. Ibid., 95.
4. Ben Golder and Pater Fitzpatrick, *Foucault's Law* (London: Routledge, 1999), 31.
5. Foucalt, *Security, Territory, Population*, 258.
6. Golder and Fitzpatrick, *Foucault's Law*, 226.
7. Ibid., 270.
8. Michel Foucault, *The Birth of Biopolitics: Lectures at the College de France, 1978–1979* (New York: Picador, 2010), 56.
9. Michel Foucault, *Society Must Be Defended: Lectures at the College de France, 1975–1976* (New York: Picador, 2003), 38.
10. Michel Foucault, *The Birth of Biopolitics*, 17.
11. Jamie Peck and Adam Tickell, "Neoliberalizing Space," *Antipode* 34.3 (2002): 388–89.
12. Nikolas Rose, *Powers of Freedom: Reframing Political Thought* (Cambridge: Cambridge University Press, 1999), 178.
13. Foucault, *Security, Territory, Population*, 107–8.
14. George Pavlich, *Governing Paradoxes of Restorative Justice* (London: Routledge, 2005), 9.
15. Mitchell Dean, "Sociology after Society," in *Sociology after Postmodernism*, ed. David Owen (New York: Sage, 1997), 213.
16. Barry Hindess, "A Society Governed by Contract?" in *The New Contractualism*, ed. Glyn Davis et al. (London: Palgrave Macmillan, 1997), 22.
17. Karl Polanyi, *The Great Transformation: The Political and Economic Origins of Our Time* (1944; rpt. New York: Beacon, 2001), 18.
18. Hyman P. Minsky, "Hyman P. Minsky (1919–1996)," in *A Biographical Dictionary of Dissenting Economists*, ed. Philip Arestis and Malcolm Sawyer (New York: Elgar, 2000), 411–16.
19. Costas Lapavitsas, "Mainstream Economics in the Neoliberal Era," in *Neoliberalism: A Critical Reader*, ed. Alfredo Saad-Filho and Deborah Johnston (London: Pluto, 2005), 32.
20. Alvin H. Hansen, *Full Recovery or Stagnation?* (London: Adam and Charles Black, 1938); Hyman P. Minsky, *John Maynard Keynes* (New York: McGraw-Hill, 2008); Michal Kalecki, *Theory of Economic Dynamics: An Essay on Cyclical and Long-Run Changes in Capitalist Economy* (New York: Monthly Review Press, 2011).
21. John Maynard Keynes, *General Theory of Employment, Interest, and Money* (1935; rpt. New York: Martino Fine Books, 2011), 376.
22. U.S. Treasury Secretary Henry Morgenthau, quoted in Leo Panitch and Sam Gindin, "Finance and American Empire," in *Empire Reloaded: Socialist Register 2005*, ed. Leo Panitch and Colin Leys (New York: Monthly Review Press, 2005), 49–50.
23. Bill Gross, quoted in Niall Ferguson, *The Ascent of Money: A Financial History of the World* (New York: Penguin, 2009), 109.
24. "The Death of Equities: How Inflation Is Destroying the Stock Market," *Business Week*, August 13, 1979.
25. Bank of International Settlements (BIS), *Forty Ninth Annual Report* (Basel: BIS,1979), 3.
26. Susanne MacGregor, "The Welfare State and Neoliberalism," in Saad-Filho and Johnston, *Neoliberalism*, 142.

27. Anthony Carty, "Marxism and International Law: Perspectives for the American (Twenty-First) Century?" in *International Law on the Left: Reexamining Marxist Legacies,* ed. Susan Mark (Cambridge: Cambridge University Press, 2008), 170.

28. Juan Gabriel Valdez, *Pinochet's Economists: The Chicago School in Chile* (Cambridge: Cambridge University Press, 2008).

29. David Harvey, *A Brief History of Neoliberalism* (New York: Oxford University Press, 2007), 29. Bankers forced New York to accept "fiscal discipline" as the cost of a bailout—curbing municipal unions, layoffs in public employment, wage freezes, cuts in social provisions, and imposition of user fees. See William K. Tabb, *The Long Default: New York City and the Urban Fiscal Crisis* (New York: Monthly Review Press, 1982); and Robert Fitch, "Explaining New York City's Aberrant Economy," *New Left Review* 1.207 (1994): 17–48.

30. Mark D. Harmon, *The British Labor Government and the IMF Crisis* (London: Palgrave Macmillan, 1997).

31. David Harvey, "Neoliberalism as Creative Destruction," *Annals of American Academy of Political and Social Science,* 610.1 (2007): 31.

32. Gerard Dumenil and Dominique Levy, *Capital Resurgent: Roots of Neoliberal Revolution* (Cambridge, Mass.: Harvard University Press, 2004), 69, 165.

33. Paul Volcker, "The Triumph of Central Banking?" Jacobson Lecture, Per Jacobson Foundation, Washington, D.C., September 23, 1990, 5, http://www.perjacobsson.org/lectures/1990.pdf.

34. Joseph E. Stiglitz, *Freefall: America, Free Markets, and the Sinking of the World Economy* (New York: Norton, 2010), 142.

35. Panitch and Gindin, "Finance and American Empire," 65.

36. "The Bond Vigilantes: The Disciplinarians of U.S. Policy Makers Return," *Wall Street Journal,* May 29, 2009.

37. Paul Volcker and Toyoo Gyohten, *Changing Fortunes: The World's Money and the Threat to American Leadership* (New York: Three Rivers Press, 1993), 167.

38. Panitch and Gindin, "Finance and American Empire," 63.

39. James K. Galbraith, Olivier Giovannoni, and Ann J. Russo, "The Fed's Real Reaction Function: Monetary Policy, Inflation, Unemployment, Inequality, and Presidential Politics," Levy Economics Institute Working paper, No. 511, August 2007, http://ideas.repec.org/p/lev/wrkpap/wp_511.html.

40. William Greider, *Secrets of the Temple: How the Federal Reserve Runs the Country* (New York: Simon and Schuster, 1987), 429.

41. Edwin Dickens, "The Great Inflation and U.S. Monetary Policy in the Late 1960s: A Political Economy Approach," *Social Concept* 9.1 (1995): 49–81; Dickens, "The Federal Reserve's Tight Monetary Policy during the 1973–75 Recession: A Survey of Possible Interpretations," *Review of Radical Political Economy* 29.3 (1997): 79.

42. Michael Mussa, "U.S. Monetary Policy in the 1980s," in *American Economic Policy in the 1980s,* ed. Martin Feldstein (Chicago: University of Chicago Press, 1994), 112.

43. George Mellon, "Some Reflections on My 32 Years with Bartley," *Wall Street Journal,* December 16, 2003.

44. Gerard Dumenil and Dominique Levy, *The Crisis of Neoliberalism* (Cambridge, Mass.: Harvard University Press, 2011), 59, 58, fig. 4.1.

45. Ibid., 46, fig. 3.1.

46. William Bonner and Addison Wiggin, *The New Empire of Debt: The Rise and Fall of the Epic Financial Bubble* (New York: Wiley, 2009), 203.

47. David McNally, "From Financial Crisis to World-Slump: Accumulation, Financialization, and the Global Crisis," *Historical Materialism* 17 (2009): 60.

48. Quoted in John B. Taylor, "Changes in American Economic Policy in the 1980s: Watershed or Pendulum Swing?" *Journal of Economic Literature* 33 (1995): 778.

49. Quoted in David M. Smick, *The World Is Curved: Hidden Dangers to the Global Economy* (New York: Portfolio Trade, 2009), 217.

50. Martin Jay Levitt and Terry Canrow, *Confessions of a Union Buster* (New York: Crown Publishers, 1993), 217.

51. Dan Clawson and Mary Ann Clawson, "What Happened to the U.S. Labor Movement: Union Decline and Renewal," *Annual Review of Sociology* 25 (1999):100–101.

52. Ibid.
53. Jacob S. Hacker and Paul Pierson, *Winner-Take-All Politics: How Washington Made the Rich Richer—and Turned Its Back on the Middle Class* (New York: Simon and Schuster, 2010), 56.
54. Bureau of Labor Statistic, U.S. Department of Labor, news release, January 21, 2011, http://www.bls.gov/news.release/pdf/union2.pdf.
55. Ibid.
56. Steven Greenhouse, *The Big Squeeze: Tough Times for the American Worker* (New York: Knopf, 2008), 243.
57. Clawson and Clawson, "What Happened to the U.S. Labor Movement," 97.
58. Bureau of Labor Statistics, Department of Labor, table 1. Work stoppages involving 1,000 or more workers, 1947–2010, http://www.bls.gov/news.release/wkstp.t01.htm.
59. Lawrence Mishel et al., *The State of Working America, 2008/2009* (Ithaca, N.Y.: Cornell University Press, 2009), 201, table 3.32.
60. Ibid., 202, table 3.33.
61. Ibid., 207, table 3.36.
62. Ibid., 201, table 3.32.
63. Ibid., 209, 208–11, fig. 3AA, table 3.38, and fig. 3AB.
64. Mishel et al., *State of Working America*, 47, table 1.2.
65. Ibid., 128, table 3.2.
66. Fred Magdoff, "The Jobs Disaster in the United States," *Monthly Review* 63.2 (2011): 24.
67. Ibid., 30.
68. Ha-Joon Chang, *23 Things They Don't Tell You about Capitalism* (New York: Bloomsbury Press, 2010), 17.
69. Dumenil and Levy, *Crisis of Neoliberalism,* 62, fig. 4.3, 355n8. 70. Chang, *23 Things They Don't Tell You,* 19–20; William Lazonick and Mary O'Sullivan, "Maximizing Shareholder Value: A New Ideology for Corporate Governance," *Economy and Society* 29.1 (2000): 13–35.
70. William Lazonick, "The Buyback Boondoggle," *Business Week*, August 24, 2009.
71. Chang, *23 Things They Don't Tell You*, 19.
72. Magdoff, "Jobs Disaster in the United States," 26, table 1.
73. Ibid., 26, 36.
74. Sudeep Reddy, "Downturn's Ugly Trademark: Steep, Lasting Drop in Wages," *Wall Street Journal*, January 11, 2011.
75. Gerald A. Epstein, ed., *Financialization and the World Economy* (New York: Elgar, 2006); Hengyi Feng et al., "A New Business Model? The Capital Market and the New Economy," *Economy and Society* 30.4 (2001): 467.
76. McNally, "From Financial Crisis," 56.
77. Joanna Chung, "Multi-Layered Patchwork Will Be Tough to Unpick," *Financial Times*, April 24, 2008.
78. Frederic S. Mishkin, *The Economics of Money, Banking, and Financial Markets* (New York: Addison Wesley, 2000), 41.
79. Martin Wolf, *Fixing Global Finance* (Baltimore, Md.: Johns Hopkins University Press, 2010), 78, fig. 4.14.
80. Panitch and Gindin, "Finance and American Empire," 69; emphasis added.
81. "The O'Neill Doctrine," *Economist*, April 25, 2002.
82. Wolf, *Fixing Global Finance*, 4.
83. McNally, "From Financial Crisis," 63.
84. Riccardo Belloriore and Joseph Halevi, "A Minsky Moment? The Subprime Crisis and "New" Capitalism," in *Credit, Money, and Macroeconomic Policy: A Post-Keynesian Approach*, ed. Claude Gnos and Louis-Philippe Rochon (Cheltenham, U.K.: Elgar, 2011), http://gesd.free.fr/wp200904.pdf.
85. Dumenil and Levy, *Crisis of Neoliberalism,* 146, fig. 10.3.
86. Stephen Roach, "US Not Certain of Avoiding Japan-Style 'Lost Decade,'" *Financial Times*, January 14, 2009.
87. Dumenil and Levy, *Crisis of Neoliberalism*, 104.
88. Ibid., 150, fig. 10.6.
89. John Bellamy Foster and Fred Magdoff, *The Great Financial Crisis: Causes and Consequences* (New York: Monthly Review Press, 2009), 29, table 1.1.

90. Dumenil and Levy, *Crisis of Neoliberalism,* 65–66.
91. Magdoff, "Jobs Disaster in the United States," 30–31.
92. Ibid., 31.
93. "Credit Card Statistics, Industry Facts, and Debt Statistics," http://www.creditcards.com/credit-card-news/credit-card-industry-facts-personal-debt-statistics-1276.php.
94. Dumenil and Levy, *Crisis of Neoliberalism,* 147, fig. 10.3.
95. Will Bonner and Addison Wiggin, *The New Empire of Debt: The Rise and Fall of an Epic Financial Bubble,* 2nd ed. (New York: Wiley, 2009), 203.
96. Susanne Soederberg, "Cannibalistic Capitalism: The Paradoxes of Neoliberal Pension Securitization," in *The Crisis This Time: Socialist Register 2011,* ed. Leo Panitch, Greg Albo, and Vivek Chibber (New York: Monthly Review Press, 2010), 229, table 1.
97. Andrew Leyshon and Nigel Thrift, "The Capitalization of Almost Everything: The Future of Finance and Capitalism," *Theory, Culture, and Society* 24.7–8 (2007): 106.
98. Anastasia Nesvetailova and Ronen Palan, "A Very North Atlantic Credit Crunch: Geopolitical Implications of the Global Liquidity Crisis," *Journal of International Affairs* 62.1 (2008): 168.
99. Quoted in Leonard Seabrooke, *U.S. Power in International Finance: The Victory of Dividends* (New York: Palgrave Macmillan, 2001), 150.
100. Gregory Elliehausen, quoted in Peter Gosselin, *High Wire: The Precarious Financial Lives of American Families* (New York: Basic Books, 2008), 183.
101. For an insightful refutation of the exclusion thesis in the context of race relations, see Denise Ferreira da Silva, *Toward a Global Idea of Race* (Minneapolis: University of Minnesota Press, 2007).
102. Fiona Allon, "Speculating on Everyday Life: The Cultural Economy of the Quotidian," *Journal of Communication Inquiry* 34.4 (2010): 368.
103. Andrea Fumagalli, "The Global Economic Crisis and Socioeconomic Governance," in *Crisis in the Global Economy: Financial Markets, Social Struggles, and New Political Scenarios,* ed. Andrea Fumagalli and Sandro Mezzadra (Los Angeles: Semiotext(e), 2010), 64.
104. Robert Wade, "The First-World Debt Crisis of 2007–2010 in Global Perspective," *Challenge* 51.4 (2008): 30.
105. For details, see Edward M. Gramlich, *Subprime Mortgages: America's Latest Boom and Bust* (Washington, D.C.: Urban Institute Press, 2007).
106. Wade, "First-World Debt Crisis," 31; emphasis added.
107. Louis Hyman, *Debtor Nation: The History of America in Red Ink* (Princeton, N.J.: Princeton University Press, 2011), 243.
108. Allon, "Speculating on Everyday Life," 377.
109. Leonard Seabrooke, "What Do I Get? The Everyday Politics of Expectations and the Subprime Crisis," *New Political Economy* 15.1 (2010): 56.
110. Christian Marazzi, "The Violence of Financial Capitalism," in Fumagalli and Mezzadra, *Crisis in the Global Economy,* 31.
111. Nesvetailova and Palan, "Very North Atlantic Credit Crunch," 166.
112. Dumenil and Levy, *Crisis of Neoliberalism,* 197–98; Greg Ip, "Did Greenspan Add to Subprime Woes?" *Wall Street Journal,* June 9, 2007.
113. Wade, "First-World Debt," 35.
114. Dumenil and Levy, *Crisis of Neoliberalism,* 185–87.
115. Simon Johnson and James Kwak, *13 Bankers: The Wall Street Takeover and the Next Financial Meltdown* (New York: Vintage Books, 2010), 123.
116. Leonard Seabrooke, *The Social Sources of Financial Power: Domestic Legitimacy and International Financial Orders* (Ithaca, N.Y.: Cornell University Press, 2006), 125–30.
117. Guy Stuart, *Discriminating Risk: The U.S. Mortgage Lending Industry in the Twentieth Century* (Ithaca, N.Y.: Cornell University Press, 2003), 110.
118. Johnson and Kwak, *13 Bankers,* 124–25.
119. Dawn Burton, *Credit and Consumer Society* (London: Routledge, 2008), 81, table 4.4.
120. Seabrooke, *Social Sources of Financial Power,* 126–27. By 2008 this had grown to US$5.3 trillion.
121. Richard Roll, "Benefits to Homeowners from Mortgage Portfolios Retained by Fannie Mae and Freddie Mac," *Journal of Financial Services Research* 23.1 (2003): 36.
122. Sharan Dietrich, "Work Reform: The Other Side of Welfare Reform," *Stanford Law and Policy Review* 9 (1998): 57.

123. Richard S. Belous, *The Contingent Economy: The Growth of Temporary, Part-Time, and Subcontracted Workforce* (Washington, D.C.: National Planning Association, 1998), 15; Stanley Nollen and Helen Axel, *Managing Contingent Workers: How to Reap the Benefits and Reduce the Risks* (New York: AMACOM, 1995), 9–10.

124. Kenneth L. Kart, "The Coming Crisis of Work in Constitutional Perspective," *Cornell Law Review* 82 (1997): 523.

125. Stephen F. Beford, "Labor and Employment Law at the Millennium: A Historical Review and Critical Assessment," *Boston College Law Review* 43 (2002): 368.

126. Scott Lash and John Urry, *Economics of Signs and Space* (New York: Sage, 1994).

127. Richard Sennett, *The Corrosion of Character: The Personal Consequences of Work in the New Capitalism* (New York: Norton, 1998).

128. Gosselin, *High Wire*, 142.

129. Carlo Vercellone, "The Crisis of the Law of Value and the Becoming-Rent of Profit," in Fumagalli and Mezzadra, *Crisis in the Global Economy*, 91.

130. Antonio Negri, "Interpretation of the Class Situation Today: Methodological Aspects," in *Theory and Practice*, vol. 2 of *Open Marxism*, ed. Werner Bonefeld et al. (New York: Pluto, 1992), 85.

131. Michael Hardt and Antonio Negri, *Commonwealth* (Cambridge, Mass.: Harvard University Press, 2011), 155.

132. Jeff Howe, *Crowdsourcing: Why the Power of the Crowd Is Driving the Future of Business* (New York: Crown Business, 2008).

133. Marazzi, "Violence of Financial Capitalism," 38–39.

134. Andrea Fumagalli, "The Global Economic Crisis and Socioeconomic Governance," in Fumagalli and Mezzadra, *Crisis in the Global Economy*, 81–82.

135. Yochai Benkler, *The Wealth of Networks: How Social Production Transforms Markets and Freedom* (New Haven, Conn.: Yale University Press, 2007); John Banks, "The Labor of User Co-Creators: Emergent Social Network Markets," *Convergence: The International Journal of Research into New Media Technologies* 14.4 (2008): 401; Manuel Castells, *The Rise of the Network Society: The Information Age: Economy, Society, and Culture*, 2nd ed. (New York: Wiley-Blackwell, 2010).

136. For an articulation of the hypothesis of cognitive capitalism, see Carlo Vercellone, "From Formal Subsumption to General Intellect: Elements for a Marxist Reading of the Thesis of Cognitive Capitalism," *Historical Materialism* 15 (2007): 13–36; Bernard Paulre, "Cognitive Capitalism and the Financialization of Economic Systems," in Fumagalli and Mezzadra, *Crisis in the Global Economy*, 171–96.

137. Marazzi, "Violence of Financial Capitalism," 41.

138. Federico Chicchi, "On the Threshold of Capital, at the Thresholds of the Commons: Sidenotes on the Ambivalences of Biopolitical Capitalism," in Fumagalli and Mezzadra, *Crisis in the Global Economy*, 144.

139. Andrew Ross, *No Collar: The Humane Workplace and Its Hidden Costs* (Philadelphia: Temple University Press, 2004).

140. Tim O'Reilly, "What Is Web 2.0 Design Patterns and Business Models for the Next Generation of Software," September 30, 2005, http://oreilly.com/web2/archive/what-is-web-20.html.

141. Alison Wolf, *Does Education Matter? Myths about Education and Economic Growth* (London: Penguin Global, 2003), 264.

142. John Bellamy Foster, "Education and the Structural Crisis of Capital," *Monthly Review* 63.3 (2011): 6–37; Pauline Lipman, *The New Political Economy of Urban Education* (New York: Routledge, 2011).

143. Tamar Lewin, "What's the Most Expensive College? The Least? Education Dept. Puts It All Online," *New York Times,* June 30, 2011.

144. Ibid.

145. Josh Mitchell and Maya Jackson-Randall, "Student-Loan Debt Tops $1 Trillion," *Wall Street Journal,* March 22, 2012; Tom Raum, "Student Loan Debt Threatening Economic Recovery," Huffington Post, April, 3, 2012.

146. Edward A Ross, *Social Psychology* (New York: Macmillan, 1917), 89.

147. A business manager, quoted in Charles H. Whitaker, *The Joke about Housing* (1920; rpt. College Park, Md.: McGrath Publishing, 1969), 9; emphasis added.

148. David Graeber, *Debt: The First 5,000 Years* (New York: Melville House, 2011), 40.

149. Geoffrey Ingham, *The Nature of Money* (Cambridge: Polity, 2004), 90.

150. Ferguson, *Ascent of Money*, 98–100.

151. Cheryl Payer, *Debt Trap: The International Monetary Fund and the Third World* (New York: Monthly Review Press, 1974).

152. Tayyab Mahmud, "Is It Greek or Déjà vu All Over Again: Neoliberalism and Winners and Losers of International Debt Crises," *Loyola University Chicago Law Journal* 42.4 (2011): 629–712.

153. Gordon Hanka, "Debt and the Terms of Employment," *Journal of Financial Economics* 48:3 (1998): 245–82.

154. Foucault, *Birth of Biopolitics*, 269.

155. Vercellone, "Crisis of the Law of Value," 107.

156. Jamie Peck, *Workfare States* (New York: Guilford, 2001), 23.

157. R. Kent Weaver, *Ending Welfare as We Know It* (Washington, D.C.: Brookings Institution Press, 2000).

158. "Consensus over Welfare," *Washington Post*, August 20, 1996.

159. Frances Fox Piven and Richard Cloward, *Regulating the Poor: The Functions of Public Welfare* (New York: Vintage, 1993), 396.

160. Douglas J. Besharov and Karen N. Gariner, "Paternalism and Welfare Reform," *Public Interest* 122 (1996): 84.

161. Peck, *Workfare States*, 6.

162. The bible of the human capital theme remains a book sponsored by the consulting firm Arthur Anderson: Brian Friedman, James Hatch, and David M. Walker, *Delivering on the Promise: How to Attract, Manage, and Retain Human Capital* (New York: Free Press, 1998).

163. Foucault, *Birth of Biopolitics*, 225.

164. Mitchell Dean, "Governing the Unemployed Self in an Active Society," *Economy and Society* 24.4 (1995): 559–83.

165. Chicchi, "On the Threshold of Capital," 149.

166. Liz McFall, "The Disinterested Self: The Idealized Subject of Life Insurance," *Cultural Studies* 21.4–5 (2007): 591–609.

167. Shaun French and James Kneale, "Excessive Financialization: Insuring Lifestyles, Enlivening Subjects and Everyday Spaces of Biosocial Excess," *Environment and Planning D: Society and Space* 27.6 (2009): 1030–53.

168. George Gilder, *Wealth and Poverty* (Ithaca, N.Y.: ICS Press, 1993), 110.

169. Peter A. Ubel, *Free Market Madness: Why Human Nature Is at Odds with Economics—and Why It Matters* (Cambridge, Mass.: Harvard Business School Press, 2009).

170. Pat O'Malley, *Risk, Uncertainty, and Government* (London: Routledge-Cavendish, 2004), 131.

171. Paul Langley, *The Everyday Life of Global Finance; Saving and Borrowing in Anglo-America* (Oxford: Oxford University Press, 2008), 47.

172. Martin, *Financialization of Daily Life*, 12.

173. Ibid., 17; Nicholas J. Kiersey, "Everyday Neoliberalism and the Subjectivity of Crisis: Post-Political Control in an Era of Financial Turmoil," *Journal of Critical Globalization Studies* 4 (2011): 23–44.

174. Martin, *Financialization of Daily Life*, 16–17; Alyssa Katz, *Our Lot: How Real Estate Came to Own Us* (New York: Bloombury, 2009).

175. Michel Foucault, "Technologies of the Self," in *Technologies of the Self: A Seminar with Michel Foucault*, ed. Luther H. Martin et al. (Amherst: University of Massachusetts Press, 1988), 17.

176. Paulre, "Cognitive Capitalism," 193.

177. Chicchi, "On the Threshold of Capital," 147.

178. Stefano Lucarelli, "Financialization as Biopower," in Fumagalli and Mezzadra, *Crisis in the Global Economy*, 125.

179. Randy Martin, *Financialization of Daily Life* (Philadelphia: Temple University Press, 2002); Shaun French and Andrew Leyshon, The New, New Financial System? Towards a Conceptualization of Financial Reintermediation," *Review of International Political Economy*, 11.2 (2004): 263–88.

180. Rob Aitkin, *Performing Capital: Towards a Cultural Economy of Popular and Global Finance* (New York: Palgrave Macmillan, 2007).

181. Paul Langley, "The Making of Investor Subjects in Anglo-American Pensions," *Environment and Planning D: Society and Spaces* 24.6 (2006): 919–34.

182. Dumenil and Levy, *Crisis of Neoliberalism*, 151.

183. Dawn Burton, *Credit and Consumer Society* (London: Routledge, 2007), 53.

184. Ibid., 53.

185. Stephen E. G. Lea et al., "The Economic Psychology of Consumer Debt," *Journal of Economic Psychology* 14.1 (1983): 85–119.
186. Massimo Amato and Luca Fantacci, *The End of Finance* (Cambridge: Polity, 2011), 227.
187. Pierre Bourdieu makes a parallel analogy by way of "the Left hand" of the state, which protects and expands life chances through Keynesian welfare, and is supplanted by the "Right hand," that of coercion (*Acts of Resistance: Against the Tyranny of the Market* [New York: New Press, 1998], 1–10).
188. Joel F. Handler, *The Poverty of Welfare Reform* (New Haven, Conn.: Yale University Press, 1995), 137.
189. David Garland, *Culture of Control: Crime and Social Order in Contemporary Society* (Chicago: University of Chicago Press, 2002).
190. Loïc Wacquant, "The Penalization of Poverty and the Rise of Neoliberalism," *European Journal of Criminal Policy and Research* 9 (2001): 401–12.
191. Loïc Wacquant, *Punishing the Poor: The Neoliberal Government of Social Insecurity* (Durham, N.C.: Duke University Press, 2009), 305.
192. Ibid., 7.
193. Lauren E. Glaze, "Correctional Population in the United States, 2010," *U. S. Department of Justice Bulletin of Justice Statistics* (2011), 3, table 1, http://bjs.ojp.usdoj.gov/content/pub/pdf/cpus10.pdf.
194. Michelle Alexander, *The New Jim Crow: Mass Incarceration in the Age of Colorblindness* (New York: New Press, 2010); Loïc Wacquant, *Deadly Symbiosis: Race and the Rise of the Penal State* (London: Polity, 2009); Michael Tonry, *Malign Neglect: Race, Class, and Punishment in America* (New York: Oxford University Press, 1995); David Cole, *No Equal Justice: Race and Class in the American Criminal Justice System* (New York: New Press, 2000); Becky Pettit and Bruce Western, "Mass Imprisonment and the Life Course: Race and Class Inequality in U.S. Incarceration," *American Sociological Review* 69 (2004): 151–69.
195. Wacquant, *Punishing the Poor*, 117, fig. 1.
196. Ibid., 115, table 6.
197. Ibid., 153.
198. Ibid., 160. For the inverse relationship between expenditures on public housing and corrections, see page 160, figure 4.
199. For growth of private imprisonment, see Wacquant, *Punishing the Poor*, 170, fig. 5; Alexis M. Durham, "Origins and Interest in the Privatization of Punishment: The Nineteenth and Twentieth Century American Experience," *Criminology* 27.1 (1989): 107–40; Charles Logan and Sharla Rausch, "Punish and Profit: the Emergence of Private Enterprise Prisons," *Justice Quarterly* 2 (1985): 303–18.
200. Wacquant, *Punishing the Poor*, 172.
201. International Monetary Fund, "Global Financial Stability Report: Navigating the Challenges Ahead," October 2009, http://www.imf.org/external/pubs/ft/gfsr/2009/02/pdf/text.pdf; United Nations, "World Economic Situation and Prospects," 2010, xii–xiii.
202. Nelson D. Schwartz, "Unemployment Surges around the World, Threatening Stability," *New York Times*, February 14, 2009; and James Kwame Sundaram and Felice Noelle Rodriguez, "Structural Causes and Consequences of the 2008–2009 Financial Crisis," in *Aftermath: A New Global Economic Order*, ed. Craig Calhoun and Georgi Derluguian (New York: New York University Press, 2011), 109.
203. Ferguson, *Ascent of Money*, 5–6, 63, 228.
204. Manuel Castells, "The Crisis of Global Capitalism: Towards a New Economic Culture?" in *Business as Usual: The Roots of the Global Financial Meltdown*, ed. Craig Calhoun and Georgi Derluguian (New York: New York University Press, 2011), 199.
205. Binyamin Appelbaum and Eric Dash, "S & P Downgrades Debt Rating of U.S. for the First Time," *New York Times*, August 6, 2011.

Gambling with Debt: Lessons from the Illiterate

Sarita Echavez See

You are mortgaging your whole future.
—Carlos Bulosan, "The Romance of Magno Rubio"

By asking us to consider the debt that we owe the subprime debtor rather than the other way around, Fred Moten has sounded an important call for interrogating dominant constructions of the subprime debtor, which draw on stereotypes of lower-middle-class and working-class people and especially of black women.[1] The refrain is all too familiar: the subprime debtor is a hapless, naive victim of smarter, educated folk. He is a contractual illiterate whose inability to read the instruments he signed led to the global economic meltdown of 2008. She is greedy and tries to cheat the system like her predecessor, the welfare queen dreamed up by the political Right during Reagan and Thatcher's era. She wants to get rich quick and buy her dream home without working long and hard at a decent job like decent folk do. The social-climbing subprime debtor gambled with debt on a micro-economic scale, and her behavior enabled macro-economic forms of gambling with debt, ending in collapse on a national and global scale. We see how these stereotypes start to go in circles, chase their own tails, and contradict themselves. Subprime debtors are, on the one hand, victims of their own pathos and ignorance and, on the other, willful, knowing, and amoral cheats. Yet these images and perceptions still enthrall.

Even, and perhaps especially, liberal and progressive commentators routinely if unintentionally make links between the financial devastation wreaked on the subprime debtor and his or her purported lack. For example, the authors of the otherwise excellent June 2010 study commissioned by the Center for Responsible Lending, "Foreclosures by Race and Ethnicity: The Demographics of a Crisis," emphasize the "vulnerability" of communities of color, yet that vulnerability rhetorically is connected to lack and lag: "As the foreclosure crisis threatens the financial stability and mobility of families across the country, it will be particularly devastating to African-American and Latino families, who

135

already lag their white counterparts in terms of income, wealth and educational attainment."[2] Moreover, such families tend to have "higher unemployment rates."[3] This is not to dismiss or deride the report. On the contrary, the report contains important insights and statistics about the demographics of the foreclosure crisis, for example, the fact that 82 percent of completed foreclosed loans between the years 2005 and 2008 involved owner-occupied, primary residencies and not investment properties. The report also calls attention to especially hard-hit places like Prince George's County, Maryland, one of the country's largest African American–majority counties.[4] My point is that, despite the best of intentions, there is an insidious tendency to turn the blame back onto the victims of the foreclosure crisis, a rhetoric and ideology of "personal responsibility" that usually is moored to tenets of white supremacy that manifest themselves as meritocratic, self-disciplined individualism. Let me turn to a more explicit example. Among the online comments responding to a 2007 article titled "Minorities Hit Hardest by Housing Crisis" and published by the online progressive gazette *Common Dreams*, one reader expresses his or her irritation with the author's focus on "minorities" and asks, exasperatedly: "Okay, I agree that 'these people' are being targeted, and that's wrong, but for heaven's sake, what happened to personal responsibility? . . . If something seems 'too good to be true,' it generally is. What is needed is more education. I was raised to avoid debt, and to pay it off as rapidly as I can. That has served me well. . . . Todays [*sic*] debtors will be tomorrow's indentured servants. Minorities should be taught this."[5] However, as we are continuing to learn from the ongoing investigation of the foreclosure crisis, the need for "more education" seems to have been even direr. According to lawyers defending home owners in foreclosure cases, bank employees who processed the mortgages seem to have been barely literate themselves, the so-called "robo-signers" who "couldn't define the word 'affidavit.'"[6]

This essay responds to this call for "more education." But it tries to do so by reversing the direction of learning and edification. Let us for once consider the lessons that the illiterate offer to the literate rather than the other way around. In the readings that follow of Carlos Bulosan's fiction from the era of the (other) Great Depression and its contemporary adaptation for the stage, I argue that what today's subprime debtor achieved is a literalization of the logic of debt that structures capital. The contractually illiterate spelled out for all of us what was and is so clearly a systemic hoax. It is a hoax that implicates all of us, the educated and the uneducated, but that also binds us in ways that potentially spell other forms of belonging to and with one another—alternative, *other* forms of debt. This essay in turn calls for renewed attention to the prescience of Bulosan's short story "The Romance of Magno Rubio," published in the 1940s, and for attentiveness to the staged adaptations that have been circulating in Filipino America for years preceding and now succeeding the 2008 fiscal crisis. By focusing on the naïveté and illiteracy of Bulosan's title character Magno Rubio, I argue that the U.S. Filipino diaspora returns to and transforms modes of storytelling that return to and transform anticapitalist traditions of reciprocity, mutuality, and obligation. In this way, we might be able to glimpse what an alternative ethical economy of anti-accumulation might look like. In other words, if we take seriously rather than sneer at the ways in which Magno gambles with, throws away, and "mortgag[es] [his] whole future," we might be able to glimpse other reasons and worldviews underpinning the decision to sign those bad contracts.

At first glance it makes no sense at all to sign those subprime mortgage loans. So in some ways it is understandable that the turn to commonsensical explanations of the subprime debtor's psyche invoke her desire to take a short cut to home ownership and the realization of the American Dream. Indeed, the (white settler) American Dream can be said to be symbolized and embodied by the dream home. So the subprime debtor's attempts to enter or at least get nearer to the "general neighborhood of home ownership, wherein the normative conception, embodiment and enactment of wealth, personhood and citizenship reside," are interpreted as manifestations of aspirational assimilationist desire, an embarrassing investment in the whiteness of belonging.[7]

Yet perhaps what was and is desired is not so much the American Dream and its concomitant dream home but rather shelter, pure and simple. Rather than an assimilationist "investment" in the American Dream, how might the actions of Magno Rubio and the subprime debtor be explained by reverting to *other* values and economies that are impelled by a belief in "our common capacity to live beyond our means" rather than the logic of capitalist accumulation that underwrites assimilationist desire?[8] For people who historically have had no chance in generations at getting anywhere near the "general neighborhood of home ownership," perhaps the decision to sign those contracts was a worthy risk. Perhaps it was a form of squatting. Perhaps it was a worthy gambit so as to provide shelter for, typically, multiple generations under one roof according to the laws of reciprocity and other forms of debt, like *loob* (debt) and *kapwa* (the self in the other) in the indigenous Filipino worldview.[9] In other words, it is only through the terms of a different system of valuation that it becomes clear that *foreclosure is another form of enclosure.*

Gambling with Words

But first let us learn about the stakes of gambling with words. "The Romance of Magno Rubio" and its adaptation for the stage have proved immensely popular among a variety of theater audiences in Filipino North America. How do we reckon with this story of fieldworkers throwing their money away on gambling, pornography, dance halls, prostitution, and drink, thus invoking all the stock stereotypes of Filipino men and working-class and underclass masculinity in general? How do we account for the contradictions of its homosocial economy of outrageous exploitation and extravagant generosity? What do we make of its doubled portrayal of aspirational assimilationism and anti-accumulative reciprocity?

"The Romance of Magno Rubio" and its theatrical adaptation are set in the fields of Depression-era California and during the U.S. colonial period (1899–1942). It is a story of the lives, desires, and exploited labor of Filipino American men who occupied the legal limbo of noncitizen, nonalien, or "national," one of the official terms for the status of Filipinos at the time. We see the Filipino reduced to nothing but labor, the laboring body. Yet Magno Rubio is desperately in love with a white woman, Clarabelle, whom he has never met. He is illiterate, yet his romance blossoms through written correspondence, letters penned by a coworker who at first charges him "five dollars per letter" and then up to "twenty dollars per letter" while they each earn only "two dollars fifty cents a day" as seasonal laborers. A literary form of prostitution, if you will. Magno shells out dollar after dollar and takes out loan after loan from his foreman to pay his coworkers to write letters for him and, eventually, to buy and send increasingly extravagant presents to Clarabelle. A big rube indeed, Magno counts how many heads of lettuce or tomatoes will buy him the words "I love you." Language is literally composed of the fruits and vegetables whose harvest—the repeated act of picking—facilitates the alienation of Magno and his comrades from their own labor. This is an alienation preceded by earlier dispossessions from the Philippine land and augmented by the vicious segmentation of the workers (by the workers themselves) into a racialized, classed pecking order of who is illiterate and who is not, who is an "Igorot" and who is not, who is a "peasant" and who is not. In other words, Magno insists on a literal reading of the act of picking peas as that which will allow him to buy the letter "p"; and that illiterate reading allows us, Bulosan's supposedly literate readers, to begin to grasp the processes and repercussion of what we have been trained not to read: the creation and exploitation of living labor.

It generally is assumed that the immigrant achieves assimilation and the American Dream by accumulating material goods and cultural capital. So the title character of Bulosan's story has been read—and dismissed—as a dupe, a stupid naïf and an illiterate peasant who gets taken in by his foolish desire for the white woman, who allegorically stands in for America. But I would like to analyze the story against the grain of that reading. I am interested in the naive and the illiterate. I am interested in people who make the worst, most glaring, and embarrassing calculations and decisions because, as it turns out, Magno Rubio is an unexpected source of literacy for American studies and Filipino American studies today. It is precisely his naïveté and literalism that allow Bulosan to traverse multiple modes of capitalist abstraction and that ironically offer knowledge about the brutality of what it means to pursue the romance of money and love in the United States. Magno allows us to see what is glaringly obvious. For when it comes to both the wages of romance and the romance of wages, we do not see what is right before our eyes.

Foreign in a Domestic Sense

There are of course several aspects to the problem of recognition and non-recognition when it comes to the intersection between the commodification of racialized, gendered living labor and the noncitizen nonalien. But I would like to highlight the dimensions of the problem of nonrecognition or invisibility that I find most relevant for Filipino Americans especially in relation to the broader narratives and paradigms current in Asian American studies and American studies. The problem of Asian American invisibility generally has been defined in terms of exclusion from the body politic. The narration of Asian American history has been subtended by the logic of exclusion, a civil rights framework underpinned and motivated by the desire to be included. Thus the solution in Asian American studies to the problem of exclusion has been that of inclusion. Ironically, this involves following rather than undercutting the logic of the imperial, racial state, which depends on the linear and developmental narration of American history as inevitably progressing toward that perfect future nation even as that future horizon is ever receding and even as the frontiers of America's manifest destiny continue to expand. The "perniciousness" of the "myth of America," as David Palumbo-Liu argues, "lies in the fact that it is more than the externally identified 'myth' so easily debunked by social reality." He continues: "It is rather the more deep-seated myth of America's ultimate justness *despite every social fact*."[10] The logic of such a myth moreover is entwined with the desire to become the subject of "transparency," in Denise da Silva's phrasing, and to emerge as a full individual bestowed with all the powers of thought, history, and civilization that the subjects of "affectability" innately lack.[11] To put it crudely: the problematic of assimilation in Asian American studies critique has been too quickly and abstractly tied to the desire for home and for belonging to the nation when the object of that desire also could be that of shelter.

Moreover, as several scholars have pointed out, the problem for Filipino Americans has been that of "forced inclusion" and not exclusion.[12] The Philippines and other new "territories" were deemed "foreign to the United States in a domestic sense," the phrase that the U.S. Supreme Court coined at the turn of the last century to describe the predicament that the new colonies posed for the American constitutional republic. Thus the Filipino "national" is a perfect example of that experience of being inside and outside, indeed of being externalized in order to be internalized. That is to say, Filipinos are the external other to the internal contradictions of the imperial, racial state. Yet few scholars in Asian American studies and American studies have commented on the similarity between this special positioning of Filipinos and the dynamics of capitalism, even though Bulosan's writings have called for such an analysis for well over half a century. Historically, legally, rhetorically, and materially, the problem that Filipinos pose for America has revolved around the innate and *endless* violence of the conversion of land and people into objects, the capitalist colonial logic of power. Why endless?

"Your greatest want is, you want much," says the title character of Shakespeare's *Timon of Athens* to the bandits who intend to rob him.[13] Following David Harvey's work, we understand that overaccumulation is the problem that capitalism inexorably generates for itself. Harvey thus is revising Karl Marx's concept of primitive accumulation, which is configured as an originary and specific moment in the history of capital. But Harvey comes up with the phrase "accumulation by dispossession" vis-à-vis Hannah Arendt and Rosa Luxemburg to suggest the ongoing nature of accumulation. It is the "endless accumulation" driving capitalism that requires the "endless accumulation of political power," the ability to continuously open up (noncapitalist) territories to capitalist development.[14] Luxemburg baldly and powerfully phrases it thus: "Expansion becomes a condition for existence."[15] Harvey also draws on Luxemburg's work for the key insight that capitalism has to have something "outside of itself" to stabilize it. According to Luxemburg, it has an "inner dialectic . . . forcing it to seek solutions external to itself."[16] Indeed, capitalism "needs other races."[17] In the United States the Filipino exactly fulfills that role, the role of the outside constantly being incorporated—foreign in a domestic sense. There is, moreover, an additional violence innate to this process that has to do with the continual *occlusion* of that process of permanently unincorporating people and lands. As Oscar Campomanes has noted, the forgetting of the Filipino is integral to the imperial constitution of the United States as a free and democratic republic.[18]

Staging the Wages of Romance

The recent resurgence of interest in Bulosan's short story in Filipino America thus constitutes an undoing of the unincorporation of the Filipino. Ma-Yi Theatre Company is a not-for-profit, pan-Asian American Theatre Company based in New York City, and about ten years ago it commissioned the playwright Lonnie Carter to adapt "The Romance of Magno Rubio" for the stage. Along with Carter, the director Loy Arcenas, the lyricist Ralph Peña, and the original New York City cast won eight OBIE awards in 2003. (The OBIE is the Off-Broadway theater award awarded annually by the *Village Voice* newspaper to theater artists and groups in New York City.) The play has been staged in New York City (Ma-Yi Theatre, 2002), Laguna Beach, California (Laguna Playhouse, 2003), Manila and other cities in the Philippines (May-Yi and Tanghalang Pilipino, 2003–2004), Chicago (Victory Gardens, 2004), Toronto (Carlos Bulosan Theater, 2005), Honolulu (Kumu Kahua Theatre, 2008), Stockton, California (Bob Hope Theatre, 2008), and most recently in Los Angeles (Ford Theatre, 2011).

The original New York City cast and crew staged it in Stockton in 2008 in the Central Valley, informally dubbed the foreclosure capital of the nation.[19] The Stockton production was a fund-raiser for the Little Manila Foundation, which is devoted to the historic preservation of Filipino American sites in Stockton, where Bulosan lived on and off. Much of the buzz leading up to the Stockton production focused on how historically momentous it was for Bulosan's story to come "home" to Stockton, which from the 1920s to the 1950s was the largest Filipino American community in the United States because it was near menial agricultural jobs. According to the historian Dawn Mabolon, whose tour of the Little Manila area I joined in October 2008, Stockton was for Filipinos the place to be—to find jobs, to reunite with friends, to gamble, to eat some Chinese or Filipino food, to join a fraternal society, to go to church, or to find out about the unions.[20]

Trapped among the Central Valley's dusty fields, Bulosan's Magno Rubio is desperately in love with his pen pal Clarabelle, whom he discovers through an advertisement in a Lonely Hearts magazine. She lives in distant Arkansas, and he learns from her letters that she is "twice [his] size sideward and upward."[21] He corresponds with the giant blonde but he has never met her. He hires a coworker, Claro, to write letters for him. And so of course the similarity between the names "Claro" and "Clarabelle" signal to the reader the story's allegorical nature as well as the potential connection between the two: if Clarabelle might be considered a forerunner of today's telephone or cyber sex workers, might we think of Claro as Clarabelle's john? At the same time, Magno's name has at least two possible meanings or translations: He is a great rube as well as a big ("magno") blond ("rubio"). Who is the john and who is the prostitute? Given the charges of plagiarism and other forms of literary criminality that plagued Bulosan during his lifetime and that mar his reputation today, how might Bulosan be providing us with what Kimberly Alidio calls an "avenue towards overturning the moralism" of the terms "prostitute" and "plagiarist," an avenue that opens up through a nexus of "overlapping underground economies [and] 'black markets'"?[22]

Claro at first writes in exchange for bottles of wine from Magno. But he quickly leaves the barter system and begins to charge Magno money, at first five dollars per letter and then eventually up to twenty dollars per letter, based on a fee of ten cents per word, while they each earn only $2.50 a day as fieldworkers. (They make twenty-five cents per hour picking tomatoes, for example.) As readers of Bulosan's short story and as audience members watching Carter's adaptation, we are bewildered yet entranced by Rubio's willingness to pay to be exploited. The title character is seemingly knowingly exploited. He has a knowing kind of naïveté as he shells out dollar after dollar for the words and the gifts to persuade and romance the six-foot-tall Clarabelle, the "Arkansas Arkanssassin."[23] This is presented—in Carter's play and in Bulosan's story—in realist ways. Yet the workings of allegory are always present. We understand that Clarabelle stands in for the "United Snakes of America."[24] We see how the lives of these men are allegories for the relations between colonizer and colonized, for exploited labor, and for racist antimiscegenation laws. So what are some ways to interpret Bulosan's allegory of naive literal-minded illiteracy?

The dramaturge-critic Joi Barrios-Leblanc brilliantly contextualizes the adaptation of Bulosan's story by reading it within Filipino traditions of political satire such as the "sainete" (short comic play) and the "drama simboliko."[25] Such readings do depend on figuring Rubio as a dupe, however. Barrios-Leblanc implies that Rubio is a model minority figure and that the story and play pedagogically and politically tell a story of assimilation and of "interrupted" cosmopolitanism.[26] In her own translation of the play into Filipino—for the

Ma-Yi tour of the Philippines—Barrios Leblanc dealt with what she perceived as assimilationist elements of the play by including references to the neocolonial conditions of today, including the National Democratic movement in the Philippines.

The Wages of Colonial Romance

But I would like to argue otherwise and to propose an interpretation of Magno Rubio's naïveté, illiteracy, and literalness that is an alternative to the assimilationist reading. The play is assimilationist only if one conducts a literal-minded reading of Magno's literalness. Read otherwise or nonliterally, we see how the story is structured brilliantly around a combination of the abstract and the literal. Ridiculing Magno's conception of love, one of his compatriots declares in Bulosan's story: "Words, words, words! They don't mean a thing."[27] But when it comes to the colonial subject's idealization of money, whiteness, and imperial romance, it is clear that Bulosan is showing us that words do, after all, "mean a thing." Bulosan portrays the conversion—the abstraction—of produce into labor into wages into money, gifts, and words for the white woman. However, while Marxian analysis calls our attention to the abstraction of the conversion of social meaning and processes into things, Bulosan performs one more turn of the screw. Magno literally is counting how much asparagus or how many tomatoes will buy him the words "I love you." Bulosan can be said to be responding to Marx's call for attention to the abstraction of the representative form of money and wages by creating an illiterate character like Magno who insists on treating *the* form of representation—language—totally literally. Rubio picks peas in order to buy the letter "p," thus recalling and transforming Marx's marvelous formulation: "All commodities are perishable money; money is the imperishable commodity."[28]

Bulosan's story has embedded in it a complex repetition, circulation, and rhythm of racialized work and words. Carter's staged adaptation draws on Bulosan's repetition of a passage that produces a deliberately vicious caricature of Magno even as it contains hints of lyric verse: "Magno Rubio. Filipino boy. Four-foot six inches tall. Dark as a coconut. Head small on a body like a turtle. Magno Rubio. Picking peas on a California hillside for twenty-five cents an hour. Filipino body. In love with a girl he had never seen. A girl twice his size sideward and upward, Claro said."[29] Versions of this passage appear five times in a short story that is only sixteen pages long, and it is passages like this that inspires Carter to write most of the play in lyric verse. Indeed, the staging of the play is highly percussive and tightly choreographed, utterly dependent for its success on the fluidity and synchronicity of the ensemble cast who cannot afford to miss a line or a beat.

If we follow this rhythm of racist insult, sexual desire, and exploited labor, we begin to grasp Bulosan's investment in the forms that he uses to depict various acts of putative exchange, an economy that the Filipino enters in order to be converted into money. In other words, we start to understand the relation between the form and content of the wages of colonial romance.

In *Marx beyond Marx: Lessons on the Grundrisse*, Antonio Negri usefully describes the relation of form to content when it comes to money:

> Marx notes, if money is an equivalent, if it has the nature of an equivalent, it is above all *the equivalence of a social inequality.* . . . Money hides a content which is eminently a content of inequality, a content of exploitation. *The relation of exploitation is the content of the monetary equivalent:* better, this content could not be exhibited.[30]

What I am suggesting is that there are common characteristics between, on the one hand, how money "hides the content" of exploitation and, on the other, how Filipino American labor disappears, how what Campomanes calls the "invisibilization" of colonized Filipino subjects is achieved.[31] Thus Carter's achievement is that of translating for the stage Bulosan's remarkable condensation of labor, desire, and language, interlocked as they are by the operations of abstraction.

At the same time what is at stake in "The Romance of Magno Rubio" is the clash between two perspectives on gambling. There are a number of scenes in which the men drink and gamble, in search of pleasure and relief from boredom and loneliness. These scenes of gambling of course signal racial as well as socioeconomic type, particularly Filipino men's innate moral turpitude and their inexorable path to financial debt and ruin. Of course this is a not unfamiliar stereotype for other men of color and white working-class men. Generally, gambling signals the opposite of heteronormative behavior, that of the virtuous family man who devotes himself to accumulation rather than to squandering and who devotes himself to saving and assimilation rather than expenditure, extravagance, and various forms of waste and transgression.

"The Romance of Magno Rubio" turns the tables on gambling. In this portrayal of exploitation and the men's refusal to accumulate, capitalism is revealed as a form—*the* form—of gambling with debt. Ferdinand Braudel defines Western capitalism as "a collection of rules, possibilities, calculations, the art both of getting rich and of living," and he notes that these include "gambling and risk." He continues: "The key words of commercial language, *fortuna, ventura, ragione, prudenza, sicurta*, define risks to be guarded against."[32] As Anthony Trollope portrays so powerfully in the novel *The Way We Live Now* and of course as we know from the 2008 collapse of the market, capitalism is an elaborate form of gambling with debt. But Bulosan also depicts instances of extravagant generosity among the men, underground economies and unfathomable acts of giving it all away under some of the worst working conditions, which I understand as the manifestation of *other* modes of debt and obligation.

In contrast with capitalist forms of gambling with debt, the five workers in "The Romance of Magno Rubio" follow protocols of kinship that draw on other kinds of "debt," captured by the Filipino words *loob* and *kapwa*. If, as Marx has it, money is a "social bond, a social *thing* connecting unsocial individuals," Bulosan's characters embody and perform a sociality that operates according to a wholly other system of obligation.[33] The everyday phrase *utang na loob* literally means "inner debt," and it refers to a range of interiorized feelings of social obligation. *Kapwa*, often defined or translated as a "shared inner self," can be understood as a worldview based on profoundly collective forms of mutual recognition. According to *sikolohiyang Pilipino* scholars like Virgilio Enriquez who forward the study of "indigenous Filipino psychology," in the colonial context *kapwa* can be interpreted as a kind of friendliness, hospitality, and even naïveté to be exploited and integrated in a master-slave relationship especially in combination with feelings of *utang na loob*.[34] Instead, *sikolohiyang Pilipino* scholars remind us of a definition of *kapwa* as an invitation and introduction to an economy of values based on reciprocity. But what Bulosan incisively points out is that there is no simple side-stepping, opposing, or exiting the forces of capitalism. Rather, the rhythm of both Bulosan's story and Carter's play teaches us that one must gamble away everything to begin to access and enter the *other*—rather than the oppositional—economy of debt. In other words, Bulosan's characters throw it all away in an *exemplary* way.

And there is something especially resonant about the performative dimensions of Carter's dramatic translation of Bulosan's gambling with words. Let us turn to the rhythm and economy of language in Carter's staged adaption. Below are examples of the different characters' speech and my attempts at rhythm analysis, which I hope illustrate Carter's metrical and lyric complexity and range.

Here is what Magno Rubio sounds like when he describes the rhythm of his and his compatriots' work in the fields:

> For every pod of pea I pick
>   one mill is what I earn
> For every little mill I get
>   one word is what I buy
> For twenty ears of corn I shuck
>   one cent is what I put away
> For fifty heads of lettuce plucked
>   two cents will buy—"With love I burn!"
> For every bunch of cherries snapped
>   "I miss you"'s what I sigh
> One hundred stalks of 'sparagus
>   for "Love you love you love you, love"
>   I work the livelong day[35]

Carter establishes a direct ratio between piecemeal labor and the number of words that Magno can purchase for his correspondence with Clarabelle. Thus the playwright brings to life Bulosan's insistence on *literalizing* the metaphorical nature of wages and the money form. The Chorus then responds to Magno:

> Words words words, now here's the matter
>   monkey boy in heat
> Words words words, more veg – e – tables,
>   Rubio, more fruit
> Fruit fruit fruit, the bigger harvest
>   sooner you two meet . . .
> Work words work, she loves your chatter
>   monkey boy in heat
> Words work words, she needs you at her,
>   wants you to repeat[36]

Here the Chorus uses a regular four-stress pattern that at times breaks into rhyming couplets, so generally the effect is comic and parodic.

The cook, Prudencio, is an older, gentler character who moves a little more slowly on Carter's stage. While most of the play's language is quite bawdy and riotous, Prudencio uses blank verse (nonrhymed verse) when he tries to console Magno and when he talks about missing his own wife:

> Why are you weeping, little one?
> How long have you been at this?
> This life which makes us all old without cease
> What is it when we have no work?
> What is it even when we do?
> Weep for that that keeps us here

Playing games of cards, so ripped and bent,
    my back so stripped and bent
    with four or five *manongs* like me
And always one off to the side
    with his solitaire
Or strumming battered guitars with broken strings
The wattles of my rooster neck shaking with anger
    like a dog with an old shoe in his stinking mouth
Why are you weeping, little one?
Why is your face broken?
How long have you been at this
This life that makes us old without release
What is it when we have no work
What is it even when we do
Weep for coming here across the waters
When we had hope that this land
Would open its arms
And yes it has—open—now shut around us
    "parang sawa" [like a large snake]
The United Snakes of America
Little one, go ahead and weep[37]

Prudencio's speeches are elegaic, and they powerfully convey his and his co-workers' loneliness.

In contrast, the character Clarabelle uses verse that is metrically irregular, so the effect is comic. During the one and only encounter between her and Magno, Clarabelle addresses Nick, who acts as their interpreter. Carter wonderfully mixes the "tiempo" of her pulse with the temperature of her passion when she meets Magno and is baffled by his inability to speak English:

Doesn't he speak, ah what? Inglese?
He's been writing me all these letters. You should see them, Nickie boy.
The things he says—mooey delicioso!
Are you sure you don't, how you say—Tenga la bonedad un poco tiempo
Take my tiempo, feel my tiempo, racing mucho
    uno mas uno uno mas[38]

Notably, Clarabelle is played by one of the (male) actors in gestural and aural drag. He uses highly exaggerated falsetto while he faces the audience and speakes into an old-fashioned microphone that recalls 1950s radio. In a scene that powerfully melds the promise of miscegenated sex with the technology for transcontinental remittance, Clarabelle begs Magno to "please, please, Western Union me":

Tomorrow tomorrow
          tomorrow please Western Union me
My daddy most of all is pleased
          and anxious for us two
To be so joined in Holy Mat-
          rimony, that's the glue
That sticks me to you you to me
          until death do us part
In meantime Daddy has such bills
          they mangled up his heart
Tomorrow tomorrow
          tomorrow please Western Union me
Back to your sweet proposal, dear,
          I have it with me now
My heart is with you now and then
          I'm there ASAP
I think of you much every day
          you say you to me bow
So, darling, handsome Magno love
          express your dough to me
Tomorrow tomorrow
          tomorrow you Western Union me[39]

Clarabelle's plaintive plea to "please, please, Western Union me" contains a crucial pun: her seduction of Magno involves the promise of miscegenated union with the Western woman in exchange for cash remittance through the transcontinental telegraph system.

But the play's erotic economy becomes even more interesting if we queer the triangulated relationship between Magno, Clarabelle, and Claro. As I noted above, Magno's name translates to "Big Blond," which connects him to Clarabelle, whose name of course is the feminine version of Claro. So who is the blond(e)? Who is the source of clarity and light? Who is the giver and who is the receiver of sexual excitement and pleasure? Who is pimping whom?

Generally speaking, Clara is configured as the prostitute and Magno as the client, because he is paying her for her service of affording him sexual pleasure. But if we pay attention to the play's erotic economy, an alternative interpretation emerges. Because the medium is that of text, the genre is that of the epistle, and participation in this relationship requires literacy, Magno is paying Claro and then Nick to write the letters. In an early scene in Carter's play, Magno asks Nick to translate and set down in a letter his words to Clarabelle. But words fail Magno. All he manages to utter is "ikaw" ("You") three times before falling silent. At that point, another one of his coworkers produces a guitar out of thin air, and the entire ensemble breaks into a serenade with each line beginning with *ikaw*. So Nick, together with the Chorus, becomes the author-prostitute that provides words of courtship and seduction that send Magno—and not, ironically, Clarabelle—into thrills of ecstasy. Twirling a chair and then dancing by himself with his arms embracing empty air, Magno is caught up in a reverie about the Big Blonde, and he nearly swoons by the end of the serenade.

Finally, Nick, nicknamed "college boy" by his coworkers, recites sonnets that indicate his higher level of education and his mastery of a "classic" and classy form. For example, puzzled by Magno's boundless naïveté, Nick delivers the following speech, which takes the form of a classic, Shakespearean sonnet:

> What quality of soul sustains a man
> To have such faith in someone he's not seen
> What possibly can he be thinking? Can
> He hold such hope when all about him mean
> To tell and do tell him he's lost his mind?
> When he, beyond all reason and belief
> Who should have given up, as others find
> No solace in anything, no relief
> Except who touches them and whom they touch;
> Is this untouchable, this wretched ram
> Whose only good would seem to be so much
> Of picking, stacking, carting—Jesus damn!
>
> Or does he, Magno Rube, know more than we
> And should we turn ourselves so loose—and free[40]

Because of this speech, scholars like Barrios-Leblanc have critiqued the play for its valorization of model minority assimilation. Yet according to the ending of both the story and the play, Magno never assimilates. He shows no interest—and, I would argue, neither the story nor the play shows interest—in the individuated process of accumulation that underwrites assimilation. At the end of both story and play, Clarabelle betrays Magno and goes off with another man. While Nick is devastated, Magno merely shrugs and says that they should go back to their cabin and eat before the rest of the crew finishes the food. He seems to have no interest in possession, and Bulosan seems to have no interest in satisfactory or neat narratological resolution.

It is tempting to think of the story and play as a tragic depiction of Magno's naïveté and literalism and his inability to recognize how he is getting had. Magno will not learn from Nick. Rather, it would seem that Nick the "college boy" can learn from Magno about the freedom of oblivion. But I want to resist the easy interpretation of Bulosan's story as simply a refrain about the bliss of ignorance. While Nick does learn a lesson from Magno, it is another kind of lesson altogether. To my mind, the play implies that it is from Magno that Nick learns to simply give away money with no profit or accumulation in sight. To not save money. To fritter. To squander. To dissipate. To do so means to refuse mobility and all that comes with it, for example, the heteronormative, nuclear family. To refuse the path of aspirational accumulation. In a crucial scene, Nick in fact gives his roll of money to Claro, who has shown no sign that he will do anything other than throw it all away. Claro is, after all, off to find El Dorado, the fabulous country of gold. In this way, we are reminded of the false promises of education, which is supposed to be about literacy but instead is an institution devoted to aspirational accumulation.

Magno throws away his wages on his correspondence with Clarabelle, an epistolary form of prostitution. Indeed, the repeated appearance of the prostitute in Bulosan's writings indexes the trace of appositional economies of reciprocity and mutuality in the name of the art and act of survival. These appositional economies have persisted in living on ironically—or perhaps necessarily—in the form of transactions and activities deemed immoral or criminal, such as prostitution, gambling, and drinking. For the lesson here for Nick and for the readership-audience is about the false promises of education, assimilation, and accumulation. Carter's play has been called "drunk with language," and, from what we know of Bulosan's own life, he did drink a lot. That is how he got his writing done. In the staging of transgressive forms of excess like intoxication, gambling, and prostitution, Bulosan and Carter have produced a brilliant indictment of the workings of capitalism, the relation between the form and content of exploitation. If we can but listen more closely and hear better, we would perhaps heed their call for, following Negri, the "destruction of exploitation and the emancipation of living labor. *Of non-labor.*"[41]

To reiterate: It is the naïveté and literalism of the central character that allow Bulosan to traverse multiple modes of capitalist abstraction and that ironically offer knowledge about the brutality of what it means to pursue the romance of money and love in America. Bulosan both literally and abstractly spells out the violence and contradictions of being foreign in a domestic sense. The achievement of "The Romance of Magno Rubio" lies in its productive failure to produce heroes or hagiography and, instead, to focus on the worst stereotypes of Filipino American men. Gamblers. Sex-obsessed wastrels. Illiterates. Drunkards. Yet who really are the wastrels and the thieves?

Bulosan tells a history for the present. In bringing *The Romance of Magno Rubio* to Stockton, the community organization Little Manila Foundation reminds us in all too timely ways of the devastating consequences of the theft of labor and also of alternatives to that regime of accumulation. If we read Bulosan alongside Moten's insights into the debt that we owe the subprime debtor, we can appreciate that the values of Magno Rubio are not yet dead. The subprime debtor usually is configured as the object of either condemnation or condescension. These debtors are not literal illiterates. They are contractual illiterates. How could they have signed those deeds? Either they were trying to take a shortcut to accumulation and failing or they were too stupid and naive to understand the contract.

But what if there is another way to read the scenario of signing the subprime mortgage? What the subprime debtor achieved is a literalization of the logic of debt that structures capital. The contractually illiterate spelled out for all of us what is so clearly a systemic hoax, even as they signed those contracts to provide shelter for multiple generations under one roof according to the laws of *loob* and *kapwa*, according to the presumption of abundance rather than lack, and according to the principles and logics of generosity rather than accumulation. It is the illiterates who insist on finding better ways to cohabit and live with one another, unown-ing rather than disowning one another in a world devoted to a radically different kind of dispossession.

Only with the kind of clarity provided by the so-called illiterate can I myself begin to fathom my aunt's unforgivable decision to buy a house she could not afford on her son's—my cousin's—credit at the peak of the mortgage frenzy. Only then can I begin to pay tribute to her and the shelter and child care that she provided and continues to provide to the grandchildren in the family. Only then can I begin to understand what I owe her, rather than what she owes the bank or the family, when she had to foreclose on the house over a year and a half ago. This is the lesson that my aunt and the other subprime debtors spelled out for all of us, and with that lesson I can begin to forgive the debt that I owe to my aunt.

Clarity. Claro. Clarabelle.

Notes

For their feedback on earlier versions of this essay I am thankful to Denise Ferreira da Silva and Paula Chakravartty for their editorial acuity, patience, and generosity; Kimberly Alidio, Rick Berg, Joseph Keith, Monica Kim, David Lloyd, Venky Nagar, Hiram Pérez, and an anonymous reader; and most especially Fred Moten.

1. Fred Moten, "The Subprime and the Beautiful," unpublished manuscript, 8. Moten also notes: "In the United States, whoever says 'subprime debtor' says black as well" (6). See also Fred Moten and Stefano Harney, "Debt and Study," *e-flux* 14 (2010), http://www.e-flux.com/journal/debt-and-study/.

2. Debbie Gruenstein Bocian, Wei Li, and Keith S. Ernst, "Foreclosures by Race and Ethnicity: The Demographics of a Crisis," Center for Responsible Lending, June 18, 2010, 3, http://www.responsiblelending.org/.

3. Ibid., 6.

4. Ibid., 8, 12.

5. Comment posted by reader-user "Jan Steinman," November 26, 2007, in response to Dana Ford's "Minorities Hit Hardest by Housing Crisis," *Reuters*, November 26, 2007, republished by *Common Dreams*, http://www.commondreams.org/archive/2007/11/26/5441.

6. See, for example, Michelle Conlin, "Banks' Foreclosure 'Robo-Signers' Were Hair Stylists, Teens, Walmart Workers: Lawsuit," *Associated Press*, October 13, 2010, updated December 13, 2010, re-published by Huffington Post, http://www.huffingtonpost.com/2010/10/13/meet-banks-robosigners-fo_n_761698.html.

7. Moten, "Subprime and the Beautiful," 13.

8. Ibid., 7–8.

9. Generally speaking, according to *sikolohiyang Pilipino*, or indigenous psychology scholars, *loob* refers to a range of interiorized feelings of social obligation. As I explain later in the essay, the concept of *kapwa*, the "self in the other," can be understood as a kind of friendliness or hospitality that, in the colonial context, is interpreted and exploited as naïveté rather than as an invitation and introduction to an indigenous economy of values based on reciprocity (ethical, political, cultural, philosophical, and material). See Virgilio Enriquez, *Decolonizing the Filipino Psyche: Philippine Psychology in the Seventies* (Quezon City, Philippines: Philippine Psychology Research House, 1982) and *From Colonial to Liberation Psychology: The Philippine Experience* (Diliman, Quezon City: University of the Philippines Press, 1992); and Karin de Guia, *Kapwa: The Self in the Other: Worldviews and Lifestyles of Filipino Culture-Bearers* (Pasig City, Philippines: Anvil, 2005).

10. David Palumbo Liu, *Asian/American: Historical Crossings of a Racial Frontier* (Stanford, Calif.: Stanford University Press, 1999), 402.

11. Denise Ferreira da Silva, *Toward a Global Idea of Race* (Minneapolis: University of Minnesota Press, 2007).

12. See, for example, Rachel Lee, "Fraternal Devotions: Carlos Bulosan and the Sexual Politics of America," in *The Americas of Asian American Literature: Gendered Fictions of Nation and Transnation* (Princeton, N.J.: Princeton University Press, 1999), 17–43; and Oscar Campomanes, "The New Empire's Forgetful and Forgotten Citizens: Unrepresentability and Unassimilability in Filipino-American Postcolonialities," *Critical Mass* 2.2 (1995): 145–200.

13. William Shakespeare, *Timon of Athens*, 4.3.417.

14. David Harvey, *The New Imperialism* (New York: Oxford University Press, 2003), esp. 139–40.

15. Rosa Luxemburg, *The Accumulation of Capital* (New York: Routledge, 2003), 12.

16. Quoted in Harvey, *New Imperialism*, 141.

17. Ibid., 343.

18. See Campomanes, "New Empire's Forgetful and Forgotten Citizens."

19. For a recent analysis of Stockton's collapse, see Sasha Abramsky, "Stockton Goes Bust," *Nation*, February 14, 2011, 14–19.

20. See also Dawn Mabolon's contributions to the Little Manila Foundation's invaluable web site: http://www.littlemanila.org/; and also Mabolon, "Losing Little Manila: Race and Redevelopment in Filipina/o Stockton, California," in *Positively No Filipinos Allowed: Building Communities and Discourse*, ed. Antonio T. Tiongson Jr., Edgardo V. Gutierrez, and Ricardo V. Gutierrez (Philadelphia: Temple University Press, 2006), 73–89.

21. Carlos Bulosan, "The Romance of Magno Rubio," in *Fiction by Filipinos in America*, ed. Cecilia Manguerra Brainard (Quezon City: New Day, 1993), 78.

22. Kimberly Alidio, e-mail to the author, January 13, 2012. I also am grateful to Joseph Keith for pointing out that Bulosan also is manifesting a form of anxiety about his own position of getting paid to write. With the characters of the illiterate Magno Rubio, the "college boy" Nick, and the seamy Claro who eventually charges Magno up to twenty dollars per letter, Bulosan is expressing his own anxiety about his role in translating Filipino American workers' experiences and getting paid for it. In *America Is in the Heart*, Bulosan writes letters for other people and translates Filipino migrant experience, and of course "migrant" here has the doubled meaning of transnational, cross-border migration and of seasonal migrant labor. I imagine that, if Keith is right about Bulosan's anxiety about a form of writerly prostitution, this anxiety translated productively into the creation of a "personal history," the crucial subtitle to *America Is in the Heart*. Yet Bulosan was plagued during his lifetime by charges of plagiarism and theft, for example, of ostensibly stealing the ideas for "Romance" from the Italian American writer John Fante's short story "Helen, Thy Beauty Is to Me." At a glance, though, one can tell that Fante's story is composed of caricature, a stilted and static portrait of the "Filipino boy" Julio Sal. In stark contrast with Bulosan's Magno whose illiteracy, I argue, generates knowledge, Julio's naïveté about Helen's work as a taxi-hall dancer reproduces racialized stupidity. Shot through with sentimentalism about the fatuousness of the "Filipino boy" and the dream about Helen that forms in his "Malay brain," Fante's story confirms racial type in its insistence on reducing the Filipino to the possession of a "Malay brain," which translates into the lack of a brain.

23. Lonnie Carter with Loy Arcenas, *The Romance of Magno Rubio*, in *Savage Stage: Plays by Ma-Yi Theater Company*, ed. Joi Barrios-Leblanc (New York: Ma-Yi Theater Company, 2006), 309.

24. Ibid., 323.

25. Joi Barrios-Leblanc, "The Politics of Romance: A Study of Ma-Yi Theatre Company's *The Romance of Magno Rubio*," in Barrios-Leblanc, *Savage Stage*, 385–481. See also the republication of the essay in *Philippine Studies: Have We Gone beyond St Louis?* ed. Priscelina Patajo-Legasto (Diliman, Quezon City: University of the Philippines Press, 2008), 514–36.

26. Barrios-Leblanc, "Politics of Romance," 399.

27. Bulosan, "Romance of Magno Rubio," 79.

28. Karl Marx, *Grundrisse: Introduction to the Critique of Political Economy* (Baltimore, Md.: Penguin, 1973), 149.

29. Bulosan, "Romance of Magno Rubio," 78, 82, 86, 89, 94.

30. Antonio Negri, *Marx beyond Marx: Lessons on the Grundrisse* (Brooklyn, N.Y.: Autonomedia, 1991), 26.

31. Antonio Tiongson Jr., "On Filipinos, Filipino Americans, and U.S. Imperialism: Interview with Oscar V. Campomanes," in Tiongson, Gutierrez, and Gutierrez, *Positively No Filipinos Allowed*, 40.

32. Ferdinand Braudel, *The Structures of Everyday Life: The Limits of the Possible* (New York: Harpers and Row, 1979), 513–14.

33. Marx, *Grundrisse*, 17.

34. See, for example, Enriquez, *Decolonizing the Filipino Psyche*; and Enriquez, *From Colonial to Liberation Psychology*.

35. Carter, *Romance of Magno Rubio*, 318–19.

36. Ibid., 319.

37. Ibid., 323.

38. Ibid., 328.

39. Ibid., 320.

40. Ibid., 321.

41. Negri, *Marx beyond Marx*, 83.

Realty Reality: HGTV and the Subprime Crisis

Shawn Shimpach

If the social machine manufactures representations, it also manufactures *itself* from representations—the latter operative at once as means, matter and condition of sociality.
  —Jean-Louis Comolli, "Machines of the Visible," *The Cinematic Apparatus*

We honestly asked ourselves, "Have we been part of this?" I think we reflected the enthusiasm that people had around their homes. In some cases that meant that people were making big investments in their homes, and we tried to help them make smart decisions. But it's a stretch, and I think it's unfair, to say that HGTV fueled a housing bubble.
  —Jim Samples, "Reality Check for Real Estate Shows"

At the start of 2009 the *Wall Street Journal* ran an op-ed piece by a senior vice president of an Ohio-based advertising agency, titled "Blame Television for the Bubble." The piece soon refined its target, stating: "The cable network HGTV is the real villain of the economic meltdown."[1] This piece was hardly a lone voice. Less than a year earlier Miami University professor Ron Becker had asserted much the same idea while sheepishly confessing his own pleasure in watching the cable channel: "I am ashamed because as much as any corner of the television universe, HGTV reflects and in its way, I'd suspect, has helped fuel the unfettered consumerism and neoliberal politics that have helped put millions of American home owners into foreclosure and bankruptcy."[2] The *New York Times* meanwhile has referred to HGTV as both the channel "more closely associated than any other with the country's housing crisis"[3] and "a cable network that fed—and feasted on—the fantasies and delusions of the housing bubble."[4] By March 2009 *Time* magazine had listed the "programming czar" at Scripps Networks, HGTV's corporate parent, among the "25 people to blame for the financial crisis."[5]

These judgments arrived amid the worst global financial crisis since the Great Depression,[6] in which unemployment in the United States alone more than doubled between 2007 and 2009,[7] and literally millions of people lost their homes to foreclosure.[8] This era, in which the wealthiest 1 percent of the U.S. population had a total net worth more than twice that of the bottom 80 percent,[9] is constituted by what Toby Miller has called a "bizarre reconcentration of wealth . . . unprecedented in world history since the advent of working-class electoral franchises."[10] The not-yet-addicted might be forgiven for wondering how a formerly benign and banal basic cable channel like HGTV—which considers 2 million viewers a very good day—came to be considered so central to global geo-economics.[11]

On one level, such public targeting of HGTV represents a particular crisis in television programming. HGTV is a television channel available to most cable system and satellite television subscribers in the United States. Its programming is consistently focused on home improvement, decorating, and real estate. Its wide distribution, relative popularity (for a cable channel), and overt programming content make it a familiar and superficially logical target amid a crashing residential real estate market popularly perceived as the impetus for the global financial crisis.[12] As Scripps Networks' CEO explained to investors in 2010, "some of the negative associations with the housing market caught us a little off guard." Programming, he suggested, now needed to be "a little more relevant to the times and a little more relevant to what the American public is going through."[13] The very things that had made this cable channel popular and financially successful had suddenly become liabilities, publicly associated with the catalysts and causes of a ballooning housing market now burst.

On another level, however, while the accusations therefore appear to fit the accused, they also seem to beg the question and too eagerly attribute motives of global financial malfeasance. Indeed, if we are meant to take at face value a direct link between HGTV's programming and the current financial crisis, then we must discard more than four decades of audience, cultural, and textual studies in favor of a critique that posits a more or less direct correlation between "content" and "behavior." We would stand ready to accuse HGTV of explicitly and transparently conditioning its viewers to act uncritically against their own self-interests. Indeed, we would ultimately have to blame those most adversely affected by the crisis for causing the crisis.

Instead, it is perhaps the case that HGTV's low-budget, ostensibly didactic, "reality" shows combined with an almost exclusive focus on residential home improvement and ownership offer simply a convenient site for what amounts to attacks on the channel's perceived democratization of the appeals, desires, and entitlements of home ownership. Lacking the textual markers of "quality" television, HGTV's public sphere "narrativization and performance" of the domestic and the everyday functions to make its programming suspect by virtue of whom it is presumed to address. As Ruth McElroy observes, for some, HGTV "is indicative of an unhealthy shift (unhealthy, that is, for the body politic) from a public sphere characterized in media terms by hard news, quality drama, and documentary, toward one marked by soft news, affective/sensational dramas, and makeover shows."[14] Perceiving this unhealthy shift has animated the critical drawing of a straight line from HGTV to bloated demand for subprime mortgages. Yet in an era of domestic financialization and crisis, this line seems inevitably to lead through a morass of largely un-examined presumptions about both who watches HGTV and who might be "responsible" for the financial crisis.

HGTV's real estate and home improvement shows, noticeably more so than most American television channels, regularly feature people of color, gay and lesbian couples, and clear class differences. With 73 percent of its viewers female and a prominent emphasis on diversity and difference across its pro-gramming, accusations about HGTV's role in the financial crisis evoke very specific cultural anxieties.[15] By regularly making visible so many people formerly excluded from the "dream" of home ownership, HGTV announces itself as a site for contesting the limits of access to this dream under crisis conditions.

So let us be clear. The current financial crisis was not caused by duped viewers of basic cable television. It was not the result of "over-reaching" minority homebuyers, or the activities of the "at risk," the supposed "nanny state" Fannie and Freddie beneficiaries. It was not the result of amateurs and greedy (would-be) home owners reaching beyond their place only to find the economic equivalent of divine retribution. It was instead caused by the profes-sional activities of supposed experts speculating without oversight.

Yet HGTV can be a significant and revealing site for understanding the rather more complex, nuanced relationship between textual representation and politi-cal economy. To be sure, HGTV has been complicit with, indeed continues to participate in, the political economy of early-twenty-first century neoliberal capitalism. This complicity is most profoundly manifest in *the economic* basis for HGTV, in which HGTV's commercial purpose, ownership, and distribu-tion structure make it ultimately indifferent to any outcome other than bald profitability. Arising from this economic basis are at least two more realms in which HGTV has been complicit: *the ideological*, in which HGTV's program-ming is produced within, naturalizes, and reproduces a neoliberal worldview granting financial markets autonomy and individual subjects self-interested, fiscally driven motives; and *the disciplinary*, in which the cable channel's re-gime of low-budget "lifestyle" programming teaches viewing subjects about presentation of self, the limits of possibility, and the ubiquity of surveillance.

As an accessible and popular site of cultural representation, HGTV evokes a range of responses, from pleasure to anxiety, and has become a focal point for—to borrow one of its own popular terms—"staging" the public negotiation of contradictory responses to current economic conditions. Indeed, it is precisely this complex arousal of such "curious feelings of guilt, titillation, and flooding bourgeois pleasure"[16] (e.g., "I am ashamed to admit I am obsessed with HGTV")[17] that has led Terry Castle to evocatively invoke the term *house-porn* to describe this genre of programming.

Thus the association of HGTV with the "crisis of the subprime" offers an important site for considering the role of textual representations at the intersection of class, gender, race, and text in a critique of the economy. Rather than reductive "blame" that begs the crucial questions and too readily engages in the gendered and racialized logics at play during the housing boom and bust, it is worth considering the complexity of the processes by which political economies become textualized and what this might tell us.

Complicity: The Economic

HGTV was launched in 1994, as the "Home, Lawn, and Garden Channel," at once announcing its content and targeting prospective sponsors. Backed by the Ohio-based newspaper publisher E. W. Scripps Company,[18] the new channel was explicitly aimed at home-owning, middle-class television viewers (and those aspiring to join that demographic). Programming was developed with the intention of simultaneously attracting that audience and providing a "comfortable environment" for potential advertisers. Combining do-it-yourself, lifestyle, and real estate advice programming into a schedule of "shelter TV" was, as the industry trade journal *Advertising Age* explained, "particularly appealing to advertisers in the home category since it affords them a chance to more closely align thematically with content that matches their brands."[19] This industry logic—in which a channel defines all its programming around uniting a particular audience segment with specific advertisers—was the outcome of years of multichannel growth in the American television industry and part of much larger political and economic project of deregulation and globalization (that, in a parallel fashion, affected the financial industries). Government regulatory oversight was replaced by market logics, only to witness the field of market competitors merge until just a few massive conglomerates now control most of the television industry. Citizenship, meanwhile, was conflated with consumerism and subdivided along predetermined (and product-friendly) demographic and psychographic categories, representing different "lifestyles" to be reached through programming and advertising strategies. These audience categories, Sasha Torres explains, "now might plausibly be conceived as composed of multiple minoritarian segments, each with merely a partial claim to the status of 'national' audience."[20] One result has been HGTV's conscious efforts at growing on-screen diversity with the idea of attracting multiple audience segments. Although 81 percent of HGTV's viewers have been identified by the channel's own research as white, with 13 percent black, and 5 percent Hispanic,[21] this is nevertheless enough diversity to position HGTV as one of the most popular cable channels for home-owning African American audiences along with a "higher-than-average" number of upscale Latino/a viewers composing its national composite audience.[22]

While compiling this audience, even as the "Lawn" was soon dropped from the name, HGTV, by all accounts, performed very well and grew rapidly. By summer 1995 the channel had nearly 6 million subscribers. That number doubled in less than a year. It became profitable within its first four years ("12 months ahead of schedule and far earlier than the industry norm of six to seven years").[23] By 2010 the entertainment industry trade journal *Daily Variety* estimated that HGTV was worth $4.9 billion, grossing $556 million in ad revenue that year. HGTV today currently reaches approximately 99 million homes in the United States.[24] In 2008 Scripps spun off its consistently growing cable channel holdings into a separate "lifestyle media" company, Scripps Networks Interactive.[25] HGTV is estimated to contribute approximately 38 percent of the new company's revenue,[26] which also includes the DIY Network, the Food Network, Great American Country, Travel Channel, and Cooking Channel.[27] Scripps also runs highly integrated websites, a recently launched print magazine, and an HGTV Home branding effort associated so far with paint, flooring, and bedding. In addition, Scripps continues to expand its market globally with HGTV programming alone licensed in over sixty-nine countries and territories.[28] Meanwhile, recent rumors of a sale were followed by a $1 billion stock buyback, demonstrating how HGTV and parent Scripps Networks have become desirable and valuable assets with an increasingly global presence.

Yet global corporate branding paired with demographic-niche marketing is not the only way in which HGTV is complicit with and participates in the new economy of the twenty-first century. For example, even as HGTV grossed over $550 million in advertising revenue in 2010, it spent only $221.4 million on total production costs.[29] That it was able to program an entire channel at so (relatively) little cost speaks in part to its liberal use of rerunning program episodes and also its (noticeably) frugal production practices. These practices extend to HGTV's heavy reliance on what Andrew Ross calls the "cultural discount" of precariously employed media labor, in which "the cultural labor problem figures primarily as the challenge of maintaining a steady supply of workers willing to discount the price of their labor for love of their craft."[30] Such workers are frequently freelance, sacrificing both employment security and benefits, in addition to salary, for love of their craft. Thus HGTV effectively subcontracts out much of its program production work. Its roster of reality shows is typically produced by small, independent production companies that compete vigorously for contracts, often relinquishing ownership rights—from format to library to home video to global distribution—even on shows they conceived and pitched to the channel, in order to win the contract. In such cases, "the bulk of lucrative revenues" goes to someone other than the company actually making the show. Such companies find that "it's virtually impossible to make much money off a $200,000-per-episode show, a usual charge for a cable series [in 2004]." As the cofounder of one company that supplies episodes of several of HGTV's programs, Los Angeles–based Pie Town Productions, told the industry trade journal *Broadcasting & Cable*, "volume is the only way we can afford to do these shows and offer year-round employment for our staff."[31] The relatively small Pie Town produces more than five hundred episodes of dozens of programs for several cable channels.

Thus despite its "shelter TV" programming content, HGTV's production, contract, and employment practices reproduce the conditions of insecure, precarious employment that contribute to the high risk of lengthy mortgage commitments. HGTV participates in and is complicit with the economic practices associated with neoliberal market deregulation (with its attendant precarious employment, globalization, market fragmentation, and ownership consolidation). Yet complicity and participation in broad global economic practices are not quite the villainies of which HGTV has stood accused. For that we need to look further into the programming "environment" HGTV developed since its start to bring specific audience segments together with advertisements from specific kinds of industries.

The Ideological

Television, the home, and financial investment have a long and complicatedly intertwined history. Raymond Williams famously coined the phrase "mobile privatization" to capture the contradictory impulses greeting television's introduction to the home in the middle of the twentieth century.[32] Television offered a virtual window from the home, letting into the private domestic realm the glare of the public world of commercials, business, news, and finance at a time, particularly in the United States, when new technologies of transportation and communication coupled with federal and state economic incentives fostered the growth of suburban commuter living.

As such television found comfortable footing in the emerging "ideology of domesticity," which also emphasized home ownership, privacy, self-help—"a campaign, both political and commercial, which took up existing aspects of respectable life" and recentered them from an individual's comportment to the home.[33] Television helped facilitate the transition from "dwelling" as site of labor and production to "home" as site of consumption.[34] Fostered within postwar commercial, social, and political policies encouraging individual home ownership (not to mention the growth of mass media), television grew to be associated with, as John Hartley suggests, "the company it kept—personal experience, private life, suburbia, consumption, ordinariness, heterosexual family-building, hygiene, the 'feminization' of family governance."[35]

HGTV draws on this history of associations to stage home improvement and ownership within the ideology of domesticity. While capitalist entertainment is always on some level about property acquisition, HGTV explicitly embraces the ideology of domesticity as the very subject matter of its entire programming schedule and brand association (a point made somewhat brutally by a recent bit in *McSweeney's* that lists ten titles—for example, *Bought and Sold, The Unsellables, Not For Sale, Buy Me*—and asks: "HGTV Program or Film about Human Trafficking?").[36] As McElroy has noted, such programming "places the acquisition, exhibition, inhabitation or transfer of homes at the centre of lifestyle programming. It makes the idea and material realities of property ownership mundane, common, exhilarating and compelling."[37] HGTV's programming provides viewers access to the "dream" of home ownership by making its everyday components visible to all basic cable subscribers.

The programming on HGTV has always and continues to simply presume the normality of home ownership and then repeat it ad infinitum. The programming thus normalizes, routinizes, and naturalizes the facts and practices of investing in domestic property, by displaying and narrativizing, through sheer repetitive volume. It allows the ideology of domesticity to not simply underlie the commercial programming but to be visualized, made accessible, imaginable, and desirable, associating home with comfort and achievement, on the one hand, and with labor and investment, on the other. Moreover, this visualization is noticeably inclusive of difference. It has made benignly visible, on widely watched television, people whose sexuality, race, ethnicity, or class remain rare on prime-time television in the United States yet are here simply included (rather than spectacularized or problematized) as participants in this ideology of domesticity.

In this sense HGTV programming can be understood to be complicit with the Bush Jr. mantra of an ownership society, in which home ownership is offered as the preferred alternative to welfare dependency. As James Hay has summarized, this policy makes "a virtue explicitly of private and personal ownership and implicitly of an entrepreneurial (self-starting, self-directed, self-responsible) citizenship."[38] The ownership society logics predate the second Bush era in the United States and are supported not only by nationalized mythology—the "American dream" of home ownership—but also by years of legislative policy. As Randy Martin notes, "Homeownership is treated as one of the criteria for membership" in the expanding "investor class" poised to capitalize on government policies "of tax cuts and incentives as a means of distribution of wealth."[39]

HGTV's combination of naturalizing residential property ownership and DIY maintenance and improvement therefore demonstrates and reproduces the logics at work in the so-called housing bubble. As the *New York Times* simply put it: HGTV contributes to the "glorifying mythologies of ownership."[40] The logic of this ideological complicity has been explained by John McMurria "as cultural reinforcements for encouraging multiple generations to find fulfillment through laboring to attain and maintain property."[41]

This is not, however, to suggest a systematic agenda imposed by a monolithic television industry. In fact, the rapid growth and success of HGTV took most in the industry by surprise. In 2004, at the peak of the home-investment boom, *Advertising Age* was still trying to explain HGTV's success to its readers. The trade paper suggested that the growth of "shelter" programming like that on HGTV had resulted from the fact that "the cocooning trend wrought by 9/11 still lingers, and low interest rates arrived in a timely fashion to herald a boom in home sales and remodeling." HGTV is presented in this analysis as the rather fortunate beneficiary of an unlikely conflation of broader socioeconomic conditions, rather than the genius provocateur systematically implementing a heightened regime of domestic ideology.[42]

Indeed, just a few years earlier the channel's content had been seen as a liability in its efforts to attain cable system carriage. Prior to HGTV, very little on American television was explicitly focused on decorating, gardening, or home ownership (rare exceptions include PBS's popular *This Old House* and the *Martha Stewart Living* syndicated program). As the *Wall Street Journal* put it in 1998, "despite the proliferation of 'shelter' magazines, cable companies questioned whether viewers would be willing to watch a 24-hour network devoted to 'paint drying and grass growing.'"[43] Scripps pitched HGTV to cable system operators and advertisers as a channel that addressed programming to "a niche the big entertainment companies had all but ignored: the growing legions of do-it-yourselfers and nesting baby boomers."[44] Home ownership by the end of the twentieth century had already reached the historically high level of two-thirds in the United States, nearly 50 percent higher than a century before.[45] That is, in the 1990s HGTV, rather than the cause of the housing boom, presented itself as the first channel to discover and program for the "growing legions" of home-owning, "nesting," investing, and refurbishing cable subscribers already in existence.

The Disciplinary

Regardless of cause and effect origins, HGTV's programming not only fits ideologically with a neoliberal market philosophy but also can be understood to be actually instrumental in making the practices associated with this ideology thinkable, training viewers to manage their own lives within this realm. As Anna McCarthy suggests, such reality shows are "an important arena in which to observe the vernacular diffusion of neoliberal common sense."[46] With a programming schedule comprised almost exclusively of low-budget "reality TV" about domestic property, HGTV serves as a constant reminder of the potential to have one's home and one's self subject to unscripted, televisual surveillance.[47] The threat and the ideals of televisual presentation become part of the lessons learned in each of the channel's pedagogic programs. Through positive and negative example, guided by self-proclaimed expertise, viewers are taught discernment, taste, and self-discipline as learned skills that are desirable, ethically appropriate, and self-empowering. As one HGTV viewer told *Newsweek* in 2008, "You want to see something really ugly, to be able to say 'Man, those people have bad taste.'"[48] Indeed, this combination of constantly evoked surveillance in the context of pedagogic programming can be understood to have the effect of transforming the viewing subject.

The disciplinary, in this sense, might be summarized as referring to the "lifestyle" in HGTV's lifestyle programming. The techniques, skills, practices, hints, and help offered across HGTV programming teach viewers about comporting themselves, cumulatively setting the limits, contexts, and range of possibilities for people who own and invest in property. In Hay's summary, HGTV (and its ilk) basically literalize Michel Foucault's notion of governmentality: "As ongoing training, advice, and rules, these programs operated as technology for the government of the self, *empowering* citizen-consumers to help themselves and in that way affirming the virtues of entrepreneurial citizenship."[49] The emphasis on design and DIY improvements and investments, paired with the repetition of sales, investment, and refurbishment strategies through HGTV's daily schedule, effectively blur the distinctions between self-expression and the "financialization of daily life." Home ownership, as domicile and investment strategy, becomes a form of self-actualization.[50] As Martin suggests, "The current financial mode is not simply spectacle, an eye-catching economic view, but an invitation to participate in what is on display as a fundamental part of oneself."[51] Good consumer–citizen status, viewers are literally instructed, involves the enterprising "need to capitalize on one's home and to maximize financial security and risk-management through one's home."[52] The ideology of domesticity is again extended, from dwelling to home and, now, to investment.

HGTV's programs frequently use superimposed graphics to remind viewers of the "budget" involved in projects or the "value" of home on display. For DIY programs, viewers are frequently reminded how much was spent, how long it took, and what the home is now worth because of this "investment." The home is slyly presented as a site of financialization, the place in which it pays to invest. Similarly, real estate shows remind viewers of the house hunters' budget, or the seller's asking price, and visually display the types of expectations to be associated with those numbers in various locations around North America and the world.

Crucially, this is explicitly shown to be accessible to everyone. HGTV's exceptionally prolific (for American television) representations of normalized diversity across racial, sexual, class, and lifestyle identity arrive without spectacle or stereotype. Compared with most American television, HGTV offers "a differently contoured public." As Charlotte Brunsdon urges, there is something "positive to be said about the varieties of people that these shows construct as ordinary."[53] Even more so because, as National Public Radio's *Morning Edition* has observed, HGTV not only prominently displays difference but also "shows minorities as tastemakers, arbiters, decision-makers."[54]

Racial difference is not "staged" on HGTV as spectacle, as social problem, or even as a site of "at risk" behaviors. "Successful non-white couples, including blacks, Asians, and Latino/as," Anna Everett insists, "are shown not as societal threats, menaces and perils, but as 'everyday people' . . . *normal* and helpful suburban neighbors."[55] Inclusion, however, extends only as far as commercial imperatives and consumerist logics allow, and thus representations of (relative) empowerment fit well within the disciplinary role of the programming. For example, "It is notable how 'successful' operates here to link normality to the ownership of property," McElroy notes. Full citizenship is contingent on and conveyed through home ownership. Staged in this way, the U.S. legacy of systemic oppression and disparity is effectively effaced. Displays of the "exceptionalism of the non-white middle class" can neither equalize housing disparities nor transform the role gender, class, and race play in constructing citizenship.[56] Instead, the systematic disciplinary lessons in neoliberal cultural participation on HGTV mean that, as NPR concluded, "in spite of all this great diversity on HGTV, everybody ends up wanting exactly the same things . . . granite and stainless steel."[57]

Diversity becomes another way to enact the logics of privatization and the dismantling of government assistance. The drive for additional consumer choice as a substitute for political efficacy,[58] however, has clear implications when that consumer choice gets so readily linked to political repercussions, as in the aftermath of financial collapse. It is these shows, featuring these people, after all, that stand blamed for the crisis.

Yet the programming's noticeable diversity does suggest that viewing HGTV includes pleasures beyond instrumental instruction. It does not necessarily diminish the possibility of disciplinary effects to suggest that pedagogic instruction on HGTV might operate for many viewers as the alibi rather than the reason for viewing. Whether or not people watch realty TV for simple instruction in how to govern their own behaviors, it is partly what they encounter. That HGTV explicitly claims to instruct, however, might serve as convenient means to disavow other, less explicit, pleasures to be found in these shelter programs.

Certainly many viewers harbor no such need to disavow the repetitive pleasures or the consumerist lessons HGTV offers through its programming. As *USA Today*'s television critic recently opined about HGTV, "There is something very satisfying in watching people come to the realization that today's economy, and common sense, require adjusting expectations to realities while finding a pleasant place to live in the bargain. As a bonus, you get to recoil in horror at the worst houses, root for the best and guess which they'll pick."[59] *Newsweek* quoted one viewer of HGTV in 2002 who noted the low-key, easy access appeal of the network: "With Martha Stewart, there's so much high anxiety, you end up feeling that unless you have unlimited time and money, there's just no hope. HGTV is for real people."[60] On the other hand, the *Philadelphia Inquirer* suggests, in a postfinancial crisis world, that HGTV might be credited "with turning viewers into savvy shoppers conversant with matters of housing value and renovation, if not always fluent on the nuances. Reality TV's impact has been discernible and keeps them on their toes, builders and contractors say."[61] The *New York Times*, meanwhile, suggested that being a "student of HGTV" has "taught us that investing a few hundred dollars in repairs, painting and accessories can yield thousands of dollars from the sale."[62]

Yet viewing pleasures are not all fiscal, or strictly educational. It can also be pleasurable to ignore the financializing advice and simply enjoy access to other people's private spaces and a (albeit mediated) sense of proximity to their lives. This "browsing through scenes of national domesticity," as McElroy describes it, signals a viewing pleasure premised on "a transgression of boundaries that makes the private world intimately known and familiar on the national screen."[63] Indeed, what makes the visibly diverse public HGTV presents so appealing and enticing is the way it is incorporated into the channel's generically repetitive programming. This programming continually rehearses "the desire to aspire and be mobile within the nation."[64] Such aspirations are multiplied for populations formerly excluded from participation at all. Indeed, there is another form of work performed by HGTV's programming, perhaps equally central to understanding the channel's role in contemporary political economic matters, that does not become clear unless we examine the programs closely.

The Textual: HGTV's *House Hunters*

My buyers will walk into a house and immediately comment, "Oh, this house has been staged," just as they see it done on television. So many people watch . . . that their expectations of how a house should "show" have been heightened.
— Quoted in Alan J. Heavens, "Reality TV Changed the Reality of Buying a House," *Philadelphia Inquirer*

Our viewers know they won't see anything anxiety-provoking or disturbing, we see that when the news in the world is dark, people tune in. We're a safe haven.
— Ed Spray, quoted in Peg Tyre, "Watch the Paint Dry!" *Newsweek*

"Shelter TV" is called such not simply because it literally involves people's domestic dwellings as its subject matter but also because it presents this subject matter in comforting, predictable, and straightforward ways. This genre of programming is not about complex narrative, stylish formal innovations, surprise, or challenging ideas. Lacking these markers of "quality" TV, it instead appeals to its viewers by appearing simply predictable, reliably benign, and thus reassuringly comfortable.

HGTV, perhaps more so than any other channel on television, doggedly adheres to a programming lineup that is low budget, inflexibly straightforward, unspectacular, and rigidly formulaic. These cheap reality shows are almost determinedly *uninteresting* at the aesthetic, formal, and narrative levels. The bulk of stylistic presentation on HGTV makes John Caldwell's "zero-degree" production style of the 1970s look downright spectacular.[65] As Pie Town cofounder Jennifer Davidson once told *Daily Variety*, "It's very lean-and-mean television. It takes a certain mentality to be able to produce programming on these budgets."[66]

Simplicity of form is not the same as absence of form, however, so it is important to consider how the stripped-down formal aspects of HGTV programming affect their experience and interpretation. Since the genre—indeed, all "reality TV"—must keep close to the documentary evidence of visible truth, HGTV has habitually resisted narrative elaboration, complex plots, character development, or even unhappy (or ambiguous) endings. It reliably eschews current conventions of complex "quality" television. The channel's repeatedly simple formalism instead encourages a sense of transparency. Viewer attention is not explicitly drawn to the structure, arrangement, or appearance of the programs' stylistic elements. Camera angles and movement, lighting, editing, sound, even narrative appear merely functional, allowing us to simply and clearly see what is happening in front of the camera. These low-key formal arrangements nearly require that when we watch, we look right through them, as it were, seeing only the program's "content" of home owners and fixer-uppers.

But all television is representational. Rather than actual transparency, these formal characteristics help define the channel's textuality. After all, we're not *really* seeing "through" form into pure content. Choices are made and consistently applied. Our experience and interpretation is merely shaped by a formal strategy that seems to draw less attention to its own existence. Transparency in this case is actually the result of formal self-effacement. And this is clear if we look at how a typical HGTV show is staged.

House Hunters (1999–present) is HGTV's longest running and among its highest rated programs (episodes average between 1 and 2 million viewers, "a very respectable figure for a reality show on a basic cable network").[67] Certain evenings of HGTV programming have been composed of nothing else than blocks of the program (and its near-identical twin spin-off, *House Hunters International*). Together these two programs have documented one thousand home purchases in their first dozen years (six years for *International*).[68] At one point in 2011, episodes of *House Hunters* made up one-third of HGTV's entire schedule.[69] In 2010 it drew ad revenue of about $83.2 million (up from about $57.6 million in 2008).[70] The program also combines the channel's glaringly simple formal structure and repetitive style with an explicit emphasis in content on home ownership. *House Hunters*, in the context of the broad political economy, is clearly not a radical or even obviously subversive text. Inasmuch as it does not function to undermine or explicitly draw out the contradictions of the dominant ideology, it tends to reinforce it. It represents precisely the programming intended by critics of HGTV's role in the subprime crisis, offering all the offending attributes and viewer gratifications of any HGTV program.

Of course, the program is itself a product of the new economy, in which "individual freedom" is equated with mobility, market choice, and precariousness. Like much of its programming, HGTV outsources the production of *House Hunters*. Several independent production companies have shot episodes for HGTV, including High Noon Entertainment and Pie Town Productions.[71]

To describe any episode of *House Hunters* is to describe a typical episode, as there is room for very little variation in the formula. As the *Los Angeles Times* notes about *House Hunters International*, "in this corner of reality TV, there are no gut-wrenching financing issues, no mortgage worries, no tedious weekends full of overpriced open houses." Instead, "this real estate fairy tale unfolds in the same fashion [every time]: a buyer looks at three houses and, like Goldilocks, picks the one that's just right."[72] The half-hour episodes are actually about twenty-two minutes long (with remaining minutes filled by commercials, promotions, and teasers). Originally, *House Hunters* featured a host—the erstwhile comedienne Suzanne Whang, playing it blandly, if pleasantly, straight—introducing this episode's house hunters, made up of, over the years, an impressive diversity of people, looking on their own, in various pairings, or as various types of families.[73] Such diversity within such a rigid formula reinforces the utter routine of domestic realty acquisition as accessible for any and everyone. As each episode's house hunters are introduced, the program briefly signals their need (and some specific desires) for a new home. These situations can hint at the complexities of residential property that are rarely followed through in any detail in the rest of the program ("their lease expires in one month" or "just took a new job in Atlanta" or, more recently, "she's looking to downsize"). While house hunters are frequently people formerly excluded from the dream of home ownership, this fact, as well as specific reasons for any limits on the stated budget, is left largely uncommented on.

Early episodes were always vague about the location of the house hunt and never revealed the house hunters' budgets (or, then, the price of the homes on display). This was apparently initially a decision based on the fact that early episodes were shot almost entirely in Los Angeles. Thus, "so as not to scare off viewers in the rest of the country, prices for the Los Angeles–area houses [were] never specified."[74] The program's popularity grew after the decision was made to specify where the house hunting was taking place and how much the hunters had budgeted for a new home and what each home's asking price was. The increased access to other people's personal finances increased viewership apparently without loss of willing subjects. As HGTV executive Beth Burke has explained, "people would rather be on television than not say the price of their house."[75] In each episode the house hunters' budget is repeated in voice-over and on-screen graphics throughout the episode, along with each home's asking price.

The realtor is then introduced before the episode's narrative truly commences. The first five or so minutes offer the most variation between episodes: each house hunter and their location vary considerably from episode to episode (even as their ultimate property desires vary rather less). It is also the most formally innovative part of the program. Here the editing is quicker, the camera more mobile, the angles on action more often canted, than throughout what follows.

The bulk of each episode follows the house hunters and their realtor as they view three distinct properties that broadly fit the budget and desires described at the start. Footage of each significant room in each house is shot with handheld camcorders. While an occasional quick edit or rapid camera movement is allowed, these shots remain almost brutally static, nearly rivaling the impassive camerawork viewable on the Home Shopping Network and tempting the extraordinarily patient camera operator to zoom, tilt, or pan, almost imperceptibly. Yet any variation from these near-static shots would be inconceivable and utterly unsatisfying for viewers, as the entire point here is to produce a kind of formal transparency so that each room can be simply seen. The point is to invite temporary inhabitation of the space rendered before the camera. Sequences like this are not about watching television, they are about seeing into someone's home. Extremely slow pans, tilts, or zoom-outs constitute all the movement, so that home viewers may scan the screen for a full image of the room. (This formal transparency is undermined only in retrospect, upon consideration of how rare these brightly lit, high key, static shots are in our contemporary media-landscape.) In postproduction these shots are complemented with Muzak-style instrumentals. Meanwhile, graphics appear on-screen reminding viewers of the home's price and the house hunters' budget (and sometimes their location). Transitions between locations or sequences are done with wipes accompanied by sound effects and chunky graphics.

Bumpers before each commercial break tease the forthcoming sequences mercilessly, voice-overs completely resummarize the episode after each commercial break, and the same footage is edited into sequences again and again. Narratively, everything but the denouement is shown and repeated at least four or five times during the episode's half-hour block of time. The denouement segment, nonetheless, begins with yet another condensed montage revisiting, again, each of the three homes, as voice-over and on-screen graphics repeat home size, price, location, and house hunters' general impression. Then the house hunters are shown "casually," if stiffly, discussing the pros and cons of each home sequentially—again intercut with by-now-familiar footage of the home under discussion—in some blandly neutral setting. Finally, the voice-over asks: "So which one did they choose?" Again, a static shot of each home is returned to, with low-budget, "game show" style suspense music and a punning graphic title summarizing their impression of each home. Suspense is held for a second or two before this program's version of the classic reality show "reveal," borrowed from makeover shows, in which the house hunters tell the camera their choice. Recently some episodes have attempted to extend the suspense by allowing the house hunters to first "definitely eliminate" one of the three choices.

A final segment involves a secondary set of "reveals." The house hunters are documented through footage shot at a later date to have taken occupancy over a quick cut that temporally collapses anywhere from a few days to many months. Once in a while the voice-over will explain a complication in taking ownership—bidding war, vague financing trouble, short sale, and so forth—but much more typically the choice of the home is simply equal to the ownership and occupancy of the home. This is demonstrated by a (relatively) rapid series of before-and-after shots of main rooms in the newly acquired home.

This indexical proof of occupancy is inevitably accompanied by unanimous assertions that purchasing this home was "the best decision" and the former house hunters are "so happy" to have the "perfect place" for them at this time. There has not been a single episode of *House Hunters* or its spin-offs where the new owners are revealed to be displeased or admit to having made a mistake in purchasing the home.[76] While difficult financial conditions are sometimes referenced (more since the financial crisis, such as the inconvenience of dealing with bank "short sales"), the new home owners at the end of each episode are never exposed as suddenly underwater, surprised by mortgage terms, or otherwise fiscally or emotionally unequipped to enjoy their role as new home owners. Neither are they ever revealed to be displeased with (or disliked by) new neighbors, dissatisfied with schools, or unwelcome in the neighborhood. In *House Hunters*, buyer's remorse does not exist. Every purchased home is always exactly what buyers needed and wanted, and they could never be happier with their choice.

This, however, is largely the result of something else the program never reveals: *House Hunters* is staged. The simple, seemingly straightforward reality we encounter many times each day on HGTV has been constructed from production choices rather than simply recorded as it unfolded before the camera. While apparently belying the program's "reality" genre, few viewers, upon any reflection, should be surprised that the repetitive editing, camera work, locations, and characters, and relentlessly predictable narrative, have been chosen intentionally rather than serendipitously stumbled on while filming.[77] Upon further reflection, it might be more than coincidence that the featured buyers on this program always and only see three potential homes before making a final decision to buy a house. Perhaps less obviously, the spaces they see have often been "staged" by HGTV (or Pie Town or High Noon), with furniture rearranged, removed, or transformed; lighting changed and heightened; clutter cleaned and removed. Indeed, conversations, reactions, and direct-to-camera "confessions" are also frequently "staged" and often reshot again and again for a usable take. Any one of the three homes featured in the half-hour episode typically takes an entire day to shoot (not much time in terms of television production, but a lot more time than ever appears on-screen). Participants speak of forty-hour shoots reduced to twenty minutes of screen time. More shocking, still, to avid viewers is news that in many cases the featured house hunters are no longer hunting for a house by the time they are being filmed. To be sure of a consistent ending to each episode (with new buyers happily ensconced in new home), shooting often begins after buyers have made a decision, and frequently when they are already in escrow, thus reversing the real-world chronology.

Pie Town helpfully explains all this staging to prospective participants on their website: "This is 'reality-style' television, which means that although we aim to remain true to events as they happen, there are times we may need to direct the action. For instance, we may ask you to re-do some things, so that we get a better shot or a different camera angle, or ask you to repeat certain answers in order to tell your story in a succinct way."[78] In all, to be a house hunter, you must submit an audition tape and must be completing your home search. Should you be chosen to appear on the program, you will be offered $500 in exchange for five (by all accounts, long) days of shooting. You will be asked to relook at the home you have already chosen and act surprised, make up cons to go with the pros of this and two other homes, which you will then visit—having or perhaps not having seen them when originally looking. You should not say anything that might tip off viewers about which home you (already) chose. In each case you might be asked to alter your comments or repeat yourself (for better sound, lighting, angle, or succinctness). The *Chicago Tribune* reported on one area realtor who "found herself having to say the same things over and over, while the camera crew shot her conversations . . . from different angles, and had to be careful not to tip off viewers to which property was chosen."[79] Such realtors, by the way, are asked to escort clients without compensation from the television producers, but with usually positive, repeated exposure on national television.

All this staging is important to do and useful to know about because it constitutes the necessary practices for producing the reliable, predictable, familiar, and repetitive gratifications that *House Hunters* offers (unlike reality). *House Hunters*, through its staging of apparent transparency, more than anything else, seeks to make *visible* the seemingly abstract content of the residential real estate market. But this visibility is necessarily constituted by leaving some things unseen. It is here that the supposed transparency suggested by the "invisible" formal characteristics and the repetitive genre conventions begins to reveal a secondary level of effacement. Even as *House Hunters* is produced to mask the work of its own production and appear as if it simply happened in front of the camera, it is also produced to efface the labor and the risk that exists and is inherent to its content. The "reveal" of the house hunters' choice, which through formal repetition effaces differences in buyers, is followed immediately by proof of occupancy, skipping over and masking, in the space of a single edit, the work, the transactions, the bidding, the negotiations, even the sellers involved in turning a consumer choice into a "happy ending." Risk, meanwhile, is here mitigated through temporality. Both in the program's staging (shot in reverse chronology, with the house hunter having already selected a home) and the program's narrative structure (wherein risks to home life, personal finance, and domestic investment are presented—if at all—at the start of the program, as reasons *for a* new purchase, which the new purchase is *always* shown to resolve), the production is organized around producing a transparency that effaces its own constructedness as well as its subject matter's risk.

Consider the program's diversity of minority house-hunting participants. This diversity within the rigid formulaic sameness of the program's formal structure similarly works to effectively efface the reality of home ownership inequalities. In *House Hunters* all house hunters, regardless of race or ethnicity, are represented as equal participants and are shown to be equally (completely) satisfied with their home purchase by each episode's end. Yet according to U.S. census data, in 2007, at the start of the subprime crisis, with total home ownership in the United States at 68 percent, the rate of white householding was above the national average, at 72 percent. In contrast, householders who were black had home ownership rates of 47 percent, and Hispanic householders (of any race) had a 50 percent home ownership rate—both well below the national average.[80] These data seem to belie the premise of HGTV's equal-access programming. Moreover, as Paula Chakravartty and Dan Schiller report, this racial disparity can be found in the mortgage terms for homebuyers as well.

"Home loan figures from 2006 show that 53.3% of loans issued to Black borrowers were high-cost sub-prime, along with 46.2% of loans to Latinos, compared to 17.7% to white borrowers."[81]

Whereas much of television programming—from police/doctor/lawyer procedurals to reality contests to news coverage—is about narrativizing and spectacularizing risk, most of HGTV's shelter TV schedule offers safe harbor from even the very risks inherent to its apparently straightforward subject matter. As one realtor involved in the production suggested, "'House Hunters' is house candy. It's not realistic. It's directed. You don't learn anything about buying. You learn about real estate values. You learn about how houses look." Viewing these programs is much more a formal game than a window into empirical reality. We are formally encouraged (through recaps, dramatic pauses, lists of pros and cons) to see the homes and come to our own conclusions. Viewers are encouraged through visual and narrative redundancies, as well as through HGTV promos and teasers for the program, to "play along" while they watch: which home *will* they choose? Which home *should* they choose? Which home *would I* choose?[82] This is a televisual game, drawing pleasure from the program's textuality rather than the "reality" of what is represented.

This strategy of mitigating and effacing real and knowable risk through televisual production practices actually operates for HGTV as product differentiation. HGTV provides a retreat for viewers and a comfortable environment for advertisers. It takes the fact of risk as an opportunity for differentiation and profit (through its effacement).

"Staging" the Economy

There is of course at least one other realm in which the real risks of residential property ownership have been understood as opportunities for profit. Parallel with the replacement of governmental oversight by market logic in the television industry, "the deregulation of financial markets," Luc Boltanski and Eve Chiapello explain, "their decompartmentalization, and the creation of 'new financial products' have multiplied the possibilities of purely speculative profits, whereby capital expands without taking the form of investment in productive activity." The resultant fact that "capital profitability [is] now better guaranteed by financial investment than industrial investment"[83] means that nearly 40 percent of corporate profit now comes from a financial sector that employs merely 5 percent of private-sector workers.[84] Investment in infrastructure, industry, and other sources of productive capital, employment, and opportunity have diminished in favor of seemingly byzantine global trading practices and spiralingly abstract speculations that are as striking as cultural allegories as they are as fiscal practices.[85]

Consider one's individual residential property mortgage. Rather than sit with the original lender who might modestly profit off the attached interest, it has found investors and entered into a larger set of speculations. Perhaps it has become part of a mortgage-backed security (MBS). This is essentially a pool of home mortgage loans purchased from lenders and grouped together, secured with the promise of repayments, with the value of the properties as (implied) collateral. Such a bet on an aggregate of future payments has limits, and investment in them is not without potential risks: there is the risk that interest rates will rise, and mortgage lenders may end up borrowing money at a more expensive rate than the loans they previously made; there is the risk of default and foreclosure; there is even the risk of prepayments that would "return principal to investors precisely when their options for reinvesting those funds may be relatively unattractive."[86]

These risks have themselves been financialized, however, serving as the occasion for new financial products and thus as an additional opportunity for investors.[87] For example, risk is codified and somewhat mitigated in MBSs by channeling the flow of money (i.e., people's monthly mortgage payments) through a hierarchical series of tranches, with senior tranches paid out first, junior tranches thereafter. These securities are then themselves repackaged to form larger and more diversified collateral—and thus some protection against default risk—into collateralized mortgage obligations, which are backed by the total worth of all the mortgages bundled together. At this point, for investors, the "promise of future payments" is only distantly derived from any actual mortgage of any individual home owner. What is being bought and sold are bets about aggregate mortgage payments, the percentages of certain categories of mortgages being paid regularly, regardless of whether any individual home owner was suddenly underwater or faced financial difficulty.

Yet further opportunities to bet on (or "manage") risk use these bundles as their basis. Credit default swaps allow investors to either bet that a security will pay or will not pay, even if they have not invested directly in that security. These bets can then also be bundled and sold. Such derivatives can continue to escalate (ever away from the original mortgages) while inspiring additional instruments of financial speculation.

The trading of many of these speculations on speculative trades is done en masse, often faster than can be humanly perceived through networked computers, according to proprietary algorithms, across global markets. Any one investor may on some occasions "own" one of these securities for mere fractions of a second, profiting instead through arbitrage on minute differences in their trading value across different global markets.

Continuous, around-the-clock global trading in the financial markets has a material basis in the telecommunication infrastructure, computer hardware, and algorithmic trading software that makes it physically possible. The rapid (in the case of arbitrage, humanly imperceptible) trading of potentially massive quantities over potentially unlimited space also has the effect of further abstracting trading practices from material sources or implications, rendering the market in its only tangible form as screen representation.[88]

All these "globally traded instruments of financial speculation" represent but a subset of the "new financial products" produced and sold on a purely speculative basis. The distant basis in bets on actual home owners need not even be visible to traders, (remaining) regulators, or certainly the public, even while the "low interest rates—particularly, for mortgage and credit—that working and middle class people were offered were a response to this demand for financial investment venues."[89] That borrowers became home owners (with loans they could not afford) was essentially a side effect of this demand for more and new financial products. Minority and other populations formerly excluded from home ownership were increasingly encouraged to now participate largely because investors were looking to expand financialization opportunities. In other words, "working and middle class debt was an instrument of capital accumulation for the wealthy,"[90] part of a larger systemic movement toward the upward distribution of resources. Hence deflated former Federal Reserve Board chairman Alan Greenspan's suggestion that "the big demand was not so much on the part of the borrowers as it was on the part of the suppliers who were giving loans which really most people couldn't afford." The links between these speculations and actual homes only became clear as the liquidity crisis finally worked down the various—seemingly abstract—levels and called on the material value of the underlying mortgages.

Trading like this is not only facilitated but made at all knowable through specific, material representational practices. Hence the fashioning of "the market" as an intangible, but empirical, entity.[91] It is only accessible, knowable, visible through the screen representations in which it has been staged. The market is staged in identical, overlapping, and coordinated screen presentations. "On each of these screens, the same market has a vigorous presence; traders worldwide who deal in the same financial instrument watch the same screen content, which is delivered to them by globally operating firms."[92] This is a practice that emulates nothing so much as television!

Indeed, the same growth of narrow-focused, specialized programming for distinct audience segments that made HGTV's programming possible has also fostered the growth of cable channels catering to audiences interested in financial markets. As Chakravartty and Schiller note, television's financial channels effectively blur "market news and advertising into infotainment [which has] not only provided a venue for promoting investment interests, but also helped spearhead a culture of credit, risk, and individual responsibility and the potential of unprecedented reward."[93] Moreover, these channels represent the (seemingly abstract) risk and potential rewards of financial transactions through graphically pleasing, personality-driven, entertaining, and seemingly transparent visual forms. Screens on Fox Business News, Bloomberg TV, CNBC, and the like are typically oversaturated with information. Modeled on the "windows" interface of a personal computer or workstation, screens are multiply split, news updates scroll in different directions, live-seeming market numbers fill quadrants of the screen, and pleasant news readers occupy additional screen space, all simultaneously. This, for any interested basic cable customer, is what abstract financial markets have come to look like: numbers, information, simultaneity. After all, as Martin reminds us, "only a minority of individual investors trade more than twice a month." Awash in all this market data, the real function of these channels is to offer a "medium through which people imagine that they are living in the same world" as rapid, abstract financial trading markets.[94]

Yet, as Caitlin Zaloom argues, this imaginary is not limited to armchair investors at home. It is a staging that forms the very basis for financial markets to exist. The social context fostering both the creation of new trading paradigms and new financial products as well as the competitive desire among individuals to pursue aggressive trading strategies are influenced by the material staging of trading markets, the literal "blend of devices, social forms, and human skills that are necessary to make them work" in combinations that Zaloom calls the "socio-technical arrangement" of financial markets. Crucially, this material staging is not simply the arranging of preexisting financial markets but their very foundation. "Markets *are* socio-technical arrangements of material devices and the competitive individuals that these arrangements create."[95] Markets, too, are staged.

To suggest that this all came tumbling down because too many of the actual mortgages were "high risk" (and thus more likely to default), however, seems to be missing the point. It was not actual defaults that "caused" the current global economic crisis but the complex, yet lucrative, economy of risk that was built up from and capitalized on the promises of individual home owners to make their monthly payments yet was represented as managed risk through formally standardized screen representations on remote traders' computer screens. The economy of risk was staged as its own sort of game, with its own specific representational strategies, and it was a different game than home owners were playing (or even encouraged by the likes of HGTV to play).

Yes, we found out the games were linked, but only indirectly. Nonetheless, this linkage, however tenuous, gets used to suggest that particular, "subprime," individual borrowers are to be blamed for the collapse of the whole system. In such cases, reductive blame does more to contribute to the ongoing crisis, by effacing the staging that led to it, than it does to explain it.

Conclusion

Staging allows home buyers to imagine their own inhabitation of a space. This means effacing the actual, current status of the property (owned by the seller) by producing a preferred, future status (inhabited by the buyer). Staging does not show off how the home has been lived in, but how it might be. The spaces of the home are staged specifically to show potential buyers the most pleasing and desirable arrangement, regardless of how attainable or livable that arrangement might actually prove to be.

Staging is therefore deceptive, yet it does not really expect to actually fool anyone. Savvy homebuyers recognize when a home has been staged (the detritus of everyday life conspicuously evacuated from the property) and understand it is not "real." Nevertheless, house hunters increasingly expect—indeed desire—to view homes that have been thoughtfully staged. It is a pleasant, if transparent, and yet effective, deception.

A popular trope in shelter TV, staging is an intensely temporal project, operating now, but only temporarily, to provoke an imagination of the future. It makes the possibility of occupancy not only thinkable but desirable. In this way staging is also a useful metaphor for thinking through the relationship between ownership, finance, and textuality and race, class, and gender. In residential property, staging is a practice intended to facilitate a sale. Its correlates in financial markets, on television, and in representational practices operate similarly.

HGTV and its public associations with the financial crisis offer an important site for considering how these staging practices operate and how they might (and might not) correspond. HGTV's programming offers a prominent and consistent image of race-blind access to home ownership for all populations, including those long excluded from the centerpiece of the American dream. It stages racial difference in commodity form to construct a coalition viewership in lieu of the mass national audience once claimed by television channels for sale to advertisers. In a time of financial crisis associated with mortgage default, this has opened the channel to accusations of indiscriminately encouraging home investment to unqualified buyers, more broadly constructed as overreaching minority beneficiaries of government assistance.

Yet a closer look at HGTV's programming reveals it has been remarkably successful in arranging the textual representations it programs to offer not just lessons in commodity culture but also a peak behind private doors, imaginatively staging for viewers the possibility of access, control, and presence. In the context of increasingly global, increasingly abstract, highly financialized ways of being in the world, this textual staging offers much more than lessons in the mundanities of middle-class life: it also offers a way to imagine participation and proximity to others. It effaces the reality of a continuing legacy of significant racial disparities in access to this middle-class life by staging the way to imagine it as accessible to all.

Of course for HGTV, the point has been to make television, not reproduce reality. Yet knowing that reality TV, in shows like *House Hunters*, is the end product of a series of stagings, that it is constructed, allows us to consider the specific priorities directing its construction and how that construction has circulated and become meaningful. Producing "shelter TV" that is reassuring and comforting allows racial difference to feature as product differentiation, even amid alarmist targeting of the channel's supposedly duped viewers. In this context a program like *House Hunters* has no less efficacy for being staged; it has more.

Notes

1. Jim Sollisch, "Blame Television for the Bubble," *Wall Street Journal*, January 3, 2009, 7.
2. Ron Becker, "Horribly Guilty Television," *Flow*, April 24, 2008, http://flowtv.org/2008/04/horribly-guilty-television-hgtv-and-the-promotion-of-americas-ownership-society/.
3. Brian Stelter, "Reality Check for Real Estate Shows," *New York Times*, May 24, 2009, www.nytimes.com/2009/05/24/arts/television/24stel.html?pagewanted=all.
4. Alessandra Stanley, "On HGTV, Fixing Home and Hearts," *New York Times*, March 18, 2010, http://tv.nytimes.com/2010/03/18/arts/television/18hgtv.html?ref=alessandrastanley.
5. Quoted in Stelter, "Reality Check." See also "25 People to Blame for the Financial Crisis," www.time.com/time/specials/packages/article/0,28804,1877351_1877350_1877332,00.html (accessed August 23, 2011).
6. See, for example, www.reuters.com/article/2009/02/27/idUS193520+27-Feb-2009+BW20090227 (accessed August 31, 2011).

7. See U.S. Department of Labor Bureau of Labor Statistics website. http://data.bls.gov/timeseries/ LNU04000000?years_option=all_years&periods_option=specific_periods&periods=Annual+Data (accessed September 3, 2011).

8. See, for example, www.businessweek.com/the_thread/hotproperty/archives/2009/01/over_one_millio. html (accessed August 31, 2011).

9. For details, see http://sociology.ucsc.edu/whorulesamerica/power/wealth.html (accessed September 9, 2011).

10. Toby Miller, *Makeover Nation: The United States of Reinvention* (Columbus: Ohio State University Press, 2008), 9.

11. See, for example, Wayne Freidman, "Cablers History, FX on Upswing, While CNBC, Fox News Plummet," *MediaDailyNews*, March 1, 2011, www.mediapost.com/publications/?fa=Articles. showArticle&art_aid=145905&passFuseAction=PublicationsSearch.showSearchReslts&art_ searched=hgtv&page_number=0.

12. See, for example, Jeremy J. Seigel, "The Lehman Crisis: An Unhappy Anniversary," *Business Week*, September 20, 2009, www.businessweek.com/investor/content/sep2009/pi20090918_770685. htm?chan=investing_investing+index+page_top+stories.

13. Scripps Networks CEO Ken Lowe, speaking to investors about HGTV's (it turns out, fairly brief) ratings decline in 2009. Quoted in David Goetzl, "HGTV Adjusts Shows to Match Consumer Experience," *MediaDailyNews*, September 23, 2010, www.mediapost.com/publications/index.cfm?fa=Articles. showArticle&art_aid=136313&passFuseAction=PublicationsSearch.showSearchReslts&art_ searched=hgtv&page_number=2.

14. Ruth McElroy, "Property TV: The (Re)making of Home on National Screens," *European Journal of Cultural Studies* 11.1 (2008): 44.

15. See www.hgtvadsales.com/AboutUs/research.pdf (accessed March 30, 2012).

16. Terry Castle, "Home Alone: The Dark Heart of Shelter-Lit Addiction," *Atlantic*, March 2006, www. theatlantic.com/doc/200603/house-porn.

17. Becker, "Horribly Guilty Television."

18. Scripps's interesting history is worth exploring. See, for example, Gerald J. Baldasty, *E. W. Scripps and the Business of Newspapers* (Chicago: University of Illinois Press, 1999).

19. Daisy Whitney, "Marketers Feel at Home in Shelter TV," *Advertising Age*, April 5, 2004, S4. The extent to which their intentions have been fulfilled might be discerned from a 2010 study of 225 advertising media executives, in which 75 percent found HGTV to be a "desirable programming environment on which to advertise." See Wayne Friedman, "Ad Execs See Higher Cable Ad Budgets, ESPN, Food Top List," *MediaDailyNews*, March 16, 2011, www.mediapost.com/publications/?fa=Articles. showArticle&art_aid=146818&passFuseAction=PublicationsSearch.showSearchReslts&art_ searched=hgtv&page_number=0.

20. Sasha Torres, "Television and Race," in *A Companion to Television*, ed. Janet Wasko (Malden, Mass.: Blackwell, 2005), 395–408.

21. See www.hgtvadsales.com/AboutUs/research.pdf (accessed March 30, 2012).

22. See www.wbur.org/npr/135353192/if-youre-looking-for-a-little-diversity-on-television-try-hgtv (accessed March 30, 2012).

23. Leslie Cauley, "Scripps Quickly Proves an Outsider Can Start a Cable-TV Network," *Wall Street Journal*, November 13, 1998.

24. The HGTV website reports "over 89 million" (www.hgtv.com/about-us/about-us/index.html [accessed August 27, 2011]). Parent company Scripps Networks Interactive's website instead reports "more than 99 million U.S. household as of February 2011" (http://scrippsnetworks.com/newsitem.aspx?id=90 [accessed September 2, 2011]). Other sources suggest as many as "100 million subscribers." See "HGTV Remodel Rolls with Changing Landscape: Cable Net Spruces Up Its Lineup after Housing Bust," *Daily Variety*, October 18, 2010, 14; and Wayne Friedman, "Scripps Cable Nets Feasts on Higher Revs," *MediaDailyNews*, August 9, 2011, www.mediapost.com/publications/?fa=Articles.showArticle&art_ai d=155578&passFuseAction=PublicationsSearch.showSearchReslts&art_searched=hgtv&page_number=0.

25. Scripps Networks website, www.scrippsnetworks.com/ (accessed August 28, 2011).

26. David Goetzl, "Scripps Spins Off TV Section," *MediaDailyNews*, July 2, 2008, www.mediapost.com/ publications/index.cfm?fa=Articles.showArticle&art_aid=85893&passFuseAction=PublicationsSearch. showSearchReslts&art_searched=hgtv&page_number=6.

27. Formerly Fine Living, but rebranded after the financial crisis. See David Goetzl, "New Dish: Fine Living Rebranded as Cooking Channel," *MediaDailyNews*, October 8, 2009, www.mediapost.com/publications/index.cfm?fa=Articles.showArticle&art_aid=115124&passFuseAction=PublicationsSearch.showSearchReslts&art_searched=hgtv&page_number=4.

28. http://scrippsnetworks.com/newsitem.aspx?id=90 (accessed August 31, 2011).

29. See "HGTV Remodel Rolls with Changing Landscape."

30. Andrew Ross, "The Mental Labor Problem," *Social Text* 18.2 (2002): 6.

31. Allison Romano, "Table Scraps," *Broadcasting and Cable*, July 26, 2004, 1.

32. Raymond Williams, *Television: Technology and Cultural Form* (London: Fontana, 1974).

33. John Hartley, *Uses of Television* (London: Routledge, 1999), 105.

34. Ibid. See also Williams, *Television*; John McMurria, "Desperate Citizens and Good Samaritans: Neoliberalism and Makeover Reality TV," *Television and New Media* 9.4 (2008): 305–32; James Hay, "Too Good to Fail: Managing Financial Crisis through the Moral Economy of Realty TV," *Journal of Communication Inquiry* 34.4 (2010): 382–402; and Shawn Shimpach, "Viewing," in *The Handbook of Media Audiences*, ed. Virginia Nightingale (Oxford: Wiley-Blackwell, 2011), 62–85.

35. Hartley, *Uses of Television*, 107.

36. At least one was both! See David Harnden-Warwick, "HGTV Program or Film about Human Trafficking?" *McSweeney's*, www.mcsweeneys.net/articles/hgtv-program-or-film-about-human-trafficking (accessed July 15, 2011).

37. McElroy, "Property TV," 44.

38. Hay, "Too Good to Fail."

39. Randy Martin, *An Empire of Indifference: American War and the Financial Logic of Risk Management* (Durham, N.C.: Duke University Press, 2007), 37.

40. Gina Bellafante, "Every Home's a Castle, Cinderella," *New York Times*, June 5, 2011, www.nytimes.com/2011/06/06/arts/television/for-hgtv-and-bravo-the-housing-market-is-still-booming.html?scp=2&sq=gina%20bellafante%20every%20home's%20a%20castle&st=Search.

41. McMurria, "Desperate Citizens and Good Samaritans."

42. Whitney, "Marketers Feel at Home," S4.

43. Cauley, "Scripps Quickly Proves an Outsider Can Start a Cable-TV Network."

44. Ibid.

45. Randy Martin, *Financialization of Daily Life* (Philadelphia: Temple University Press, 2002), 19.

46. Anna McCarthy, "Reality Television: A Neoliberal Theater of Suffering," *Social Text* 25.4 (2007): 17–41.

47. Mark Andrejevic, *Reality TV: The Work of Being Watched* (New York: Rowman and Littlefield, 2003).

48. Daniel McGinn, "With Lust in Our Hearts," *Newsweek*, January 14, 2008. The article ran in the real estate section, as an excerpt from McGinn's 2008 book *House Lust: America's Obsession with Our Homes* (New York: Currency Books/Doubleday, 2008).

49. Hay, "Too Good to Fail."

50. See Laurie Ouellette and James Hay, *Better Living through Reality TV* (Malden, Mass.: Blackwell, 2008).

51. Martin, *Financialization of Daily Life*, 16–17.

52. Hay, "Too Good to Fail."

53. Charlotte Brunsdon, "Lifestyling Britain: The 8–9 Slot on British Television," *International Journal of Cultural Studies* 6.5 (2003): 17–18.

54. Linda Holmes, "If You're Looking for a Little Diversity on Television, Try HGTV," April 13, 2011, www.wbur.org/npr/135353192/if-youre-looking-for-a-little-diversity-on-television-try-hgtv.

55. Anna Everett, "Trading Private and Public Spaces @ HGTV and TLC: On New Genre Formations in Transformation TV," *Journal of Visual Culture* 3.2 (2004): 157–81.

56. McElroy, "Property TV," 57.

57. Holmes, "If You're Looking for a Little Diversity on Television."

58. Sasha Torres, "Television and Race," in *A Companion to Television*, ed. Janet Wasko (Malden, Mass.: Blackwell, 2005), 403.

59. Robert Bianco, "Critic's Corner," *USA Today*, June 27, 2011, 6.

60. Peg Tyre, "Watch the Paint Dry!" *Newsweek*, November 18, 2002, 64.

61. Alan J. Heavens, "Realty TV Changed the Reality of Buying a House," *Philadelphia Inquirer*, May 21, 2010.

62. Brian Stelter, "Housing Slump Helps the Draw of Fixer-Upper TV," *New York Times*, June 12, 2008, www.nytimes.com/2008/06/12/business/media/12flip.html?scp=1&sq=Brian%20stelter%20housing%20slump%20helps&st=Search.

63. McElroy, "Property TV," 50.

64. Ibid., 57.

65. John Thornton Caldwell, *Televisuality: Style, Crisis, and Authority in American Television* (New Brunswick, N.J.: Rutgers University Press, 1995), 58.

66. Patricia Saperstein, "Pie Town Delivers Product for Varied Tastes," *Daily Variety*, December 14, 1999, A16.

67. Carolyn Kellogg, "House Hunting the Globe from Your Comfy Couch," *Los Angeles Times*, July 24, 2011, D1.

68. This according to production company Pie Town's website: http://www.pietown.tv/Shows/hh.html (accessed September 3, 2011).

69. Georg Szalai, "Food Network Ratings Drop 10% in Key Demo," *Hollywood Reporter*, January 20, 2011, www.hollywoodreporter.com/news/food-network-ratings-drop-10-73923.

70. Brian Steinberg, "Home-Improvement TV Still Going Strong on Cable Despite Soft Market," *Advertising Age*, July 24, 2011, 13.

71. Saperstein, "Pie Town Delivers Product," A16.

72. Kellogg, "House Hunting the Globe," D1.

73. In 2008 Suzanne Whang left the series and the program has since operated without a host, instead sufficing with merely a disembodied narrator (frequently the voice-over artist Colette Whitaker).

74. Saperstein, "Pie Town Delivers Product," A16.

75. Quoted in McGinn, "With Lust in Our Hearts." The article ran in the real estate section, as an excerpt from McGinn's 2008 book *House Lust: America's Obsession with Our Homes.*

76. On incredibly rare occasions, more prevalent on *International*, an episode will end without the house hunter taking occupancy—usually explained by unusually slow or complex "foreign" real estate protocols, more rarely still by the house hunter's apparent apathy.

77. Although anyone familiar with the production of so-called unscripted television should not really be shocked, this realization has become something of a point of conversation for many fans of the program. See, for example, http://hookedonhouses.net/2010/06/02/the-truth-about-house-hunters-on-hgtv/ or www.associatedcontent.com/article/1167564/the_top_five_hgtv_shows.html?cat=6 (accessed July 25, 2011).

78. PieTown FAQ, www.pietown.tv/Shows/hh_FAQ_Buyer.html (accessed August 16, 2011).

79. Mary Ellen Podmolik, "In Reality, Those Real Estate Shows Are Really Fake," *Chicago Tribune*, December 4, 2009, http://articles.chicagotribune.com/2009-12-04/entertainment/0912020969_1_reality-television-real-estate-agent.

80. See www.census.gov/hhes/www/housing/hvs/annual09/ann09t22.xls (accessed March 30, 2012).

81. Paula Chakravartty and Dan Schiller, "Global Financial Crisis: Neoliberal Newspeak and Digital Capitalism in Crisis," *International Journal of Communication* 4 (2010): 670–92.

82. McGinn, "With Lust in Our Hearts."

83. Luc Boltanski and Eve Chiapello, *The New Spirit of Capitalism* (London: Verso, 2005), xxxvii.

84. "The Gentleman's Bailout," *Nation*, April 7, 2008, 3–4; and "Wall Street Crisis," *Economist*, March 22, 2008, 11–12; both cited in Toby Miller, *Makeover Nation: The United States of Reinvention* (Columbus: Ohio State University Press, 2008), 8.

85. For examples of such a treatment, see Fredric Jameson, "Culture and Finance Capital," *Critical Inquiry* 24.1 (1997): 246–65; Benjamin Lee and Edward LiPuma, "Cultures of Circulation: The Imaginations of Modernity," *Public Culture* 14.1 (2002): 191–213, expanded and published as Edward LiPuma and Benjamin Lee, *Financial Derivatives and the Globalization of Risk* (Durham, N.C.: Duke University Press, 2004).

86. See www.sec.gov/answers/mortgagesecurities.htm (accessed August 10, 2011).

87. "Over the Counter, Out of Sight," *Economist*, November 12, 2009, www.economist.com/node/14843667.

88. Caitlin Zaloom notes that at the same time this also "creates an opportunity to transform the social arrangement of the market, bringing in the women and minorities whose identity-based 'perspectives' now orient the collectivity of the market" (Zaloom, "Markets and Machines: Work in the Technological Sensoryscapes of Finance," *American Quarterly* 58.3 [2006]: 827).

89. Jyotsna Kapur, "Capital Limits on Creativity: Neoliberalism and Its Uses of Art," *Jump Cut: A Review of Contemporary Media*, no. 53, Summer 2011, www.ejumpcut.org/currentissue/kleinhans-creatIndus/index.html.

90. Ibid.

91. Zaloom, "Markets and Machines," 815–37.

92. K. Knorr Cetina and U. Bruegger, "Global Microstructures: The Virtual Societies of Financial Markets," *American Journal of Sociology* 107.4 (2002): 924.

93. Chakravartty and Schiller, "Global Financial Crisis."

94. Martin, *Financialization of Daily Life*, 123.

95. Emphasis added. Zaloom, "Markets and Machines," 833; see also Donald MacKenzie and Yuval Millo, "Negotiating a Market, Performing Theory: The Historical Sociology of a Financial Derivatives Exchange," *American Journal of Sociology* 109.1 (2003): 108; Michel Callon, ed., *The Laws of the Markets* (Oxford: Blackwell, 1998), 2.

Coloring in the Bubble: Perspectives from Black-Oriented Media on the (Latest) Economic Disaster

Catherine R. Squires

> Part of our contemporary crisis is created by a lack of meaningful access to truth . . . [and] our capacity to face reality is severely diminished as is our will to intervene and change unjust circumstances.
>
> —bell hooks, "A Revolution of Values:
> The Promise of Multicultural Change"

The subprime crisis was caused by a cascade of factors that include radical deregulation of the financial markets; corruption within and across financial institutions; a mix of irresponsible and inaccurate reporting on the housing market boom; and plain old human vices like greed.[1] Many have claimed since the bubble burst in 2007–8 that they saw it coming, but had insufficient influence or power to change the minds of the Wall Street titans and federal investigators who should have known better. While it is worthwhile for historians to chronicle exactly which signs were misread, why whistleblowers were dismissed, and who was responsible, the question we face now is how do we remedy the extreme losses and prosecute the now-proved illegal practices that led to the worst economic fallout since the Great Depression? More specifically for this essay, how do black media account and suggest remedies for the fact that disproportionate numbers of African American homebuyers and neighborhoods have suffered the worst effects of the subprime debacle?

The crisis is not just a matter of governmental financial regulation; the ways in which our watchdog press fell asleep on the job is indicative of a broader, problematic cultural shift to neoliberal, postracial discourses. These ideologies have become normalized and entrenched in many parts of the mediated public sphere, as well as government-sponsored discourses of economic and social policy.[2] None of the dominant media outlets—whether broadcast, cable, print, or online—waved sufficient red flags about the burgeoning bubble. As hooks's quote suggests, we continue to be in dire need of intellectual, critical, and popular spaces where quality information about the economy and racial inequality can engage wider publics. Traditionally, the black public sphere has supported such spaces, fostering oppositional economic thought in critiques of racial capitalism, imperialism, and antilabor practices. This history suggests that existing black media outlets should provide more alternatives to the neoliberal depictions of the crisis found in most mainstream news and financial media.

Given the depth of the corruption and the near complete lack of oversight and prosecution exercised during the Bush era, it is unclear whether one could have reasonably expected newspapers and magazines with fewer investigative resources, personnel, and financial support than players like CNBC or the *New York Times* to break the stories that would have fostered more skepticism of Alan Greenspan or SEC practices. What we could reasonably expect, given the black press's legacy of critiques of capitalist excesses and racial discrimination in the marketplace, is that some significant proportion of black-oriented media would be on the front lines offering alternative, progressive responses to the crisis and its related racial disparities once the bubble burst. That is, for those publications that promote themselves as serving underserved black audiences, we need to ask to what extent their discussions of the impact of the subprime crisis on black communities and the prescribed means to recover from it focus on neoliberal and postracial strategies, or race-aware, progressive understandings of community action and the continuing operation of racist practices in the marketplace.

This essay explores how assorted black-oriented media responded to the subprime crisis. First, I summarize discussions of the ways postracial and neoliberal discourses are intertwined, promoting a view of empowered, multicultural individuals now unhindered by racism, free to maximize their choices to reap consumer comforts. Second, I discuss the historical role of the black press in producing and circulating a range of counterdiscourses of capitalism and consumer identities in black public spheres. In that section, I also outline the changing landscape of black-oriented news media and lay out questions about the impact of new technologies and altered economic configurations on black media. Third, I analyze how three black-oriented news outlets—*Black Enterprise*, TheRoot.com, and *Colorlines*—framed the subprime crisis and relevant actions readers should take in its wake. These media outlets were chosen to explore if and how different models of economic and institutional support result in varying approaches to describing the subprime crisis and its disproportionate impact on black home owners. Looking across a set of different types of informational media that emerged in the post–civil rights era may provide some coordinates for where neoliberal logics have been incorporated into black media vehicles set up ostensibly to provide information and opinions not widely circulated in dominant media and public spheres. Finally, I reflect on the comparison of the three outlets and suggest other lines of inquiry.

Postracial, Neoliberal Media: People of Color "Choosing" to Fail

A growing group of scholars have described the emergence of "postracial" discourses in American media. Mainstream media serve up visions of a society that has already reaped sufficient benefits from the civil rights movements of the mid-twentieth century and needs no more government or social activism to achieve equal opportunity.[3] This vision of an already achieved multicultural nation draws on neoliberal assumptions of market individualism, where race/ethnicity presents us with specific kinds of choices to be negotiated: whether to display or not display racial affinities, whether to consume or not consume the cultural products of other groups.[4] I concur with those scholars and political commentators who have argued that postracial is a naive term at best and a product of cynical strategizing at worst. Postracial popular discourses emerged at a time when the human genome project "proved" that there are not "different races"; that we humans are more alike than different; that race is a social construct, not a constituent element of humanity. However, as Eric K. Watts summarizes, "Treating 'race' as merely a social construction misses a crucial facet of its nature; the power of tropes of race . . . [that are] coded into the institutions we inhabit and the social relations regulated by them. . . . Saying that 'race' is a 'fiction' does very little to disable its vigorous affects."[5]

Postracial discourse obfuscates the continued oppressiveness of institutional racism by highlighting individual-level identity choices, thereby dovetailing with neoliberal discourses that place the blame for continuing racial and economic inequalities on individuals who, ostensibly, just made the wrong choices for themselves and/or their families.

Helene Shugart demonstrates how the synergies of neoliberal and postracial logics are on display in television shows such as *Judge Joe Brown*. The failures and foibles of the largely African American, Latina/o, and poor white litigants are contrasted with the bootstrapping life story and harsh advice of Judge Brown, an African American who exhorts personal responsibility as the route out of their troubles. Brown and his reality TV judge counterparts consistently employ racist and sexist stereotypes as they viciously impugn the morals and life paths of the participants in the trials. Poverty, unemployment, single parenthood, and lack of connections with economic means are explained as the result of poor choice making and failure to educate oneself.[6] Similarly, when reports of sky-high foreclosures in black and Latino neighborhoods filled the headlines, many commentators in the news framed the issue in terms of the failure of black and Latina/o homebuyers to educate themselves on "the fine print" or to choose the best mortgage deal. The evidence of fraudulent loan practices, redlining, and discriminatory rate-setting was swept aside in favor of a neoliberal, postracial view of a marketplace that faltered only because of inexperienced or greedy individuals. Whereas the banks were "too big to fail," the disproportionate number of people of color with mortgage woes seemed doomed to failure in these accounts.

In an earlier analysis of mainstream coverage of the crisis, I found that many dominant news articles framed the subprime crisis as the result of bad decisions by ignorant borrowers and shady lenders. For example, in early 2008, the *Los Angeles Times* printed a masthead editorial titled "How to Spell Solvency." After acknowledging that redlining had denied housing opportunities to "people solely based on race, sex, surname, or address" in the "not-so-distant past," the editors proclaimed that the subprime crisis was a function of a new pathology: financial illiteracy. "This time around, we're limited by too many choices rather than too few . . . financial illiteracy is the new redlining."[7] Other stories that focused on statistical reports, lawsuits, and proposed legislation ping-ponged between quotes from mortgage bankers and their allies and statements made by fair housing activists and victims. But striving for "balance" does not necessarily result in an accurate picture of what the data show and what the realities on the ground mean. For example, the *New York Times* printed two articles about studies by the Center for Responsible Lending.[8] In these stories, journalists "balanced" hard data from the reports with denials and opinions from mortgage lenders and conservative think-tanks, who argued subprime lenders were only guilty of "expanding homeownership by going into neighborhoods not served by others."[9] None of the comments from business people or their conservative allies utilized data to refute the studies.

Other commentators insisted that too much regulation—specifically the Community Reinvestment Act (CRA), which requires banks to invest in minority neighborhoods that were subjected to redlining—was the real cause of the crisis. One *New York Times* op-ed piece stated: "One cannot say with any certainty whether the more important cause . . . was affordable housing mandates or the actions of investment banks and investment agencies."[10] It concluded that the nation "can't afford" aspects of the CRA and that the modern system of credit scores allow banks and other lenders to evaluate "the merits of individual households" in a colorblind fashion, so they will not need any government agencies "to push lenders to make loans just to please regulators." These samples from mainstream news not only deny racial discrimination in the *current* housing and mortgage markets, they place blame on consumers of color, who are financially illiterate, and color-aware policies that try to remedy racism. Although there were some editorials and comments in news articles that suggested institutional causes and remedies, for the most part mainstream news responses hewed to neoliberal frames.

Black Public Spheres and Counterdiscourses

As I have argued elsewhere, the question is not whether there is a black public sphere—there exist multiple black publics in the diaspora; rather, the question is, under current conditions, are the institutions of any particular black public sphere providing discursive and other resources that foster counterpublic consciousness that precedes coordinated political activism?[11] In the face of the subprime crisis, then, we might ask, are black-oriented media institutions—those set up to serve black publics—providing sufficient discursive resources to deconstruct and resist the neoliberal, postracial framing of the crisis that dominated mainstream media? Moreover, in deconstructing those discourses, are black-oriented media providing black publics with alternative understandings of the origins of the crisis and suggestions for community-based responses or strategies to remedy the economic hardships that disproportionately harm and undermine black and Latino communities?

Perhaps one could argue that, in the era of strict legal and social segregation, the "counter" of the black public sphere was easier to constitute, as people of African descent could readily agree on the evils and absurdities of de jure racism. Although black publics have always contained multiple approaches to the question of gaining freedom, the nadir of the 1950s–1960s civil rights struggles brought momentous accomplishments and highly visible differences on how to go forward. As Amin Ghaziani writes, social movement theorists have focused mostly on how oppositional groups assert their differences in the process of fighting for redistributive justice; but in the era of the proliferating "posts" (postfeminist, -racial, -gay), there has been more emphasis—reinforced by radical visions of individualism and backlash against freedom movements—on sameness rather than difference.[12] But appeals to "we're more alike than different" and "working within the system" resonate with the conclusion that the legal gains won in the 1960s provided the necessary and sufficient conditions for all individuals to compete in the marketplace on equal footing without need for state intervention. Moreover, any attention to racial/ethnic/gender/sexual difference should be the result of individual choice making, not collective action.

From this perspective, any discomfort or discrimination experienced by people of color, gays and lesbians, or heterosexual women of any color are the result of bad choice making, not institutional practices. Asserting that discrimination has occurred usually results in accusations that the victim is "playing the race card" or taking things too seriously, not having a sense of humor. Thus, as black publics debate when, how, and to what degree racial identity still matters, we need to discern when and where discussions of racial inequalities in black publics resonate with neoliberal and postracial discourses that dominate public discussions of race. That is, how are dominant neoliberal and postracial discourses affecting what Houston Baker refers to as "the active working imagination" of a black public sphere?[13] It is in the imagination where visions of resistance emerge, where tactics and strategies are crafted, where different subjectivities and futures are designed. What options are imagined in black media and presented to black audiences, then, is a pertinent question, and we cannot assume that the answers will contain the same range of counterdiscourses over time and across intragroup differences.

From the Great Society to the Ownership Society

Many historians and sociologists have recounted the uneven impact of the deindustrialization of the U.S. economy on black and Latino workers and communities.[14] The shift from production to service/consumption was accompanied by the resurgence of right-wing political gains and economic policies that worsened the already fragile position of those in the black middle class and decimated working-class communities. From Richard Nixon's 1970s lip-service to black capitalism to Ronald Reagan's 1980s demonization of the "welfare queen" to Clinton's promise to "end welfare as we know it," successive administrations undercut the fledgling programs of the Great Society. Democrats like Clinton often couched their "reforms" of public programs as necessary compromises to regain "independent" white voters; Republicans framed their policies in the name of reinstilling "American values" of thrift, entrepreneurialism, and hard work. Discourses of "modern racism," or what some called "cultural racism," replaced biological reasoning for the economic subordination of African Americans with the argument that "black culture" was "pathological" and not securely assimilated to "American" bootstrapping values.[15] Exceptional black people who retrained themselves to dissociate from that pathology might succeed, but government intervention was not necessary because it was doomed to fail given the black cultural morass.

In the 2000s President George W. Bush, under the tutelage of strategists who realized the demographic changes in the United States required, at the very least, a less rabid discourse on race and ethnicity, introduced the ideas of "compassionate conservatism" and the "ownership society" as vehicles to bring more people of color into the middle class (and hopefully, the GOP).[16] Bush articulated a vision of citizenship through property and stock ownership. As Robert Asen writes, Bush's formulation of citizenship as ownership positions the owner-citizen as someone who "keeps an eye on Washington" but does not participate in governance herself. "In this way, President Bush circumscribed the agency of participants, construing a passive mode of citizenship . . . a separation of seeing from knowing and doing."[17] In the ownership society, the most important thing an American citizen can do is invest in the marketplace in order to demonstrate and "see" her "stake" in the country, but what she should do if she sees malpractice in the marketplace or government is unclear. Here the problem with people of color is that they have not been part of the owner class, and so public policies should support their entry into it. Not only does this approach dovetail with neoliberal scorn for the commons, but also it suggests that "ownership is a necessary condition of political participation," and attempts by nonowners to be part of political debate are illegitimate.[18] Moreover, Bush's proposals neither addressed nor redressed the stark realities of wealth disparities, employment discrimination, and financial redlining that keep so many people of color out of the ownership class, let alone the fact that many of the financial products being sold required access to complex mathematical and statistical skills.[19] Pretending that all "average Americans" could easily navigate and master Wall Street or the mortgage markets without regulatory or educational support, the "compassionate conservative" approach requires significant amnesia about the realities of race and class in the United States.

The Black Press and Capitalism's Excesses

The black press has often promoted counternarratives to laissez-faire capitalism, from antislavery arguments about the corruptness of making humans commodities to socialist warnings about unfair labor conditions and imperialism. Many writers in the black press have crafted insightful, fierce critiques of how racism plays a role in the exploitative aspects of capitalism and the dangers of too little oversight.[20] Columnists during both World Wars accused the United States and its European allies of speaking double-talk about democracy while oppressing people of color worldwide via colonial domination.[21] Daily and weekly black papers in labor strongholds such as Detroit supplied regular critiques of capitalist excesses and stood for workers' rights in the 1930s and 1940s.[22] The editor and activist Charlotta Bass's *California Eagle* provided consistent support for socialism and labor actions.[23] In the 1960s, periodicals such as *Freedomways* and, most famously, the Black Panther Party's paper issued scathing critiques of racist capitalism and imperialism.[24]

Aside from a few specialty periodicals, such as the *Messenger*, most of the daily and monthly black publications contained a mix of economic ideologies and advice. At the same time that papers trumpeted the rights of everyday laborers, they also lavished attention on the material successes of black athletes and actors, and schooled their readers in the ways of bourgeois norms and tastes. The *Chicago Defender*, *Ebony*, and other widely circulated periodicals celebrated the exploits and consumptive choices of the small but growing black bourgeoisie in the postwar era, prompting E. Franklin Frazier to dismiss the press as an engine of wish fulfillment and magical thinking.[25] Along with the focus on consumption, many papers advocated self-reliance, whether drawing from ideas popularized by Booker T. Washington after Reconstruction or pursuing separatist strategies like Marcus Garvey's *Black World* and the Nation of Islam's *Final Call* (or a mix of both). Many black periodicals contained regular admonitions to create a class of black entrepreneurs, "buy black," and win the game of capitalism in order to foster self-sufficiency in black communities. These trends continue in publications such as *Essence*, which fields column after column on self-help style articles, and local weeklies like *N'Digo*, which focuses on the up-and-coming business owners, fund-raisers, and trendsetters in black Chicago.

While the emphases on consumption and self-help may be lopsided, especially in larger commercial entities such as the Johnson family's magazine empire, others have pointed out that there are other ways to read the focus on fashion and celebrity in the black press. Maren Stange argues that *Ebony* magazine's focus on what its editors referred to as "the happy side of Negro life" provided different points of identification for black readers who were not used to seeing respectful visions of their faces, bodies, and homes in newspapers. The photos of middle- and upper-class black life in its pages provided an important alternative to the usual visual representations of black people as "spectacular and/or degraded Others." In its focus on consumption and entertainment, its photos "naturalized and sanctioned [black images] of respectability, achievement, and American national identity."[26] Roopali Mukherjee summarizes work that asserts a political dimension to black conspicuous consumption. For example, scholars have argued that whites' violent reactions to black property ownership and ability to buy a wider range of consumer goods demonstrate that many whites viewed black material gain as a threat to what was once an unambiguous marker of white superiority: the ability to consume rather than to be an object of consumption.[27] Others emphasize that as the black middle class grew in the postwar era, performing consumption signified its claims to equal citizenship in American society.

Discourses and images of wealth and consumption are multivalent and incorporated in different, unpredictable ways by audiences. Whether considering different images of black selves or contemplating the ability to be equal via consumption choices, these practices constitute part of the "imaginary" work Baker describes, albeit it is not always as explicitly political as boycotts or sit-ins as some might want to see. I would, however, like to suggest that we must pay particular attention to how black consumption choices are presented to other publics. Mukherjee describes how hypervisible black wealth has been used to argue against the need for social justice programs. Here black wealth is offered as "proof of the democratizing power of consumerism [and is] a ready shorthand for cultural transformations toward the post-racial."[28] Simultaneously, the same displays of consumption are framed as excessive and/or tacky, repathologizing black choice-making abilities by reviving "age-old scripts that black Americans are, at base, ill-equipped to manage wealth and are deserving of racist ridicule" and white consumer avoidance.[29] Indeed, some advertising firms and high-end brands have expressed the fear that too many black clients will scare away white patrons or devalue the brand.[30]

Given the continued racialized understandings of consumer behavior, it is imperative that we interrogate the types of discourse that result when a major financial meltdown disproportionately affects black people. If it is so easy for dominant voices to delegitimate the choices of *rich* blacks who can afford "bling," it's reasonable to predict that those same voices will be quick to demonize those who lost their homes after the bubble burst. The question then becomes, how do media institutions that address a black public respond to the crisis and dominant discourses of the crisis? We should ask, what responses do they imagine will best serve those who have been hit hardest, and what do their communities and the nation need to do—if anything—to make it right? In short, do black-oriented media offer collective or individualistic means for understanding the crisis and what it will take to prevent another?

Black-Oriented Media: Continued Relevance and Negotiations in the Multicultural Marketplace

I argue that the public should have access to black-oriented publications that feel an obligation to provide counterdiscourses to audiences. Importantly, many black citizens continue to seek and expect alternative information and opinions from black media, and express greater trust in black media.[31] Research on black audiences continues to suggest that many black people hold reservations about how "mainstream" media depict black individuals and communities.[32] Media economists also note that black audiences are underserved in the marketplace (particularly broadcast) and are undervalued by advertisers. Black-oriented media, therefore, continue to fill a need, addressing the continued reluctance of dominant media firms to expand their offerings for audiences that desire more black-focused cultural or information content. This does not mean, however, that the traditional black press has not been affected by either the economic or sociocultural changes that occurred since the end of de jure segregation. As Armistead Pride and Clint Wilson III document, from the 1960s to the 1980s scores of black newspapers went out of business because of changes in opportunities for black writers and editors as well as competition from television news.[33] Likewise, deregulation of broadcasting in the 1990s led to decreases in the small gains in black television and radio ownership that occurred in the 1970s. This is not to romanticize how segregation created a larger "natural" market for black-owned and -oriented news products; rather, it illustrates how the shifting of media habits and the unpredictable structures of new opportunities for consumers and producers of black news led to radical changes in the fortunes of the black media, but not the elimination of black-owned or -oriented media. As evidenced in the explosion of Web sites and success of new glossy monthlies, black-oriented media continue to draw significantly large and diverse audiences.

As Anna Everett writes, "It is not difficult to regard the black press's new guard as the proverbial Phoenix arisen from the ashes" of its predecessors.[34] Some of the "new guard" imagine themselves reshaping the black media to fit the aesthetic expectations of black people (what Neal would call the "post-soul" generation) raised on "integrated" media.[35] For example, Everett quotes *Black Enterprise*'s 1989 explanation that "'the end of civil rights and the advent of integration have spawned a generation of young black adults who are unimpressed with black papers that don't display the spit and polish of mainstream newspapers.'"[36] The Internet, with its lower cost of production and ever-changing modes of advertising and fund-raising methods, provides a more-level playing field than the glossy magazines, full-color newsprint operations, or television studios. Simultaneously, many media firms are pursuing "multicultural" audiences, reading the tea leaves of demographic projections and repositioning themselves to provide content to different slices of the audience. Thus, as traditional black news media find footholds online, Everett argues that the "new guard" of black-oriented digital media makes clear "the fact that new conditions of digital production have radically altered the nature and status of black publication."[37] I would add that we must recognize that the new guard is made up of those who seek to continue old traditions and make new ones, as well as entrepreneurs whose drive to get into black media markets is connected not to traditions of protest and solidarity with black people but to visions of fragmented ethnic audiences with varying levels of disposable income to be delivered to advertisers.

Everett focuses on the online publications that explicitly devote themselves to carrying on the advocacy traditions as a way to delimit "an otherwise endless and unreliable slide of racial signification" by sampling "websites established by legitimate and prominent" black-owned presses.[38] This essay follows her caution that it is not possible to glean a set of "authentic" black press institutions online, given the exponential number of search terms and results one might get from a search for "black news." However, instead of turning only to well-established, black-owned and -oriented publications that have migrated online, this essay looks to sample from black-oriented publications that represent different configurations of ownership and financial support while still avowing service to black communities and allies of black communities.

Today, trends in multicultural marketing encourage this embrace of capitalism as racial uplift. *Ebony* founder John H. Johnson is considered a pioneer for creating black upscale publications to convince advertisers that black consumers were worth their attention. Today, multiculturalism in advertising is "common sense" and produces often contradictory partnerships in black-oriented media. Affirmative action reforms in hiring have led to internal and external diversity specialists, navigating community relations as well as watching trends to stay ahead of the market.[39] Firms develop specific appeals for different demographic groups, hiring specialty "diversity marketing" consultants or subcontractors to focus attention on black consumers and to translate "ethnic" cultures across racial, ethnic, and national lines. Some think these efforts reek of tokenism; others see true efforts at diversifying a field that continues to face lawsuits and protests over discrimination in hiring, as well as continued dismay at the often stereotypical representations in advertising.[40]

Much of the critical scholarship on diversity marketing and African Americans is focused on how the entertainment and fashion industries have appropriated and resold black popular culture to global audiences. Paul Gilroy aptly reminds us that this development is not a result of a "pure" oppositional culture being exploited by cynical corporations. Certainly, many of these transactions are suspect; however, black individuals and institutions have profited from these developments and often articulate their success with rubrics of black self-determination. Gilroy suggests Spike Lee's partnership with advertising behemoth DDB Needham exemplifies how black cultural producers serve as a "hip cultural vanguard in the business of difference" in an era when "the appeal of black faces and styles need no longer be restricted to black consumers."[41] Thus Spike Lee's articulation of his work (40Acres+AMule) with reparations and black social activism provides the street credibility that corporations need to develop and sell products to the multicultural, youth-oriented marketplace. Lee helps Needham translate black culture into a "marketable 'reading'" for audiences outside black communities.[42]

Lee's elite position reflects some of the multifaceted ways in which "diversity" has changed corporate media tactics for selling goods and establishing brands. Activists have long called for more aggressive integration in the media industries to rectify decades of discrimination and misrepresentations; hiring Lee and other black executives is part of the "diversity work" response to protest movements. It also achieves public relations benefits: firms trumpet their efforts to diversify their workforce, to reach out to and serve marginalized communities of color. One way to communicate business commitments to diversity is through advertisements in "ethnic" and alternative media. This has the potential to amplify contradictions in the black press, traditionally a watchdog for African Americans against racism and exploitation, much of which has been perpetrated by corporations. Where the neoliberalism and postracial multiculturalism combine to provide opportunities for black publications, it may result in pitfalls for their audiences.

Even as black culture is appropriated to sell goods and services to multiple demographic segments, media economists have shown that advertisers continue to undervalue black-oriented media and their audiences.[43] Whereas the elite-focused financial media discussed earlier have lucrative advertising opportunities given the income level and status of their core audience, black-oriented media have to work harder to gain and maintain advertising revenues, often depending on down-market items to make ends meet.[44] Hence there is an overrepresentation of unhealthy products and dubious services advertised in black media; from hard liquor to cigarettes and fast food, many activists have argued that firms are targeting vulnerable communities with toxic products, contributing to skyrocketing rates of cancer, obesity, diabetes, and other public health nightmares.[45]

The lack of consistent or lucrative advertising revenue means that black papers are less able than their mainstream news counterparts to pay for the kind of investigative and in-depth reporting needed to cover complex issues.[46] As such, overtures from large corporations to place "diversity" ads are often welcome, even if the products or services are not beneficial to black communities. From McDonald's ads that celebrate Black History Month to Wells Fargo and Freddie Mac ads touting black home ownership, various firms buy ad space in black media to promote their identities as equal opportunity employers and friendly to black consumers. Dependence on toxic ads and corporate PR results in contradictory messages: articles on obesity or asthma rates among black children reside a few pages away from ads for a McDonald's training camp for aspiring black franchisers or Kool cigarettes.

One might imagine, then, that interaction with and dependence on the advertising industry could result in neoliberal explanations for the housing bubble in the black press. However, these news media derive some, if not all, of their legitimacy from the tradition of speaking to and for the interests of black publics. While some editors may translate those interests through the lens of neoliberalism, not all do or will. Being close to the experiences and political interests of their communities and articulating those interests when mainstream media do not are the two main advantages that media serving black people might retain. So some outlets will interpret neoliberalism as a bane, others as a boon, depending on their assessment of audience opinions and desires. Moreover, as all news media rethink business models in the Internet era, some people of color-oriented media have gravitated toward different partnerships and funding streams in response to the economic realities and opportunities brought by the Web. While many of these outlets have been affected by the same social and market forces that encourage neoliberal framing, that does not guarantee those frameworks will dominate reporting to black publics.

Although collective and historical experiences with racism in the market are not a sufficient buffer to neoliberalism, they suggest a space for resistance exists in at least some media outlets serving black publics. The next section of this essay provides examples of how black-oriented news outlets have responded to the subprime crisis, highlighting places where neoliberal discourses mesh with black capitalist yearnings and places where critiques emerged of neoliberalism and its collusion with race-based target marketing. As with my earlier analysis of op-ed pages, both of these approaches exist in the pages of the black news; however, the different news vehicles described here illustrate how different models for producing black-oriented news may correlate with the range of critiques available to readers.

Responses to the Subprime Crisis in Black-Oriented News

I analyzed articles in three publications: *Black Enterprise* (*BE*), TheRoot.com, and *Colorlines*. These three publications represent different approaches to survival in the news business. *BE* is a monthly, glossy magazine that targets a specialty market: upper-middle-class African Americans and aspirants, drawing revenue from a mix of subscription fees and advertising. In contrast, TheRoot. com is a Web-only publication and is not black-owned. It is a division of the *Washington Post*, one of the leading mainstream newspapers in the nation, and derives revenue from its parent corporation and advertising; there are no subscriptions. *Colorlines*, a paper and online magazine, is published by the Applied Research Center (ARC), a nonprofit research center that focuses on social and economic justice issues, as well as cultural trends, that affect communities of color. *Colorlines* is supported by the ARC and collects some moneys from newsstand sales of and subscriptions to the print version of the magazine. There are some advertisements in the pages of the print magazine, mainly from social justice organizations, independent presses, and other nonprofit institutions.

All three of these publications explicitly state commitments to black and other communities of color. *BE* pledges to connect with "African Americans who are serious about success" and, through its multiple media vehicles, to offer "a detailed, perceptive look at social forces and trends shaping modern African American life."[47] TheRoot.com highlights the "leadership of Professor Henry Louis Gates, Jr" in its founding and promises to "raise the profile of black voices in mainstream media."[48] Although *Colorlines* is not meant for only black readers, its spirit of advocacy for communities of color and the preponderance of articles about African Americans situate it in the tradition of the black press. Its tagline, "The National Magazine on Race and Politics," situates it as a go-to place for people interested in engaging with race issues.

Black Enterprise: *Neoliberalism with a Black Twist*

In January 2009 *Black Enterprise* proudly dispatched the "mantra" of its CEO, Earl "Butch" Graves Jr.: "Wealth building, from investing to entrepreneurship, is the key to the progression of African American professionals and entrepreneurs." With this mantra, the magazine describes its target readership: affluent and aspirant black Americans. And, in the next statement about the CEO's philosophies, *BE* declares wealth building is the key to ameliorating racial inequalities as well: "The ills that plague the African American community—whether they involve education, health, or technology—can largely be fixed by closing the wealth gap."[49] This conclusion provides the backdrop for *BE*'s announcement of a redesign and reboot of its "Black Wealth Initiative" to guide readers to "take the appropriate action to place you on to achieving your goals" in a sputtering economy. And with this flourish, *BE* energizes its African American spin on neoliberal faith in the market to always provide to those who work hard enough: black communities will make gains when individuals maximize opportunities to build wealth.

This is not to say that the wealth gap between whites and people of color is not troubling but that, as is made clear by *BE*'s other articles and editorials, the problem of the wealth gap is communicated mainly as a problem to be solved by individual effort, despite the fact that the gap was created by institutionally structured and sanctioned racism against individuals and communities. Some of the articles even emphasize how black individuals might even profit from the crisis.[50] It may be of little surprise that *BE* presents its readers with a black-oriented spin on neoliberalism, given its title and focus on the business world. What is shocking is the extent to which the magazine's editor and publisher discount and dismiss the role of financial institutions, as well as the lack of civil rights enforcement, in creating the crisis.

BE's publisher and CEO, in their regular letters to the readers, did acknowledge some residues of racism made the financial crisis hit black people harder than whites. They included statistics about disparities in subprime loans in their remarks, the magazine also featured one lengthy story about the credit crisis in the pages of the January 2009 edition that criticized conservative pundits' attempts to pin the blame on minorities. Publisher Earl Graves Sr. drew on visions of black fortitude and sacrifice to rally his readers' spirits. He noted that record layoffs and unemployment hit blacks harder, since they "often remain the last hired, first fired, or . . . are employed in dying industries." But he quickly turned away from these residues of structural racism to discuss individual efforts to survive financial meltdown. Graves compared his Depression-era childhood to the current time. He recounts how he witnessed his parents and their neighbors as they "maintained their households and advanced their families by scaling back on expenditures. . . . These times require you to demonstrate the same level of sacrifice. . . . It may mean forgoing the family vacation, carpooling, or devising a plan to generate new streams of income."[51]

Nowhere in his sentimental celebration of Depression-hardy black families is any inkling of the collective struggles for better livelihoods that blacks participated in during the 1930s and 1940s. Graves does not recognize that many black families survived the Depression because of labor agitation by the likes of A. Philip Randolph, which led to expanded job opportunities for African Americans during World War II. Reforms such as food aid programs, public housing, and Social Security are not named in Graves's reminiscence either. For Graves, the only lesson to be learned from that time of intensive black agitation is self-sufficiency. Nor are there any lessons about the deregulation of banking reforms set in place after the Depression to guard against the kind of financial disaster that has harmed the "disproportionate number of Black families in danger of losing their homes" he invoked in an earlier paragraph.

The absence of any references to structural factors that contributed to the crisis hitting African American communities continues in subsequent editorials by Graves Sr. and "Butch" Graves Jr. Indeed, in his December letter to readers, Graves Sr. lamented that Lehman Brothers might have to retract a $10 million gift to Spelman College to build a Center for Global Finance and Economic Development because of the meltdown, but without any sense that the financial giant was brought low by the corruption of its own and other banks' schemes that ensnared black home buyers.[52] Instead, he exhorted readers to stop paying attention to discussions of what the government might do to alleviate the burdens on citizen-consumers who lost so much in the crisis in favor of bootstrapping actions. "While the debate remains over what we can expect from our government in the way of bailouts and economic stimuli . . . our most immediate source of economic relief lies not in what might be done for us, but in what we are willing to do for each other." And what might that be? Giving donations to charities and shopping at black businesses. Generating support for progressive economic policies and petitioning Congress to reinstate bank reforms demolished by neocons, apparently, is not something we can do for each other.

Butch Graves likewise brushed aside questions of the government's responsibilities in the financial crisis with ease—and with venom toward individual home owners. Citing "public resentment" toward home owners who "purchased properties they couldn't afford," Graves Jr. went on to "unequivocally stress that taxpayers should not subsidize irresponsible behavior. Even though he admitted that the crisis was severe enough that some government intervention was necessary, in his editorial he named no alternative policies to those put forth by the outgoing Bush administration or those of the Obama team. Instead, he chastised a "segment of the American public—including some readers of this magazine—" who, apparently, believe that Obama's election "means that their debts will be absolved." Those folks, he continues, are facing foreclosure because they wanted to "keep up with the Joneses" and used "credit cards to finance a posh lifestyle."[53]

Graves Jr.'s defamation of the character of "some readers" of *BE* is all the more galling—and ironic—because in the same issue, the magazine printed a letter from a reader who praised *BE* for its January 2009 news feature on the credit crisis. The writer congratulated *BE* journalists for exposing the faults in the conservative pundits' accusations that blacks and Latinos were irresponsible borrowers. She concluded, "Now more than ever, 'our' print media must keep us informed and educated."[54] Her feedback, though, and the content of the earlier exposé were continually undermined and contradicted by the advice given to readers by the magazine's leaders and columnists. Graves Jr. continued the drumbeat of blame the victims in another "Executive Memo," where he lambasted black home owners for not taking "serious action to correct their finances or sell their homes due to an emotional attachment . . . or a false idea of what it's worth." He advised underwater home owners to be like his family: "My parents' generation believed when you bought a home, you didn't try to time the real estate market. . . . It may seem old school, but we all need to embrace the basics of homeownership."[55] That the housing market—regardless of pricing of individual homes—was at its lowest ebb in decades was irrelevant and went unmentioned. Rather, the bad choices and irrational behavior of home owners were to blame for houses languishing on the market.

While wrapped in the rhetoric of doing the right thing for black families and communities, these missives from the editors of *BE* replicated and reinforced the worst of the neoconservative blame games that circulated in the mainstream press. The sprinkling of references to black fortitude in the face of hardship and championing of black entrepreneurship merely recycled the faulty assumptions of an earlier black capitalist advocate who put the burden of effort on the shoulders of blacks individuals: Booker T. Washington. From one Gilded Age to another, we find believers in the market who are fond of telling black people that if they only strive hard enough, they will prosper in America and insulate themselves from any racial problems that may exist. Any deviation from the path of hard work and self-improvement is folly. Pursuing politics is a sign that one is looking for a handout or wants to be dependent on others for well-being. When contrasted with writings in TheRoot.com and *Colorlines*, *BE*'s advice rings quite hollow, and its diagnoses and advice look ridiculous.

TheRoot.com

TheRoot.com writers were much more concerned about the racial disparities in lending than their *BE* colleagues. They provided evidence from studies and investigations that showed redlining and steering, as well as the use of repugnant racial stereotypes by mortgage bankers themselves.

> First, mortgage industry defenders have repeatedly asserted that the wave of subprime and other exotic loans that flowed over black neighborhoods did plenty of good, too. It drove up the black home ownership rate to an historic high of nearly 50 percent (alongside a rapid increase in home ownership across the racial spectrum). As we now see, however, that gain was illusory. It was based upon predatory, unsustainable loans. . . .

Fewer than half of blacks and just 53 percent of Latinos owned homes. Subprime brokers preyed upon this disparity—which was created through generations of publicly financed discrimination in the lending market—and gave everyone the impression that housing equality was on its way. Well, it wasn't.[56]

Some writers at TheRoot.com, as with *BE*'s investigative piece, accused mainstream media for recirculating neoconservative talking points and racial resentment.

The offensive new vogue in cable TV talking points goes something like this: Wall Street is melting down because the government forced banks to make loans to poor people—especially poor minorities. . . .

The fake story line reintroduces the trope of the irresponsible welfare queen who was given a house but who was so stupid and unthankful as to lose it all in an entrepreneurial misadventure. . . .

The campaign to racialize a global financial meltdown operates in a fact-free zone. A national study of the performance of banks covered by the Community Reinvestment Act (CRA) shows that these government-backed banks were much less likely than other lenders to make the kinds of risky, high-cost home purchase loans that helped fuel the foreclosure crisis.[57]

Beyond demonstrating the dishonesty of the pundits, other writers took government regulators to task for being, at best, ignorant of what seems plain as day in hindsight: rampant racial bias and other corruption in mortgage lending.

It's not only low-income borrowers: A new mortgage study shows that wealthy blacks and Hispanics pay higher interest rates than wealthy whites and Asians. . . .

Why aren't federal investigators looking into how badly some banks have conducted their affairs? Indeed, if racial discrimination in mortgage lending is illegal and immoral, why do these banks seemingly display an even-handed level of racial and ethnic discrimination?

The simple reason is that nobody has demanded that they do better. There's no powerful lobby for minority banking customers. As outlined in a July report by the Center for Responsible Lending . . . "Consumer protection often went neglected, if anything, an afterthought or a box to check," the report said. "Federal regulators' failure to restrain abuses that led to today's credit crisis demonstrates the need for a single agency focused on protecting consumers to ensure financial institutions flourish in a sustainable way."[58]

Though the emphasis in most articles was on institutional wrongdoing and fingerpointing, a few articles on TheRoot.com focused on individual stories and financial advice in ways that resonated with *BE*'s conclusions about the subprime crisis: black people need to take care of it themselves. In an interview with Iyanla Vanzant, the Q&A began to take on a new-age spin on neoliberalism as they discussed how even a best-selling author could get caught in the crisis.

TheRoot: **You are a best-selling author, TV personality and attorney. What else was going on financially that prevented you from saving your home?**
Vanzant: I'm self-employed, and my income is tied to what I do on a daily basis. My daughter had been diagnosed with a fatal form of cancer, and I had gone through a very painful divorce. . . .

TheRoot: **You, Michelle Singletary and others on the panel implied that this crisis is not only a financial awakening in our country but a spiritual awakening.**
Vanzant: I think it's more of a spiritual awakening than anything else. For me it was very challenging, very painful, very difficult for having lost my daughter, my husband and my home. But that house was a thing. It was just a thing. And so some of us are fighting and struggling to hold on to things when we need to look at the other blessings that we have. . . . When I grew up, anytime family got in trouble, they came to our house. And they slept on the sofa, in the basement or we bunked up. Now you got four siblings, everybody has a townhouse and everybody's struggling. I say get one house; everybody bunk up together like we used to.[59]

Like the Graves, Vanzant draws on sentimental memories of resilient families scrimping and sacrificing to make things work. TheRoot.com's financial advice columnist, Stacey Tisdale, also mirrored *BE*'s advice-givers, telling readers that they had themselves to blame for not being "financially literate."

It's not just Wall Street; we have to stop being stupid about money.
It will be interesting to see how people reflect on this economic crisis in years to come. Will it be remembered for the trillions of dollars the government will likely throw at the problem before it's over? Will it be remembered for the failures of financial industry giants like Bear Stearns and Lehman Brothers? Will it be remembered as the era in which millions of people lost their homes due to the predatory practices of some unscrupulous lenders? Will it be the defining issue for a president past or future?
. . . Quite frankly, it's what I'm not hearing that is making me nervous. . . . At its heart, this financial crisis is a story of financial illiteracy: People signed up for mortgages they did not understand.[60]

In another column, Tisdale insisted that black consumers could get the right information to become "financially literate" from mainstream news sources— the same sources indicted by scholars and progressive media for facilitating the mortgage bubble. Like *BE*'s editors and writers, she insisted that thinking about what the feds might do was beside the point—it is all about self-education.

Struggling financially? It's up to you to get a clear picture of how to make ends meet.
. . .
While we hopefully wait for our leaders in Washington to bring financial education into the mainstream by requiring it at schools, Congresswoman Lee said, "financial education should be part of employee benefits at companies." But we can empower ourselves.

> There has never been an easier time to find the financial information you need. Web sites such as *Market Watch, CNN Money* and *Smart Money* have beefed up their sites with more emphasis on personal finance. Simple searches on the Internet, "minorities and mortgages," for example, can help get you information on how lenders are likely to treat you as well as fair market rates. There has never been more information on TV about financial issues, and newspapers are also overloaded with great info.[61]

This advice—to consult mainstream media for financial guidance—is incredibly suspect given the evidence that these same outlets initially served as cheerleaders for the unsustainable practices of the mortgage industry and have returned to largely uncritical acceptance of the market's logic.[62]

Clearly TheRoot.com does a better job undermining the main arguments of conservatives in mainstream news, and more consistently offered data and analysis from reports on the crisis than *BE*. However, even as it did so, it rarely strayed far from the types of sources that dominate the parent company's pages: business and government officials. Moreover, other than calling for additional consumer protections or enforcement of existing laws, writers did not promote progressive voices and ideas that went beyond the Beltway remedies. And, as will be clear in the comparison to *Colorlines*, TheRoot.com writers did not question the premise that home ownership is (usually) a win-win for individuals and society.

Colorlines: *Community Focus and Action*

Like TheRoot.com, *Colorlines* writers countered neoliberal discourses that blamed individual blacks and Latinos for their plight and the burst mortgage bubble. The magazine also spoke to the history of deregulation of the financial industry and how failures to pursue or prosecute civil rights violations during the Bush administration contributed to the crisis. The articles made heavy use of ARC reports and research by other progressive think tanks, as well as government sources, to back up their assertions that more than individual consumers have to be involved "before bad mortgage loans take down an economy."[63] Much of their data overlapped with studies cited by TheRoot.com.

What made the analytic and editorial contributions of *Colorlines* different from its counterparts was how writers articulated the need for a paradigm shift in housing policy, not just reforms of the mortgage system. *Colorlines* was the only magazine that asked the question, why should everyone strive to be home owners, and asked its readers to remember the days when the phrase "affordable housing" was in wider circulation. In an editor's letter titled "Remember Affordable Housing," Managing Editor Daisy Hernandez reminded readers that a lot of effort has gone into convincing "people that they want home ownership instead of affordable housing. And before that you have to sell them on notions of personal responsibility and the free market. . . . These families were okay and making it with Section 8, but when convinced to do home loans, got sucked in and now can't afford shelter—which they had access to before."[64]

By making a connection between neglect of affordable housing policies and misguided policies for expanding home ownership, Hernandez and other writers directly challenged the paradigm of home ownership as the cornerstone of the American Dream. Describing how families who were stable before predatory lenders descended on their communities, they debunk the myth that only home owners have an ability to save money, support their families, and take pride in their neighborhoods. Although some writers at TheRoot.com made brief mentions of HUD's role in the crisis, none of them questioned the premise that increasing home ownership is an absolute social good. *Colorlines*, in contrast, called for a paradigm shift from the assumptions of the "ownership society" to concerns about keeping communities on solid footing through housing policies that support neighborhoods no matter if they are inhabited by renters or owners.

Kai Wright pursued this by linking the subprime crisis to the overwhelming increases in poverty in the United States compared with the United Nations' campaign to decrease poverty. The statistics—nearly 44 million people in poverty since the crisis began—were so stark, Wright questioned how American leaders could continue to act as if recovery and progress were a sure thing. The idea that the "American Dream" would again be attainable by a majority of Americans was bankrupt, unless major changes in public policy were implemented to reverse these trends:

> Stop and try to digest this data: More than a third of all black and Latino kids are growing up destitute. With numbers like that, how can we talk meaningfully about a future of any kind, let alone a better one?[65]

This question asks the reader to rethink the grand narrative of progress and prosperity that anchors American exceptionalist discourse. Wright follows up by reminding readers that many of the 44 million were "most vulnerable to the housing market predation that pushed the country's economy off the cliff. We now know that banks wrote bad loans deliberately, and that regulators ignored ample real-time signs."[66] America did not present a level playing field to these aspiring home owners: what was exceptional about the crisis was how predatory and callous the institutions of the market and government were as the most vulnerable people tried to achieve the Dream.

As they called into question the underpinning assumptions of the American Dream, *Colorlines* writers often wove in a "miner's canary" approach to the subprime crisis that was completely absent in *BE* and rarely available in The-Root.com. In *The Miner's Canary*, Lani Guinier and Rodolfo Torres illustrate how racial inequalities are indicative of broader social problems that, in fact, all Americans pay for and suffer from.[67] The fact that whites and people of color share these problems can be seen best when one imagines our society as a coal mine, with racial minorities as the canaries, and dominant white groups as the miners. The canary, whose extrasensitivity to noxious gases informs all occupants of the mine that the environment has gone bad, always suffers from the problem first. Once the miners and others see the canary suffering, the best course of action is to heed the warning and figure out how to fix or change the environment.

For example, in an article that returned to check in on a family who lost their Detroit home, Seth Freed Wessler drew on the ARC's "Race and Recession" report to convey the connection between the nation's economic health and the health of marginalized communities of color. "The report finds that the economic crisis is not only impacting communities of color at disproportionate rates, but that the country's long failure to address systematic racial inequity through public policy threw the whole economy into free-fall."[68] The advantage of *Colorlines'* connection to ARC is clear: data and analysis are at the ready for writers, whose online and printed discussions and translations of research on race provides readers with evidence to counter neoconservative and postracial claims about the market and public policy.

Finally, *Colorlines* was better at attaching its critiques and recommendations for policy reform to activism and organization on the ground. Some writers at TheRoot.com called for expressions of outrage; *BE* instructed readers to "create your own economic stimulus plan," *Colorlines* was unique in reporting on community organizations that worked for (or against) specific policy initiatives. Thus, where TheRoot.com sprinkled some stories with heart-wrenching accounts from individuals who lost their houses after their ARMs blew up, *Colorlines* followed on these narratives with descriptions of what some foreclosure victims were doing to solve their housing problems—solutions that were derived from interactions with grassroots organizations, nonprofits, and, sometimes, government bureaus.

Compare the profile of Vanzant, for example, with the words of Sam Jackson, featured in *Colorlines* magazine as he continued his fight to get back into housing after being displaced by Hurricane Katrina five years earlier: "'We had nowhere to stay when we got back, and I said, 'we should go and make some noise even though we had only a few residents here to protest,' Jackson recalls." The double whammy of the hurricane and the subprime crisis made it nearly impossible to find affordable housing when his family and friends returned home. Jackson and others organized a press conference and other protest events. Since then he has "traveled to Indonesia and Thailand as part of an international delegation to . . . share rebuilding strategies."[69] Thus *Colorlines*' article made the issue of housing about human rights and connected U.S. failures to a worldwide crisis in affordable, safe housing, a crisis made visible by humanmade and natural disasters.

Other stories featured the protests of the National People's Action and Maine People's Alliance outside banker meetings in Washington, D.C. Pictures like that of a multiracial group of home owners, marching with signs indicting the Wells Fargo "Stagecoach from Hell," were also published regularly in the online and print versions of the magazine.[70] By showcasing organized protests and a variety of policy demands, *Colorlines* was the only publication that provided readers with a sense of resistance and awareness of organizations and individuals who were working to change the system—or at least hold it accountable.

Closing Remarks

The three media outlets compared here represent different responses to the changing marketplace of "ethnic" segmentation, deregulation, and post–civil rights opportunities to address black audiences still underserved by "integrated, mainstream" media. The trends found here are troubling, especially for those who remain invested in the power of counterpublics and counterdiscourses to foster social action. Counterframing the subprime crisis is part of creating the means for promoting alternative policy solutions and opposing the neoliberal dogma that continues to be represented—often unchallenged—as economic common sense.

Certainly, *Colorlines* is not the only publication that gives readers access to more progressive policy debates and activism tools. However, given the pride of place and trust that publications oriented toward communities of color often enjoy, it is imperative for us to ask that they do more to foster innovative and imaginative alternatives to those easily accessed in dominant media. As *BE* and TheRoot.com suggest, the synergies between mainstream advertising, news, and "multicultural" publications provide opportunities to broaden access to voices of people of color, but this does not mean that the most progressive voices or counterframes will occupy those spaces opened up by desires to gain market share in communities long-neglected by corporate media. However, as

I have argued elsewhere, progressive scholars should take these For-Us-By-Us publications—whether they are run by corporations or nonprofits—up on their stated commitment to supporting communities of color. Contributing essays, analysis, and quotations to media that serve communities of color is one way to participate in wider counterpublic discussions, discussions that sorely need more explicit challenges to neoliberal and postracial discourses.

Reflecting on these findings, one thing that comes to mind is how they reveal different strategies for rearticulating goals and success for black publics in the post–civil rights era. In the long buildup to the movements of the 1950s and 1960s, black public success was articulated with visions of communal uplift, collective action, antiracist expression, and reconstruction of cultural images of blackness. For thinkers like bell hooks, one of the most corrosive effects of the neoconservative backlash and ideological turn of the past forty years is the emphasis on individualism and materialism as vehicles to equality. "After the slaughter of radical black men, the emotional devastation of soul murder and actual murder, many black people became cynical about freedom. They wanted something more tangible, a goal that could be attained."[71] In hooks's reckoning, too few black leaders continued to mine the habit of being critical of capitalism and its part in exploiting black labor. Instead, too many turned toward "black capitalism" and material success as a benchmark for liberation. Messages touting dignity via money and power circulated with much more ease than messages of gaining dignity via shared struggle and caring, whether in black-oriented or mainstream media. She identifies some of the problem in the fact that most successful black-oriented media outlets—print, electronic, or otherwise—have not given adequate space to counterhegemonic voices that might encourage new ways of seeing and defining dignity, success, and the good life.[72] Thus it is not only that, as Gandy observed, the devaluation of black audiences leads to fewer and lower-quality news or information media but also that the frameworks for explaining socioeconomic and political phenomena are constrained.

Online media resources, Cathy Cohen suggests, allow folks to "network" and through those connections invite people to take on specific political subjectivities.[73] The three publications evaluated here suggest particular ways of responding (or not responding) to the crisis hooks describes and invite readers to respond in particular ways to the individual material route to salvation offered by so many media outlets and cultural messages.[74] *Black Enterprise* deepens the channels running to the neoliberal positioning of black individuals, urging trust in the marketplace and counseling personal financial literacy. Financed by multinational corporate sponsors, it amplifies the message that the system works for everyone who is willing to be entrepreneurial enough. TheRoot.com's commentary and criticism gestures toward counterhegemonic discourse and action, but stops short of suggesting frameworks for collective action. Each of these news products leaves a vacuum in terms of programs for rethinking the economic situation and one's relation to it. *Colorlines*, in contrast, realizes a different type of networking via discussions of public protest and mobilization along with the critiques of the systemic failure and racial unfairness of the subprime market. This approach encourages audiences to imagine themselves not as individual players in the market but as people who share common experiences, outrage, and, most importantly, opportunities to join others to challenge the system.

Building up and sustaining oppositional consciousness is a long-term process of struggle, experimentation, frustrations, and incremental victories. In a multimedia system dominated by multinational firms, even the Internet is not a guarantee to the fostering and sustenance of opposition to neoliberal, postracial frameworks for understanding socioeconomic patterns and crises. Clearly the emergence of outlets such as *Colorlines*—as well as Web-born sites such as Colorofchange.org and the Adbusters-sponsored, new-media-realized Occupy Wall Street (OWS) phenomenon—showcases the incredible potential for publics to exchange and network via counterpublicity. Moreover, the rapid swell of support for OWS and popularity of "the 99%" as a clarion call for a return to fairness and regulation suggests an opportune moment for black (and all) media to reconsider how bold they can be in not only providing critiques of laissez-faire, neoliberal policies but also advocating alternatives and public action against the status quo. Scholars and activists should continue to examine media outlets that purport to serve black publics for evidence that these producers innovate in ways that reimagine black audience information needs and political desires. As OWS evolves, perhaps other black-oriented publications will reconsider the elements of capitalist critique that were more evident in the past. Articulating black standpoints on the fate of the 99% would, I gather, be welcome in many quarters of black public spheres.

Notes

1.   Simon Johnson and James Kwak, *Thirteen Bankers: The Wall Street Takeover and the Next Financial Meltdown* (New York: Pantheon Books, 2010); "Where Credit Is Due: A Timeline of the Mortgage Crisis," *Mother Jones*, July–August 2008, www.MotherJones.com.

2. An impressive number of scholars have been describing and unpacking the ways neoliberalism works in mainstream media. See Paula Chakravartty and Dan Schiller, "Neoliberal Newspeak and Digital Capitalism in Crisis," *International Journal of Communication* 4 (2010): 670–92; Henry Giroux, *Against the Terror of Neoliberalism* (Boulder, Colo.: Paradigm, 2008); Laurie Ouellette and James Hay, "Makeover Television, Governmentality, and the Good Citizen," *Continuum: Journal of Media and Cultural Studies* 22.4 (2008): 471–84; Aimee Carrillo Rowe, Sheena Malhotra, and Kimberly Perez, "The Rhythm of Ambition: Power Temporalities and the Production of the Call Center Agent in Documentary Film and Reality Television," in *Critical Rhetorics of Race*, ed. Kent Ono and Michael Lacey (New York: New York University Press, 2011), 197–213.

3. Roopali Mukherjee, "'Bling-Fling': Commodity Consumption and the Politics of the 'Post-Racial,'" in Ono and Lacey, *Critical Rhetorics of Race*, 178–96; Catherine Squires, *Dispatches from the Color Line: Multiracial Identity in the News* (Albany: State University of New York Press, 2007); Ralina Joseph, "'Hope Is Finally Making a Comeback': First Lady Reframed," *Communication, Culture, and Critique* 4.1 (2011): 56–77.

4. bell hooks, *Black Looks: Race and Representation* (Boston: South End, 1992); Mary Thompson, "'Learn Something from This!': The Problem of Optional Ethnicity on *America's Next Top Model*," *Feminist Media Studies* 10.3 (2010): 335–52; Traise Yamamoto, "Millennial Bodies," *Signs* 25.4 (2000): 1243–46.

5. Eric K. Watts, "The Nearly Apocalyptic Politics of Post-Racial America: Or, 'This Is Now the United States of Zombieland,'" *Journal of Communication Inquiry* 34 (2010): 216.

6. Helene Shugart, "Ruling Class: Disciplining Class, Race, and Ethnicity in Television Reality Court Shows," *Howard Journal of Communications* 17 (2006): 79–100.

7. Catherine Squires, "Bursting the Bubble: A Case Study of Counter-Framing in the Editorial Pages," *Critical Studies in Media Communication* 28.1 (2011): 28–47.

8. Erik Eckholm, "Black and Hispanic Homebuyers Pay Higher Interest on Mortgages, Study Finds," *New York Times,* June 1, 2006; Manny Fernandez, "Racial Disparity Found among New Yorkers with High-Rate Mortgages," *New York Times*, October 15, 2007.

9. Eckholm, "Black and Hispanic Homebuyers Pay Higher Interest."

10. Squires, "Bursting the Bubble."

11. Catherine R. Squires, "Rethinking the Black Public Sphere: An Alternative Vocabulary for Multiple Public Spheres," *Communication Theory* 12.4 (2002): 446–68.

12. Amin Ghaziani, "Post-gay Collective Identity Construction," *Social Problems* 58.1 (2011): 99–125.

13. Houston Baker Jr., "Critical Memory and the Black Public Sphere," in *The Black Public Sphere*, ed. Black Public Sphere Collective (Chicago: University of Chicago Press, 1995), 5–38.

14. Michael Dawson, "A Black Counterpublic? Economic Earthquakes, Racial Agendas, and Black Politics," in *The Black Public Sphere*, 199–227; Manning Marable, *The Great Wells of Democracy: The Meaning of Race in American Life* (New York: Basic Books, 2002); William Julius Wilson, *When Work Disappears: The World of the New Urban Poor* (New York: Knopf, 1996); Melvin Oliver and Tom Shapiro, *Black Wealth, White Wealth: A New Perspective on Racial Inequality* (New York: Routledge, 1997).

15. Robert Entman, "Manufacturing Discord: Media in the Affirmative Action Debate," *Press/Politics* 2 (1997): 32–51; Wahneema Lubiano, "Like Being Mugged by a Metaphor: Multiculturalism and State Narratives," in *Mapping Multiculturalism*, ed. Avery F. Gordon and Christopher Newfield (Minneapolis: University of Minnesota Press), 74–75; Michael K. Brown et al., *Whitewashing Race: The Myth of a Colorblind Society* (Berkeley: University of California Press, 2004); Patricia H. Collins, *Black Sexual Politics: African Americans, Gender, and the New Racism* (New York: Routledge, 2004).

16. Steven Teles, "The Eternal Return of Compassionate Conservatism," *National Affairs*, Fall 2009, 107–26.

17. Robert Asen, "The Ownership Society, or Bourgeois Publicity Revisited," in *Public Modalities: Rhetoric, Culture, Media, and the Shape of Public Life*, ed. Daniel C. Brouwer and Robert Asen (Tuscaloosa: University of Alabama Press, 2010), 122–23.

18. Ibid., 125.

19. Ibid., 123.

20. Theodore Vincent, ed., *Voices of a Black Nation: Political Journalism during the Harlem Renaissance* (Trenton, N.J.: Africa World Press, 1990); Cary Wintz, ed., *African American Political Thought, 1890–1930* (New York: Sharpe, 1996); Todd Vogel, "The New Face of Black Labor," in *The Black Press: New Literary and Historical Essays*, ed. Todd Vogel (New Brunswick, N.J.: Rutgers University Press), 37–54.

21. Penny Von Eschen, *Race against Empire: Black Americans and Anti Colonialism, 1937–1957* (Ithaca, N.Y.: Cornell University Press, 1997).

22. Henry Louis Suggs, ed., *The Black Press in the Middle West, 1865–1985* (Westport, Conn.: Greenwood, 1996).

23. Charlotta Bass, *Forty Years: Memoirs from the Pages of a Newspaper* (Los Angeles: Charlotta Bass, 1960); *The Black Press: Soldiers without Swords* (dir. Stanley Nelson; California Newsreel, 1998).

24. Jane Rhodes, *Framing the Black Panthers: The Spectacular Rise of a Black Power Icon* (New York: New Press, 2007); Esther Cooper Jackson, ed., *The Freedomways Reader: Prophets in Their Own Country* (Boulder, Colo.: Westview, 2000).

25. E. Franklin Frazier, *The Black Bourgeoisie* (Glencoe, Ill.: Free Press,1957).

26. Maren Stange, "Photos Taken in Everyday Life": *Ebony's* Photojournalistic Discourse," in Vogel, *Black Press*, 208.

27. Mukherjee, "'Bling Fling,'" 184.

28. Ibid., 180–81.

29. Ibid., 186.

30. Leonard Baynes, "White Out: The Absence and Stereotyping of People of Color by the Broadcast Networks in Prime Time Entertainment Programming," in *Media Diversity and Localism: Meaning and Metrics*, ed. Philip Napoli (Mahwah, N.J.: Erlbaum, 2007).

31. Catherine Squires, "Black Talk Radio: Community Needs and Identity," *Harvard International Journal of Press/ Politics* 5.2 (2010): 73–95; Squires, "Black Audiences, Past and Present: Common Sense Media Critics," in *Say It Loud! African American Audiences, Media, and Identity*, ed. Robin R. Means Coleman (New York: Routledge), 45–76; Timothy Vercellotti and Paul R. Brewer, "'To Plead Our Own Cause': Public Opinion toward Black and Mainstream News Media among African Americans," *Journal of Black Studies* 37.2 (2006): 231–50.

32. Means Coleman, *Say It Loud!*; Squires, "Black Talk Radio."

33. Armistead Pride and Clint Wilson III, *A History of the Black Press* (Washington, D.C.: Howard University Press, 1997).

34. Anna Everett, "The Black Press in the Age of Digital Reproduction: Two Exemplars," in Vogel, *Black Press*, 246.

35. Mark Anthony Neal, *Soul Babies: Black Popular Culture and the Post-soul Aesthetic* (New York: Routledge, 2002).

36. Everett, "Black Press," 246.

37. Ibid., 248.

38. Ibid.

39. Alfred Schreiber, *Multicultural Marketing: Selling to the New America* (Chicago: NTC Business Books, 2006).

40. Leon Wynter, *American Skin: Pop Culture, Big Business, and the End of White America* (New York: Crown Publishers, 2002); Baynes, "White Out."

41. Paul Gilroy, *Against Race: Imagining Political Culture beyond the Color Line* (Cambridge, Mass.: Belknap Press of Harvard University Press, 2001), 242.

42. Ibid.

43. Philip Napoli, "Audience Valuation and Minority Media: An Analysis of the Determinants of the Value of Radio Audiences," *Journal of Broadcasting and Electronic Media*, 46.2 (2002): 169–84.

44. Oscar Gandy Jr., "Privatization and Identity: The Formation of a Racial Class," in *Media in the Age of Marketization*, ed. Janet Wasko and Graham Murdock (Creskill, N.J.: Hampton Press, 2007), 109–30.

45. D. Kirk Davidson, *Selling Sin: The Marketing of Socially Unacceptable Products* (Westport, Conn.: Praeger, 2003.)

46. Gandy, "Privatization and Identity."

47. www.blackenterprise.com/about-us.

48. www.theroot.com/aboutus.

49. "A New Era," *Black Enterprise*, January 2009.

50. See, for example, "The Giant Slayers," Blackenterprise.com, October 15, 2010, which congratulated the owner of a black financial firm for expanding its business by hiring people from failing financial firms.

51. Earl Graves Sr., "Publisher's Page: Your Trusted Resource in a Tough Economy," *Black Enterprise*, September 2008.

52. Graves, "Publisher's Page: Let Our Economic Recovery Begin with Us," *Black Enterprise*, December 2008.
53. Earl Graves Jr., "Executive Memo: Create Your Own Economic Stimulus Plan," *Black Enterprise*, April 2009.
54. Pamela Kirkland, "Letters: We're Not to Blame," *Black Enterprise*, April 2009.
55. Earl Graves Jr., "Executive Memo: Your House Is Not an ATM," *Black Enterprise*, June 2010.
56. Kai Wright, "More Proof Blacks Are Losing the Most Homes," TheRoot.com, May 13, 2009.
57. Emma Coleman Jordan, "Wall Street in Black and White," TheRoot.com, October 6, 2008.
58. Sam Fulwood III, "More Money, More Problems," TheRoot.com, September 15, 2009.
59. Jeneé Darden, "Starting Over: How Iyanla Lost Her Home," The Root.com, March 16, 2009.
60. Stacey Tisdale, "Market Crash Course," TheRoot.com, October 28, 2008.
61. Stacey Tisdale, "Talking the Talk about Money," TheRoot.com, May 11, 2009.
62. Chakravartty and Schiller, "Neoliberal Newspeak," 670–71, 683–84.
63. Daisy Hernandez, "Editor's Letter: Remember Affordable Housing?" *Colorlines*, May–June 2009.
64. Ibid.
65. Kai Wright, "One Step Forward, Two Steps Apart on UN Poverty Goals," Colorlines.com, September 17, 2009.
66. Ibid.
67. Lani Guinier and Rodolfo Torres, *The Miner's Canary: Enlisting Race, Resisting Power, Transforming Democracy* (Cambridge, Mass.: Harvard University Press, 2003).
68. Seth Freed Wessler, "Race and Recession: Foreclosure Losses Still Mounting," Colorlines.com, July 8, 2009.
69. Tram Ngyuen, "Pushed Out and Pushing Back in New Orleans," Colorlines.com, April 7, 2010.
70. See, for example, Shani O. Hilton, "Foreclosed Families Descend on Capitol to Make Wall Street Pay," Colorlines.com, March 8, 2011; Jamilah King, "Wells Fargo 'Stagecoach from Hell' Loses Wheels," Colorlines.com, July 8, 2010.
71. bell hooks, *We Real Cool: Black Men and Masculinity* (New York: Routledge, 2004), 15.
72. Ibid., xvii.
73. Cathy Cohen, "Politics, New Media, and Inequality: From the Occupy Movement to the 2012 Elections," address to the Gender, Sexuality, Power, and Politics Colloquium, University of Minnesota, Minneapolis, January 12, 2012.
74. In addition to the kinds of media referenced earlier in this article, commentators have begun to intensify scrutiny of discourses of wealth-as-salvation in black churches as another source of neoliberalism. See, for example, comments by Fredrick C. Harris, "'Prosperity Gospel' vs. the King Legacy," *New York Times*, February 2, 2012, http://www.nytimes.com/roomfordebate/2012/02/02/.

New Racial Meanings of Housing in America

Elvin Wyly, C. S. Ponder, Pierson Nettling, Bosco Ho, Sophie Ellen Fung, Zachary Liebowitz, and Daniel J. Hammel

> In the twilight of materialism, the meaning of housing will be simplified and clarified, with a renewed emphasis on shelter and neighborhood. The false hope that everyone can get rich from real estate will be laid to rest for another fifty years, or perhaps for all time.
> —John S. Adams, "Housing Markets in the Twilight of Materialism"

> Equality begins at home.
> —Anita F. Hill, "Marriage and Patronage in the Empowerment and
> Disempowerment of African-American Women"

> Mr. Martin's "suspicious" profile amounted to more than his black skin. He was profiled as young, loitering, non-property owning and poor. . . . Why is a child dead? The rise of "secure," gated communities, private cops, private roads, private parks, private schools, private playgrounds—private, private, private—exacerbates biased treatment against the young, the colored, and the presumably poor.
> —Rich Benjamin, "The Gated Community Mentality"

Ideals of housing and home have always shaped periods of social and political transformation in America.[1] For more than a century these ideals have been intertwined with segregation and the structured inequalities of capital and race.[2] Challenges to class inequality and racism have been repeatedly deflected and co-opted by the complex social and political construct of the "American Dream" of home ownership. We should not be surprised, therefore, that the worst financial crisis since the Great Depression of the 1930s has destabilized the social relations of racial categories and identities in America's ongoing drama of racial formation.[3] For decades, the simultaneous acceleration of privatization and debt allowed white privilege to ignore Derrick Bell's call "to 'Get Real' about race and racism in America," to deal honestly with "the increasingly dismal demographics that reflect the status of those whose forebears in this country were slaves."[4] Housing—and especially the expansion of mortgage debt—was crucial in deflecting the more fundamental demands for redistribution and genuine economic justice that grew out of the civil rights movement. Risky, deceptive practices in the "subprime" mortgage market were particularly effective in replacing the old rigid justifications for *exclusionary* racism with more flexible, entrepreneurial forms of *inclusionary* discrimination that promised opportunity and access to the wonders of the market. The American Dream: no money down!

Predatory home-financing schemes were perfected in subaltern America, among the people and places marginalized by social relations of class, race/ethnicity, gender, and metropolitan spatial restructuring. For years, well-documented cases of targeting and predatory exploitation were waved away by policy elites as "anecdotal." High-profile legislative and regulatory debates typically featured economists and U.S. senators—almost always white men—sternly assuring everyone that the free market was delivering widespread benevolence and that we should not worry too much about these isolated cases. There are striking parallels between the way policymakers casually and repeatedly dismissed the mounting evidence of systemic targeting of African American women in predatory housing finance and the way women of color were treated in other high-stakes political encounters.[5] In October 1991, when Anita Hill testified about sexual harassment by Clarence Thomas, she did so alone, without the (white male) "patron to confer legitimacy at official proceedings . . . and to navigate the corridors of power."[6] The penalties of speaking truth to power as an individual were severe. One white male senator (Arlen Specter) accused Hill of "flat-out perjury," another (Orrin Hatch) accused her of fabricating her allegations based on a passage from *The Exorcist*, and another (Alan Simpson) complained, "The stuff we listened to, I mean, you know, come on—from the moon."[7]

A generation later, all the "anecdotes" of exploitative, racialized lending were again forgotten amid a spreading global financial crisis, and it was thus a bittersweet realization in October 2011 that Bell had died the night before the conference "Context and Consequences: The Hill-Thomas Hearings Twenty Years Later." The gathering of legal scholars at Georgetown Law showcased what has changed—and what has not—in the politics of race, gender, and power in America. In a new book on the financial crisis and the meanings of home in America, Hill offered optimism:

Today I am privileged to witness the coming of age of a generation that seeks to move beyond historic race and gender divisions. For them, the American Dream means nothing if it is not inclusive. Because of the financial crisis, and because of their having grown up in an era of less strident racial discrimination and in homes where women are breadwinners, they will be less willing and able to pay a premium to live in a racially-isolated (predominantly white) community.[8]

Figure 1.
Professor Anita Hill, October 2011.
Courtesy of Elvin Wyly.

Hill's analysis is valuable and hopeful. Yet two incidents in America's long housing crisis—one from the central-city African American neighborhoods of northern industrial cities, another from the expanding suburban frontiers of the Sun Belt—illustrate the troubling mixture of continuity and change. For several years, an elderly African American widow in Akron, Ohio, was drawn into a series of risky, highly leveraged loans from Countrywide Mortgage; eventually, Addie Polk fell behind on the payments, and foreclosure proceedings began on the home she had bought in 1970 with her husband, Robert, a tire factory worker. In October 2008, with sheriff's deputies pounding on the front door to enforce an eviction order, Addie stayed upstairs in her bedroom and shot herself twice with a long-barreled handgun. Addie, ninety, survived the wounds, but died in a nursing home a few months later.

Several years later, another gun was fired. This time it was not self-inflicted, but a gunshot motivated by another person, with (1) a deep desire to protect a community where the housing crisis has frayed the social fabric, (2) an in-your-face personality sharpened by several encounters with law enforcement, (3) a suspicion of young black men, or (4) some combination of all factors. Seventeen-year-old Trayvon Martin was walking back from a convenience store to the home where his father was staying with his fiancée, in a gated community just outside Orlando, Florida. George Zimmerman, twenty-eight, saw Trayvon and called 911; Zimmerman was the coordinator for the neighborhood watch in the Retreat at Twin Lakes, where property values have fallen by half since the new community was completed six years ago; "a 'significant number' of foreclosures . . . have prompted investors to buy the properties at a discount and then rent them out."[9] Zimmerman told the 911 dispatcher he was concerned about recent break-ins, "and there's a real suspicious guy." Zimmerman ignored the dispatcher's instructions to wait for the police, and chased down Trayvon; a struggle ensued, and the unarmed teen was shot dead. After persuading the police he acted in self-defense, Zimmerman was released. Indignant rage spread quickly—an unarmed boy was dead, and no one was even arrested—until a special prosecutor filed second-degree murder charges. Public debate focused on Zimmerman's identity, biography, and racial attitudes: a Catholic altar boy whose father was a U.S. Army intelligence veteran of the Vietnam War and whose mother was a Peruvian immigrant. After high school graduation, Zimmerman moved to Florida and became a real estate broker as the market flourished. He was making more than $10,000 a month by his early twenties, but when the market collapsed he held a series of service-sector jobs before landing a full-time position at a "fraud-detection company," Digital Risk, that "helps institutions like Bank of America and Freddie Mac to rid their balance sheets of the kinds of toxic loans that led to the 2008 banking crisis. Mr. Zimmerman was among hundreds of auditors who work in a four-story office building . . . mining borrowers' files, sniffing out lies and scrutinizing hardship letters."[10]

A despondent elderly black women is alone in her bedroom, blaming herself for borrowing too much from the nation's largest mortgage lender, described by its cofounder and CEO as "having helped 25 million people buy homes and prevented social unrest by extending loans to minorities, historically the victims of discrimination."[11] A young black teen is profiled as "young, loitering, non-property owning and poor," and shot by the vigilant protector of a Sun Belt suburban gated community, a man who knows the importance of surveillance, real estate, and property values.[12] "Welcome to gate-minded America,"[13] where "an 'us vs. them' mentality festers" and property values are sustained "by creating an external enemy—those people outside the walls."[14]

These stories demand a reconsideration of American racial and ethnic relations—and in particular, changes in the connection between individual experiences of discrimination and the wider structures of inequality in American housing. In this article, our purpose is to analyze legal and institutional changes that have rescaled parts of America's racial political economy. Our analysis draws on theories of racial formation and the racial state[15] and legal analyses of American federalism and banking regulation[16] to identify regional and local variations in the racialized inequalities of housing and home.[17] We focus specifically on the inequalities of the high-risk, subprime segment of American mortgage credit.[18] Despite a vast, interdisciplinary literature, many of the spatial inequalities of racialized risk remain unexplored.[19] As we shall show, however, space was crucial in transforming America's discriminatory racial state. The predatory exploitation of the urban core has gone mainstream, altering the spatial relations of privilege on the expanding frontiers of Sun Belt suburbia (fig. 2).

New Laws of Spatial Organization

A generation ago, John S. Adams and other housing analysts suggested that postindustrialism was eroding the old foundations of scarcity—ending the long period of easy speculative real estate gains delivered through the steady suburbanization of the modern industrial metropolis.[20] The information economy would erode the arbitrage opportunities of geography, history, and urbanization. Housing would no longer promise to make everyone rich,[21] but would instead become a partly decommodified realm governed by the socially necessary use values of home, neighborhood, and community. Adams and his colleagues could not have predicted the speed and power of neoliberal policy decisions in the 1980s and 1990s that created a "global circulation of mortgages" that transformed local housing into "an electronic instrument,"[22] as the local lives and needs of individual home owners making monthly payments became the "postindustrial widgets" of mortgage-backed securities.[23] Housing-related debt was only part of the broader financialization of the American economy—before the collapse, the financial sector accounted for more than two-fifths of all U.S. corporate profits—but risky mortgage lending was a crucial site of innovation and exploitation that connected local inequalities with global circuits of investment, risk, and speculation.[24]

Postmaterialist interpretations of housing reflected broader debates over the nature of postindustrial society and were quickly subsumed within the economic theorists' view of a world freed from the messy constraints of real-world geographies.[25] These visions guided key policy decisions on banking deregulation for an entire generation. Our central argument is that deregulated market innovation reconfigured the relations between local housing markets and transnational financial circuits. Preexisting local racisms were integrated into wider spatial networks. But the insatiable "appetite for yield" enabled a ruinous

Figure 2.
Las Vegas, December 2008. Courtesy of Elvin Wyly. Between 2004 and 2006, Wall Street and local lenders funneled more than $20 billion in high-risk, high-cost subprime mortgage credit to consumers in the Las Vegas area. Compared with otherwise similar non-Hispanic whites, African American, and Latina/o borrowers in the region were twice as likely to be pushed into subprime credit.

competition that now threatens to undermine the political foundations of America's racial state.[26]

In America's utopia of spatial form, housing markets are defined by a regime of spatial segregation that keeps the other at a safe distance to protect white property values.[27] For many years, this regime was reproduced through pervasive practices of segregation in development and neighborhood social relations.[28] Yet the law and economics of housing finance were also crucial—particularly the division between "traditional" forms of closely regulated prime credit of white privilege and scarcity and its "nontraditional" others.[29] At first, this other entailed systematic exclusion from the institutions of mainstream credit. Over time, however, more and more marginalized people and places were incorporated into an expanding field of high-risk subprime and predatory debt.[30] The expansion of debt in turn fueled an acceleration in home prices, encouraging further innovations in leveraged risk—generating a steady stream of fees and investment returns for everyone in the industry.[31] "Nontraditional" forms of credit became an ever more important source of income for *local* realtors, mortgage brokers, and appraisers, for *regional and national* banks and bank holding companies, and for Wall Street investment houses and investors around the world lured by the promise of high risk-adjusted yields. But yields require volume. The *rate* of exploitative profits has always been highest among the segregated and marginalized, but market volume is another matter: housing finance starkly illustrates Slavoj Žižek's parallax view. Between 2004 and 2010 high-risk subprime mortgages accounted for more than 39 percent of all mortgage loans made to single, non-Hispanic African American women—almost four times the share for non-Hispanic white male-female couples, and more than five times the rate for non-Hispanic Asian or Hawaiian/Pacific Islander traditional couples; these disparities are reduced only somewhat when we account for African American women's lower incomes and other factors.[32] Yet non-Hispanic whites remain a dominant plurality even in the subprime market, accounting for 45.9 percent of the 10.9 million high-cost loans made in these years (fig. 3).

From the perspective of marginalized communities, it is impossible to ignore the deeply racialized and gendered dimensions of the subprime boom and today's foreclosure disaster. Nationwide, foreclosure starts and serious delinquency rates in predominantly minority neighborhoods are more than twice as bad as those in predominantly white communities (table 1).

But a different view appears from the perspective of Wall Street and transnational investors. As the market accelerated between 2004 and 2005, the subprime share among single black women shot up from 36.2 percent to 52.4 percent, dwarfing the comparable rates among non-Hispanic white male-female couples (from 9.5 percent to 14.5 percent). Yet each percentage point increase in subprime share among single black women delivered fewer than 5,800 new customers—each one an opportunity for deceptive fees and charges on the front end and an ongoing stream of returns from leverage and speculation through securitization. By contrast, each percentage-point advance in subprime market share among non-Hispanic white couples delivered more than thirty-four thousand new prospects. By the time the global circulation of mortgages really took off in the first decade of the twenty-first century, America's most deeply marginalized communities—mostly but not exclusively, inner-city and inner-suburban neighborhoods of non-Hispanic African Americans—had been thoroughly devastated by generations of various kinds of exploitative financial schemes (fig. 4).[33] New volume for the newest forms of capitalist predation required new targets: suburbanizing African Americans and Latina/os, and eventually some of the traditional beneficiaries of America's institutions of Anglo white privilege.[34] Half of all mortgage volume in the 2004–7 credit binge went to neighborhoods where non-Hispanic whites comprised at least

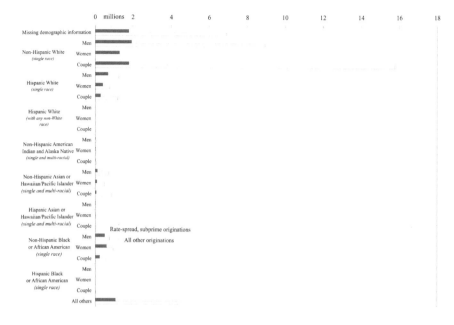

Figure 3.
Race, ethnicity, and gender in subprime lending. Number of rate-spread (subprime) originations and all other originations, 2004–2010. Source: Federal Financial Institutions Examination Council, *Frequently Asked Questions about the New HMDA Data* (Washington, D.C.: Federal Financial Institutions Examination Council, 2005–2011).

Table 1. Race, Risk, and Capital.

Minorities as share of census tract population	Average tract subprime market share	*Block group estimates*		
		Mortgage volume 2004-2007	Estimated foreclosure starts, Q32009-Q32010	Average serious delinquency rate, Q32010
< 20	20.1	21,400,752	914,282	6.81
20-39	22.8	8,435,290	460,778	8.19
40-59	28.4	3,957,123	255,536	9.75
60-79	32.7	2,712,836	203,328	11.51
>80	43.0	3,065,190	272,949	14.25

Data Source: Calculated from Neighborhood Stabilization Program, Phase 3 data, matched with tract-level HMDA census characteristics. See US Department of Housing and Urban Development (2011), FFIEC (annual).

Table 1.
Race, risk, and capital, calculated from Neighborhood Stabilization Program, Phase 3 data, matched with tract-level HMDA census characteristics. Source: U.S. Department of Housing and Urban Development, *Neighborhood Stabilization Program 3 Downloadable Data Files* (Washington, D.C.: U.S. Department of Housing and Urban Development, 2011); and Federal Financial Institutions Examination Council, *Frequently Asked Questions about the New HMDA Data* (Washington, D.C.: Federal Financial Institutions Examination Council, 2005–2011).

Figure 4.
Cleveland, July 2010. Courtesy of Elvin Wyly. Cleveland was once an American icon, famous for making things. Then it became famous for deindustrialization, environmental catastrophe, and depopulation. Then came the predatory lending boom. More than $5 billion in subprime loans were made in the Cleveland metropolitan area at the height of the boom; these high-cost loans were about five times more likely to be sold to Wall Street and other private investors than conventional prime loans. Now the ongoing foreclosure crisis is making Cleveland famous yet again, this time for tearing down houses. Cleveland has about fifteen thousand vacant and abandoned homes, and dealing with them is described by the county land bank president as "the root canal of community development." Source: B Dennis, "The Foreclosure Crush," *Washington Post*, October 15, 2011.

80 percent of the population. White privilege in accumulated wealth enables most of these communities to better resist the devalorization of the ongoing crisis—foreclosure and delinquency rates are half those in the most racially marginalized and segregated neighborhoods—but volume again tells a different story. Two-fifths of all foreclosure starts nationwide are in predominantly white neighborhoods (table 1).

This is where the spatial constitution of American racial formation has been destabilized. In the second half of the twentieth century, the vast wave of suburbanization retained a predominantly white spatiality: middle-class aspirations conjoined upward *economic* mobility with *outward* residential mobility and *whiteward* institutional mobility through the privileged realms of education, job markets, and of course housing markets. For most of this period, the innovations of predatory capital were safely contained by the spatial separations of the city-suburb divide and neighborhood-level processes of class difference and racial and ethnic segregation. But things changed dramatically after 2001, when the appetite for yield required volume—thus necessitating an expansion of predation into the markets of whiteness in American housing. To understand the present instability of American racial formation, therefore, we need to consider the spatial reorganization that enabled and encouraged a direct pipeline between inequalities usually experienced as local (i.e., racial segregation) and the speedy flows of credit and debt in national and transnational capital markets.

All That Is Solid Melts into TARP

It is now widely recognized that the stable, locally oriented "golden age" of American housing and banking disappeared some time ago. Gone is the tightly regulated regime dominated by savings and loans connecting local borrowers and savers, reliant on the standard, thirty-year self-amortizing mortgage held on the lender's books; we now have something much more spatially complex, dynamic, and risky. The empirical details of this transformation are well documented in a vast and interdisciplinary literature.[35] For most of the post–World War II period, American housing was a Keynesian arrangement, in which the economics of supply-side housing construction cycles were governed by the "fundamentals" of demand for housing as a consumption good, paid for by the wages of an industrial economy. But postindustrialism and deregulated financialization created a more unstable post-Keynesian network of supply-side profit opportunities that were partly unhinged from wages and other fundamentals. Homes, borrowers, and financial obligations became the vehicles for capital accumulation backed by (and driven by) the steady rise in home prices.[36] Housing became a nexus between the slow materialities of place and the accelerating velocity of financial innovation and regulatory evasion. Mortgage finance became a sector with its own partly autonomous dynamics of production, consumption, and speculation.

Housing finance opened a thick pipeline for a capital "switching" crisis first predicted in the 1960s. Henri Lefebvre first hypothesized a switching process in which declining profit rates in the primary circuit of capital accumulation gradually encouraged an increase in investment and then speculation in a secondary circuit that provided the infrastructure that sustained capitalist social relations. Real estate turned out to be the part of this infrastructure that was the easiest to commodify for speculative purposes. Lefebvre's insight inspired a central part of David Harvey's analysis of urbanism and the connections between local, urban forms of exploitation and higher level processes of capital accumulation and financial speculation.[37] Harvey's work in turn encouraged generations of researchers to analyze various kinds of real estate trends to test the theory.[38] Ironically, the mixed results of these tests reflected data limitations that also blinded the neoclassical economists in charge of public policy—making it impossible, for instance, to measure how mortgage-backed securities were interwoven with the giant, unregulated, and undisclosed global market of trillions of dollars of credit default swaps. As the financial crisis swept the globe from the spring of 2007 into the fall of 2008, the daily headlines appeared as summaries of Lefebvre and Harvey: Marxist analyses of accumulation and financialization were eerily echoed in widespread discussions of Ben Bernanke's suggestion of a "global savings glut" flooding into U.S. financial instruments, Alan Greenspan's attempt to minimize the scale of the exploding subprime crisis by reassuring investors that "arbitrageable long-term assets are worth close to a hundred trillion dollars," and the dozens of obscure bailouts and guarantees begun with the Troubled Asset Relief Program (TARP).[39] Harvey's analyses of fictitious capital seemed almost mainstream by the time central bankers from around the world applauded the Federal Reserve's success at the annual conference in Jackson Hole, Wyoming, in August 2009: "Economists say Mr. Bernanke's most important accomplishment was to create staggering amounts of money out of thin air."[40] All that is solid melts into TARP.[41]

Financialized Federalism

The scale of the global financial crisis shocked a broad spectrum of mainstream and conservative analysts, and made it clear how much had changed in the politics of geographic scale—the level or arena of decisions and actions that are usually divided into (deceptively) neat categories: local, urban/regional, state, federal/national, transnational/global.[42] In the United States, the fundamental scale conflict in law and politics involves the state-federal tensions first negotiated through the Federalist Papers.[43] The state-federal axis has been remade slowly over time, with evolving geographies of urbanization, immigration, electoral competition, and the regional contours of racial and ethnic identity. The American racial state, therefore, can be understood as the sequence of legislative and judicial attempts to adapt and interpret a seventeenth-century document written by slave-owning merchant classes yearning to be free—to cope with the jurisdictional battles as capital circulates more widely and encompasses growing shares of people and places once defined as racially and economically "marginal." For a short but important period in the twentieth century, these contradictions were partly resolved through the spatiality of the modern metropolitan welfare state—symbolized by high-modernist, high-rise public housing at the core, and white middle-class owner-occupied housing on the expanding suburban fringe. The local white-ethnic political machines of northern industrial cities got federal help to rebuild their inner-city slums without disturbing established regimes of neighborhood segregation, while the broad coalitions of national and regional conservatism reaped the rewards of racially exclusionary FHA mortgage insurance, tax subsidies for ownership, and massive investments in the interstate highway system. Ironically, the largest welfare program in American history—the vast greenfield vistas of suburban houses for middle-class whites—is falsely remembered as a golden age of the private market. By contrast, the most concentrated loci of affirmative efforts to help the racialized victims of housing market failure—federally funded, publicly owned housing—were built only in those cities that actively sought the money, and only for a few years. Ever since Nixon imposed a moratorium on new public housing construction in 1973, this component of the "racial-state spatial fix" has been demolished bit by bit. Bipartisan policy shifts have forced tenants of public housing projects to become couriers delivering subsidies to private landlords (through Section 8/Housing Choice Voucher certificates) and investors (those purchasing Low Income Housing Tax Credits) (fig. 5). Eventually, a demonstration program crafted to deal with the specificities of racial and class segregation in one of the iconic centers of the urban welfare state (Chicago) was used as a template for a comprehensive but locally adaptable federal makeover of public housing.[44] Other commitments of the national Democratic coalition were reconsidered, and programs with explicit potential for political conflicts over race-class redistribution were "reinvented" (i.e., destroyed). But home ownership—and especially mortgage finance—would be different. For Democrats, public policies designed to "tap new markets" would connect minorities and the poor "to the regulated banking industry in a politically visible way."[45] Republicans, meanwhile, sought "to use increased rates of home ownership among blacks and Latinos to lure a slice of these culturally conservative but economically excluded groups away from the Democratic Party" and toward the Right.[46]

Legal Spatial Fixes

The bipartisan appeal of mortgage finance was enhanced by a mixture of deliberate and unintentional changes in the laws and regulations governing banking and lending. The first significant cracks in the foundation of the stable postwar

Figure 5.
South Side Chicago, July 2010. Courtesy of Elvin Wyly. The empty green corridor to the right of the Dan Ryan Expressway is where the Robert Taylor Homes once stood. The projects were built in the late 1950s on the site of the old Federal Street slum, and demolished beginning in 1998. Source: K. Easterling, "Subtraction," *Perspecta* 34 (2003): 80–90.

housing finance system appeared in the late 1970s. The Supreme Court's 1978 *Marquette* decision allowed national banks to "take their most favored lender status across state lines and preempt the usury laws of the borrower's home state."[47] South Dakota and Delaware moved first to repeal usury limits as an economic development strategy, and soon the process of "regulatory exportation" intensified competition that weakened nearly all states' usury laws. Then, in response to the corrosive inflation and disintermediation of the late 1970s, Congressed passed the Depository Institutions Deregulation and Monetary Control Act (DIDMCA) of 1980. DIDMCA eliminated interest rate caps for first-lien residential mortgages and allowed other types of depository lenders (not just national banks) to take advantage of the *Marquette* decision.[48] Shortly thereafter, the Alternative Mortgage Transactions Parity Act (AMTPA) preempted, for nearly all types of lenders, state restrictions on "alternatives" from the standard, fully amortized fixed-rate loan—allowing variable rate terms, negative amortization, balloon payments, and other creative possibilities. The interactions between *Marquette*, DIDMCA, and AMTPA created intricate, non-Euclidian spaces of permissible financial transactions: *Marquette* disconnected the rules from the state where a borrower lived, DIDMCA freed depository lenders from common state restrictions, and AMTPA liberalized certain types of nontraditional *loans*, regardless of whether they were made by deposit-taking banks or independent mortgage companies.

These laws provided the *necessary* conditions for the growth of high-risk mortgage lending, and by the 1990s the market was studded with niche sub-prime products targeting inner-city neighborhoods and rural mobile-home owners, particularly in renovation and refinance lending.[49] The *sufficient* conditions for a broader expansion required other changes in technology, regulation, financial competition, and transnational investment. Enhanced consumer credit surveillance, credit scoring, default modeling, and automated underwriting promised increased accuracy in extracting profits from consumers once viewed as too risky to serve.[50] Mortgage-backed securities, launched tentatively in 1968 by the government-sponsored Ginnie Mae, finally began to grow after the 1984 Secondary Mortgage Market Enhancement Act resolved tax issues and state regulations.[51] At the time, however, secondary market growth was slowed by the exploding savings and loan crisis—itself a product of deregula-tion—and the bad publicity made it hard for Wall Street's lobbyists to achieve more sweeping relaxation of Depression-era laws on securities and banking. Yet whenever regulatory capture and pressures on lawmakers failed, entrepreneurial innovation in legal evasion took up the slack: Wall Street quickly found new ways to subvert the old laws through products that fell through the cracks of existing laws, regulations, or narrow paths of enforcement. *The products fell through the cracks because they were designed exactly for this purpose.* One example comes from the bizarre, obscure sole-purpose companies established to handle the flow of mortgages and other asset-backed securities marketed to institutional investors around the world. Sometimes these entities were called special purpose entities (SPEs), sometimes special purpose vehicles (SPVs). Much of what makes them special is that they break the chain of legal liability, insulating investors from claims over violations of law committed by brokers or originators getting borrowers into the mortgage.[52]

Another factor was the widespread fear of budget surpluses. Debt itself is a partly autonomous circuit of capital investment, subject to its own switch-ing crises. Projecting surpluses to infinity under then current budget laws, Clinton's Treasury Department announced in 2001 a plan to phase out the thirty-year "long bond." Suddenly, the universally recognized global safe harbor and benchmark for evaluating debt and credit risk was set to disappear, and anxious institutional investors around the world cast about for alternatives.[53] The securities of the government-sponsored enterprises (GSEs), Fannie Mae and Freddie Mac, became popular replacements.[54] They were soon joined by the private-label mortgage-backed securities offered in ever-greater volume by the growing, deregulated Wall Street investment banks.[55]

So far, so good. All of this regulatory history is now well-known.[56] What makes it relevant to our claims about a new spatiality of racial inequalities in housing finance is the peculiar configuration of banking and financial regulation in American federalism. From the earliest days of the republic, the states viewed any kind of federal initiative in the realm of finance—a common currency, the creation of a central bank—as a dangerous threat to their sovereignty. Between Andrew Jackson's veto of the Second Bank of the United States in 1832 and the creation of the Federal Reserve in 1913, many of the state-federal tensions were negotiated only through a complex web of functional and geographic-legal divisions that placed careful limits on federal power. Only the Great Depression brought clear and consistent federal regulation—and even then, the most potent interventions were laid atop the existing framework that already separated national and state banks. There has never been a single regulator, therefore, supervising institutions involved in mortgage finance. Supervision depends on whether an institution has a state or national charter; whether it accepts customer deposits or exists solely to make mortgages; and whether it serves a mixture of business and consumers, or functions solely as a savings and loan. By the late 1990s the mortgage market was split across six regulatory agencies: the Office of the Comptroller of the Currency, the Federal Reserve Board, the Federal Deposit Insurance Corporation, the Office of Thrift Supervision, the National Credit Union Administration, and the U.S. Department of Housing and Urban Development. After the repeal of Depression-era banking laws with the Gramm-Leach-Bliley Act in 1998, the regulatory matrix become even more complex with large, multisubsidiary holding companies.[57] George W. Bush's federal agencies led the way, "pre-empting" state laws on predatory lending for federally regulated lenders,[58] while in *Watters v. Wachovia* the Supreme Court struck down even modest requirements for subsidiaries of national banks to register to do business in a state.

This all makes for complicated geographies. While Adams hoped for a "renewed emphasis on shelter and neighborhood,"[59] deregulation and financialization created an intricate landscape of institutions whose behavior could not be regulated by local rules or, increasingly, by state laws that were preempted by weak and easily evaded federal regulations. The *where* of a consumer's interaction with mortgage finance still mattered to local brokers and small-time mortgage firms, but more of these local actors brought their business to (or were acquired by) the large, multisubsidiary national banks and holding com-

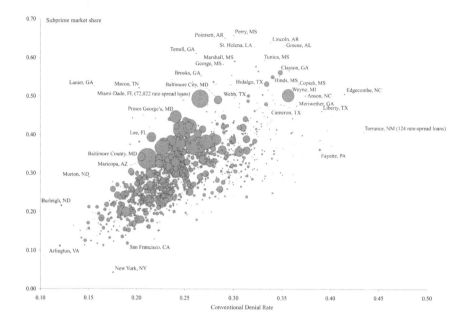

Figure 6.
Conventional mortgage denial rates and rate-spread market penetration, by metropolitan county. Circle sizes are scaled proportional to total number of rate-spread originations. Source: Federal Financial Institutions Examination Council, *Frequently Asked Questions about the New HMDA Data* (Washington, D.C.: Federal Financial Institutions Examination Council, 2007).

panies. For these expanding conduits of national and transnational capital, the combination of subsidiary-structure, preemption, and financial deregulation created a thoroughly post-Cartesian, non-Euclidian space of law and accumulation.

Mapping the New Racial State

These new institutional spaces reconfigured the relation between localized racial-ethnic inequalities and broader spaces of finance. We can glimpse some of these new spaces if we explore the variation of subprime lending across the American urban system. Consider first the relations between old and new types of exclusion (fig. 6). Subprime market penetration rises smoothly with increasing local denial rates. Approximately half the variance in subprime market share in the nation's metropolitan counties can be attributed to a single factor—differences in conventional mortgage denial rates. The eye is drawn to the large circles representing the big markets with the highest subprime market penetration—Miami-Dade, Florida, and Wayne County, Michigan (Detroit)—and the exploitation of people in these places is indeed very important (fig. 7). Yet even

Figure 7.
Detroit, July 2010. Courtesy of Elvin Wyly. The view is to the north-northwest, just beyond Detroit's downtown core. In the foreground are the Brewster-Douglass Housing Projects, built on the site of Detroit's Black Bottom community. Wayne County, Michigan, is the nation's largest urban area with the worst combination of high mortgage denial rates and deep subprime market penetration. Blacks were more likely to be pushed into subprime loans compared with whites with similar incomes, and this disparity was deeply intertwined with neighborhood segregation.

more extreme cases at the top of the graph highlight a vast, diverse array of landscapes across the South—from the border cities of South Texas (Hidalgo County, just north of McAllen) to the growing suburban black middle-class communities south of Atlanta (Clayton County, Georgia), to several small-town counties across Louisiana, Alabama, Mississippi, and Arkansas.

These urban patterns are deeply shaped by historical and contemporary regional contexts of race and ethnicity (figs. 8, 9). For African Americans, the pattern still reflects the antebellum settlement fabric of small towns that emerged from the old plantation network across the Piedmont South, from Virginia to Mississippi.[60] Yet the Great Migration between World Wars I and II also made the "dream of Black Metropolis" a reality in Harlem, Chicago's South Side, Detroit, and other expanding industrial centers of the North.[61] After the civil rights movement of the 1960s, service-sector growth in the rising Sun Belt nourished a growing black middle class in Atlanta, while federal efforts to rectify discriminatory hiring and promotion in the civil service made the suburbs of Washington, D.C., an epicenter of African

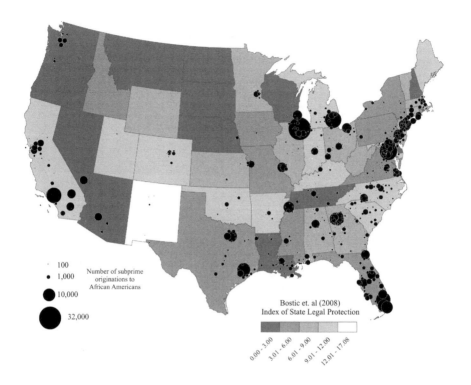

Figure 8.
Subprime loans to African Americans and state regulation.
Sources: Federal Financial Institutions Examination Council, *Frequently Asked Questions about the New HMDA Data* (Washington, D.C.: Federal Financial Institutions Examination Council, 2007); and R. W. Bostic, K. C. Engel, P. A. McCoy, A. Pennington-Cross, and S. M. Wachter, *The Impact of State Anti-Predatory Lending Laws: Policy Implications and Insights* (Cambridge, Mass.: Harvard University Joint Center for Housing Studies, 2008).

American upward mobility. For Latinas and Latinos, by contrast, the housing and credit boom was deeply regionalized in the urban landscapes of Southern California, Florida, Texas, and Arizona. For both African Americans and Latinas/os, however, there is no clear relationship between intra-urban racial and ethnic diversity and the landscape of state-level attempts to restrict the worst abuses of predatory lending.

The patterns change when we analyze the segmentation of individual borrowers into risky credit, while using logistic regression to account for income, loan amount, and other borrower characteristics (fig. 10). Compared with otherwise similarly qualified non-Hispanic whites, African American home owners and home buyers in the suburbs of St. Louis, Missouri, are six and a half times more likely to wind up with high-cost credit. At the other extreme,

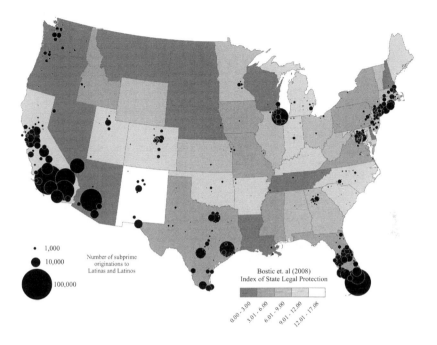

Figure 9.
Subprime loans to Latinos and Latinas, and state regulation.
Sources: Federal Financial Institutions Examination Council,
Frequently Asked Questions about the New HMDA Data
(Washington, D.C.: Federal Financial Institutions Examination
Council, 2007); and R. W. Bostic, K. C. Engel, P. A. McCoy,
A. Pennington-Cross, and S. M. Wachter, *The Impact of State
Anti-Predatory Lending Laws: Policy Implications and Insights*
(Cambridge, Mass.: Harvard University Joint Center for
Housing Studies, 2008).

the ratio drops to 1.74 for African Americans in Prince George's County, one of the nation's largest communities of black middle-class professionals in the suburbs east of Washington, D.C. Just on the other side of town, however, suburban Fairfax County, Virginia, posts the worst inequalities for Latina and Latino borrowers: a massive six-to-one disparity compared with otherwise similar non-Hispanic whites.

These variations in racial inequality are not entirely random: the massive black-white disparities toward the right of the graph, for example, clearly highlight the old southeast and northern deindustrialization. But the overall pattern is also not consistent or systematic. Additional regression analysis indicates that adding a vector of county measures of regional demography and industrial structure yields little improvement in model fit, after we control for borrower characteristics. This does not mean that local variations are insignificant—just that these local variations can be explained in terms of targeting

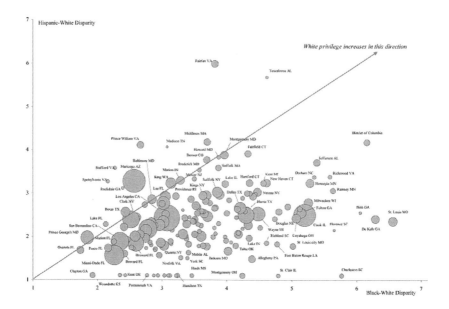

Figure 10.
White privilege in mortgage lending, by county. Odds ratios from logistic regressions of subprime segmentation, after controlling for applicant income, loan amount, and other borrower and lender characteristics. Circle sizes scaled proportional to total number of subprime loans; analysis restricted to metropolitan counties with at least five hundred subprime originations to African Americans. Not all counties are labeled. Source: Federal Financial Institutions Examination Council, *Frequently Asked Questions about the New HMDA Data* (Washington, D.C.: Federal Financial Institutions Examination Council, 2007).

and discrimination against certain *borrowers* by different kinds of *institutions*. Once these structures of inequality have been considered, however, other unique circumstances of regional context fade into the background. Inequalities once understood as local, neighborhood-level processes have been interwoven with national and transnational investment circuits.

Securities, Subsidiaries, and Space

Urban and regional context have been reshaped by institutional restructuring. Logistic regressions of the prime-subprime division indicate that institutional configurations of mortgage capital played an independent role, even after accounting for class inequalities and the individual-level effects of racism and white privilege. Even after accounting for the segmentation of *individual* African Americans and Latinas/os into risky credit, for example, borrowers were much more likely to get subprime loans if they dealt with a lender specializing in

Figure 11.
St. Louis, Missouri, August 2007. Courtesy of Elvin Wyly. Comparing the odds of receiving high-risk subprime loans among whites and otherwise similar African Americans gives us what we might call an "exploitation ratio" for America's mortgage mode of accumulation. In the city of St. Louis this ratio is almost five; in the county, it's well over six. These inequalities are tightly integrated into transnational investment and debt markets. Todd Swanstrom estimates that direct costs of recent foreclosures in St. Louis County approach $1 billion (Swanstrom, *St. Louis County's Billion-Dollar Problem: Foreclosures* (Berkeley: Institute of Governmental Studies, University of California, 2011).

black and Hispanic markets. For a customer approaching a lender whose African American market share was one standard deviation higher than the industry average, the subprime odds jumped by a factor of 2.40. For Latina/ Latino market specialization, the corresponding effect is 1.53. Secondary-market networks are also crucial: compared with loans held on the books, a mortgage sold to a purchaser in the "other" category (typically, an SPV) is 2.1 times more likely to be subprime. Credit outcomes cannot be explained solely in terms of borrowers' needs or characteristics, but also depend on factors decided by industry actors.

Regulatory climate also matters, but only for those institutions that have not reorganized themselves to evade restrictions (table 2). For the market overall, Raphael W. Bostic et al.'s measure of state lending protection does not significantly affect subprime segmentation.[62] But this national aggregate conceals a stark divide in financialized federalism: when the models are strati-

Table 2. Multivariate Models of Institutional Circuits.

Standardized Odds ratios I from Logistic Regression — Avery Code I or Institution Type

Variable	Full Market	Bank Holding Company	Foreign Banking Organization as a Bank Holding Company	Federally Chartered Credit Union	Financial Holding Company as Bank Holding Co. (foreign/domestic c)	Financial Holding Company as Foreign Banking Organization	Federally Chartered Savings Bank	Independent Mortgage Bank	Nationally Chartered Commercial Bank	State Chartered Commercial Bank, not Federal Reserve Member	Savings and Loan Association	State Chartered Credit Union	State Chartered Commercial Bank, Federal Reserve Member	State Chartered Savings Bank
Intercept	0.08	0.67	0.00	0.46	0.03	0.00	0.01	0.02	0.90	0.20	0.03	0.44	0.50	0.43
Applicant income*	0.88	0.74	0.93	0.63	0.77	0.74	0.96	0.98	0.54	0.80	0.77	0.69	0.72	0.76
Loan to income ratio*	1.10	1.15	1.00	1.19	1.10	1.29	1.10	1.03	1.13	1.42	1.11	1.10	1.28	1.13
Owner occupied	0.62	1.49	3.94	0.64	0.65	0.36	0.44	0.61	1.57	0.49	1.39	0.43	1.43	0.62
Subordinate lien	1.14	0.40	4.74	0.38	0.78	1.61	1.60	1.82	0.33	2.64	1.31	0.72	0.04	0.42
Jumbo loan	0.77	0.79	0.93	0.64	0.51	0.53	0.93	1.05	0.89	0.77	0.59	1.42	0.55	0.96
Pre-approval requested	0.34	0.66	0.89	0.25	0.35	1.20	0.71	0.33	0.98	0.35	0.32	0.57	0.23	0.74
Validity or quality edit failure	1.20	1.99	3.07	2.61	1.63	1.07	1.28	0.63	1.95	0.64	1.97	2.74	1.91	2.39
Home improvement	0.65	0.65	0.71	0.76	0.81	0.63	0.49	0.99	0.70	0.32	0.53	0.79	0.89	0.55
Refinance	0.85	0.88	0.56	0.58	0.84	0.70	0.70	0.95	0.93	0.72	0.56	0.62	1.11	0.65
Demographic information unknown	1.12	0.82	0.84	1.19	1.23	0.94	1.09	1.05	0.90	1.04	1.16	1.37	0.58	0.72
Female primary applicant	1.08	1.15	1.18	1.03	1.09	1.01	1.09	1.03	1.23	1.14	1.10	1.05	1.03	1.16
Hispanic	1.42	1.63	1.86	0.98	1.50	1.02	1.43	1.35	1.29	1.31	1.32	1.29	3.12	1.31
Native American	1.25	1.35	0.60	1.27	1.22	1.07	1.27	1.33	1.16	1.39	1.31	1.23	2.20	1.25
Asian	0.93	1.00	1.08	0.73	0.83	0.74	0.94	1.01	1.03	0.87	0.78	1.14	0.66	0.74
African American	1.74	1.50	1.36	1.23	2.08	1.38	1.77	1.46	1.22	2.10	1.75	1.62	0.75	1.51
Sold to GSE	0.23	0.13	0.61	0.25	0.23	2.08	0.41	0.30	0.03	0.31	0.21	0.39	0.00	0.23
Sold to private securitization	2.40	0.55	0.01	0.12	2.89	0.47	1.78	2.86	0.00	1.25	0.87	7.81	...	...
Sold to bank	1.47	0.22	0.08	0.10	2.01	1.22	0.80	1.29	0.09	0.11	1.30	0.41	0.00	0.38
Sold to finance company	1.78	0.30	0.69	6.52	2.13	2.20	1.85	1.46	0.45	0.25	0.13	2.01	0.06	0.24
Sold to affiliate	1.06	0.27	0.25	0.53	0.81	0.81	1.61	1.26	...	0.49	0.94	1.32	...	0.23
Sold to other purchaser	2.10	0.37	0.01	0.92	6.11	66.72	0.43	1.14	0.39	0.04	0.94	0.38	1.26	1.35
Lender share demographic unknown*	1.53	1.07	0.56	0.67	1.26	1.23	1.70	2.46	1.15	0.73	1.13	0.80	1.20	0.92
Lender share female*	1.16	1.03	1.08	1.12	1.44	1.41	1.46	1.32	1.15	1.42	1.21	1.10	0.93	1.28
Lender share Black*	2.40	1.28	2.16	0.80	1.41	1.23	2.67	2.83	1.04	2.61	1.82	1.11	1.56	1.43
Lender share Hispanic*	1.53	1.39	1.72	0.89	1.16	2.76	1.94	1.63	1.30	1.63	1.36	1.33	1.51	1.07
Lender share Native American*	1.09	1.11	1.38	1.08	1.02	1.44	0.71	1.10	1.11	1.05	1.04	1.13	...	1.14
Lender share Asian*	0.63	0.75	0.92	0.32	0.61	0.97	0.58	0.76	1.00	0.99	0.80	0.66	1.13	0.61
Bostic (2008) legal index*	0.98	0.85	0.98	0.92	0.99	0.98	1.00	0.98	0.86	0.99	1.02	0.77	0.34	0.57
Tract to MSA income percentage*	0.73	0.72	0.79	0.83	0.72	0.74	0.74	0.80	0.65	0.76	0.77	0.78	1.01	0.76
Tract minority percentage*	0.95	0.93	1.09	1.14	0.94	0.85	0.94	1.01	0.84	0.94	0.95	0.87	1.13	0.96
Number of observations, subprime	3,302,131	76,636	3,626	9,164	961,084	170,085	264,503	1,537,060	1,050	199,338	69,488	6,483	275	3,147
Number of observations, all other	7,698,334	424,553	27,657	250,325	3,426,637	342,994	627,489	1,869,298	5,239	227,910	240,064	187,754	2,042	53,508
Nagelkerke (1991) max-rescaled R-squared	0.47	0.20	0.30	0.22	0.41	0.77	0.65	0.47	0.25	0.65	0.38	0.11	0.35	0.24
Percent concordant	86.4	76.8	82.5	81.0	84.4	95.6	91.9	85.9	80.1	91.8	84.2	73	85.5	83.8

*Continuous variable; odds ratios for continuous measures report the change in odds with a one standard deviation increase in the respective predictor variable.

... Coefficient not estimated.

Data Sources: FFIEC (2007); Avery (2010).

Table 2.

Multivariate models of institutional circuits. Sources: Federal Financial Institutions Examination Council, *Frequently Asked Questions about the New HMDA Data* (Washington, D.C.: Federal Financial Institutions Examination Council, 2007); and R. Avery, *HMDA Lender File, 2008 Filing Year* (Washington, D.C.: Board of Governors of the Federal Reserve, 2009).

fied by lender type, subprime segmentation is significantly reduced for three institutional forms: state chartered credit unions, state chartered commercial banks that are part of the Federal Reserve, and state chartered savings banks. For all other institutions, the standardized odds ratios are all quite close to 1.00, indicating no significant effect. For those institutions regulated by states, legislators' response to the deception of predatory lending *did* have an effect on how borrowers were treated in the market for high-cost loans. Unfortunately, the insignificant results for all other lending types confirm the effectiveness of the Bush administration's selective assault on federalism. Lenders simply reorganized themselves and traded a restrictive charter for a permissive one. Building on the bipartisan federal enchantment with a laissez-faire approach to financial-sector innovation that began in the Clinton years, George W. Bush's administration mobilized conservative forces in an "active obstruction of state and local legislative attempts to rein in predatory lending."[63]

The liberation of federal pre-emption was most crucial for the highly mobile and postindustrial factions of mortgage capital. For the market as a whole, selling loans to Wall Street—the SPVs coded as "other purchaser"—reflects and reinforces subprime segmentation; all else constant, a loan sold to an SPV is twice as likely to be high cost. But the odds ratio skyrockets to more than six for lenders organized as financial holding company as bank holding company," a regulatory category that includes both domestic and transnational institutions. For many years, banks and financial holding companies with gold-plated reputations dismissed predatory lending concerns by pointing to the more egregious behavior of nonbank, independent mortgage companies. But subprime profits were irresistible, and by 2006 financial holding companies were fast closing on independent mortgage companies and made $144.6 billion in high-cost loans. For these factions of capital, securitization was the name of the game. All the loan-sale circuits post high odds ratios, while the value below parity for affiliates (0.81) indicates that these institutions were careful about drinking their own poison. The low value for GSE sales (0.23) is also crucial, although this effect is common to nearly all the other lender types as well.[64] This result confirms that the GSEs "followed rather than led Wall Street and other lenders in the rush for fool's gold."[65] We can visualize this division between the hybrid public/private channels of the GSEs and the back-channel private-label route if we graph each of the 8,886 lenders and subsidiaries separately (fig. 12). Tellingly, the largest exception to the GSE-subprime trade-off is Countrywide, which at the peak was the nation's largest mortgage originator. "Since its foundation in 1969," Cassidy recounts, "Countrywide had portrayed itself as a conservative issuer of prime loans, but it had also adapted a 'match-

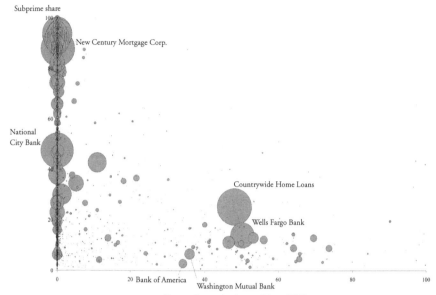

Figure 12.
Same-year mortgage sales to GSEs and subprime share. Circle sizes are scaled proportional to total number of rate-spread originations. Source: Federal Financial Institutions Examination Council, *Frequently Asked Questions about the New HMDA Data* (Washington, D.C.: Federal Financial Institutions Examination Council, 2007).

ing strategy,' which committed it to offering its customers any deal that its rivals were offering."[66] The crescendo of competition between 2004 and 2006 drove Countrywide into loans that Angelo Mozilo knew were dubious (judging from the private e-mails that have circulated in the press and legal proceedings). But as the nation's largest originator, Countrywide had to move into the "new market" of middle-class whites to maintain volume, in a multivariate loan model of subprime segmentation, income makes no difference, although the lender was apparently reserving its prime products for the larger loans. Tract minority composition measure is close to parity. Disparities for African Americans and Hispanics (2.1 and 1.4, respectively) are not as bad as many other lenders.

Mozilo famously declared in a Milken Institute speech that the firm had been forced to lower its lending standards and "the industry faced special pressure from minority advocates to help people buy homes."[67] Investigative journalists later discovered exactly where the pressure had come from. Shortly after becoming chief executive of Fannie Mae, Daniel H. Mudd traveled to Mozilo's office in the hills northwest of Los Angeles, where Mozilo warned him that Fannie's reluctance to buy the firm's more risky loans threatened their long-standing partnership; Countrywide now had the option of bypassing the GSEs and selling directly to Bear Stearns, Lehman Brothers, and Goldman Sachs. "You're becoming irrelevant," Mozilo reportedly told Mudd; "You need us more than we need you . . . and if you don't take these loans, you'll find you can lose so much more."[68]

Alternative Cartographies

Understanding these new spaces of unequal risk requires that we view states, cities, and neighborhoods from the perspective of financial institutions. This means taking seriously Peter Gould's quip that "space is not a wastepaper basket that sits there waiting for us to fill it with things, but something we define to suit our needs."[69] One way to accomplish this definition involves using the mathematical transformations of multidimensional scaling to map crucial facets of the boom and the subsequent crash,[70] in the context of varied state regulations on predatory lending.[71]

The resulting two-dimensional mathematical projection charts the contours of a painful housing collapse (fig. 13). This is not a chart but a map: states to the "south" on this map have laws establishing standards well above the weak federal limits. The strongest state laws are found south of a line running just above New Jersey, Washington, D.C., and New York, and extending south of Colorado to curve up, including Georgia and Texas. Highly leveraged subprime borrowers with low credit scores are more prevalent to the "east," while low-doc loans are more common to the "west." The housing boom drove prices up the most in the northwest quadrant of the map, and it is here where prices fell the farthest in the crisis: on the ride up from 2001, real house prices increased more than 90 percent in an arc stretching from New York through what the business press dubbed the "sand states" (California, Florida, Nevada, and Arizona) to Maryland; by early 2010, prices had fallen at least 39 percent in the sand states. Fully 30 percent of the subprime loans outstanding in Florida were in some stage of foreclosure in May 2010.

This alternative cartography presents an unusual view of the states, but it is not entirely abstract. The upper-right-hand section of the map has few state restrictions, generally higher subprime market penetration, and a subprime profile oriented toward highly leveraged, low-credit borrowers; most of the Confederacy remains in this section of the map, a reminder that "a pall of debt" still "hangs over" the land more than a century after W. E. B. Du Bois's eloquent analysis.[72] From the perspective of lenders and the housing boom, the midsection of the map stretches all the way from Oregon to Montana,

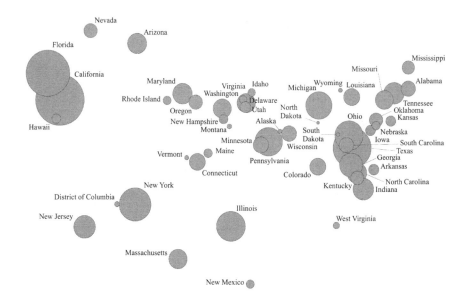

Figure 13.
U.S. states in housing finance space, 2004–2010. Map created with classical multiple dimensional scaling algorithm. Circle sizes are scaled proportional to total number of rate-spread originations. Sources: Federal Financial Institutions Examination Council, *Frequently Asked Questions about the New HMDA Data* (Washington, D.C.: Federal Financial Institutions Examination Council, 2007); Federal Reserve Bank of New York, *Nonprime Mortgage Conditions in the United States* (New York: Board of Governors of the Federal Reserve, 2010); and FHFA (2011).

Michigan, and Pennsylvania, with middle-range scores on most indicators. The regulatory battlegrounds are New Jersey, New York, Massachusetts, Illinois, and New Mexico. New Mexico stands out as exceptional, with Governor Bill Richardson working with a coalition of church officials to pass major predatory lending legislation in 2003.[73] But in the non-Euclidian space of housing finance and regulation, the state next door is far away, at the epicenter of deregulatory growth that collapsed in California, Florida, Nevada, and Arizona.[74]

Other spatial contortions are apparent elsewhere on the map: New York is right next to Washington, D.C., which is itself reconfigured in turn by legal geographies. In terms of consumer protection, the leafy streets of northwest Washington and the disinvested blocks of Anacostia are closer to the distant, working-class small towns of the Appalachian ridge-and-valley section of Virginia than to the adjacent suburbs of Maryland and West Virginia. And in one of those Virginia suburbs, about half of all the debt claims of mortgage borrowers across all of America's states, cities, and suburbs are legally claimed by a single company, Mortgage Electronic Registration Systems (MERS).[75]

Capital and law are constantly reconstructing this map of American federalism. The integration of persistent local segregation processes with broader networks of securitization, however, may destabilize the gerrymandered electoral geographies that have long favored conservative and reactionary factions in the United States.[76] Subprime expansion beyond the confines of northern inner cities into the expanding Sun Belt suburbs has devastated housing wealth—and all the conservative ideological promises of home ownership—in precisely those places where Democratic and Republican competition is most fierce, and where the coalition of economic and cultural conservatives is most unstable. This becomes clear from the foreclosure and delinquency estimates compiled as part of the Neighborhood Stabilization Program.[77] While many of the highest local delinquency rates appear in the safe Democratic seats of northern deindustrializing cities, the largest *number* of foreclosures hit hardest in a mixture of Democratic and Republican districts in the states that appear in the upper-left corner of figure 13: parts of North Las Vegas, Victorville, and other centers across Riverside and San Bernardino counties in California's Inland Empire, the Phoenix area, and Miami-Dade. The single hardest-hit neighborhood in the nation, a block group with more than two thousand foreclosure starts as of May 2010, is in a patchwork of master-planned communities in the San Tan Valley in Arizona's Sixth Congressional District, southeast of Phoenix. This is Goldwater territory, about two-thirds Anglo white and one-quarter Latino, represented by the rock-solid conservative commitments of Jeff Flake. Flake is now running for John Kyl's Senate seat, and in October 2012 he will receive the "Defending the American Dream Award" at the Sixth Annual "Defending the American Dream Summit" sponsored by the Koch Brothers' Americans for Prosperity Foundation. Flake's opposition to foreclosure relief—in early 2009, he tweeted, "my constituents wonder why they have to keep paying for others' mistakes"—nicely symbolizes the Right's attempts to restore the natural affinity of home ownership with the cult of John Galt heroic individual entrepreneurialism. The Right's coalition of cultural and economic conservatives seems to be holding for now. But the alliance is unstable, and it is becoming harder to find scapegoats for the devastation of the home equity premiums once provided by suburban white privilege.

Conclusions: A Paler Shade of the American Racial State?

"As he traveled across South Carolina on Tuesday, Mr. Santorum . . . said the party can win back the White House only by offering a 'clear contrast' with President Obama.

'We need contrasts,' Mr. Santorum said, 'not just a paler shade of what we have.'"
    —Jeff Zeleny, "Santorum Cites a Local Legend," *New York Times*

> The present moment constitutes a bundle of contradictions in respect to racism. How is it possible to have persistent forms of racial inequality in a period in which colorblindness is the hegemonic racial ideology and most whites claim that racism is no longer relevant?
> —Michael Omi and Howard Winant, *Racial Formation in the United States: From the 1960s to the 1990s*

Housing in America, once the foundation of a national identity of domestic family security and economic upward mobility, is deeply unstable in today's rapidly shifting racial state. Housing was at the birth of America's latest lurch to the right: Rick Santelli's call for "a tea party" went viral after the financial anchor screamed about "bailing out the losers" when news broke in early 2009 that the Obama administration was considering plans to write down a small part of the principal for some mortgages. The administration quickly backed off and was able to get Congress to agree to only very limited programs helping borrowers—most of them requiring the voluntary participation of mortgage servicers. We are now half a decade into the American Housing Depression. By the time the Republican primary contest heated up in early 2012, the American Right was working furiously to restore the ideological stability of capital accumulation, consumer responsibility, and corporate rights. Gone was the "shocked disbelief" of a Fed chairman forced to admit in open congressional testimony that his "whole intellectual edifice" had collapsed. Once again, the national conversation went back to the Right's familiar Reagan mantra: government is not the solution to the problem, government *is* the problem.[78] In the populist conservative imagination, it is all about public debt, and too much government spending going to help others—*those* people, everyone but me, us, and ours—all those *others*.

American capital achieves its fixes through a hybrid racial state. One part of the racial state is the fluid, dynamic interplay of images, discourses, and ideologies used to fight over the meanings of racial categories and their political mobilization.[79] Thus we have Herman Cain's meteoric trajectory as a one-hit-wonder Republican primary candidate achieving popularity with his "9-9-9" tax plan that maps the way to the Steve Forbes flat-tax world. When sexual harassment allegations sent Cain's campaign into a nosedive, Cain joked that he wondered if Anita Hill might not endorse him. A few months later he appeared on Bill Maher's "Real Time" in front of a poster advertising the "documentary" film *Runaway Slave: From Tyranny to Liberty*. *Runaway Slave* "discovers the unknown history of the Civil Rights Movement" and "exposes the NAACP as a mouthpiece of the Democratic Party, and the NAACP's leaders as the ultimate 'race hustlers' who perpetuate—and profit—from a victim mentality that hurts the African-American community."[80] Produced by

Dick Armey's Freedom Works, *Runaway Slave* declares that "while the African-American community has triumphed over the scourge of physical slavery, many still suffer from a mental slavery—to government."[81]

This simulacra racial state moves fast: racial images, categories, and politics move like mercury. It does have serious performative consequences, and thus the critical Left must always be in the arena to challenge the evasive new constructions of white privilege manufactured by the powerful coalitions of capital and racism. But another part of the project must devote attention to the old-fashioned material inequalities that are still quite literally *located* in real places and real neighborhoods. This part of the American racial state involves the layering of fast capital on a mixture of urban landscapes—some of them rapidly growing, others quickly declining, others slow and stable. The interplay of suburbanization, history, demography, and all the hidden biases of market practices and public policy help reinforce many of the old inequalities. The evidence from the foreclosure disaster tells a painfully familiar story: using the most widespread ways of measuring segregation in the nation's one hundred largest metropolitan areas, J. S. Rugh and D. S. Massey find that black–white residential segregation has a significant, independent effect on foreclosure.[82] The magnitude of the effect, moreover, "clearly exceeds that of other factors linked by earlier studies to inter-metropolitan variation in foreclosures."[83] Even as old forms of discriminatory exclusion gave way to new kinds of segmented inclusion, residential segregation remained a crucial site of tensions and contradictions in American housing.

America's subprime boom reconfigured the scale of class-monopoly rent.[84] Local loan sharks were replaced by a vast food chain of predators in pinstripes, each claiming a share of the surplus value extracted from borrowers, or of the fee income thrown off by the manufacture of fictitious mortgage capital. Loan sharks know they are loan sharks. But today's predators deny all intent to deceive, or discriminate. For many, this claim may be an honest defense: millions of ordinary middle-class investors around the world received quarterly financial statements on portfolios that, inevitably, included substantial investments in mortgage-backed securities—many of them those famous "tranches" backed by the monthly payments of subprime borrowers who may have been pushed into usurious obligations by deceptive local brokers. But we can acknowledge the absence of discriminatory intent in the newly transnationalized commodity chain of class-monopoly rent without denying the persistence of deeply racist processes, structures, and outcomes: this is the crucial legal distinction between *disparate treatment* and *disparate impacts*. Good intentions are no match for the powerful structures of law and capital accumulation. Perspective also matters, in the simple numerators and denominators of all those statistics. If you care about a particular marginalized community, then the high rates of market penetration are what matters. Between 2004 and 2010 the market share of high-risk subprime mortgages to single black women was almost four times the share for Anglo white couples. But Wall Street sees a different view: Anglo white couples outnumber single black women three to one. Wall Street made it clear that local brokers and lenders could target any submarket, any community that made sense in a particular urban and regional context—so long as borrowers were delivered to feed the vast securitization machine.[85] In the expansion, grabbing market share meant adapting some of the old abuses used to strip wealth from the black inner city to the broader multicultural mosaic of the Sun Belt suburbs—including a growing proportion of Anglo whites. Now, in the Depression, the old exclusionary disparate impacts are making a comeback in a troubling equilibrium of white privilege. Nationwide loan-level models of black-white mortgage segmentation (controlling for income and other factors) fell from 3.1 in 2006 to 1.6 in 2009, but the old black-white denial disparities shot up from 1.9 to 2.5 in the same period.

The evidence presented in this article documents the crucial role of institutional and legal strategies in reshaping the relations between neighborhood racial inequalities and national and transnational networks of financialization. The devastation wrought by deregulated mortgage capital exploited the loopholes of federalism in ways that may have destabilized the long-established role of racial segregation in maintaining American class inequality. In the familiar story of inner-city and inner-suburban segregation, financial exploitation reproduced relatively stable forms of gerrymandered political marginalization. But now we have a more confusing story in the vast archipelago of gated communities in Sun Belt suburbs, where even the racially and ethnically integrated master-planned subdivisions are trapped by the fears of losing the home equity premium so long promised by American white privilege. Anita Hill is right that "the American Dream means nothing if it is not inclusive," but so is Derrick Bell when he demands that we "'Get Real' about race and racism in America."[86] One part of getting real involves building the infrastructure of discrimination enforcement that was stripped out of civil rights legislation in the 1960s and 1970s to avoid Southern filibusters.[87] That might offer a first step toward the "simplified and clarified" meaning of housing in America, "with a renewed emphasis on shelter and neighborhood" as well as genuine equality.[88]

Notes

We are grateful for the valuable comments from the anonymous *AQ* referee, as well as helpful recommendations from guest editors Paula Chakravartty and Denise Ferreira da Silva. Any remaining deficiencies remain the responsibility of the first author.

1. Gwendolyn Wright, *Building the Dream: A Social History of Housing in America* (New York: Random House, 1981).
2. A. Leon Higginbotham Jr., "An Open Letter to Justice Clarence Thomas from a Federal Judicial Colleague," *University of Pennsylvania Law Review* 140 (1991): 1005–28; Anita Hill, *Reimagining Equality: Stories of Gender, Race, and Finding Home* (Boston: Beacon, 2011).
3. Michael Omi and Howard Winant, *Racial Formation in the United States: From the 1960s to the 1990s* (New York: Routledge, 1994).
4. Derrick Bell, "After We're Gone: Prudent Speculations on America in a Postracial Epoch," *St. Louis Law Review* 34 (1989): 393.
5. Elvin Wyly and C. S. Ponder, "Gender, Age, and Race in Subprime America," *Housing Policy Debate* 21.4 (2011): 529–64.
6. Anita F. Hill, "Marriage and Patronage in the Empowerment and Disempowerment of African-American Women," in *Race, Gender, and Power in America: The Legacy of the Hill-Thomas Hearings*, ed. Anita F. Hill and Emma Coleman Jordan (Oxford: Oxford University Press, 1995), 274.
7. Ibid., 275, 289.
8. Hill, *Reimagining Equality*, 167.
9. Dan Barry, Serge F. Kovalevski, Campbell Robertson, and Lizette Alvarez, "In the Eye of a Firestorm," *New York Times*, April 1, 2012.
10. Ibid.
11. Financial Crisis Inquiry Commission, *The Financial Crisis Inquiry Report* (Washington, D.C.: National Commission on the Causes of the Financial and Economic Crisis in the United States, 2011), 105.
12. Rich Benjamin, "The Gated Community Mentality," *New York Times*, March 29, 2012.
13. Ibid.
14. Edward J. Blakely, "Us versus Them: Gated Communities Provide False Sense of Security," *Washington Post*, April 15, 2012.
15. Omi and Winant, *Racial Formation*; Omi and Winant, "Thinking through Race and Racism," *Contemporary Sociology* 38.2 (2009): 121–25; and David Theo Goldberg, *The Racial State* (Malden, Mass.: Blackwell, 2002).
16. Kathleen C. Engel and Patricia A. McCoy, "A Tale of Three Markets: The Law and Economics of Predatory Lending," *Texas Law Review* 80.6 (2002): 1255–381; Engel and McCoy, *The Subprime Virus* (New York: Oxford University Press, 2011).
17. Hill, *Reimagining Equality*.
18. Daniel Immergluck, *Foreclosed* (Ithaca, N.Y.: Cornell University Press, 2009); Gillian Tett, *Fool's Gold* (New York: Free Press, 2009); A. R. Sorkin, *Too Big to Fail: The Inside Story of How Wall Street and Washington Fought to Save the Financial System—and Themselves* (New York: Viking, 2009); Financial Crisis Inquiry Commission, *Financial Crisis Inquiry Report*; J. P. Relman, *Second Amended Complaint, Mayor and City Council of Baltimore v. Wells Fargo Bank, N.A.*, Case 1:08-cv-00062 JFM, filed April 10, 2010, Baltimore, U.S. District Court for the District of Baltimore; and Engel and McCoy, *Subprime Virus*.
19. For a valuable exception, see Alex Schafran and Jake Wegman, "Restructuring, Race, and Real Estate: Changing Home Values and the New California Metropolis, 1989–2010," *Urban Geography* 33.5 (forthcoming).
20. John S. Adams, "The Meaning of Housing in America," *Annals of the Association of American Geographers* 74.4 (1984): 515–26; Adams, "Housing Markets in the Twilight of Materialism," *Professional Geographer* 38.3 (1986): 233–37; James W. Hughes and George Sternlieb, *The Dynamics of America's Housing* (New Brunswick, N.J.: Center for Urban Policy Research, 1987).
21. Adams, "Housing Markets."
22. Saskia Sassen, "When Local Housing Becomes an Electronic Instrument: The Global Circulation of Mortgages," *International Journal of Urban and Regional Research* 33.2 (2009): 411.
23. Kathe Newman, "Post-industrial Widgets: Capital Flows and the Production of the Urban," *International Journal of Urban and Regional Research* 33.2 (2009): 314–31.

24. Manuel B. Aalbers, ed., *Subprime Cities: The Political Economy of Mortgage Markets* (West Sussex, U.K.: Wiley-Blackwell, 2012).

25. Daniel Bell, *The Coming of Postindustrial Society* (New York: Basic Books, 1973).

26. Phil Ashton, "An Appetite for Yield: The Anatomy of the Subprime Crisis," *Environment and Planning A* 41.6 (2009): 1420–41.

27. David Harvey, *Spaces of Hope* (Berkeley: University of California Press, 2000).

28. Douglas Massey and Nancy Denton, *American Apartheid: Segregation and the Making of the Underclass* (Cambridge, Mass.: Harvard University Press, 1993).

29. Joseph E. Stiglitz and Andrew Weiss, "Credit Rationing in Markets with Imperfect Information," *American Economic Review* 71.3 (1981): 393–410.

30. Engel and McCoy, "Tale of Three Markets"; Gregory D. Squires, ed., *From Redlining to Reinvestment* (Philadelphia: Temple University Press, 1992); Squires, ed., *Organizing Access to Capital* (Philadelphia: Temple University Press, 2003); and Jeff R. Crump, Kathe Newman, Eric S. Belsky, Phil Ashton, David H. Kaplan, Daniel J. Hammel, and Elvin Wyly, "Cities Destroyed (Again) for Cash: Forum on the U.S. Foreclosure Crisis," *Urban Geography* 29.8 (2008): 745–84.

31. Immergluck, *Foreclosed*.

32. Wyly and Ponder, "Gender, Age, and Race." These figures, and all of the original tables and charts presented in this article, are built from publicly available data sets on individual loan applications, originations, and lending institutions (Federal Financial Institutions Examination Council, *Home Mortgage Disclosure Act, Raw Data* [Washington, D.C.: Federal Financial Institutions Examination Council]; U.S. Department of Housing and Urban Development, *Neighborhood Stabilization Program 3 Downloadable Date Files* [Washington, D.C.: U.S. Department of Housing and Urban Development, 2011], http://www.huduser.org; R. Avery, *HMDA Lender File, 2008 Filing Year* [Washington, D.C.: Board of Governors of the Federal Reserve, 2009]). Our data sets define "subprime" according to the "rate-spread" trigger specified in Home Mortgage Disclosure Act (HMDA) regulations. Rate-spread loans are those obligations with total annual percentage rate borrowing costs (including points and fees) more than three percentage points above Treasury security yields of comparable maturity for first-lien loans, and more than five percentage points for subordinate liens. For further details, see http://www.geog.ubc.ca/~ewyly/replication.html#aq.

33. David Harvey, *Social Justice and the City* (London: Edward Arnold, 1973); Harvey, "Class-Monopoly Rent, Finance Capital, and the Urban Revolution," *Regional Studies* 8.3–4 (1974): 239–55; see also Crump et al., "Cities Destroyed (Again)."

34. Many middle-class whites sought to use the years of easy credit and rising house prices to regain the equity windfalls they lost with the end of the 1990s stock market boom. Countrywide's CEO told the Financial Crisis Inquiry Commission that "housing prices were rising so rapidly—at a rate that I'd never seen in my 55 years in the business—that people, regular people, average people got caught up in the mania of buying a house, and flipping it, making money" (*Financial Crisis Inquiry Report*, 5).

35. Immergluck, *Foreclosed*; Tett, *Fool's Gold*; FCIC, *Financial Crisis Inquiry Report*; Relman, *Second Amended Complaint*; Engel and McCoy, *Subprime Virus*.

36. Newman, "Post-industrial Widgets."

37. Harvey, *Social Justice and the City*, 312–14; Harvey, "The Urban Process under Capitalism: A Framework for Analysis," *International Journal of Urban and Regional Research* 2 (1978): 101–31; Harvey, *Urbanization of Capital* (Baltimore, Md.: Johns Hopkins University Press, 1985).

38. See, e.g., R. J. King, "Capital Switching and the Role of Ground Rent: 1. Theoretical Problems," *Environment and Planning A* 21 (1989): 445–62; Robert A. Beauregard, "Capital Switching and the Built Environment, United States, 1970–89," *Environment and Planning A* 26 (1994): 715–32; and Kevin Fox Gotham, "Creating Liquidity out of Spatial Fixity: The Secondary Circuit of Capital and the Subprime Mortgage Crisis," *International Journal of Urban and Regional Research* 33.2 (2009): 355–71.

39. Ben Bernanke, "The Global Saving Glut and the US Current Account Deficit," Richmond, Virginia Association of Economists, March 19, 2005; and Alan Greenspan, "US Moving Closer to Recession," *ABC News This Week*, December 16, 2007.

40. Edmund Andrews, "Bernanke, a Hero to His Own, Can't Shake Critics," *New York Times*, August 20, 2009.

41. Marshall Berman, *All That Is Solid Melts into* Air (New York: Simon and Schuster, 1982).
42. Neil Brenner, "The Urban Question as a Scale Question: Reflections on Henri Lefebvre, Urban Theory, and the Politics of Scale," *International Journal of Urban and Regional Research* 23.2 (2000): 361–78.
43. Daniel J. Elazar, *American Federalism: A View from the States*, 2nd ed. (New York: Crowell, 1970).
44. Elvin Wyly and Daniel J. Hammel, "Capital's Metropolis: Chicago and the Transformation of American Housing Policy," *Geografiska Annaler* 83B.4 (2000): 181–206.
45. Herman Schwartz, "Finance and the State in the Housing Bubble," in *Subprime Cities*, ed. M. B. Aalbers (West Sussex, U.K.: Wiley, 2012), 54; and David Listokin, Elvin Wyly, Larry Keating, Kristopher Rengert, and Barbara Listokin, *Making New Mortgage Markets: Case Studies of Institutions, Home Buyers, and Communities* (Washington, D.C.: Fannie Mae Foundation, 2000).
46. Schwartz, "Finance and the State," 54.
47. Patricia A. McCoy and Elizabeth Renuart, *The Legal Infrastructure of Subprime and Nontraditional Home Mortgages* (Cambridge, Mass.: Harvard Joint Center for Housing Studies, 2008), 5.
48. McCoy and Renuart, *Legal Infrastructure*.
49. Cathy Lesser Mansfield, "The Road to Subprime HEL Was Paved with Good Congressional Intentions: Usury Deregulation and the Subprime Home Equity Market," *South Carolina Law Review* 51 (2000): 473–559.
50. Margaret J. Miller, ed., *Credit Reporting Systems and the International Economy* (Cambridge, Mass.: MIT Press, 2003).
51. Simon Johnson and James Kwak, *Thirteen Bankers: The Wall Street Takeover and the Next Financial Meltdown* (New York: Pantheon, 2010), 73.
52. Engel and McCoy, *Subprime Virus*, 234–36.
53. J. Wiggins and Vincent Boland, "U.S. Treasury Completes the Eclipse of the Long Bond," *Financial Times*, November 2, 2001, 24.
54. Robert D. Hershey, "Learning to Love Fannie and Freddie," *New York Times*, November 4, 2002.
55. Johnson and Kwak, *Thirteen Bankers*.
56. Crump et al., "Cities Destroyed (Again)"; Engel and McCoy, "Tale of Three Markets"; Engel and McCoy, *Subprime Virus*; Daniel Immergluck, *Credit to the Community* (Armonk, N.Y.: M. E. Sharpe); Immergluck, *Foreclosed*; Newman, "Post-industrial Widgets"; Squires, *Organizing Access*.
57. Viral V. Acharya, Thomas F. Cooley, Matthew P. Richardson, and Ingo Walter, eds., *Regulating Wall Street: The Dodd-Frank Act and the New Global Architecture of Global Finance* (Hoboken, N.J.: Wiley, 2010).
58. Engel and McCoy, *Subprime Virus*.
59. Adams, "Housing Markets," 234.
60. W. E. B. Du Bois, *The Souls of Black Folk* (1903; rpt. New York: Barnes and Nobles Classics, 2003).
61. Robert L. Boyd, "New York, Chicago, and the 'Black Metropolis' of the Early 20th Century," *Urban Geography* 32.7 (2011): 1066–83.
62. Raphael W. Bostic, Kathleen C. Engel, Patricia A. McCoy, Anthony Pennington-Cross, and Susan M. Wachter, *The Impact of State Anti-Predatory Lending Laws: Policy Implications and Insights* (Cambridge, Mass.: Harvard University Joint Center for Housing Studies, 2008).
63. Engel and McCoy, *Subprime Virus*, 9.
64. The sole exception to this pattern—the one lender type with a GSE odds ratio over 1—involves financial holding companies organized as foreign banking organizations. The largest player in this category is HSBC, whose 2002 purchase of the notorious subprime lender Household International accelerated the transnational integration of high-risk American borrowing with the high net savings rates of Asian depositors (Andrew R. Sorkin, "HSBC to Buy U.S. Lender for $14.2 Billion," *New York Times*, November 15, 2002; Michael Lewis, *The Big Short* [London: Allen Lane, 2010], 16–18).
65. Financial Crisis Inquiry Commission, *Financial Crisis Inquiry Report*, xxvi.
66. John Cassidy, *How Markets Fail* (New York: Farrar, Straus and Giroux, 2009), 246.
67. Gretchen Morgenson and Geraldine Fabrikant, "Countrywide's Chief Salesman and Defender," *New York Times*, November 11, 2007.
68. Charles Duhigg, "Pressured to Take More Risk, Fannie Reached Tipping Point," *New York Times*, October 5, 2008.
69. Peter R. Gould, *The Geographer at Work* (London: Routledge and Kegan Paul, 1986), 202.
70. J. B. Kruskal, "Nonmetric Multidimensional Scaling," *Psychometrica* 29 (1964): 115–29; J. B. Kruskal and M. Wish, *Multidimensional Scaling* (Thousand Oaks, Calif.: Sage, 1978).

71. For each state, we included measures of the inflation-adjusted rise and fall of home prices (between 2001 and the first quarter of 2010), the share of nonprime loans in foreclosure, the share of loans made to borrowers with loan-to-value ratios over 90 percent and FICO scores below 620, and the share of low- and no-doc loans. State legal protections against predatory lending are measured with Bostic et al.'s (*Impact of State Anti-Predatory Lending Laws*) classification, describing conditions as of 2004–5.

72. Du Bois, *Souls of Black Folk*, 92.

73. Jane Lampman, "Bill Richardson: A Negotiator's Faith in Fairness and Finding the Common Good," *Christian Science Monitor*, December 6, 2007.

74. C. Lincoln Combs, "Banking Law and Regulation: Predatory Lending in Arizona," *Arizona State Law Journal* 38 (2006): 617.

75. Michael Powell and Gretchen Morgenson, "MERS? It May Have Swallowed Your Loan," *New York Times*, March 5, 2011.

76. Jacob S. Rugh and Douglas S. Massey, "Racial Segregation and the American Foreclosure Crisis," *American Sociological Review* 75.5 (2010): 629–51.

77. U.S. Department of Housing and Urban Development, *Neighborhood Stabilization Program*.

78. David Harvey, *A Brief History of Neoliberalism* (Oxford: Oxford University Press, 2005); Jamie Peck, *Constructions of Neoliberal Reason* (Oxford: Oxford University Press, 2010).

79. Omi and Winant, *Racial Formation*; Goldberg, *Racial State*; Peck, *Constructions of Neoliberal Reason*.

80. M. Kibbe, *Runaway Slave Documentary Movie Poster*, Flickr, January 15, 2012.

81. Ibid.

82. Rugh and Massey, "Racial Segregation."

83. Ibid., 641.

84. Harvey, *Social Justice*.

85. See Financial Crisis Inquiry Commission, *Financial Crisis Inquiry Report*, 104–6.

86. Hill, *Reimagining Equality*, 167; Derrick Bell, "Racial Realism," *Connecticut Law Review* 24.2 (1991): 363–95.

87. Rugh and Massey, "Racial Segregation."

88. Adams, "Housing Markets," 234.

Welcome to My Cell: Housing and Race in the Mirror of American Democracy

Ofelia Ortiz Cuevas

In June 2002, six years before the subprime crisis that would send the global economic system into a tailspin, then president George W. Bush addressed the congregation of the St. Paul AME Church in Atlanta, Georgia. The topic of his speech was a new program aimed at fulfilling the "American dream" through an ambitious domestic project to extend private home ownership to those who had hitherto been excluded from it. Explicitly acknowledging the disproportionately low percentage of African American and Hispanic home-owners, Bush's plan involved removing the barriers people of color faced when buying a home. This address, just one year after New York's Twin Towers were toppled, politically and historically linked the war on terror with a revised project of domestic racial equality:

> And as we work for a more secure world, we've got to work for a better world too. And that means as we work on our security from possible attacks by terrorists, we also work on economic security. The two securities go hand in hand. . . . And part of economic security is owning your own home. Part of being a secure America is to encourage homeownership. So somebody can say, this is my home, welcome to my home.[1]

By situating the issue of domestic home ownership and its racial inequalities within the broader discourse of national and global security, Bush (or rather his speechwriters/handlers) attempted to articulate the emergent connections between the new war(s) abroad and a renewed multicultural agenda at home.[2] Economic security, symbolized by home ownership, and global security, symbolized by the spread of U.S.-style democracy, are the refracted image of the symbol of the home in the imperial mirror of American democracy. This symbolism of home as the realization of the American dream and a basic human need hides the violent side of housing—the incarceration and incapacitation of black and brown peoples domestically and abroad.[3]

The notion of "security" deployed by Bush circa 2002 refers not only to abstract, emotive, and ideological states but to individual financial assets, or to the certificates indicating ownership of them. At the time, investment banks were already engaging in the process of *securitization*, the transformation of mortgage debt into a commodity appropriate to the speculative requirements of modern markets. There was, of course, no mention—nor was it likely foreseen by his administration—that securitization would undermine whatever benefits the imagined "security" of home ownership might provide, particularly for African Americans and Latinos.

This article explores the dual meaning of the terms *security* and *securitization* by engaging the inversion in which the racial subject, on the one hand, is positioned as a consumer of a sophisticated financial product (a mortgage) and, on the other, is acted on as a product, a body that fills a bed in a system of incarceration and captivity. Both forms of housing find their place under the rubric of securitization, conceived in the full force of its double meaning, in terms of the transformation of debt into financial securities and of the financialization of "security," that is, of state violence and social control. I am interested in the inverted relationship to property, debt, and housing that, through the vicious dual logic of securitization, is forged at the very basis of the black and brown subject. This racial rubric of the black and brown subject are those populations formed by the carceral state's logics of racial organization embodied in the U.S. histories of war, occupation, settlement, and slavery. The historical relation of the racial body to property in the United States has always been made material through violence, whether it was blacks as property during the era of chattel slavery, the expulsion of native people from their land through not only violence but a definition of property that excluded them, or the occupation of the mestizo Southwest and the forced acquisition of Mexican land, which occurred not in opposition to but *by means of* law.

I begin by discussing the fundamental role of the notion of property in both liberal and idealist concepts of personhood and freedom, and the privileged position of the home in forming those concepts, through which home owner-ship functions as a precondition for any meaningful conception of personhood and freedom. Such a conception, though, operates on the basis of a universal-ity that is implicitly white and that, historically, has explicitly excluded black and brown people in the United States from both home ownership and the multivalent security that it ostensibly provides.

In the following section, I discuss that exclusion and trace the widespread invitation of black and brown Americans into a housing market radically trans-formed by shifts in the global economy. After decades of market liberalization, debt—and specifically mortgage debt—had become a complex and increasingly valuable financial product. Black and brown people thus entered the market not as home owners but as consumers of debt as commodity. They were cut off not only from the possibility of acquiring any real value or accumulation of wealth but also from the full personhood and freedom held out to them by the promise of home ownership.

As a result of that double exclusion, the only kind of "secure housing" they would be offered would be found on the other side of what I call the dark mirror of democratic security, in the hundreds of thousands of housing units where predominately black and brown men, women, and children are contained as security threats: in prison cells. Even statistically, the inversion was almost identical. At the time of Bush's speech, white people in the United States were 1.5 times more likely to own a home than black or brown people.[4] At the same time, incarcerated Americans were 1.6 times more likely to be black or brown than white.[5] In 2002 whites were as likely to own a home as African Americans and Latinos were to be housed in a prison, jail, or detention center. This was not a coincidence, I argue, but reveals a material reality rooted in the confluence of what home, housing, and race have come to mean in the contemporary markets of neoliberal securities, that is, both financial products such as mortgage securities and the overall state security apparatus.

In the final section, I thus map out the growth of a massive security apparatus in the form the largest carceral system in the world, which presently incarcerates 2.5 million people. This system where black and brown people disproportionately find themselves housed functions as a mirrored inversion of white freedom and home ownership. Finally, in conclusion, I examine the consequences of the long and tragic arc of this double movement of securitization by comparing the seemingly modest demands of the Pelican Bay prison strikes of 2011 to the emancipatory projects that underlay the prison uprisings of the early 1970s. What we have lost in the intervening years, I argue, is a projected future, a horizon of freedom.

It is to gain this perspective that I consider the housing crisis in the context of the era of superincarceration and the massive contemporary housing of black and brown people in prison, jails, and detention centers. From gymnasiums crowded with dozens of three-tiered bunk beds that house hundreds of men, to the standard cell that rooms two to four cellmates, to the end-of-the-line containers called maximum security housing units, in which a single prisoner inhabits a single cell alone for years on end—the imprisonment of black and brown people is the space in the rubric of securitization through which we can see the inversion of the American dream and the ontological security that house and home (property and possession) mean in the United States. Offering the opportunity of home ownership to black and brown people in the wake of September 11 shows a simultaneous reliance on the powerful discourse of material/economic security (what used to be understood to embody accumulated wealth through home ownership) and national-state security seen as the absence of threat to the national body.

Personhood, Property, and Politics

Before I turn to the other side of the mirror of imperialist democracy, however, it is necessary to grasp something of the centrality of "home" in the annals of modern Republicanism and in the constitution of modern politics. In both its liberal (Lockean) and idealist (Hegelian) conceptions, our very understanding of what constitutes personhood are founded in property and property relations. For John Locke, even the body—the material seat of the self—is regarded fundamentally as property:

> Yet every man has a property in his own person: this no body has any right to but himself. The labour of his body, and the work of his hands, we may say, are properly his. Whatsoever then he removes out of the state that nature hath provided, and left it in, he hath mixed his labour with, and joined to it something that is his own, and thereby makes it his property.[6]

Man's labor and its material products were his property, but in the Lockean tradition that informs American law, so were his rights. Not only did one have a right to property, but one's relationship to one's body and one's rights assumed the form of a property relation: personhood could not even be conceived except by way of property. One's humanity is something one *owns*. As David Abraham puts it, "There is property in rights as well as a right to property."[7] Hence the latter right worked as a pragmatic precondition to the full exercise of other political rights (for most of the first half of the nineteenth century, only white, male property owners were allowed to vote) and hence to full political personhood. Even when it appears absent, the law is saturated by property, as Abraham writes: "One result has been that even in those arenas of the law presumptively removed from issues of property, property governs conceptualization and discourse on all sides."[8] Property, in the liberal conception, is hinged on exclusivity, on exclusion. That I own a home means that no one else can claim it. Such a forceful exclusion requires the full violence of the law as the means to enforce, sustain, and continually reproduce the divisioning between inside and outside, mine and yours, ours and theirs, and so on.

Nicholas Blomley finds this violence also in the roots of the liberal notion of property, itself dependent on "a domain of non-property," conceived by Locke and later by Jeremy Bentham in racialized, colonial terms as an outside—both geographically and historically, an extrahistoric and distinctly non-European condition.[9] Blomley quotes Locke—"In the beginning, all was *America*"—and concludes, "Western notions of property are deeply invested in a colonial geography, a white mythology, in which the racialized figure of the savage plays a central role."[10] Property did not have to be explicitly denied to nonwhites (though of course it was): the very possibility of ownership was only conceivable for whites. Whoever existed outside whiteness existed outside property as well, or simply *as property*.

Similarly, Hegel situates property as the means through which the individual realizes himself as a being in the world, "superseding and replacing the subjective phase of personality,"[11] and saving it from abstractness. Here the person bestows meaning unto property as an expression of identity by applying his will (of possession) in relation to the property—with the act of possession not only to satisfy need but also to *experience freedom*—the point from which a person could engage in civil society. "Property is the first embodiment of freedom," G. W. F. Hegel writes, "and so is in itself a substantive end."[12]

The home, situated within this nexus of property, liberty, and freedom, takes on a distinctive role in Hegelian self-development. Margaret Jane Radin argues that the home has been overlooked or taken for granted in legal thought, so basic is the relation of property to personhood. The home is identified as a resource essential (even most essential) to the person, which makes it "worthier of protection than other property."[13] Radin theorizes property as occupancy: the owners must be present in the object for it to take on a status superior to that of a simple commodity. Such occupancy grants it a status greater than mere fungibility. Because it is viewed as essential to life, providing shelter, protection, and security, the home takes on a moral component as well. It is the site of family and domestic relations, of the possibility of a future, both in terms of biological reproduction and of the projection of the self through time. As such, it functions as a precondition for any meaningful conception of personhood, for without the future, the self dissolves into the evanescence of an eternally fragmented present. Home ownership thus provides what sociologists and psychologists refer to as "ontological security,"[14] the state of emotive well-being and constancy necessary for developing a stable personal identity. U.S. law hence accords the home a "sanctity" not applicable to other spaces. It is the one space secure from intervention not only from other individuals but from the state. Radin explains:

> It would be an insult for the state to invade one's home, because it is the scene of one's history and future, one's life and growth. In other words, one embodies or constitutes oneself there. The home is affirmatively part of oneself—property for personhood—not just the agreed-on locale for protection from outside interference.[15]

Radin's explanation of home as related to personhood and property presupposes the transparency and universality of the law. But black and brown people in the United States have never been protected from the sort of "insult" to which Radin refers. Their homes have never provided the presumed guarantee against state or extralegal violence that the home is understood to provide for whites. Even when they are allowed to purchase and own houses, their homes do not provide full ontological security.

The residences of people of color, even when owned by their inhabitants, do not ultimately attain the status/condition of *homes*, as Radin uses the word. They are frequently and freely subject to insult and invasion by the state, often with fatal consequences for their inhabitants. As such, they cannot provide unified ethical personhood—full possession of self and future—that Radin claims for them. They are always already outside such possession, and always subject to the violence of the state. Racial violence, argues Denise Ferreira da Silva, "does not require stripping off signifiers of humanity."[16] The very figuring of ethical personhood in the Western philosophical tradition depends on the representation of the nonwhite and non-European self as an unstable and "affectable" subject "that can be excluded from juridical universality without unleashing an ethical crisis."[17] This dehumanizing exclusion, Silva writes, "is already inscribed in raciality, which produces humanity, the *self-determined* political (ethical-juridical) figure that thrives in Ethical life, only because it institutes it in a relationship . . . with an other political figure (the *affectable* I) that stands before the horizon of death."[18]

We should thus not be surprised by the routine violence with which the homes of black and brown people are subjected to by police, frequently with fatal consequences. Take, for instance, the case of Kenneth Chamberlain Sr., a sixty-eight-year-old African American Marine Corps veteran who was fatally shot in his home by White Plains, New York, police. Officers arrived at his house in response to a call from Chamberlain's med-alert device, which went off accidently. When Chamberlain, from within the "sanctity" of his home, told officers that they were not needed and that they could not enter, the police proceeded to harass Chamberlain and subject him to racial insults, finally pulling the hinges off the door, entering his home, Tasering Chamberlain, and shooting him to death.[19] Or take the countless and literally uncounted black and brown people who have been injured or killed when militarized police SWAT teams unlawfully and apparently "mistakenly" entered their homes as part of the ongoing "war" on drugs.[20] There was, for instance, seven-year-old Aiyana Jones, killed by a Detroit SWAT team during a raid on her family's house in May 2010; seventy-six-year-old Helen Pruett who, that same month, suffered a heart attack after a police raid on her Polk County, Georgia, home; Cheye Calvo, whose status as mayor of suburban Berwyn Heights, Maryland, did not prevent a state police SWAT team from raiding his house in July 2008, handcuffing his elderly mother-in-law, and shooting his two dogs; and the African American civil rights attorney Barbara Arnwine, whose Maryland home was raided at 5:30 in the morning of November 21, 2011, and who was held at gunpoint for hours and reported being told by police that "the Fourth Amendment doesn't apply here."[21]

The home offers no ontological security. On the contrary, in the name of "security"—the state's self-preserving violence—we witness a full inversion of Radin's suggestion that the home functions as a sanctified structure in which history, growth, and the future are protected even from the state.[22] In fact, it is the site that again foretells the future of the racial subject as what is not only *not* protected but more critically *un-projected*, in which the racial subject is denied the possibility of self-determination, of projecting oneself forward in time, of a relation to the future outside the "horizon of death," to borrow Silva's term. Racial subjects, excluded from any claim on personhood from the start, have no time or life in front of them, and therefore no need for the home/shelter that will allow them to produce or reproduce life. This *unprojected* future—on the other side of what I call the mirror of securitization, in another type of housing, the prison cell—is experienced by the racial subject in the form of debt, not mortgage debt but the incalculable debt "to society" that legitimates state violence in the form of imprisonment and, in particular, in the dark mirror image of the home, the Secure Housing Unit cell in the era of the "supermax" prison. This *unprojected* future takes the shape of what Dylan Rodríguez calls a "fatal unfreedom,"[23] which is "historically articulated through imprisonment and varieties of undeclared warfare."[24]

Housing and Accumulation

Given the more fundamental exclusion of the racial subject from what Silva calls "Ethical Life," it should come as little surprise that, as the modern housing market expanded during the late nineteenth and twentieth centuries, those populations that had emerged from the building of the liberal property regime as racial others were continually and systematically excluded from the housing market in its various forms.[25] This occurred not only through geographic segregation (housing covenants and so-called red-lining, among other practices), but also through the systematic denial of mortgage credit (put another way, of the opportunity to take on debt) to nonwhites. If home ownership emerged in the twentieth century as a primary icon of Americanness, it was a very specifically white American dream that it fulfilled. For most of the century the right to exclude was the prevailing practice of white property ownership. More than exclusion, though, the right to protect and secure one's home as related to personhood was inherent in the liberal property regime. From the New Deal era—during which wealth was massively accumulated through homeownership—to the newest landscapes of gentrification, the right to protect and guarantee possession through securitization has been legitimized through the assumed rationality of law, stripped of its coercive material and symbolic violence.

By the time Bush saw fit to address the housing gap and, supposedly, to facilitate racial equality in 2002, something fundamental had shifted in the global economy.[26] David Harvey, Christian Marazzi, and others have described the increasing financialization of the economy as an attempt to recoup corporate profits lost via the rise of wages during the postwar period.[27] The result was a massive expansion of what Karl Marx called "fictitious capital," that is, capital brought about entirely through speculation.[28] "Under this distributive profile," Marazzi writes, "the reproduction of capital . . . is carried out partly thanks to the increase in the consumption of rentiers and partly thanks to the indebted consumption of wage earners."[29] In the wake of the credit crunch of the 1990s, driven by the fear of recession, the U.S. Federal Reserve kept interest rates low beginning in 2001 and for the next five years, setting the conditions for inexpensive and trouble-free loans. As Robin Blackburn puts it, the "masters of the universe seemed to be caught in a celestial machinery they did not control" and looked to "US householders, 'the consumers of last resort,' to keep the global boom going."[30]

Debt, in increasingly abstract securitized forms, became a valuable financial product. Thirty years of neoliberal economic policies had created a new world of leverage, deregulation, and financial innovation. At the same time that the financial markets fed a hunger for new, and increasingly complex, financial products, the firewall between banking and investment—the Glass-Steagall Act, passed in 1933 to ward off future financial crises—was dismantled in 1999. Banks, which had once been motivated to issue credit conservatively, discovered an apparently bottomless market for debt. No longer interested in the role of caretaker of savings or deposits, they looked to consumer debt as a new business form by converting debt into securities that could financialized and sold to investors. The home—with all its ties to personhood—has always also been a fungible commodity, but it became something new: a pretext for the issuance of debt.

Collaterized debt obligations, or CDOs, were created as a way to bundle mortgage debt and then break it up into fragments that could be bought and sold by investors to protect themselves against risks. The actual, physical house had never been more divorced from the financial processes that surrounded it. Mortgage debt became the driving force of the real estate bubble and the source of much of the economic growth of the early 2000s, as consumption increased through home owners mortgaging or refinancing to gain new credit because of the drastic and irrational rise in home prices and value. The complicated financial engineering required to allow the fictitious increases in the amount of credit over and over again—the exact process of securitization—became central to the world economy.

More and more, and ever larger, homes were built to feed the expanding market. So-called NINA ("no income/no assets") loans were issued to ensure that consumption did not slow.[31] A whole category of mortgages emerged: the subprime. That adjective ostensibly indexed the borrower's credit rating, but as the lending market expanded to include those whom it had previously excluded (nonwhites), so-called subprime mortgages were routinely issued to black and brown borrowers, regardless of their credit rating.[32] "Subprime" thus became a demographic category as much as a financial definition. It indexed the incorporation into capital markets of individuals and classes of people who had been largely excluded from both property ownership and full personhood.

Significantly, only once the market had severed itself from real property, and home ownership had become a facade for complex forms of indebtedness—properly speaking, consumers no longer bought homes, they bought mortgages—were black and brown people invited into the market with the bar lowered into the subrealm of security (-ies). That is to say, only for the briefest moment was access to home/property and shelter made universal, and only once it had been denuded of permanence and substantiality and transformed into a speculative fiction.

The proliferation of subprime and NINA loans briefly, and virtually, put title to home, property, security—the benefits of full personhood—in the hands of millions of new owners. Only later would the charade end when the bubble burst and consumers realized that they owned nothing more than their quickly ballooning debt. Their promised ontological security never appeared: it evaporated via the cruel magic of securitization. The future home, a place of permanence, for many dispossessed and surplussed black and brown Americans, would be found elsewhere, on the other side of the mirror of democratic security.

In June 2002 Bush did not appear to have any sense that the massive debt spending necessary to conduct massive war operations in Iraq, Afghanistan, and Pakistan would undermine the very possibility of embarking on an ambitious domestic program of expanding home ownership. The dual project for democracy was presented, in wholly idealistic fashion, as being well within the capacity of the Great Nation, and completely realizable through the sheer force of will and determination (after all, as we are told again and again, we are a nation that can achieve anything we set our minds to), to uplift its own citizens into the dream of property ownership and uplift the peoples of the world out of the tyrannies that prevent them from full participation in the glories of capitalist liberty.

Acknowledging that the gap between "Anglo America and African American and Hispanic homeownership [was] too big" was a significant discursive shift for a president who had shown little concern for black and brown people (at least since before being elected when he vigorously courted the "Hispanic vote" on the basis of his tenure as governor of Texas, a state with a large Latino population).[33] The government, he promised, would take an active and responsible role in alleviating this unacceptable racial gap to secure a more equitable America by fulfilling dreams that reside in ideas of shelter, home safety, freedom, and security of life. The dream that Bush presented to the congregation—which included the heads of Fannie Mae, Freddie Mac, HUD, and Wells Fargo bank—is, as he stated, one deeply ingrained in the ideology of the American republic. The home is the symbol, as Bush explained, of the freedom that the United States can provide its citizens. It is both property and personhood in its ethical and juridical understanding.[34] Interestingly, the term "ontological security,"[35] once employed only in sociology and psychology, has recently entered the discourse of international relations, extended from individuals to nation states,[36] reflecting the consistency of the term's double meaning during the Bush era. Yet both of these usages fit within the rubric of *securitization* and the abstract functioning of capital to which that word points.

If it seems strange that Bush would suddenly be concerned about racial inequality—or the equal distribution of real security—it was. Indeed, it is more likely that he had other motivations. Enduring support for a "permanent war on terror" would probably not be sustainable without continuing attacks on American soil or the distribution of tangible, material benefits from the massive military campaigns abroad. Moreover, expanding control over resources (oil, natural gas, etc.) and markets in the Middle East, Eastern Europe, and North Africa was going to require a significant expansion of domestic markets of consumption within which home construction and home buying were a critical part. In other words, at stake was not addressing the real gap in the housing market to create social, political, and economic equality but cultivating a new market of customers who had previously been excluded, in varying degrees, not only from home ownership but from the complex financial products, that is, mortgages, required to purchase a home. Black and brown people were thus allowed to enter the housing market not as active agents—in response to their legitimate need for the ontological security of home ownership—but as consumers of debt-as-commodity. In the logic of the market, the actual and material *home* was barely relevant, much less the home-as-symbol or home-as-basis-of-civic-personhood. To the market, it was not even a *house*. It functioned only as the pretext for the abstraction of mortgage debt that could be bundled, sold, and resold as a potentially limitless source of profit.

What was elided in this revamped discourse of security and its emphasis on home, however, was the fact that since the early 1980s and continuing on before 9/11 and for a considerable time after, the state has pursued its own "ontological security" by undertaking one of the most massive public housing projects in the history of the world: the incarceration of millions and millions of its citizens.

So while President Bush may have acknowledged the racial gap in access to home ownership, he was completely silent on a somewhat less visible, but no less material, link between domestic race-class policies and imperialist aggressions abroad: the central reliance of "*both*" projects (which are in fact one) on an absolute repression of the dispossessed for whom no home will ever be awaiting, the dispossessed who are more likely to say: "This is our cell, welcome . . ."

The Dark Side of the Mirror

Overlapping with the period of neoliberal financialization, another kind of housing, an inversion of the home-as-property and of any notion of home as foundation for ontological security and personhood, was being forged out of the aforementioned historical relation of property to personhood and racial violence. According to the International Center for Prisons at Kings College, London, as of 2009 more than 9.8 million people were being held in penal institutions throughout the world.[37] The global security apparatus had been expanding at an extraordinary pace since the 1990s: there have been dramatic rises in imprisoned populations on every continent, an increase that largely derives from forms of managing populations based on U.S. models of policing and imprisonment.[38]

Although the rise in prison building globally began in the mid-1990s, the colossal growth of prisons in the United States started a decade earlier. Ruth Wilson Gilmore argues that the rapid expansion of the prison system in California—the largest domestic prison-building project in the world—arose from antiblack racism as well as from a crisis of surplus land and labor. Gilmore explains the "build the jails and we'll fill them" approach to the massive state project of incarceration as a response to the intersecting logics of capital accumulation and surplus and the rebuilding of the state, "fashioned from the surpluses that the emergent post golden-age political economy was not absorbing in other ways."[39] Prison housing in California grew 500 percent between 1982 and 2001, with twenty-three new prisons at a cost of $350 million each. This surplus of labor was a product of the same process of financialization already discussed, the attempt of capital to divest itself from an industrial labor force that had grown increasingly expensive to employ, and to seek out new sources of profit. As Jamie Peck has argued, the neoliberal state functions in a surprisingly flexible, "zombie-like" manner, swelling its repressive apparatus in apparent contradiction to the antistate visions of pioneering free market ideologues.[40]

But the "ambidextrous" flexibility of the state, to borrow Peck's term, disproportionately rains blows with both arms on nonwhites. The prison population in California and elsewhere is overwhelmingly and disproportionately black and brown: because whiteness was inherently related to personhood and to property, white surplus labor could not be used/housed in the same fashion. The enormous increase in the prison population came out of the constant concern for "security" and the wars waged to pursue it: against drugs, gangs, immigrants, and terror. During this period, hundreds of new laws were passed, a process of criminalization; through laws like California's Three Strikes and tools such as gang enhancements, sentences were drastically increased, guaranteeing that cells, once built, would stay full. In the United States overall the shift was similar: state, county, and federal prisons across the country grew 370 percent, because of the criminalization of immigration status during the early assembling of the Homeland Security structure, which conflated presumed gang members, undocumented migrants, and terrorists, leading to the swift construction of an archipelago of immigrant-detention centers nationwide. At the same time, the federal government was exporting its carceral systems, building U.S. prisons abroad to help wage the "war on terror": not only at Guantánamo, Abu Ghraib, and Bagram but in a still unknown number of CIA-administered "black sites."

Just as on the other side of the mirror of securitization, where homes were being built not to house people in need of shelter but as pretexts for the issuance of mortgage-backed securities (to feed a market), prisons were constructed through an inverted market in a different form of security and debt. They were built not to house a preexisting population, but in full confidence that criminals (or terrorists) would be found, or created, to fill each empty cell. Again, they would not be paying mortgages but an incalculable "debt to society" that could never be repaid in full. Security demanded expansion—*build the jails and we'll fill them.* On both sides of the mirror, securitization would always be speculative, a futures game. On one side, the investors would profit; on the other, that of the *unprojected* future, prisoners would only lose.

It is perhaps unnecessary to specify that in all of these sites, whether in the United States or abroad, and regardless of which state agency was in charge, the bodies housed were overwhelmingly those of black and brown people. The population residing in the millions of beds in local, state, and federal jails and prisons across the country and outside it, is, as stated earlier, the inversion of the population that embodies the home. Not only by virtue of race (and its necessary exclusion from the realm of personhood) or juridical criminalization (and ensuing *legal* deprivation of civil and human rights) but by the material facts of this population's incarceration, these individuals are not just outside personhood but function as its antithesis. They are stripped of every quality that defines personhood, not only of their freedom. They have no right even to the most basic forms of property—whatever objects they may be allowed to keep in their cell can be taken away at the whim of the state. Their very bodies exist only as the property of the state. They exist on a site outside the grid on which humanness—defined in terms of property and possession—is constructed, but one that remains subject to the violence of speculation and debt. Through their imprisonment, their personhood is erased and inverted, rendering them nonpersons, beings devoid of futures.

Nowhere is the racial body (this antithesis) realized more explicitly than in the jailing structures known as supermax prisons. Although they vary in size and structure, a report by the Urban Policy Institute Justice Center defines such prisons as "a stand-alone unit or part of another facility . . . designated for violent or disruptive inmates. It typically involves up to 23-hour-per-day, single-cell confinement for an indefinite period of time. Inmates in supermax housing have minimal contact with staff and other inmates."[41] Supermax prisons feature none of the common areas typical to most prisons—exercise yards, cafeterias, libraries, and workspaces. All inmates, in other words, are kept in solitary confinement for the full length of their sentences.

The first of the stand-alone supermax facilities, Pelican Bay in Crescent City, California, opened in 1989. Riding the early wave of the prison building boom, the high-security facilities built solely to isolate prisoners grew at a marked rate. It exemplified, to use Peck's language, the hypertrophically swollen, punitive right arm of the neoliberal state. The extreme form of housing at Pelican Bay, in which enormous repressive resources were devoted to the isolated housing of each individual prisoner, appeared to fall outside any rational calculus of social (or even fiscal) profit and loss.

By 1996 more than thirty U.S. states had built supermax facilities. Collectively, they housed more than twenty-thousand prisoners. By 2004 all but six states had built a supermax facility, and full-time solitary confinement had become a normalized feature of the U.S. incarceration system.[42] According to the *New York Times*, at least twenty-five thousand, "and probably tens of thousands more" are currently held in solitary confinement, more than "in any democratic nation."[43] The desirability of supermaxes was rationalized as necessary for the stability of the prison environment, as a way to prevent prisoner violence by holding "the putatively most violent and disruptive inmates in single cell confinement."[44] More directly, their growth was sold as an economic incentive to small towns and cities struggling amid the uncertainties of a post-Fordist economic environment.[45]

For most of its history, solitary confinement has been regarded not as the norm but as an extraordinary punishment for the most disruptive inmates. First introduced in 1829 in Philadelphia's Eastern State Penitentiary, solitary confinement has been repeatedly and consistently been condemned as inhumane. It has nonetheless persisted, despite an 1890 Supreme Court finding that it caused inmates to become "violently insane" and, more than a century later, the 1995 case of *Madrid v. Gomez*, in which federal courts found that conditions at Pelican Bay "may well hover on the edge of what is humanly tolerable." In October 2011 Juan E. Méndez, the United Nations special rapporteur on torture, called for a ban on solitary confinement "except in very exceptional circumstances and for as short a time as possible," singling out the United States and making specific reference to supermax prisoners. Under no circumstances, Méndez said, should prisoners be held in solitary confinement for more than fifteen days. Couched in careful bureaucratic prose, Méndez acknowledged the dehumanizing aspect of such confinement as not only a side effect but a goal: "Social isolation is one of the harmful elements of solitary confinement and its main objective. It reduces meaningful social control to an absolute minimum."[46]

Solitary confinement stands at the extreme end of the dehumanization that begins in the smaller localities of jails around the country, at the moment of arrest and detention. As John Irwin explains in describing the holding of suspects in local jail, the initial stages of the encounter with police/force incites the processes of officially physically separating individuals from their property. As a process that he calls disintegration, he details the separation that ultimately results in a form of disorientation with the world outside. Supermax prisons and their solitary housing units, or SHUs, form the extreme version of this initial process: people are held indefinitely in cells that average fifty to seventy square feet, without windows or natural light (zero exposure to the "natural world"). They are allowed no access to educational or vocational programs and are subject to round-the-clock surveillance. Prisoners are chained at all times when in the presence of another human being and, denied all visitation rights, have no opportunity to even touch another human being (minus the occasional brush with guards). As further punishment, prisoners can be denied a bed, clothing, and all access to light, and subjected to increased food rationing. Craig Haney explains:

> Because supermax units typically meld sophisticated modern technology with age-old practice of solitary confinement, (therefore) prisoners experience levels of isolation and behavioral control that are more total and complete and literally dehumanized than has been possible in the past. The combination of these factors is what makes this extraordinary and extreme form of imprisonment unique in the modern history of corrections.[47]

Although solitary confinement was initially based on the idea of penance—that forced solitude would allow wrongdoers an opportunity to reflect on their sins—and remained an exceptional form of punishment enacted for brief periods for most of the twentieth century, it has become a routine form of confinement for years at a time. Such prolonged periods of forced isolation, writes Haney, can cause profound existential crisis, permanent physiological changes to the brain, and ultimately death. The personality breaks down, past and future become incomprehensible: the exclusion from any coherent personhood that elsewhere occurs in the realm of law and representation is here actually and forcibly imposed.

Supermax prisons have in recent decades proliferated into a superstructure of violent dehumanization that even many correctional officials have trouble justifying on rational grounds. Daniel Mears's 2006 report *Evaluating the Effectiveness of Supermax Prisons* argues that, in blunt budgetary terms, supermaxes are not even cost-effective. Mears concludes that costs are not at all measurable in regard to the stability and security that they allegedly provide or in terms of any rehabilitative effects on the prisoners themselves.[48]

In Conclusion: Two Moments of Resistance

But supermaxes do have a rational genesis. They guaranteed that there could be no return to the prison rebellions of the 1960s and 1970s, in which inmates explicitly asserted themselves as political beings entitled to a full personhood that had been denied them both inside and outside prison walls.[49] The super-maxes, though, prevent even the possibility of the formation of solidarity and organized resistance among prisoners.[50] (They thus stand out as a fantastical and almost demonic instance of the general neoliberal push to combat the formation of social collectivities: "There is no society," as Margaret Thatcher famously declared.) Increasingly sophisticated and self-conscious forms of resistance among prisoners were on the rise throughout the late 1960s and early 1970s: in 1967 there were five prison riots in the United States. In 1972 there were forty-eight, though the word *riot* diminishes the sophistication of these uprisings. Prisoners were developing comprehensive demands that related the conditions of their confinement to their own possibilities for personhood and to power relations in society outside. Incarceration, they insisted, should not mean permanent dehumanization. Temporary housing in a prison cell should not cut off the possibility of meaningful selfhood or social participation beyond the prison walls.

Striking inmates at California's Folsom prison in 1970, for instance, drafted a "bill of rights for prisoners" that went far beyond ameliorating conditions. They demanded the right to organize themselves into unions, to vote, to be allowed "access to press and media," as well as "furloughs or institutional ac-commodations to maintain social, sexual and familial ties." They insisted on their right "to have the community come into the prison," to "freedom from mental and physical brutality," and "to make restitution in lieu of further in-carceration."[51] They were thus demanding their right to belong to and interact with the community from which they had been removed, to relate to it in a productive and even reproductive fashion, to insist on a meaningful existence as social beings with a stake in their own and their society's future. They were questioning not only the immediate circumstances of their confinement but the punitive foundations of the entire carceral system. Striking prisoners at Attica went as far as to issue statements of support with the people of Vietnam and others around the world engaged in struggles against imperialism. They thus connected the state violence to which they were subject to the violence of the state abroad and felt entitled to make claims on behalf of a common humanity. They were, in short, insisting on their humanity and on the right to shape their futures; they were demanding not the bare needs of life but emancipatory requirements that explicated a horizon of freedom—a projected future.

There is perhaps no more sobering evidence of the consequences of the intervening four decades of neoliberal securitization than to compare the demands enunciated by striking prisoners at Pelican Bay in 2011. All the intervening years of warfare—the various wars on drugs, crime, and terrorism—which had created a prison population of more than 2 million and necessitated the construction of infrastructure to confine them, had also recategorized and reconstructed the prisoner. The incarcerated black or brown man or woman could no longer take up a role of resistance such as that of George Jackson, a political prisoner, or a political being at all. Decades of media representation and public policy had confined the prisoner to a series of exclusionary roles through a pathologized racial criminalization—gang member, drug dealer, terrorist, superpredator—as a threat to the security of the nation and the state. Meaningful political participation—human engagement within a community of humans—with these figures was not only dangerous but also unimaginable. They defined the limits of the social and thus could not be allowed in.

On July 1, 2011, inmates at Pelican Bay began a hunger strike. Within weeks, more than six thousand prisoners joined them across the state's penal archipelago. Despite such strength in numbers, their demands seemed relatively modest. They had five: that officials abolish the "debriefing policy" (by which inmates were required to inform on other prisoners as a condition of release from the SHU); that they "end group punishment"; that they provide "adequate and nutritious food"; that they comply with the recommendation of the U.S. Commission on Safety and Abuse to end long-term solitary confinement; and that they offer "constructive programming" for inmates indefinitely confined to the SHU. Examples of the latter included "wall calendars," "one photo per year," a "weekly phone call," and "more TV channels." Except for the passive engagement of television viewing and the occasional telephone call to family or friends, they asked for nothing that would connect them to the world outside, that would allow them to connect to the world outside, to a projected future beyond the numbered grid of a wall calendar.

The Pelican Bay hunger strikers could locate no emancipatory horizons. The logic of securitization had accomplished its work. They had been housed, but on the wrong side of the mirror. There, as black and brown men, their debts were incalculable and could never be paid. They were willing to give their lives for the right just to hang a single photo and a calendar on the wall, to imagine another life, to count the days, to make themselves at home.

Notes

I would like to thank the reviewers and editors for their careful read of and helpful comments on this article. And I am especially grateful to political and intellectual comrade Ben Ehrenreich for his continued support.

1. See http://georgewbush-whitehouse.archives.gov/news/releases/2002/06/print/20020617-2.html.
2. See Jodi Melamed's deft elaboration of neoliberal multiculturalism in "The Spirit of Neoliberalism: From Racial Liberalism to Neoliberal Multiculturalism," *Social Text*, no. 89 (2006): 1–24.
3. For a historical overview of housing and cultural construction of "home" as a primary symbol of U.S. progress, freedom, and security, see Dolores Hayden, *Redesigning the American Dream: Gender Housing and Family Life* (New York: Norton, 2002); Margaret Garb, *City of American Dreams: A History of American Homeownership and Housing Reform in Chicago, 1871–1919* (Chicago: University of Chicago Press, 2011); Gwendolyn Wright, *Building the Dream: A Social History of Housing in America* (New York: MIT Press, 1981).
4. According to the U.S. Census of Housing in 2000, 73 percent of whites owned homes (www.census.gov/hhes/www/housing/census/historic/ownershipbyrace.html).
5. The Bureau of Justice reported that in 2002 the prison and local jail population exceeded 2 million people, holding 1 in every 142 persons. African Americans represented an estimated 45 percent of all inmates but only about 12 percent of the general population. White Americans represented 34 percent of the inmate population and made up almost 73 percent of the general U.S. population. Hispanics made up 18 percent of the inmate population and about 16 percent of the general population (U.S. Department of Justice, *Bulletin: Prisoners in 2002* [Washington, D.C.: U.S. Department of Justice, July 2003]).
6. John Locke, *The Second Treaty of Civil Government*, chap. 5, http://constitution.org/jl/2ndtr05.htm.
7. David Abraham, "Liberty without Equality: The Property-Rights Connection in 'Negative Citizenship' Regime," *Law and Social Inquiry* 21.1 (1996): 5.
8. Ibid.
9. Nicholas Blomley, "Law, Property, and the Geography of Violence: The Frontier, the Survey, and the Grid," *Annals of the Association of American Geographers* 93.1 (2003): 122.
10. Ibid.
11. G. W. F. Hegel, *Philosophy of Right*, trans. T. M. Knox (Cambridge: Cambridge University Press, 1967), 45a.
12. Ibid., 45r.
13. Margaret Jane Radin, *Reinterpreting Property* (Chicago: University of Chicago Press, 1993), 48.
14. Cf. R. D. Laing, *The Divided Self: An Existential Study in Sanity and Madness* (London: Penguin, 1960); and Anthony Giddens, *Modernity and Self-Identity: Self and Society in the Late Modern Age* (Stanford, Calif.: Stanford University Press, 1991).
15. Ibid., 57.
16. Denise Ferreira da Silva, "No-Bodies: Law, Raciality, and Violence," *Griffith Law Review* 18.2 (2009): 212–38.
17. Denise Ferreira da Silva, *Toward a Global Idea of Race* (Minneapolis: University of Minnesota Press, 2007), 35.
18. Silva, "No-Bodies."
19. http://www.nytimes.com/2012/05/04/nyregion/no-charges-in-polices-killing-of-sickly-white-plainsman.html.
20. Individual chapters of the ACLU have brought suit in a number of cases, and a simple Google search yields an overwhelming number of press accounts of people of color "mistakenly" killed and injured during police raids, but I have been unable to find any comprehensive study documenting the phenomenon. In *SWAT Madness and the Militarization of the American Police* (Santa Barbara, Calif.: Praeger, 2010), Jim Fisher writes that a sizeable percentage of the fifty thousand homes raided by SWAT teams each year occur at the "wrong addresses." Few of these assaults, most of them conducted under the auspices of the war on drugs, occur in white neighborhoods.
21. www.abajournal.com/news/article/civil_rights_leader_arnwine_says_police_held_her_at_gunpoint_raided_home_wi/.
22. Much of the massive militarization of local U.S. police forces since September 2001 has occurred via federal antiterrorism preparedness grants. This violence thus occurs doubly through the rubric of security: "homeland" security on a global scale and the dubious security against criminality promised by the war on drugs.

23. Dylan Rodríguez, *Forced Passages: Imprisoned Radical Intellectuals and the US Prison Regime* (Minneapolis: University of Minnesota Press, 2004), 1.

24. Such warfare of course predates the current wars on drugs, crime, and terror, as stated earlier.

25. Melvin Oliver and Thomas Shapiro, *Black Wealth/White Wealth: A New Perspective on Racial Inequality* (New York: Routledge, 1997).

26. Recall that it was during this time that President Bush called on the members of the public to take out their credit cards and shop as a patriotic expression after the September 11 attack: "security" could be achieved by expanding consumer spending and debt.

27. David Harvey, *A Brief History of Neoliberalism* (New York: Oxford University Press, 2005); Christian Marazzi, *The Violence of Financial Capitalism* (Los Angeles: Semiotext(e), 2007).

28. Karl Marx, *Capital: A Critique of Political Economy*, vol. 3 (London: Penguin Books, 1981), 527.

29. Marazzi, *Violence of Financial Capitalism*, 33.

30. Robin Blackburn, "The Subprime Crisis," *New Left Review* 50 (March–April 2008): 65.

31. A. M. Dickerson, "Over-Indebtedness, the Subprime Mortgage Crisis, and the Effect of U.S. Cities," *Fordham Urban Law Journal* 36.3 (2010): 403.

32. J. T. Darden and E. Wyly, "Cartographic Editorial—Mapping the Racial/Ethnic Topography of Subprime Inequality in Urban America," *Urban Geography* 31.4 (2010): 431.

33. http://georgewbush-whitehouse.archives.gov/news/releases/2002/06/print/20020617-2.html.

34. P. Kenna, "Globalization and Housing Rights," *Indiana Journal of Global Legal Studies* 379 (2008): 15; L. Fox, *Conceptualizing the Home* (Oxford: Hart, 2007). The home/house is included and to a degree protected under international human rights law versus as property in U.S. domestic law.

35. Cf. R. D. Laing, *The Divided Self: An Existential Study in Sanity and Madness* (London: Penguin, 1960); Anthony Giddens, *Modernity and Self-Identity: Self and Society in the Late Modern Age* (Stanford, Calif.: Stanford University Press, 1991).

36. Cf. Brent J. Steele, *Ontological Security in International Relations: Self Identity in the IR State* (New York: Routledge, 2008).

37. R. Walmsley, *World Prison Population List*, 5th ed. (London: Research, Development and Statistics Directorate, International Center for Prison Studies at Kings College, 2004). This is not including prisoners in administrative detention in China, which would increase the number to 10.6 million.

38. Ibid. The most dramatic increases since 2006 are in Chile, up 28 percent; Brazil, 18 percent; and Indonesia, 17 percent. In Turkey and in Georgia the rise in imprisoned populations is more than 50 percent.

39. Ruth Wilson Gilmore, "Globalization and US Prison Growth: From Military Keynesianism to Post-Keynesian Militarism," *Race and Class* 40.2–3 (1998–99).

40. Jamie Peck, "Zombie Neoliberalism and the Ambidextrous State," *Theoretical Criminology* 14.1 (2010): 104–10.

41. Daniel P. Mears, *Evaluating the Effectiveness of Supermax Prisons: Research for Safer Communities*, Report of the Urban Policy Institute Justice Center, Washington, D.C., March 2006, ii.

42. Ibid. However, these numbers do not account for state and local jails' use of Security Housing Units (SHU) Maximum Security Housing, Restricted Housing Units, Special Management Housing. In a 2005 federal Bureau of Justice report, approximately 81,622 individuals were being held under some form of isolation.

43. Erika Goode, "Prisons Rethink Isolation, Saving Money, Lives, and Sanity," *New York Times*, March 11, 2012, www.nytimes.com/2012/03/11/us/rethinking-solitary-confinement.html.

44. Mears, *Evaluating the Effectiveness of the Supermax Prisons*.

45. Kevin Pyle and Craig Gilmore, *Prison Town: Paying the Price* (Northhampton, Mass.: Real Cost of Prison Project, 2005).

46. UN News Centre, *Solitary Confinement Should Be Banned in Most Cases, UN Expert Says*, http://www.un.org/apps/news/story.asp?NewsID=40097.

47. Craig Haney, "Mental Health Issues in Long-Term Solitary and 'Supermax' Confinement," *Crime and Delinquency* 49.1 (2003): 143.

48. For testimony of prison administrators, policy officials, and politicians against the cost-effectiveness of supermax imprisonment, see Mears, *Evaluating the Effectiveness of Supermax Prisons*.

49. I thank Dylan Rodríguez for directing my attention to the 2011 prison strikes taking place across the country.

50. Alan Eladio Gomez, "Resisting Living Death at Marion Federal Penitentiary, 1972," *Radical History Review*, no. 96 (Fall 2006): 58–86. Gomez provides a historical account of the response to the prison movement of the 1960s and 1970s and the techniques developed to control political organizing. This included strict segregation in what was called steel boxcars, a form of isolation that eventually became a form of the control unit (CU). Used as a tool of political repression that is reflected in its progeny, the special housing unit, Gomez cites Giorgio Agamben and states that this form of solitary confinement "collapsed the legal and physical space between life and politics—and between punishment and death" (60).

51. For the Folsom prison strike manifesto, see http://www.prisonpolicy.org/scans/instead_of_prisons/chapter9.shtml.

The Black Mohicans: Representations of Everyday Violence in Postracial Urban America

John D. Márquez

> It's like all the good kids are leaving, you know. The gangbangers are making it and our kids are dying.
> —Annette Holt, mother of a sixteen-year-old Chicago teen slain by a peer

Perhaps the most dramatic scene of *The Interrupters* (2011) portrays the funeral director, Spencer Leak, a community elder, saying: "How can the President of the United States be a Black man? . . . I never thought that I'd see that in my lifetime. But, while I'm seeing the President on television and the images of him leading the free world . . . I'm still burying Black kids. It just doesn't make sense to me."[1] Most of the scene, filmed inside of Leaks's funeral home, showed the wake of a working-class black male teenager named Jessie "Duke" Smith, who was killed in retaliation for a previous shooting of another black male teenager, a shooting that Smith did not commit. Images of the wake and Leaks's words add another painful dramatic moment to the many other accounts of deaths of young black and Latino males. With these representations, the film's director also repeats familiar statements in accounts of racial violence in Chicago, all the more so when Leaks draws a comparison between the hope that he felt when he was part of the civil rights movement as a young man and the current moment of despair. The filmmaker's decision to highlight this statement, I believe, reflects a popular perception that the Obama presidency symbolizes that African Americans have reached an unprecedented level of access to economic opportunity and electoral representation, primarily as a result of the civil rights movement.[2]

Focusing on Leaks's and the filmmaker's references to the contradiction between the images of a black president and the images of dead black male teenage bodies, this essay explores how this juxtaposition reproduces a pervasive and perverse aspect of the discourse of the postracial United States, which is portraying *exceptional* success and *ordinary* death in the description of black and Latino lives in the United States. Like Jesse Jackson, I think that such postracial statements reflect a "veneer of success," which neatly glosses over structural inequalities including the disproportionate impact of the current subprime mortgage crisis for African American and Latino communities.[3] In other words, an illusion of inclusion has proliferated in this post–civil rights era that derives from the hypervisibility of exceptional black success stories such as Chicago's own Barack and Michelle Obama, Oprah Winfrey, and Michael Jordan. In this essay, I argue that this "veneer of success" not only occludes structural inequalities but also further legitimates the culture of poverty thesis and discourses of working-class urban neighborhoods' pathology, which have been prominent since the mid-twentieth century.[4] This has led to the common-sense perception of black and Latino populations as deficient, lacking agency, lost in chaos, violent, in short, pathological—and thus in need of perpetual state guardianship or vigilant policing.[5]

My analysis shows, then, that this postracial discourse reproduces an old rhetorical strategy, which has been used in early moments of U.S. history to justify the use of the state apparatus of violence. In early U.S. history, the pairing "noble savage" versus "bloody savage," as popularized by James Fenimore Cooper's *Last of the Mohicans* and other early American novels, was deployed to justify conquest and colonial violence.[6] Media representations of a few cases of violence in postracial urban neighborhoods in Chicago, I argue, reproduce this construct when distinguishing between the urban "Mohicans," hypervisible and yet exceptional "Black success stories"[7] constructed as "noble savages," deserving all the opportunities available in America, and urban "Huron," the young working-class dead black and Latino males who, much like the "bloody savages," are in need of state violence repression and control. Focusing on the existence of the few exceptional ones, "noble savages," in Chicago, the state has deployed this binary in constructions of these deaths as causes célèbres. That is, they become moments through which state agents promote aggressive policing campaigns, mass incarceration, and other measures to purportedly rescue exceptional black and Latino youth from the bloody savagery of their peers. A key common criteria in these cases is that the victim of violence is identified as exceptional, unlike his peers: an "honors student," the "next Obama," or as a person who was primed to take full advantage of the opportunities that the civil rights movement had provided for his generation. I show how these cause célèbre cases support prevailing negative representations of black life in general. When *exceptional* "Black Mohicans" are juxtaposed with *ordinary* Hurons, the former become emblems of a more racially equitable nation because they have emerged from the urban wilderness and overcome the plague of violence, which in turn is normalized as it is seen as the self-imposed horror of black and Latino communities. Repeatedly, the measures this binary justifies—which usually results in larger number of incarcerated blacks and Latinos and a rise in police brutality—fail consistently. To be sure, their main success, like the colonial times, has been to "clear" space for urban renewal and gentrification programs, which displace black and Latino families, as their communities turn into new real estate markets and urban playgrounds for young urban professionals.[8]

Most importantly, this analysis sustains the argument that the elements of the postracial discourse helps sustain the image of crisis of urban violence—"rampant intra-minority violence"—as it naturalizes the idea that it results from cultural traits that develop and proliferate under a situation of racial (socioeconomic) exclusion. This argument prevails among urban social scientists studying the relationship between gang violence and deindustrialization.[9] This essay provides an alternative reading of that crisis, which I rename *ghetto violence*. Borrowing from Frantz Fanon's description of colonial violence, I have coined this term to highlight a condition through which racially/colonially oppressed peoples engage in violence against one another and within the segregated spaces where they have been forced to reside, a violence that only contributes to their oppression and delays decolonial struggle.[10] Few scholars are willing to advance this kind of critique because of how analyses of urban strife recall the culture of poverty and other such sociological theses. Such a risk, I believe, results from how another binary, culture versus structure—and the essentialization it reproduces—has dominated debates about this crisis for most of the twentieth and now twenty-first centuries.

Much of the culture versus structure binary derives from how race, itself, has been uncritically theorized. Recent critical works on ghetto violence stop at structural studies debunking primordial theorizations of racial difference that underlie the culture of poverty thesis and other discourses of black pathology. Moving beyond the classic statement in racial and ethnic studies that race is a social construction deployed to justify exclusion, I borrow from contemporary critical racial theorists a perspective that sees race working in a more complex and insidious way.[11] Viewing it as a defining attribute of European modernity, they conceptualize race as a product of modern knowledge that enables and sets the groundwork for political projects such as conquest, colonial dispossession, and police violence as well as socioeconomic exclusion.[12]

Focusing on the fundamentally violent, political dimension of racial oppression, I see them as operationalizing the ethical stance, for which black and Latino lives have no value. As racial others, acting violently toward one another, they are represented as human beings who see themselves as *expendable*, whereas this *state of expendability* is an effect of institutional and discursive state apparatus, which rests on the production of ghetto as a space of endemic violence, as in the cause célèbre cases I analyze here, to justify police brutality and mass incarceration. For the most part, this essay frames the analytic tool I term *racial state of expendability*. As a contribution to critical racial analysis this concept addresses the foundational effect of racial oppression, which is an existential susceptibility to obliteration with impunity, a condition that allows for all other forms of injustice to transpire. I also show how Fanon's critique colonialism offers a method that links the racial state of expendability, racial subaltern subjectivity, and ghetto violence without rendering the latter an expression of the essence of the racial other. Like urban social scientists who argue that economic displacement produces a culture of violence within the ghetto, Fanon also focuses a critical attention on the psychosocial. His approach, however, differs completely from studies that ignore the political nature of racial domination and focus on cultural or structural elements as the cause and effect of ghetto violence.[13]

In Fanon's work, I find a third space for interpretation, one that reflects many of the ideas deployed by narratives of members of major gangs I examine in the final part of the essay, gangs initially formed to defend black and Latino communities from racial violence, the racial state of expendability, a violence intended to spatially segregate Chicago during the mid-twentieth century. Fanon helps locate ghetto violence as an element within a broader spatial/ tamporal field of political embattlement characterized by the production of the aforementioned power/knowledge interfaces, the resultant racial state of expendability, and the internalization of alienation and/or inferiority within subaltern subjectivity. Ghetto violence is, in sum, political/colonial violence that buttresses colonial power and white supremacy. It is an intended outcome, psychosocially designed to subjugate and control subaltern populations, to situate the settler (the state) in a position of sole moral/ethical authority, rendering the subaltern readily suitable for either obliteration or sustained quarantine. Like Fanon, I do not believe that this condition is reversible via inclusion into the class structure, ethics, or values of the colonial authority. It is reversible only through resistance, decolonization, and self-determination.

Beyond the "Urban Jungle" Thesis

How does one provide an analysis of ghetto violence without seeing it as an expression of some sort of pathological cultural response to structural inequalities? For instance, the urban anthropologist Elijah Anderson, in *Code of the Street*, argues that economic displacement (i.e., unemployment and access to affordable housing) from the middle class is the primary reason why urban, working-class, and young men of color develop a "street code," which is a "set of informal rules governing interpersonal public behavior, including violence."[14] This street code valorizes violence against peers as a (false) method of empowerment within a unique and urban subculture.[15] In highlighting exclusion from the middle class as the sole source of a violent psychosocial adaptation, I think, both the cultural and the structural model also imply that inclusion into the middle class would negate the purpose and repercussions of the "street code." For instance, Anderson suggests that there are conditions within the inner city that can counter the hegemonic influence of the street code and its often violent consequences: "the most powerful being a strong, loving, 'decent' family committed to middle class values."[16] That is, here we find a binary between "street" and "decent" persons in the urban ghetto, the former bearing a heavier hegemonic influence and thus making the street code the primary language/ethics that all must adapt to. Precisely this binary appears in the media representations of the episodes of ghetto violence I analyze later in this essay, the cause célèbre cases that distinguish exceptional black Mohicans from the urban Huron, the bloodily savage masses, who threaten their postracial glory.

The street-decent binary reconfigures the "bloody savage" versus "noble savage" binary that has a far more extensive genealogy. Throughout the twentieth century, a number of studies have, as Roderick Ferguson and Khalil Muhammad argue,[17] produce African Americans as an antithesis to the American middle-class family, and which have been cited to justify criminalization and segregation. Functioning as *naturalizing* devices, such recurrent constructions appear in accounts of racial violence that attribute it to the fact that blacks and Latinos inhabit what Denise Ferreira da Silva calls the "scene of nature."[18] Because it is inhabited by the racial "other" whose existence enacts its own *expendability*, this literal and figurative place is in need of conquest and violent control by the state, to allow for the construction of a rational and morally sound civil society, inhabited by the "middle-class family," the one to which a few *exceptional* blacks and Latinos are also welcome, in the postracial United States.

In the following pages, I show how, when employed in characterizations of blacks and Latinos by Chicago's media and state officials, the scene of nature naturalizes the effects of structural domination, as it describes a space/condition of savagery and affectability (passion, inclination, violence), which is the norm for black and Latino life. Because this space/condition is natural—those who live there cannot change it at will—there is the need of persistent and vigilant policing by the state's law enforcement and military apparatuses. The scene of nature grants those apparatuses their moral/ethical/legal legitimacy, which is drawn out discursively, over time—in short, the base effect of what Ferreira da Silva describes as raciality, I argue, is *expendability*.[19]

The Black Mohicans: Obama as Hawkeye, the Postracial "Chief"

In the mid-nineteenth century, the contrasting image of the noble savage and bloody savage represented in the literary works of writers such as James Fenimore Cooper and others shaped popular opinions about indigenous peoples. In fact, the mythology surrounding the "noble savage" can be traced to some of the fundamental philosophies of European modernity.[20] Jean-Jacques Rousseau is widely recognized as the modern literary creator of the "noble savage" genre, as he, according to Angela Aleiss, depicts the "noble savage" as "an individual living in a 'pure state of nature'—gentle, wise, uncorrupted by the vices of civilization."[21] By contrast, the bloody savage was corrupted and psychologically damaged by modernity. He/she could not see beyond the pathology of violence as a mechanism to exert one's power or will in the world. He/she was undiplomatic, innately violent, and incapable of functioning in a modern and liberal society, because of his/her innately primitive characteristics. He/she was then relegated or produced to be deficient but a component of the "scene of nature," a literal and figurative space from which the "noble savage" evolved beyond in his/her process of becoming enlightened and/or civil. Within the context of the European colonialism, the bloody savage was fit only to be a colonial subject, to be enslaved, eliminated, or incarcerated. He/she was a fugitive that was unfit for liberalism, for capitalism, and for citizenship and was, consequentially, relegated to the status of perpetually premodern, delinquent, if not subhuman, and thus expendable.

Why exactly do recent deployments of this colonial distinction work to sustain the deployment of the state's apparatus of control and violent repression in black and Latino neighborhoods? In Fenimore Cooper's *Leatherstocking Tales* (1823–41), we see the structuring of this binary in the most famous novel of that series, *The Last of the Mohicans*. Both the novel and its film adaptations tell the tale of the "bloody savages" and "noble savages, portraying (1) the murderous and bloodthirsty Huron, who terrorized whites and their native rivals alike in acts of revenge for being displaced and/or subjugated, and appear as defensively numb to violence/expendability similar to what Fanon describes as a "pseudo-petrification," and (2) the Mohicans, dynamic, charismatic, intelligent, yet a rarity among indigenous peoples in how they sought peace and avoided violence. They were able to maneuver around white racism and often even coexist with whites to maintain a dignified life. As I show later, in today's postracial lexicon, the figures of the bloody savage and the noble savage reappear in constructions of Obama as a symbol of black success, that is, in the "veneer of success" discourse in which the distinction between "street" and "decent" black families has a crucial part.

When distinguishing between these two kinds of "savages," the ones to be obliterated and the ones to be assimilated, Fenimore Cooper uses both physical and mental traits. On the one hand, he describes the Mohicans with physical traits that are close to whites. The Mohican protagonist Uncas, Fenimore Cooper writes, was "graceful and unrestrained in the attitudes and movements of nature . . . like that of the white man, there was no concealment to his dark, glancing, fearful eye, alike terrible and calm; the bold outline of his high haughty features, pure in their native red; or to the dignified elevation of his receding forehead, together with all the finest proportions of a noble head, bared to the generous scalping tuft."[22] By comparison, the Huron leader, Magua, appears as a dark, savage, and somewhat subhuman figure who ate raw flesh and ran naked through the wilderness. In a scene where Magua kills a white baby to steal his mother's shawl, Fenimore Cooper says, "The savage spurned the worthless rags, and perceiving that the shawl had already become a prize to another, his bantering but sullen smile changed to a gleam of ferocity, he dashed the head of the infant against a rock, and cast its quivering remains to her very feet."[23]

A pivotal figure in Fennimore Cooper's imaginary was Hawkeye, depicted as a hybrid character, or a white man who has embraced the lifestyle of the Mohicans and considers Uncas and Chingachook (Unca's biological father) to be his adopted family. This concurrency is narrated as the characteristics that put him in a unique position to promote racial harmony. As Hawkeye states in a pivotal moment in Fenimore Cooper's novel and in which he is describing the bond between him and his adopted Mohican family, "The gifts of our colors may be different, but God has so placed us as to journey in the same path." Expectedly, this whitening of the Mohicans was accompanied by the deployment of hybridity to show racial harmony. This is evident in descriptions of characters such as Hawkeye and Uncas, and in Fenimore Cooper's choice to highlight the Mohicans' approval of interracial sex/marriage. Though postracialists might find it an expression of Fenimore Cooper's lack of racial prejudice, let us not forget that hybridity—which, as Robert J. C. Young has argued, is the defining characteristic of nineteenth-century British colonial literature—although often presented as an example of racial harmony or the blurring of racial categories is more of a trope for sustaining the status quo or for reinforcing racial hierarchies, in the exotic wildernesses of colonial lands.[24]

On the other hand, the Mohicans' closeness to whiteness is also represented in the description of their mental (intellectual and moral) traits; they are virtous, peaceful, progress-oriented, and intelligent. Fenimore Cooper's Mohicans share in much of the essence of modernity, much like in Frederick Jackson Turner's version of the American national identity that is forged from/in its western frontier and within its manifest destiny. Exhibiting rational thought and moral fortitude, they were able to forge multiethnic coalitions for the common good and the promise of a multicultural and democratic society. The novel expresses a belief that tribal wars were over and that a new, peaceful, social formation was transpiring. Fenimore Cooper's American nation reborn after the obliteration of the "bloody savages" is a society within which Native Americans must learn to live in harmony with European newcomers and the black slaves and/ or servants they brought with them. In his view, there was no turning back for the progress-minded, intelligent, "noble savages," who learned to forget the violence they suffered and to manipulate the new power scheme to the best of their benefit. The clever "savages," in Fenimore Cooper's novel, willfully utilized whites as allies and often started families with them. The Mohicans represented a rarity, a contrast to the corrupted native population.

Nearly two hundred years later America has yet to eliminate all the "bloody savages" from its land. In descriptions of urban jungles like Chicago, Los Angeles, Houston, and New York City, these two figures reappear both in sociological explanations, in media stories of uncountable young deaths, and in celebrations of black success. For instance, urban ethnographies, like Anderson's, reproduce the paired "bloody" versus "noble" savages, in the distinction between "decent families" and "street poeple." "Above all," he explains, "this environment means that even youngsters whose home lives reflect mainstream values—and the majority of homes in the community do—must be able to handle themselves in a street oriented environment."[25] While still living the *scene of nature*, in postracial America, like in Fenimore Cooper's reborn United States, black and Latino boys raised by "decent families," with their reflection of "middle class values," can hope to follow in the footsteps of America's first black president. President Obama's image elevates the "veneer of success" discourse to another extreme. His *exceptional* story of decency and black success renders postracial stories of racial overcoming credible. Much like Fenimore Cooper's Hawkeye, and unlike other black leaders (like Reverend Jeremiah Wright), Obama is also virtuous, embraces (racial) peace, is progress-oriented, and is intelligent. Hybridity (in his case physical) also functions to sustain his claim as a capable leader. He stresses his own whiteness to symbolize a lack or revengefulness about past antiblack racism. Like the moral vision of Mohicans, he also stood poised to progress beyond the scene of nature. Like Hawkeye, Obama is depicted to understand two worlds, an understanding derived from his biracial body. As Obama explains in his speech titled "A More Perfect Union," "I am the son of a black man from Kenya and a white woman from Kansas. I was raised with the help of a white grandfather who survived a Depression to serve in Patton's Army during World War II and a white grandmother who worked on a bomber assembly line at Fort Leavenworth while he was overseas."[26] Obama is the hybrid, the neo-Mohican—black enough, white enough, and intelligent enough to guide a post–civil rights nation. Like Fenimore Cooper's Hawkeye, he appears as a coalition builder with whites, representing a type of nobility. Like Uncas, he is also often depicted as a white man inhabiting a nonwhite phenotype.

Cause Célèbre: The Media and the New Mohicans

News coverage routinely juxtaposes the image of Obama as a signifier of racial progress with the images and sounds of the latest black or Latino youth murdered by a peer. This juxtaposition, I argue, has serious impact on the very situation of racial oppression that Obama's election had supposedly reconciled. Frequently returning pairings such as bloody savage versus noble savage, Mohican versus Huron, and street versus decent derive from the same socio-logical schema, which produces the subaltern, condemns the subaltern, and renders the subaltern *expendable* while showing that a few of them, the ones already morally elevated, deserve access to economic opportunities and the state protections available to middle-class Americans.

Since the early 1980s Chicago's media outlets and public officials repeat these dichotomies in the few cases of murders of youth of color, which have become a cause célèbre. Following each murder, state agents have announced new initiatives designed to quell the crisis. None have worked, resulting instead in mass incarceration of black and Latino youths and a sharp increase in police brutality. In the following, I describe the constructions of these victims who have become a cause célèbre in the media and the kinds of state intervention (law enforcement and policies) they justify. Here the victim, the dead Mohican, is represented as a hybrid, an Uncas or Obama, who succumbed to the bloody savagery of the scene of nature. As the analysis makes clear, both black Mohicans and black Hurons do not escape expendability; like Native Americans from the past, they cannot willfully transcend violence. The cause célèbre cases show how postracial discourse *naturalizes* ghetto violence, rendering it, once again, an expression of the intrinsic racial and cultural attributes of working-class black and Latino communities.

The "Star Athlete" and the "Honors Student/Rapper/Son of Civil Servants": Ben "Benjie" Wilson and Blair Holt

In 1984, sixteen-year-old Ben "Benjie" Wilson was killed in Chicago's South Side, one of ninety-five "gang related" deaths that year. The prototypical black Mohican, the media describes Wilson as the next basketball star to emerge from Chicago's gritty neighborhoods. Perhaps the first cause célèbre, his murder was used to justify the deployment of a major policing strategy, known as the Chicago Intervention Network (CIN). This initiative, proposed by Mayor Harold Washington immediately after Wilson's murder, had $4.9 million designated primarily for saturation policing programs. Two years after Wilson's killing, on March 7, 1986, Washington, Chicago's first African American mayor, whose election in 1983 was celebrated to mark the triumph of civil rights movement in the city, convened a meeting to advocate CIN. Edward Pleines, the Chicago Police Department's commander of its gang unit, commented: "After Ben Wilson, the city for the first time admitted that we do have a problem with gangs. That it does reside with our children." Both Pleines and Washington were lauding the CIN program as a major success and as the solution to Chicago's youth violence. Washington declared that CIN had created "a 19.4% drop in gang related homicides" and "a 21.4% increase in gang arrests . . . not by accident."[27] In their stories, both media and politicians, when lamenting the loss of the "star athlete," construct the majority of working-class blacks and Latinos, living in Chicago's "urban jungle" in expendability, in the *scene of nature*. Not surprisingly, the Chicago Intervention Network would not prevent the return of ghetto violence and at even higher rates.[28]

Twenty years later, the cause célèbre is still deployed to delineate the state of *expendability*. In 2007 a sixteen-year-old African American boy named Blair Holt was killed by another black teenager on a Chicago city bus, on his way home from school. Major political figures attended his funeral, including Mayor Richard M. Daley, Jesse Jackson, and State Representative Bobby Rush, and Jackson and Rush spoke at the funeral. Representing the decent families of Anderson's imaginary, Holt was described as an "honors student," who steered clear of gangs and was thus an exception to the scene of nature. Both of Holt's parents were college graduates, we learned, proper (home owners) and lawful members of Chicago's middle class. His father, Ron, was a nineteen-year veteran of the Chicago Police Department, and his mother, Annette, was a captain in the Chicago Fire Department. The national news program, *Dateline NBC*, filmed an hour-long documentary special about the crisis titled *Faces against Violence*. The show features an interview with Blair's mother, Annette, where she comments: "He was a great kid. It's like all the good kids are leaving, you know. The gangbangers are making it and our kids are dying." Blair's father, Ron, conveyed a similar message: "He was gonna be somebody. . . . He already knew he wanted to go to Clark Atlanta [a university]." The Holt case was being spun as a post–civil rights success story deterred by the bloody savagery of the black community. Holt emerged as a prototypical black Mohican subject, his family epitomizing the kind of *success* story that characterizes postracial United States.

Blair Holt was also a hybrid subject, an "honors student" and "aspiring rapper" named "Bizzy B" who understood the lifeststyles of "street" kids via hip-hop culture. A CNN report on his death began with a sample of his song, as the correspondent explained, "These are the words and beat of a streetwise kid from the rough-and-tumble South Side of Chicago. Just sixteen, he had already seen a lifetime of violent death." Holt was depicted as a "decent" kid who knew the street code. The correspondent reported, "Knowing . . . was one thing. Becoming one of them, a gang-banger, was a line Blair never dared to cross. His police officer father and firefighter mother made sure of that."[29]

By all accounts, Holt was a great kid whose death was an incredible tragedy. All childhood murders are tragic, yet only a select few are the subject of national news shows. This distinction is enabled by postracial discourse.

Olympic Games: Derrion Albert and Alex Arellano

On May 4, 2009, a fifteen-year-old Latino boy named Alex Arellano was beaten with baseball bats, shot in the head, run over by a car, and lit aflame by peers in his West Side Chicago neighborhood. In September 2009, sixteen-year-old Derrion Albert died after being struck in the head with a wooden board, caught in the middle of a gang brawl among peers on Chicago's far South Side. Both deaths took place when the president and first lady and other black celebrities were busy working to support Chicago's bid to host the 2016 Summer Olympic Games. Not surprisingly, then, that in 2009, the bloody-noble/street-decent binary became more pronounced in the juxtaposition of responses to Albert's and Arellano's tragic deaths, the former being hypervisible or a cause célèbre, the latter being the invisible norm forgotten.[30]

The Obamas were joined by black celebrities such as Oprah Winfrey and Michael Jordan to promote Chicago as a safe, clean, and cosmopolitan space that was well prepared to host the Olympics. In a perfect case of "the veneer of black success," the rich, famous, and black faces of this campaign strategically represented an exemplary postracial performance. Concurrently, pervasive structural inequalities helped frame Albert's death. The gang brawl he was caught in was linked to shifting school district boundaries. Albert's original high school had been shut down by Chicago Public Schools as a cost-cutting measure in 2008 and was being transformed into a military academy, forcing Albert and peers to attend a high school located within another gang's turf. Like Wilson and Holt before him, Albert appears in the news as an exceptional youth, an "honors student" who was not involved with gangs but was surrounded by them. Albert's beating was captured on video by an eyewitness's mobile phone and spread via social networking sites, the reason for much of the media attention that followed. Black deaths and the image of safe Chicago was an untenable paradox.[31]

Expectedly, President Obama took swift institutional action—more funds for yet another massive policing program. White House Press Secretary Robert Gibbs stated that "the killing of an honor student by others . . . is chilling, chilling video, and I think this is something that the administration has been working on." Days after Albert's death, Obama sent Education Secretary Arne Duncan and Attorney General Eric Holder to Chicago to announce that the federal government was earmarking $25 million in the 2010 budget for community-based crime prevention programs. Obama's Senior Adviser Valerie Jarrett also stated at a White House press conference that the Obama administration would supply "an unprecedented level of support for law enforcement" backed by a $500,000 emergency allocation to enhance safety at Albert's high school. The city of Chicago also responded by creating an "intelligence hub" to gauge violence around Chicago public schools and announcing that it would use "federal stimulus money" to enhance its "Safe Passage" program.

A year later, as if giving further confirmation that black Chicagoans cannot outlive their *expendability*, two black state representatives, John Fritchey (D) and La Shawn K. Ford (D), filed an official request for military troops to be deployed to Chicago's violence stricken neighborhoods. "As we speak," Fritchey explained, "National Guard members are working side-by-side with our troops to fight a war halfway around the world. . . . The unfortunate reality is that we have another war that is just as deadly taking place right in our backyard."[32] When suggesting that "the same thing, we've done in Iraq, we can do here in our own back yard," Fritchey further demonstrated how state violence is allowed with deployments of racial signifiers, which produce the scene of nature as a manifestation of the violence. Here the Taliban, Al-Qaeda, the Huron, and the "street" persons of Anderson's model appear as the bloody masses deserving of death or containment. The request for troops was unfulfilled. After a rash of killings in early 2012, however, the Chicago Police Department announced a new "intelligence gathering" initiative or "gang audit" being conducted by Commander James Roussell, who previously "led a Marine Reserve force that fought insurgents in Iraq and returned to Chicago in 2008."[33]

What happens then when a nonexceptional youth is killed in Chicago? Though taking place just a few months prior to the Albert's killing, Arellano's murder did not elicit the same response, from activists, politicians, or the media. There was no video evidence, but Arellano's case was still macabre. His charred, shot, beaten, and crushed body was not found until nearly a week after he died and was so severely disfigured that dental records were needed to confirm that it was him, and his family was prohibited from viewing the corpse. Similar to Albert, Arrelano's death is explained by the media as the result of gang tensions in his neighborhood, a tension that he refused to be involved with. Elements of deficiency appear in the description of Arellano. At fifteen years of age, he is described as not primed for inclusion, already succumbing to the chaos and pathology that were socionormatively ascribed to his community, the scene of nature. In the newspapers, he was referred as a child of recently arrived immigrants who "struggled in school"—in need of special education classes—rather than "honors student." There were no press conferences and no statements from the White House to speak about the tragedy of Arellano's death. No dignitaries, civil rights icons, no members of the president's cabinet, or elected officials were present at Arellano's funeral.

As the number of deaths grew in 2009, a Chicago-based antigang activist and catholic priest named Father Michael Pfleger began to ask why the state was not doing more, and this was despite the unprecedented federal support declared just two months prior after the Albert case. "We've had," he stated, "some 45 children killed this school year. A couple weekends ago, 11 people killed. 60 some shot in a weekend. Those are numbers like you have in Iraq or you have in Afghanistan." Pfleger has flown the flag at St. Sabinas upside down, explaining, "This is a distress signal we're putting up saying we need help. . . . Swine flu is a possibility that could get worse. Gun violence is worse now. It's an epidemic." In another interview he commented, "We had 250 students came through Cook County Hospital in three months with bullet wounds. What's interesting about these 36 students that died is they're all black or brown. If there was 36 white students killed in the Northwest suburbs, there would be a national outcry and every resource would be given to it to stop this."[34]

A few months after the Albert case, Pfleger, flanked by the parents of Blair Holt, introduced a $5,000 bounty for the capture of anyone guilty of murdering a child. Although his concern is commendable, Pfleger's critiques of the state reproduce the discursive binaries I have called attention to, binaries that decry mass incarceration as the solution to the crisis, without a broader political critique about expendability. Pfleger then reinforces the postracial state. Neither the state's saturation policing programs, Pfleger's vigilante justice campaign, or the work of other religious leaders has made a difference. And 2012 is already predicted to be one of the most violence years in Chicago's history.[35]

Fanon's Epidermalization, Excavating the Decolonial

The settler . . . is an exhibitionist. His preoccupation with security makes him remind the native out loud that there he alone is master. The settler keeps alive in the native an anger which he deprives of outlet; the native is trapped in the tight links of the chains of colonialism. But we have seen that inwardly the settler can only achieve a pseudo petrification. The native's muscular tension finds outlet regulary in bloodthirsty explosions—in tribal warfare, in feuds between sects, and in quarrels between individuals. Where individuals are concerned, a positive negation of common sense is evident. While the settler or the policeman has the right the livelong day to strike the native, to insult him and to make him crawl to them, you will see the native reaching for his knife at the slightest hostile or aggressive glance cast on him by another native; for the last resort of the native is to defend his personality vis-a-vis his brother. *Tribal feuds only serve to perpetuate old grudges buried deep in the memory. By throwing himself with all his force into the vendetta, the native tries to persuade himself that colonialism does not exist, that everything is going on as before, that history continues.* Here on the level of communal organizations we clearly discern the well-known behavior patterns of avoidance. It is as if plunging into a fraternal bloodbath allowed them to ignore the obstacle, and to put off till later the choice, nevertheless inevitable, which opens up the question of armed resistance to colonialism.

—Frantz Fanon, *Wretched of the Earth*

This passage from Fanon's *Wretched of the Earth* describes intra native violence, ghetto violence, as an intended outcome of domination, a strategy to deter anticolonial resistance.[36] As violence was used and expendability created to establish settler colonies, he argued, natives often normalized this violence and their expendability as an element of survival. In *Black Skin, White Masks*, this internalization appears as "epidermalization" (also often referred to as lactification) or the psychological internalization of inferiority and expendability, an internal alienation from self that is also manifest externally through the settler's violence and spatial segregation.[37] "The colonized man," he explains, "will first manifest this aggressiveness which has been deposited in his bones against his own people. This is the period when the niggers beat each other up, and the police and magistrates do not know which way to turn when faced with the astonishing waves of crime in North Africa."[38]

Fanon's account of native violence and epidermalization presents the conceptual basis for an analysis of ghetto violence that does not reproduce the three tropes of the postracial discourse, namely, bloody savage versus noble savage, the exceptional lives, and "veneer of success," and the kind of state action authorized by cause célèbre moments dicussed above. The most important aspect of Fanon's theorizing of native violence and epidermalization is that he describes it as a politically produced and therefore mutable condition, reversible politically, through self-determination, through decolonization, or through resistance to colonialism and its corollary racial state of expendability. In fact, Fanon explains that by not resisting, the colonized merely prolongs his own suffering.

It is not possible to immediately transpose Fanon's account of native violence to the analysis of ghetto violence in Chicago and other major cities. Nevertheless, this does not mean that the kind of racial violence produced by and used to justify more racial oppression is foreign to the U.S. racial political structures. In her analysis of U.S. ideological structures, Andrea Smith identifies the "three pillars of white supremacy," in which settler colonialism indicates how the United States operates as a prototypical settler colonial state, one with an in-built propensity for sustained and pervasive violence as a way to sustain itself as a nation, a violence that is legitimated within its law enforcement and military apparatuses and that has been inflicted, to a large extent, on nonwhite persons and natives in particular.[39] This violence inherent to U.S. sovereignty, I believe, is manifest through repetitive exhibition and via what Fanon described as a "preoccupation with security" intended to communicate to the colonized that "he [the settler] alone is master." The violence of settler colonialism is then a product and reflection of the racial state of expendability that, as I have described, is a base effect of raciality and that allows for all other exclusions. The violence inherent to the settler colony is its defining attribute and is, hence, irreconcilable by design or by acts of differential inclusion. Violence is how its sovereignty is legitimated, not per specific events but as a sustained and repeatedly performed prerequisite. As Patrick Wolfe argues, "settler colonialism destroys to replace" and "invasion...is a structure not an event."[40]

Reading Fanon and Smith together I am able to identify the political field of embattlement, associated with settler colonialism, as the site of production of subjects of violence (the racial other, the "street" person, the Huron, or the bloody savage) and hence also as the site within which resistance can be generated. Fanon suggests that ghetto violence can be reduced not via inclusions afforded by the state but via a decolonial struggle, a struggle that is "inevitable" yet that the subaltern often "puts off until later" by engaging in ghetto violence. In his critical interpretation of Fanon's decolonial critique, Nelson Maldonado Torres explains, "the decolonial attitude is born of when the cry of terror in the face of horrors of coloniality is translated into a critical stance toward the world of colonial death and in search of the affirmation of the lives of those most affected by such world."[41]

Such translations were vivid across Chicago's black and Latino communities from the 1950s to the 1970s, in the very gangs now being described as the source of violence, gangs formed originally to protect black and Latino families from white ethnic gangs that used terror to enforce residential segregation. These black and Latino gangs evolved from self-defense into organizations within which decolonial critiques, expressions of self-determination, began to flourish. One significant result of this evolution is that they demonstrated a remarkable capacity to to curb ghetto violence without the state's intervention.

That history has also been obscured within the noble savage–bloody savage rhetorical strategy and by postracial discourse. In U.S. history, the image of the white and male outlaw, gangster, or gunslinger has been recuperated via the trope of the noble savage and within narratives of manifest destiny or nation building. The violent and white settler has been transformed into an icon of the civilizing mission, a momentary/aberrational yet necessary representation of savagery that is historically quarantined as part of the rustic past, and certainly not the present. Black and Latino gangsters are denied this kind of recuperation. Their violence is not historical but pervasive and never noble. As Fanon suggests, they are produced antithetically to the settler, as practitioners of purposeless violence, emotionally unstable, counterproductive, threatening to civil society, the norm, and hence deserving of either death or incarceration so as to preserve the life of a Wilson, Holt, or Albert. In Chicago's history, this schism between the violence of the settler and the native is evident in hegemonic representations of white gangs and black or Latino gangs.

Besides the postracial/veneer of success images of Jordan, Winfrey, and Obama, the most iconic Chicagoan is Al Capone, an Italian immigrant and "boss" of an organized crime network called The Outfit during the early twentieth century. Capone's fame speaks to the deep origins of white ethnic gangs in Chicago's urban development. Frederic Thrasher's work *The Gang: A Study of 1,313 Gangs in Chicago*, published in 1927, was the first scholarly analysis of gang violence in the United States, arguing that southern and eastern European immigrants experienced ethnic prejudice in early Chicago and formed gangs to defend themselves and strengthen their position within the city's political economy.[42]

The violence of white ethnic gangs granted them a foothold in Chicago's early political economy, resulting in quick integration into Chicago's middle and upper classes and, eventually, the city's political and economic elite with a strong influence over law enforcement institutions in particular.[43] The Chicago Gang History Project noted that "by the 1950s, most white ethnic gangs had faded away, their members finding jobs through patronage in the Democratic machine, often as police. *The Outfit* had found a niche in Chicago's political life."[44] Chicago's most famous mayor, Richard J. Daley, is widely recognized as benefiting from his previous membership in one of these gangs, the Hapsburgs.

Black and Latino gangs were formed, in large part, to defend black and Latino families from Chicago's white ethnic gangs, a violence that the state generally turned a blind eye to. White ethnic gangs would patrol black communities and open fire on black residents from cars to maintain the rigidly segregated borders of communities on Chicago's southwest side. This spatial segregation, and its association with racial violence, reflects Fanon's concern with spatiality, or the "dividing line" between the settler and the wretched of the "native quarter." As Fanon explains, "geographical configuration" is the "backbone on which the decolonized society is reorganized."[45] Vigilantes policed this "dividing line" as a method to segregate Chicago's growing black and Latino population during the mid-twentieth century. Daley's Hapsburg gang is reputed to have been heavily involved with this violence. The Chicago Race Riot of 1919 was the result of black residents defending themselves against white terror.[46] Decades later, Latinos followed suit in the "Division Street Riots."

The self-defense origins of black and Latinos evolved into more defiant critiques of injustice during the1960s, inspired by the growth of a "U.S. Third World Left."[47] John Hagedorn has been central to recuperating this history, while not romanticizing it as essentially decolonial.[48] Much of the ghetto violence that this essay concerns itself with has indeed been inflicted in the name of the very gangs that I am now attempting to recuperate as noble. These contradictions, however, are not sufficient enough to obscure the political significance of these gangs, in their origination, as foundations for a decolonial turn.

Black gangs such as the Conservative Vice Lords, the Black P. Stones, the Black Gangster Disciples, and Latino gangs such as the Young Lords and the Latin Kings, all derived from antiracist critiques or, as a founder of the BGD's explained, "It's the gang versus the racism."[49] The Black P. Stone Rangers were established in Woodlawn on Chicago's South Side to protect African American families from white gangs. As a former member explained, "We Fight to Protect . . . because the police . . . they wasn't doing it."[50] Lance Williams, a gang biographer, explains that the Black P. Stones were the first Chicago gang to have "a main pillar of politics of the Black Power movement from the inception." The relationship between gangs like the Black P. Stones and the Black

Panther Party was a major concern for police. As Williams explains, if gangs decided to engage in revolutionary struggle, the police "would have to call in the National Guard and the military and everybody else. . . . America would have had a big problem."[51]

The Vice Lords' history is similar. It took on an decolonial profile under the leadership of Bobby Gore and a name change to Conservative Vice Lords (CVL). Bennie Lee, another leader of the CVL, explained that the group's evolution "had a lot to do with racism. Back in 1967 we were one of the first black families that moved [into a] predominantly white neighborhood. So we had to fight to go to school, fight to play." The CVL's were also wary of the political structure of ghetto violence, as a former member explains, "We were being so abused by white society that we took it out on the closest things near us—our black brothers." Lee cites Fanon as influential to this change, explaining, "in his book *Wretched of the Earth* . . . you have a group of people that's being oppressed . . . *take on the techniques of the oppressor to fight back and what happens is . . . the oppressed use those same techniques on his own people.* And I've seen it over and over and over . . . when the whites moved out of the hood we turned and looked at the new brothers coming in and got them." Besides reading Fanon, the CVLs under Gore and Lee aimed to curb this by launching an Afro-centric culture and history project headquartered in a "soul shop" named "The African Lion," a project explained as "a people's search for meaning . . . the extent to which black people can cope with ghetto life and fight to eradicate the sickness that perpetuates ghetto conditions is the extent to which our whole society will have the strength to realize the dreams we all share."[52] The history of the CVL's decolonial ethics has been highlighted in a recent exhibit titled "Report to the Public: An Untold History of the Conservative Vice Lords," organized by the Hull House of the University of Illinois–Chicago. Lisa Junkin, the exhibit's co-curator, explained that it "challenges widely held views of gang members as unredeemable thugs through an untold story of the Conservative Vice Lords fighting for the life of their community."[53]

Chicago's Latin Kings, formed in the 1940s, and Young Lords, formed in the late 1950s, originated similarly. Young Lords leader Jose "Cha-Cha" Jimenez explains: "Our community was mostly a white Anglo community. . . . We were the first few Puerto Ricans that were living there. The result of that was that every time I went to school I'd get beaten up . . . my parents had their windows broken. . . . so we started this group called the Young Lords . . . mostly for self-protection."[54] A primary concern of the Young Lords was the displacement of Puerto Rican families by the city and state's "urban renewal" programs. Jimenez and the Young Lords associated this displacement with the broader colonization of Puerto Rico. As he explains, "We wanted to keep our community where it was . . . to stabilize our neighborhood. We were seeing our community being robbed from us. So we were looking at that and then we're looking at the fact that we're Puerto Ricans and we are a direct colony of the U.S. and so we kinda . . . looked at it as the same issue."[55] Jimenez drew precise links between settler colonialism and ghetto violence. "The fact that we were fighting each other," he explained, "fighting our own brothers (we're made to fight our own brothers) the fact that we're living in a world . . . where we stayed drugged up all the time . . . because we're frustrated with life over here . . . are why we can relate to the independence of Puerto Rico. We cannot live under a colony. . . . We want to be liberated here and we want our people to be free and liberated at home."[56] Fanon was inspirational to this transformation. As he explains, "We read Che Guevara and all that, Franz Fanon, the *Wretched of the Earth* . . . becoming more intellectual at that time and learning stuff."

Jimenez's Young Lords later joined a broader and multiracial movement called the Rainbow Coalition led by Fred Hampton, chairman of the Black Panther Party and the pivotal figure in Chicago's decolonial struggles of the 1960s. Hamton established a coalition of black gangs called *LSD*, short for *Lords, Stones, and Disciples*, with up to fifty thousand members across the city dedicated to concerted antiracist activism and the aim of reducing ghetto violence.[57] Hampton was assassinated by Chicago police officers in 1969, an act that Hahn reveals as an intended strategy, coordinated with the FBI, to undermine the growing decolonial struggle.[58] As former CVL leader, Bennie Lee explains, "Fred Hampton . . . was kinda like the mastermind. . . . he became a threat, this is why I believe he was assassinated."[59]

This was more than a local campaign. Geoffrey C. Hazard Jr., an American Bar Foundation spokesperson and law professor at the University of Chicago, testified before the U.S. House Committee on Crime in 1969 that transformations of gangs into activists was a primary threat to civil authorities in the United States. As he explained, "What is happening, particularly within the Black ghettoes of the inner city, is that youth crime is becoming a self conscious act of political rebellion. . . . the politicization of youth crime is the most serious threat to the already uncertain stability of the national community. . . . [They] have become a kind of counter police force both in monitoring the community and in, certain cases, using force under claim of their own definition of legitimacy."[60] Concurrent with Hampton's assassination, Jimenez was jailed along with Jeff Fort of the Black P. Stones, Bobby Gore and Bennie Lee of the Conservative Vice Lords, and Larry Hoover of the Black Gangster Disciples.

Mike Royko's critical biography of Daley explains that this was all part of an effort to curb revolutionary change in the city. "As Daley had seen the same thing happen before," he writes, "he recalled Ragen's Colts, the Irish thieves and street fighters who became the most potent political force in Canaryville, and his own neighborhood's Hamburgs, who got their start the same brawling way before turning to politics and eventually launching his career. There lay the danger of the black gangs."[61] Daley's brutal "war on gangs" of the early 1970s exemplifies Fanon's explanation of the settler as "exhibitionist" whose pronounced security measures are intended to communicate to the native that "he alone is master."

That "war" was followed by an epic rise in ghetto violence in the 1980s and that has been sustained until the current moment. The founders of gangs like the Black P. Stones, the BGDs, the CVLs, and the Young Lords see this as a consequence of (1) the arrest or assassination of key decolonial leaders and (2) the introduction of cocaine, heroin, and military-grade weaponry into Chicago's black and Latino communities, a shift commonly alleged as a state conspiracy designed to encourage ghetto violence and further delay the decolonial turn.[62]

Conclusion: The Postcolonial Paradox

Let me conclude by returning to *The Interrupters*, the documentary about Chicago's street violence and Ceasefire, the gang violence initiative founded by a white epidemiologist named Gary Slutkin. Like Pfleger, Slutkin envisions violence as an epidemic or infectious disease. "Violence is like the great infectious diseases of all history," he explains during a scene in the film. "We used to look at people with plague, leprosy, and T.B. as bad people and evil people . . . and they were put in dungeons. What perpetuates violence can be as invisible today as the microorganisms of the past were." The Ceasefire program, which is funded by a combination of government (local, state, and federal) and private grants, assumes that (1) ex-convicts' experiences of incarceration puts them in a better position to warn others against the consequences of engaging in violent actions and (2) that imprisonment remedies ghetto violence. As portrayed by the film, Ceasefire workers attempt to prevent black and Latino youth from acts of retaliation by sharing their own story of being incarcerated, providing psychological counseling services, encouraging success in underresourced and violence-stricken schools, helping them garner low-paying service-sector jobs, or steering them toward religious faiths. As Slutkin explains, "The interrupters role, like the TB disease control workers role, is to do this initial interruption of transmission."

Slutkin has taken this disease discourse a step farther by suggesting that the brains of Chicago's black and Latino youth need to be analyzed in clinical/medical settings as a method to better understand the epidemic that they are inflicted with. As he explains, "We've learned there are particular cells and circuits [in the brain] that are for copying, and it's not conscious," meaning that systemic violence stems from an unconscious neurological response that can be remedied through the medical manipulation of brain cells.[63] This, I believe, represents an extreme, pathologizing representation dangerously similar to the rhetoric spun by eugenicists in the late nineteenth and early twentieth centuries, and that has been allowed for by the broader hegemonic influence of postracial discourse. There is no critique of expendability and its relationship to subjectivity, no social justice component, no dialogue about the alienation wrought by settler colonialism. Ceasefire has been deployed in Chicago's black and Latino communities as if the decolonial movements of the prior few decades had never happened. The political has been completely obscured by social science and now hard science discourse that fixates a gaze on the cells of human brains rather than conditions such as the proliferation of blacks and Latinos in prison cells over the twentieth century, the violence and expendability that have allowed for that outcome, and other conditions that are the direct structural consequences of white supremacy, slavery, segregation, and settler colonialism. The occlusion of these conditions is the outcome of postracial discourse and the more general postcolonial paradox that it is an element of.

What concerns me most about Ceasefire is how it has become its own cause célèbre, the subject of an award-winning and critically acclaimed documentary film, and recently awarded as one of the world's "top 100 NGOs" (no. 30) by *Global Journal*.[64] Ceasefire been exported to over one hundred U.S. cities, and to South Africa, Brazil, Jamaica, Iraq, the United Kingdom, and Trinidad and Tobago, all places where street violence has been similarly rampant, and where state agents are now embracing the violence interruption/public health methodology invented in Chicago.[65] The exportation of Ceasefire, by the U.S. State Department, to Iraq is particularly intriguing considering how Chicago's black and Latino residents have concurrently supported requests to transport U.S. troops from Iraq to quell violence in their communities. On May 29, 2012, the new Chicago police superintendent, Gary McCarthy, announced that he and Chicago's new mayor, Rahm Emmanuel, struck a deal with Ceasefire that would integrate it into the Chicago Police Department. Ceasefire's director, Tio Hardiman, declared that the city of Chicago would be contributing $1.75 million to expand Ceasefire's operations and resources, effectively making Ceasefire a quasi-state agency.[66]

As a former victim and victimizer of ghetto violence, and as an activist who has worked to combat this crisis for over twenty years now and in cities across the United States, I have often lent a hand to Ceasefire initiatives here in Chicago. I have firsthand knowledge that the work of "violence interrupters" is admirable in many ways. They have certainly interrupted acts of violence on occasion, and Ceasefire workers often face dangers while doing so. The initiative, however, has generally fallen short of fulfilling the promise of curbing ghetto violence in Chicago and has not lived up to much of the media hype surrounding it. Further, some grassroots activists have raised serious doubts over statistical reports on Ceasefire's efficacy.[67] Over the past few years, as Ceasefire itself has become a cause célèbre, violence has actually increased in Chicago's black and Latino communities—2012 could be most violent in Chicago's history, as evident in a 35 percent increase in homicide from January to June when compared with 2011.[68] How then is Ceasefire being publicized as such a grand success, grand enough to be integrated into the state, exported the world over and even to curb homicide in the postcolonies of Africa, South America, the Caribbean, and now a war-torn Iraq? How, moreover, has Ceasefire become a cause célèbre when the decolonial movements that preceded it, movements that were arguably far more effective at curbing or at least controlling ghetto violence across the city, were so heavily vilified, criminalized, and subjugated?

The answer, I believe, resides in Ceasefire's self-defined "apolitical" stance,[69] a qualification desired not only by state agents to communicate that they are concerned with this condition but also by a large segment of the U.S. polity as validation of their postracial faith and proclamations. It shuns any mention of racial oppression by describing street violence as an epidemiological and not a political condition, a crisis that originates in diseased minds and in the "cells and circuits" of the brain that Slutkin has recently mentioned. This representation adversely reinforces the prevailing image of black and Latino youth as hopelessly savage and senselessly violent, an image reinforced via the hypervisibility of cases like the Wilson, Holt, and Albert deaths. This is an effect of the postcolonial paradox, the broader and more global foundation for the United States' "veneer of success," a condition through which the spatial and socio-logical architecture of settler colonialism, the racial state of expendability, and the political origins of ghetto violence are sustained under a discursive disguise, a veneer of success that signifies postindependence or deregulation, that describes humanitarian crises as the result of epidemic/disease and not relations of power, and that positions the state as an unrivaled moral/ethical authority on whom the subaltern are dependent on for salvation because they cannot help themselves. The strategy of power that Denise Ferreira da Silva and Frantz Fanon elucidate as the production of racial subjects within the scene of nature/native quarter, or what I call the racial state of expendability, is then left intact and without much challenge.

To be sure, Ceasefire's (and Pfleger's) were not even the first initiatives to distract attention away from the political by appropriating a disease discourse. Two decades earlier, Mayor Washington's CIN program blended police enhancement with sociopsychological services for youth, a strategy that situated the jail and the clinic as sites of cure. Chicago was again central to a paradigm shift, obscuring the political critique. Carl C. Bell, a Chicago-based sociopsychologist, was one of the first in his field to argue that ghetto violence was resulting in, at least, one-quarter of black and Latino youth in working-class neighborhoods contracting a post-traumatic stress disorder (PTSD) similar to that experienced by soldiers of war.[70] Bell also suggested that the perpetrators of such violence could have been cured via clinical treatment.

This comparison between black and Latino youth and soldiers of war indicates the flawed logic spun by the postcolonial paradox. Soldiers return from the scene of war to civilian life. Youth of color never leave the scene of war, despite how it has been discursively disguised. They are produced within it, within political (juridico-economic) relationships and the architectures of settler colonialism, the political field of embattlement as the site of production of subjects of violence, of expendability. Trauma studies, and now the epidemiological position of Slutkin's Ceasefire, move too quickly away from this relationship, therefore, having a difficult time not reproducing the image of the bloody savages against whom the noble savage, as an exception, is relationally legitimated as worthy of inclusion/salvation, a legitimation that serves to delay, not destroy, the deconial turn. In sum, as noted earlier, the risk in addressing ghetto violence by privileging the psychosocial and not the structural/economic resides in that the argument may be associated with the culture of poverty thesis or its contemporary versions. This danger, however, is also a significant part of the problem, one exacerbated by the postracial, or postcolonial paradox: that is, the binary structure versus culture, when *politicized* by the media or by government officials never accounts for a subaltern perspective on expendability.

Nevertheless, the structural critique cannot be abandoned. The economic hardships wrought by deindustrialization have, indisputably, contributed to a steady rise in ghetto violence in Chicago over the past thirty years. Fanon himself did not work outside a critique of capitalism. He saw class as linked to race as essential to a comprehensive system of domination, a "double process" resulting in multiple definitions of what it means to be subprime. Fanon's

Wretched of the Earth built on Karl Marx's concept of alienation, a denial of being, of self-knowledge, that Marx argued was produced by class. The alienation of Fanon's model, his asking, "In reality, who am I?,"[71] is produced by race, the impact of expendability on subaltern subjectivity, not detached from class. As he explains, "If there is an inferiority complex, it is the outcome of a double process—primarily economic—subsequently, the internalization, or, better, the epidermalization, of this inferiority."[72] In Fanon's view, the discovery, conquest, and colonization of the racial other created Europe and its capitalism. Expendability, as a base effect of race, then precedes and sustains economic exclusion and exploitation; hence neither economic inclusion nor the postracial illusion of it can abridge it.

Notes

1. *The Interrupters* (dir. Steve James and Alex Kotloitz; Kamtequin Films, 2011).
2. Tim Wise, *Between Barack and a Hard Place: Racism and White Denial in the Age of Obama* (New York: City Lights, 2009); Cathy Cohen, *Democracy Remixed: Black Youth and the Future of American Politics* (New York: Oxford University Press, 2010).
3. Jesse Jackson, "Trayvon Martin: Look to Rosa Parks to Ensure No More Tragedies Like This," *Guardian*, March 30, 2012, www.guardian.co.uk/commentisfree/2012/mar/30/trayvon-martin-legacy-jesse-jackson.
4. Michael Harrington, *The Other America: Poverty in the United States* (New York: Simon and Schuster, 1962). See also Oscar Lewis, "The Culture of Poverty," in *Urban Life*, ed. George Gmelch and Walter Zenner (1966; Waveland Press, 1996); and Lewis, "Culture of Poverty," in Daniel P. Moynihan, *On Understanding Poverty: Perspectives from the Social Sciences* (New York: Basic Books, 1969), 187–220.
5. Henry A. Giroux, *Fugitive Cultures: Race, Violence, and Youth* (New York: Routledge, 1996).
6. Robert Berkhofer, *The White Man's Indian: Images of the American Indian from Columbus to the Present* (New York: Vintage, 1979); Neva Jacquelyn Kilpatrick, *Celluloid Indians: Native Americans and Film* (Lincoln: University of Nebraska Press, 1999).
7. James Fenimore Cooper, *The Last of the Mohicans: A Narrative of 1757* (1826; rpt. New York: Bantam Classics, 1982).
8. Gerry Smith, "Humboldt Park Residents Feel Sting of Foreclosures," *Chicago Tribune*, November 4, 2007.
9. Elijah Anderson, *Code of the Street: Decency, Violence, and Moral Life in the Inner City* (New York: Norton, 2000); Anderson, *Streetwise: Race, Class, and Change in an Urban Community* (Chicago: University of Chicago Press, 1990); Sudhir Venkatesh, *American Project: The Rise and Fall of a Modern Ghetto* (Chicago: University of Chicago Press, 2000); Martin Sanchez Jankowski, *Islands in the Street: Gangs and American Urban Society* (Berkeley: University of California Press, 1992).
10. Frantz Fanon, *The Wretched of the Earth*, trans. Richard Philcox (New York: Grove, 2004).
11. Barnor Hesse, "Racialized Modernity: An Analytics of White Mythologies," *Ethnic and Racial Studies* 30.4 (2007): 643–63; Denise Ferreira da Silva, *Toward a Global Idea of Race* (Minneapolis: University of Minnesota Press, 2007).
12. Denise Ferreira da Silva, "Toward a Critique of the Socio-Logos of Justice: The Analytics of Raciality and the Production of Universality," *Social Identities* 7.3 (2001): 421–54.
13. Further, in these explanations the culture side of that binary envisions the psychosocial as what makes the subaltern unworthy of inclusion and thus fit for condemnation. The structure side of that binary suggests that the psychosocial is but a product of exclusion that, in some instances, can damage the

subaltern to the extent that it deters their ability to take advantage of opportunities for inclusion when they are presented.

14. Elijah Anderson, "The Code of the Streets," *Atlantic*, May 1994, www.theatlantic.com/magazine/archive/1994/05/the-code-of-the-streets/6601/.

15. Anderson, *Code of the Street*.

16. Anderson, "Code of the Streets," 1.

17. Roderick Ferguson, "The Nightmares of the Heteronormative," *Cultural Values* 4.4 (2000): 419–44; Khalil Muhammad, *The Condemnation of Blackness: Race, Crime, and the Making of Modern Urban America* (Cambridge, Mass.: Harvard University Press, 2010).

18. Denise Ferreira da Silva, "No-Bodies: Law, Raciality, and Violence," *Griffith Law Review* 18.2 (2009): 212–36.

19. For Ferreira da Silva, "raciality immediately justifies the state's decision to kill certain persons—mostly (but not only) young men and women of colour—in the name of self preservation . . . such killings do not unleash an ethical crisis because these persons' bodies and the territories they inhabit always-already signify violence" ("No-Bodies," 213).

20. Terry Jay Ellingson, *The Myth of the Noble Savage* (Berkeley: University of California Press, 2001).

21. Angela Aleiss, "Le Bon Sauvage: *Dances With Wolves* and the Romantic Tradition," *American Indian Studies Center* 15.4 (1991): 91–95. It deserves mention that Terry Jay Ellingson demonstrates how Rousseau's connection to the "noble savage" idea has been exaggerated. See Ellingson, *Myth of the Noble Savage*.

22. Fenimore Cooper, *Last of the Mohicans*, 1.

23. Ibid., 205.

24. Robert J. C. Young, *Colonial Desire: Hybridity in Theory, Culture, Race* (New York: Routledge, 1995), 27.

25. Anderson, "Code of the Streets," 82.

26. Barack Obama, "A More Perfect Union," Philadelphia, March 18, 2008.

27. Citizens Committee on the Juvenile Court of Cook County Annual Meeting, March 7, 1986, A Panel Discussion On: Gangs, What Has Been Done? Guest Speaker: Mayor Harold Washington, Chicago Gang History Project, University of Illinois–Chicago, www.uic.edu/orgs/kbc/ganghistory/Info%20Era/Washgangs.htm.

28. Anne Keegan and Jerry Thornton, "Chicago Losing Ground in War on Street Gangs," *Chicago Tribune*, July 30, 1986.

29. Anderson Cooper, "Deadly Lessons: 24 Hours in Chicago," *360 Degrees*, June 1, 2007, http://transcripts.cnn.com/TRANSCRIPTS/0706/01/acd.02.html.

30. James Alan Fox Alan and Marc Swatt, "The Recent Surge in Homicides involving Young Black Males and Guns: Time to Reinvent in Prevention and Crime Control" (working paper, Northeastern University, 2008). See also John Rodriguez, "Young Voices: Pull the Trigger on Gun Violence," *Latin Trends*, www.latintrends.com/2011/02/28/young-voices-pull-the-trigger-on-gun-violence/ (accessed July 31, 2011). See also Brady Campaign to End Gun Violence, "Overview: Gun Violence, Race, and Ethnicity," www.bradycampaign.org/facts/gunviolence/factsethnicity.

31. A similar contrast was visible with the recent NATO summit in Chicago in 2012. Gary Younge, a London-based journalist, commented, "NATO claims its purpose is to secure peace through security; in much of Chicago neither exists," evident in a 50 percent increase in ghetto violence since 2011, and also in "police . . . shooting people at the rate of six a month and killing one person a fortnight" (Younge, "NATO Talks Security and Peace: Chicago Has Neither," *Guardian*, May 20, 2012, www.guardian.co.uk/commentisfree/cifamerica/2012/may/20/chicago-nato-g8-summit-inequality.

32. "Two Chicago State Reps: Bring in the National Guard," Chicago Breaking News, April 25, 2010, http://archive.chicagobreakingnews.com/2010/04/state-reps-want-to-fight-violence-with-national-guards-help.html.

33. Frank Main, "Gangs Are under Audit in Rogers Park Neighborhood," *Chicago Sun Times*, April 16, 2012.

34. David Mattingly, "Minority Youngsters Dying Weekly in Chicago's Streets," CNN, May 8, 2009, http://articles.cnn.com/2009-05-08/justice/chicago.children.slain_1_school-year-public-schools-slayings?_s=PM:CRIME.

35. In 2012 the *Chicago Reporter* concluded that "more young people are killed in Chicago than any other American city." See Fox Alan and Swatt, "Recent Surge." There are similar statistics for Latinos.

In New York City the rate of Latino victims and victimizers has steadily increased since 2008. See Rodriguez, "Young Voices." Overall, the rate of African American gun-related deaths by homicide in the United States is 84 percent; for Latinos it is 68 percent. By comparison, 80 percent of gun deaths among whites were suicides. See Brady Campaign to End Gun Violence, "Overview."

36. See also Kelly Oliver, *The Colonization of Psychic Space: A Psychoanalytic Social Theory of Oppression* (Minneapolis: University of Minnesota Press, 2004), 5.
37. Frantz Fanon, *Black Skin, White Masks*, trans. Charles Lam Markmann (New York: Grove, 1967), 11.
38. Fanon, *Wretched of the Earth*, 31.
39. Andrea Smith, "Indigeneity, Settler Colonialism, White Supremacy," *Global Dialogue* 12.2 (2010)—Race and Racisms, www.worlddialogue.org/content.php?id=488.
40. Patrick Wolfe, "Settler Colonialism and the Elimination of the Native," *Journal of Genocide Research* 8.4 (2006): 388.
41. Nelson Maldonado Torres, "La descolonizacion y el giro de-colonial," *Tabula Rasa* 9 (July–December 2008): 66.
42. Frederic Thrasher, *The Gang: A Study of 1,313 Gangs in Chicago* (Chicago: University of Chicago Press, 1927).
43. Richard Slotkin, *Gunfighter Nation: Myth of the Frontier in Twentieth-Century America* (Norman: University of Oklahoma Press, 1998).
44. Chicago Gang History Project, "A Brief History of Chicago Gangs," www.uic.edu/orgs/kbc/ganghistory/briefhistory.html.
45. Fanon, *Wretched of the Earth*, 3.
46. John Hagedorn, "Race Not Space: A Revisionist History of Gangs in Chicago," *Journal of African American History* 91.2 (2006): 194–208.
47. Laura Pulido, *Black, Brown, Yellow, and Left: Radical Activism in Los Angeles* (Berkeley: University of California Press, 2006); Cynthia Young, *Soul Power: Culture, Radicalism, and the Making of the US Third World Left* (Durham, N.C.: Duke University Press, 2006).
48. John M. Hagedorn, *A World of Gangs: Armed Young Men and Gangsta Culture* (Minneapolis: University of Minnesota Press, 2009).
49. Interview no. 103, Chicago Gang History Project, University of Illinois–Chicago.
50. *Gangland: Stone to the Bone*, dir. Art Camacho, History Channel, December 20, 2007.
51. Lance Williams, "Black Power, Politics, and Gang Banging," lecture, UIC School of Public Health, transcribed October 18, 2001, Chicago Gang History Project, University of Illinois–Chicago, www.uic.edu/orgs/kbc/ganghistory/UrbanCrisis/Blackstone/lance.htm (accessed April 27, 2012).
52. Charlotte G. Moulton, "Youth Crime Is Political," *Chicago Daily Defender*, July 31, 1969.
53. Lisa Junkin, Hull House education coordinator, University of Illinois–Chicago, press release, "Report to the Public: An Untold History of the Conservative Vice Lords" exhibit, June 22, 2012.
54. "Chicanos: Identity Recovered: Corky Gonzalez and Cha Cha Jimenez Interview by Karen Wald," *Tricontinental*, Havana, Cuba, July–October 1970, www.walterlippmann.com/klw-1970.html (accessed May 9, 2012).
55. Erika Rodriguez and Ralph Citron, "The Origins of Puerto Rican Gangs in Chicago," interview with Jose "Cha-Cha" Jimenez, June 2002, Chicago Gang History Project, University of Illinois–Chicago. See also "The Young Lords, Puerto Rican Liberation, and the Black Freedom Struggle," interview with Jose "Cha Cha" Jimenez, *OAH Magazine of History* 26.1 (2012): 61–64. See also "Cha-Cha Jimenez and the History of the Young Lords," WBEZ Radio, June 12, 2006, Chicago, www.wbez.org/episode-segments/cha-cha-jimenez-and-history-young-lords.
56. "Chicanos: Identity Recovered."
57. "'LSD' Working for a Better Black Area: Teen Gang Coalition Lending a Big Hand," *Chicago Daily Defender*, October 9, 1969, 13.
58. Jeffrey Haas, *The Assassination of Fred Hampton: How the Chicago Police and the FBI Murdered a Black Panther* (Chicago: Chicago Review Press, 2010).
59. "Former Vice Lord Leader Bennie Lee," oral history interview, Chicago Gang History Project, February 28, 2002, www.uic.edu/orgs/kbc/ganghistory/UrbanCrisis/ViceLords/Bennieleex.html.
60. Quoted in Moulton, "Youth Crime Is Political."
61. Mike Royko, *BOSS: Richard J. Daley of Chicago* (New York: Plume, 1998), 210.
62. Williams, "Black Power, Politics, and Gang Banging,"; "Former Vice Lord Leader Bennie Lee"; Rodriguez and Citron, interview with Jose "Cha-Cha" Jimenez.

63. Dawn Turner Trice, "Ceasefire Founder: Brain Research Could Help Combat Violence," *Chicago Tribune*, June 13, 2012, http://articles.chicagotribune.com/2012-06-13/news/ct-x-0613-trice-column-20120613_1_brain-research-gang-members-slutkin.

64. *Global Journal*, "The Top 100 Best NGO's," January 23, 2012, theglobaljournal.net/article/view/511/.

65. U.S. Diplomatic Mission to South Africa, "Sharing Strategies for Reducing Gang Violence: Gary Slutkin and Jalon Arthur in South Africa to Discuss Successful Ceasefire Model," southafrica.usembassy.gov/news100927a.html (accessed May 28, 2012).

66. Frank Main, "Six Ceasefire Workers Charged with Crimes in Past Year," *Chicago Sun Times*, June 1, 2012, www.suntimes.com/12894675-761/six-ceasefire-workers-charged-with-crimes-in-the-past-five-years.html.

67. Chicago Justice Project, "Social Science as a Disaster—Northwestern's Evaluation of Ceasefire (Part II of IV)," www.chicagojustice.org/blog/social-science-as-a-disaster-2013-northwesterns (accessed May 28, 2012).

68. "Chicago Murder Rate Up 35%: Police Chief Reassigns Commanding Officers," *Huffington Post*, March 30, 2012.

69. As indicated in a scene from *The Interrupters*, where Ceasefire administrators are describing their initiative to a delegation from South Africa. I have also encountered this "a-political" discourse with my own interactions with Ceasefire. This has been evident in the ways that there is very little, if any, mention of race or any similar dynamics. In fact, any mention of race has been treated as aberational if not taboo.

70. Carl C. Bell and Esther J. Jenkins, "Traumatic Stress and Children," *Journal of Health Care for the Poor and Underserved* 2.1 (1991): 2. See also Karyn Horowitz, Randall Marshall, Mary McKay, "Community Violence and Urban Families: Experiences, Effects, and Directions for Intervention," *American Journal of Orthopsychiatry* 75.3 (2010): 356–68; Stacy Overstreet and Shawnee Braun, "Exposure to Community Violence and Post-Traumatic Stress Symptoms: Mediating Factors," *American Journal of Orthopsychiatry* 70.2 (2000): 263–71; Donna E. Howard, "Searching for Resilience among African American Youth Exposed to Community Violence: Theoretical Issues," *Journal of Adolescent Health* 18.4 (1996): 254–62; Emily S. Edlynn, Noni K. Gaylord-Harden, Maryse H. Richards, and Steven A. Miller, "African American Inner-City Youth Exposed to Violence: Coping Skills as a Moderator for Anxiety," *American Journal of Orthopsychiatry* 78.2 (2008): 249–58.

71. Fanon, *Black Skin, White Masks*, 250.

72. Ibid., 11.

Blues Geographies and the Security Turn: Interpreting the Housing Crisis in Los Angeles

Jordan T. Camp

> As I see it, history moves from one conjuncture to another rather than being an evolution-
> ary flow. And what drives it forward is usually a crisis. . . . Crises are moments of potential
> change, but the nature of their resolution is not given.
> —Stuart Hall, "Interpreting the Crisis," *Soundings*

On a cordoned-off block stretching between Fifth and Sixth Streets and Gladys in downtown Los Angeles, which on most days houses a soup kitchen, a vacant lot, and a single-room occupancy hotel, Chuck D and Public Enemy performed for free at the Operation Skid Row music festival. The festival, which took place on January 15, 2012, the weekend of Dr. Martin Luther King Jr.'s birthday, was co-organized by Chuck D and the Los Angeles Community Action Network (LA CAN), a housing and hu-man rights organization. Over fifteen hundred people crammed the street to listen to Public Enemy alongside the music of LA hip-hop performers such as Freestyle Fellowship, Medusa, Kid Frost, Yo-Yo, and Egyptian Lover as well as artists from the neighborhood like the Skid Row Playas. Chuck D proclaimed, "This day of action will promote the human right to housing and reinforce the hip hop community's responsibility to social justice causes."[1] In the face of threats from the Los Angeles Police Department to shut the festival down, Public Enemy opened with one of their signature songs of defiance, "Shut 'Em Down."[2] They did so before an audience of Skid Row residents and com-munity organizers; members of social movement organizations like the Bus Riders Union, Critical Resistance, Food Not Bombs, and INCITE! Women of Color Against Violence; and fans from across the city. This effort to connect the hip-hop generation to the struggle for human rights was significant for its timing and location. During the fifth year of the worst economic crisis since the Great Depression, this festival highlighted the material conditions in Skid Row—an area in downtown Los Angeles where black people are 75 percent of the population and which has the highest concentration of poverty, policing,

Figure 1.
Chuck D and Public Enemy performing "Fight the Power" at Operation Skid Row Music Festival promoting the human right to housing. Skid Row, Los Angeles, January 15, 2012. Image by Ernest R. Savage III.

and homelessness in the United States.[3] More than just a day of entertainment, the Operation Skid Row musical festival helped circulate an insurgent critique of the housing crisis.[4]

Community organizers have taken up a dramatic fight over the meaning of the crisis by calling for the human right to housing in Los Angeles, the "First World capital of homelessness."[5] The Operation Skid Row festival was one manifestation of this effort. It gave voice to struggles for housing rights in the historical and geographic context of the gentrification and securitization of Skid Row, by which I mean the routinized militarized policing of racialized space.[6] In doing so, it enabled the circulation of what Clyde Woods calls "blues geographies" to explain the sociospatial relationships between poverty, policing, and policies designed to punish the poor and people of color being articulated by grassroots artists and activists themselves.[7] The blues represent the material conditions experienced by the working class, and of how they have resisted them.[8] Indeed, the poetic visions produced by vernacular artists articulate "truths of working-class African American life."[9] In this case Operation Skid Row confronted the truth of the crisis, that "the social formation can no longer be reproduced on the basis of the pre-existing system of social relations."[10] This effort to highlight housing struggles in downtown Los Angeles during the crisis of global capitalism shows how expressive culture provides counternarratives to the dominant definitions of events.[11]

Figure 2.
Chuck D and Flavor Flav at the Operation Skid Row music festival. Skid Row, Los Angeles, January 15, 2012. Photo by Nicholas Dahmann.

The "blues moment" represented by the crisis has compelled artists and activists to struggle over the definition of material conditions.[12] Public Enemy's performance of songs like "Fight the Power" at Operation Skid Row reflects and constitutes the struggle for hegemony—in that these lyrics do not simply reflect the crisis; they call attention to it and, in doing so, attempt to change it.[13] The performance contributed to the ability of people who have been displaced, dispossessed, and 'dissed—because of the deleterious consequences of neoliberal housing policies—to elevate their struggles for freedom to a higher scale.[14]

The politics of scale are crucial for the evicted, poor, and homeless residents of Skid Row, who are engaged in a dynamic social movement against the "securitization of the city."[15] With the number of homeless in Los Angeles higher than in any other city in the country—affecting between sixty thousand and one hundred thousand people—the struggles on Skid Row during the housing crisis have faced the deployment of racialization and criminalization, which have operated in tandem with gentrification and capital accumulation.[16] Using Woods's concept of "trap economics," I argue that these processes work together in trapping black and poor people in space to protect the interests of capital and the state.[17] Such traps on Skid Row include the mass arrest of residents for activities such as loitering, jaywalking, public urination, and public drunkenness under the guise of public safety—or the mass eviction of residents from single-room occupancy hotels in the name of reclaiming downtown through condo and loft conversions for high-end real estate development.[18] This strategy of "accumulation by dispossession" has been sustained and justified by racial narratives, which purport that poor people of color are individually responsible for their own loss of wealth, a consequence of their attitudes, behaviors, and cultures of ineptitude.[19] As Operation Skid Row underscores, the deployment of racialization and securitization to resolve crises at different scales requires us to situate trap economics in a complex dialectic of race, class, and regional factors.[20]

This article asks and answers the following research questions about these racial, spatial, and class dynamics: What has been the relationship between the housing crisis in Los Angeles and the global financial crisis? How have the dominant representations of the crisis provoked grassroots resistance and criticism at different scales? How have grassroots activists and artists adapted the black freedom struggle's historical tradition in confronting the current crisis? What kinds of ethical responses to crisis are made possible when conceived from the perspective of the social movement for the human right to housing?

Drawing inspiration from Operation Skid Row and the grassroots struggle for housing in Los Angeles I make four principal arguments. First, the racial and spatial dynamics of capital accumulation underscore the need to theorize the politics of scale in housing struggles during this precise historical moment. The struggle for the human right to housing demonstrates the importance of the "politics of signification" in spatial politics, and that is the antiracist and class struggle in ideology over the meaning of the "production of space."[21] I seek to demonstrate how the politics of signification are intimately linked to struggles for "spatial justice."[22] In doing so, I hope to challenge how struggles over the definition of events have been depoliticized through disavowals of the race and class dimensions of the crisis.[23] After all, the housing crisis results from policies that have responded to shifts in the organization of global capital since the high tide of black freedom and labor struggles in the twentieth century, which have ensured a racially and spatially differentiated organization of the landscape in U.S. cities into the twenty-first century.[24]

Second, while there are multiple methodological approaches to analyzing the current crisis, as Stuart Hall suggests, one of the most productive ways is to analyze it as a conjuncture, which is a historical moment in which political, economic, ideological, and geographic forces take a distinct shape.[25] Like Hall, I argue that while neoliberalism may be an inadequate term, it is the best language we have to define the current conjuncture dominated by finance capital, while helping us periodize the relationships between capital, the state, and social movements.[26] Through a conjunctural analysis of the struggle for housing rights, we can better understand alternatives to the "political settlement" that has come to dominate the U.S. political and cultural economy in which housing, education, and health care are assumed to represent commodities rather than a social wage.[27] A conjunctural analysis suggests that this settlement has been defined in terms of race, law and order, and security during the "long late twentieth century," the period between 1965 and the current crisis.[28] While this may seem like a long period, it is important to remember that a "conjuncture is not a slice of time" but, as Hall puts it, "can only be defined by the accumulation/condensation of contradictions."[29]

Third, I argue that racial discourses have been deployed to endorse a neoliberal security regime that justifies economic restructuring, prison expansion, and securitization through appeals to whiteness.[30] I use the concept of neoliberal racial and security regimes to theorize the modalities of political, economic, and cultural relationships among spaces of uneven capitalist development, criminalization, incarceration, and domestic countersubversion in the past half century.[31] This line of argument enables us to understand how the housing crisis has become an especially significant moment in the process by which race and class anxieties created through economic crisis came to be represented in terms of security.[32] It can also help us assess how dominant representations of the housing crisis have reinforced the logic of the current political settlement.[33] It suggests that security ideology represents the withdrawal of the social wage as symptomatic of a decline of the nation-state at precisely the moment when military, prisons, and policing have become central to the political economy of U.S. empire.[34] Such an analysis exposes how the logics of "political whiteness" have shaped neoliberal security ideology.[35]

Finally, remaining attentive to structural underpinnings of the current conjuncture, this article also examines the perspective of events articulated in the expressive culture and political visions of social movements in Los Angeles during the long twentieth century.[36] It argues that contemporary housing and homeless struggles represent a continuity of campaigns waged by civil and human rights organizations to contest racial capitalism's organization of space in Southern California.[37] These grassroots activists and artists show that the resolution of crisis by racialization, neoliberalization, and securitization is not inevitable.[38] They have produced alternative definitions of the situation, which could produce different outcomes. To develop these arguments this article proceeds in three parts: it looks at dominant depictions of the current crisis, then turns to the historical confrontation in Los Angeles between housing struggles and emergent securitization, and concludes with a consideration of what we might learn from Los Angeles about the prospects for alternative futures.[39]

Narrating the Crisis: Racialization, Neoliberalization, and Securitization

Poor communities of color have been particularly affected by the "subprime mortgage crisis," as it has come to be signified in mass-mediated discourse.[40] These communities were targeted for predatory and faulty subprime loans, and later represented as the primary culprits of the crisis. As people of color had experienced systematic racial exclusion in access to home loans because of historical practices of redlining, they were also increasingly given access to faulty subprime loans as capital deepened its strategies of financialization.[41] Before the foreclosure crisis took hold as a national phenomenon, black people lost between $71 and $93 billion dollars in assets because of subprime loans between 2000 and 2008, while Latinos lost between $76 and $98 billion.[42] The crisis only compounded a reliance on credit by the poor and people of color.[43] As mortgage rates increased while real wages went into decline and unemployment rates skyrocketed, it became increasingly difficult for people to make their payments.[44] A wave of foreclosures followed, leading to what United for a Fair Economy describes as "the greatest loss of wealth to people of color in modern US history."[45]

The subprime mortgage crisis led to a collapse in several Wall Street banks, which in turn had the effect of spreading the crisis worldwide from its historical and geographic roots in U.S. urban spaces. While the ramifications of the financial crisis have been global, Southern California has been an "epicenter."[46] By 2010 California experienced more foreclosures than any other place in the country, with a half million cases.[47] At the national scale, over half the foreclosures were experienced by African Americans and Latinos, a rate two to three times higher than for whites.[48] It also created a spike in homelessness.[49]

The history and ongoing practices of racial segregation and policing in Southern California have concentrated the deleterious consequences of the capitalist crisis in and through the "racialization of space and spatialization of race."[50] Racial segregation traps poor people of color in spaces that have been targeted by finance capital for predatory lending of subprime loans. This spatial apartheid exists alongside other parasitic finance institutions, which exploit the poor and people of color through high interest rate loans.[51] Taken together, such practices can be read as capital's efforts to trap people in space to extract wealth.[52] Finance capitalists and their deputies have exploited the geography of poverty and spatial apartheid. In doing so, they have widened the "racial wealth gap." At the same time, mass evictions have been deployed as a solution to the foreclosure crisis in the very segregated neighborhoods that had been targeted for subprime loans. The very lenders that peddled subprime loans accumulated capital by displacing and dispossessing poor people of color.[53]

Yet in narrating the housing crisis, commentators such as the vice president of the Manhattan Institute, Howard Husock, represent the poor, people of color, housing activists, and state regulation of finance capital as the "culprits" of the crisis: "One cannot say with any certainty whether the more important cause of the current housing crisis was affordable-housing mandates or the actions of investment banks and ratings agencies." Husock simultaneously asserts that denying loans to people "based on the race of the residents or other factors unrelated to their ability to repay loans is clearly wrong," and that there is no longer a need for state regulation of finance capital. In this way, he appeals to the fantasy of a raceless meritocracy where loans can be made the "old-fashioned way, on the merits of individual households."[54] Such narratives make well-established appeals to colorblindness by suggesting that the problem is "risky borrowers," thus naturalizing the sociospatial relations that produced the situation. In doing so, they function to displace class anxieties created through the uneven development of racial capitalism.[55]

Traditional intellectuals in neoliberal think tanks such as the Manhattan Institute—which I show are closely aligned with the mayor, police department, and finance capital in Los Angeles—have engaged in an ideological struggle to legitimate their "revanchist" solutions to the crisis.[56] As rationalizers of "securitized urbanism," such think tanks—which also include the American Enterprise Institute, the Cato Institute, and the Heritage Foundation—have narrated the housing crisis as part of an effort to advocate for policy that restructures space in the interest of capital's security.[57] The state's response to the crisis—bailing out the bankers who caused the problem rather than implementing concrete housing and jobs programs to meet the needs of the poor and the working class—suggests the extent to which neoliberal think tanks and finance capital shape federal policies. It also reflects the inability of liberalism to address the race and class antagonisms at the heart of the crisis.[58] By analyzing the specific forms that capital and the state's response to the housing crisis has taken at different scales, we can better understand how such responses to the crisis have been in keeping with hegemonic tendencies in the conjuncture.

To understand the race and class underpinnings of the current crisis, we also need a long historical view of how dominant "geographical interests" have shaped what Denise Ferreira da Silva calls the "security turn."[59] As the crisis of Fordism and U.S. hegemony took hold in the late 1960s, appeals to the idea of internal security threats served to displace social antagonisms through moral panics around race and crime.[60] Race and class insecurities created by the crisis of Fordism were tactically exploited by politicians to justify the expansion of policing and prisons as solutions to the crisis.[61] Security ideologies have imposed new ways of seeing this transformation of the political economy.[62] They placed notions of safety and security at the center of the political imagination during a period marked by rising unemployment, inflation, declining rates of profit, and economic restructuring.[63] As contradictions have emerged, the traditional intellectuals of the security apparatus have articulated ideological "cement" of racialization and securitization to "fix" ruptures in the social formation.[64]

One of the most persistent ruptures has been created by deindustrialized workers of color themselves: from the Watts insurrection (1965) to the Los Angeles rebellion (1992) to the persistent struggles waged on Skid Row in the current crisis, surplus workers have been at the center of political struggles over public space and access to wealth.[65] They have promoted visions of social change marked by a commitment to justice, cultural dignity, and human rights that clash with the vision of those who seek law and order, security, and social control.[66] Yet the political struggles of the poor as they engage in social protests, uprisings, and struggles for survival have been represented in state and mass-mediated narratives as increased lawlessness, crime, and irrational violence.[67] These racial narratives have treated the dissent of surplus populations—who are disproportionately composed of people of color—as irrational expressions of discontent against a rational neoliberal security state. In turn, they have naturalized gentrification, mass incarceration, and the securitization of the city.[68]

Extending Ruth Gilmore's conceptualization of the production of carceral landscapes, we can better understand how racial capitalism and the neoliberal security state's solution to protests arising among the surplus population has been to produce securitized spaces.[69] Mass-mediated representations of the surplus populations engaged in social protest as symbols of violence and crimi-nality have legitimated the direction of resources away from the social wage and toward securitization.[70] This shift in the state form has been accompanied by a form of racism articulated by an authoritarian populist bloc—with historical and geographic roots in Southern California—whose persistent refrain has been to disavow any link between pervasive and persistent white supremacy and the impoverishment of poor people of color.[71] This bloc has coalesced around an "anti-statist" libertarian ideology that represents public housing, health care, jobs, and education as bureaucratic restrictions on the putative freedom provided by capitalist markets and entrepreneurism.[72] Such racist and populist rhetoric has been effective in winning consent to expanding the state's coercive security apparatus.[73] The housing crisis and the economic meltdown that followed need to be interpreted as the logical result of a half-century-long political project bent on destroying the welfare state, criminalizing dissent, and expanding militarized policing, prisons, and the security apparatus to violently enforce consent to the abandonment of the social wage by capital and the state.[74]

This neoliberal ideology has promoted austerity measures and urban structural adjustment as commonsense solutions to crisis, and therefore widespread cuts in public expenditure for education, health care, and housing. It has also represented the resulting racial hierarchies as natural and inevitable.[75] These representations underscore how the political logics of whiteness have shaped the transformation of the "urban security landscape."[76] While cuts in the social wage have disproportionately affected the working class community of color, the representations of this statistical reality in mass-mediated discourses have regularly obscured how class structures racist hierarchies. That is, the numerical majority of the impoverished have been poor whites, but as Cedric Robinson puts it, "The stigmata of poverty, the 'deviancy' of crime—and much of the political responsibilities of critical dissent" have been transferred to black people and other people of color.[77] Consider, for example, the fact that while the black poor make up the disproportionate percentage of the U.S. homeless population at between 40 and 56 percent (making them 3.5 times more likely to be homeless), poor whites also make up between 32 and 39 percent of the population at the national level. Ideologies of whiteness have redirected attention away from engaging with the multiraciality of poverty and homelessness.[78] They have shifted attention away from the declining material conditions for the working class in general and in doing so rationalized what Jodi Melamed calls the "new racial capitalism."[79]

The linkages between uneven capitalist development, revanchist attacks on the social wage, prison expansion, and the deployment of racial discourse to justify the consolidation of "securitocracy" constitute the terrain that I argue is most fruitfully understood as neoliberal racial and security regimes.[80] Racial discourses have sustained the proliferation of "more or less permanent 'states of exception' and emergency,"[81] and have become essential to the practices of the contemporary capitalist state.[82] At the same time, security ideologies have legitimated the denial of aggrieved and insurgent communities' human rights and naturalized authoritarianism through populist appeals.[83] This populist ideology seeks to prevent multiracial class alliances by scapegoating the poor, people of color, LGBTQI communities, immigrant workers, and radical organizers (which are not mutually exclusive categories) to displace anxieties caused by economic crisis and restructuring. It endorses the mass criminalization of dissent, a central facet of militarism.[84]

While security narratives have provided justification for transforming the political economy, this rhetoric rests uneasily alongside pervasive poverty, precarious employment, punitive housing policy, and persistent prison expansion that produces "group-differentiated vulnerabilities to premature death."[85] Thinking conjuncturally, we can begin to discern the structure of social relations that are otherwise difficult to observe.[86] The current crisis can also enable a fidelity to the unfinished business of freedom struggles from the long twentieth century.[87]

The Housing Question and the Security Turn

And when it comes to housing—why we could use the 300,000 housing units authorized annually in the administration bill among Negroes alone and we'd still be in a terrible fix for a decent place to live.
—Paul Robeson, *Paul Robeson Speaks*

The federal government should be subsidizing housing activities on such a scale that all American housing meets at least minimal standards of adequacy. Housing is too important to be left to private enterprise without only minor government effort to shape policy. We need the equivalent of a Medicare for housing.
—Dr. Martin Luther King Jr., *Where Do We Go From Here: Chaos or Community?*

In 1948 the legendary singer, actor, and internationalist Paul Robeson performed in Los Angeles at a fund-raiser for the Civil Rights Congress (CRC).[88] The concert, along with many others like it, was organized to support the CRC's campaigns against racism and segregation and to build solidarity.[89] The CRC organized social protests challenging racist restrictive covenants, segregated schools, and police violence.[90] Historically trapped in areas with poor housing, black workers in Los Angeles had limited access to quality education and meaningful employment.[91] The fight for jobs, relief for the unemployed, and public housing was therefore a struggle against the more general exclusions of racial capitalism.[92] Such fights had been persistently waged by labor and civil rights organizations since the Great Depression.[93]

By the late 1940s and early 1950s groups like the CRC increasingly faced political repression. Against their efforts to end police brutality, racist violence, segregation, and civil and human rights violations, the Subversive Activities Control Board declared that the CRC represented a "communist front."[94] Such political repression was part and parcel of the postwar red scare that marked the emergence of Cold War racial liberalism. Despite these attacks, the CRC continued to organize to demonstrate how racism persistently violated the human rights of black and brown working people. Perhaps the most prominent example of this effort at the international scale occurred in 1951 when the executive director of the CRC William Patterson submitted the study *We Charge Genocide* at the United Nations in Paris—at the same time as Robeson submitted the document to the U.N. in New York.[95] In a speech he delivered in New York City on November 12, 1951, at a release event for the study, Patterson explained that it represented the struggle against what he called the "premature death" created by racist violence and segregation.[96] U.S. state officials prevented the U.N. from considering the petition. Then the national security state intensified its systematic campaign of repression against black radicals and the Left—such as W. E. B. Du Bois, Patterson, and Robeson—which included surveillance, arrest, show trials, denial of passports, exclusion from employment, and incarceration. Appeals to moral panics around communism helped win consent to coercive securitization and the diversion of expenditures away from the social wage.[97]

With its strategically located means of cultural production in Hollywood and postwar expansion of the military-industrial complex, Southern California became an epicenter of the Cold War counterrevolution.[98] California countersubversives launched an organized political attack on labor and civil rights activists.[99] These counterinsurgents recognized that black workers entering the defense industry who were experiencing racial segregation would be sympathetic to efforts to promote equality, the redistribution of wealth, and civil rights.[100] Richard Nixon and Ronald Reagan rose to prominence through carrying out domestic counterinsurgency campaigns that practiced "anticommunism as governmentality."[101]

As Gerald Horne's research shows, efforts by civil rights organizers and the multiracial Left to resist segregation were demonized by anticommunists.[102] The promotion of public housing as a solution to housing shortages was represented in the "counterinsurgent narratives" as a "creeping socialism."[103] Even where black workers gained access to public housing, quotas were used to limit it. At the same time, deindustrialization began wiping out jobs in segregated neighborhoods. Waves of foreclosures followed.[104]

In November 1964 Proposition 14 was passed by California voters, which undid the Rumford Fair Housing Act that had sought to restrict racial segregation in housing.[105] This was key in fanning the flames among residents, who perceived it as the latest in a long history of efforts to trap them in segregated neighborhoods. Indeed, the "housing question" was a major motivating factor among black workers' engaged in the events of 1965.[106] As Daniel HoSang puts it, "Persistent housing segregation—and the segregated schools, workplaces, and social settings it produced and naturalized—fueled the fires of Watts."[107]

DECEMBER 17, 1951 - PAUL ROBESON PRESENTS WE CHARGE GENOCIDE BY
WILLIAM PATTERSON, TO U.N. SECRETARIAT IN NEW YORK

Figure 3.
Paul Robeson and the Civil Rights Congress submitting *We Charge Genocide* petition to the United Nations Secretariat, New York, December 17, 1951, *Daily Worker/Daily World* Photographs Collection, Tamiment Library, New York University.

The Watts rebellion occurred just days after the passage of the historic Voting Rights Act, drawing national attention a visit by King to Los Angeles to meet with the participants in the dramatic events.[108] In the wake of this encounter, King and his colleagues worked to articulate alternatives to the slums. He concluded that the insurrection represented the emergence of a new moment in the struggle, and there was no turning back. He came to the ethical position that "something is wrong with capitalism. . . . there must be a better distribution of wealth, and maybe America must move toward a democratic socialism."[109] He intensified his organization for redistributing social wealth, arguing that the civil rights movement was engaged in the class struggle.[110] As he carried out this organizing, he was shunned by prominent Cold War liberals and ultimately assassinated in Memphis on April 4, 1968, writes Vincent Harding, "in the consciously chosen company of the poor."[111]

James Baldwin, a key figure in the "Blues literary tradition," was living in Hollywood and working on a film version of *The Autobiography of Malcolm X* when he learned about King's murder.[112] "An old world is dying," Baldwin wrote, "and a new one . . . announces that it is ready to be born."[113] In penning these words, Baldwin echoed Antonio Gramsci's theory of crisis and change. As Gramsci famously put it, "The crisis consists precisely in the fact that the old is dying and the new cannot be born; in this interregnum a great variety of morbid symptoms appear."[114] As Gramsci had grappled with the meaning of fascism's ascendancy with the Italy of the 1920s, Baldwin also took stock of the particularly morbid systems that appeared with Reagan's rise to the governor's mansion in California during the 1960s.[115] Baldwin remembers,

> that was a very ugly time—the time of the Black Panther harassment, the beginning (and the end) of the Soledad Brothers, the persecution and trial of Angela Davis. I saw all that, and much more, but what I really found unspeakable about the man was his contempt, his brutal contempt for the poor.[116]

In making this intervention in the conjuncture, Baldwin extended the radical critique of white supremacy, capitalism, and the national security state articulated by activists such as Du Bois, Patterson, Robeson, and King.[117] His words could not have articulated more vividly the importance of the politics of signification.[118] They underscore the pressing need for scholars of neoliberalism to analyze its historical and geographical roots in the racist counterrevolution against the Second Reconstruction."[119] They provide a blues archive for scholars to tap in examining the roots of the conjuncture.[120] Since Reagan's office became a war room for the development of revanchist solutions to crisis, the neoliberal effort to undo the access won to the social wage won by black freedom and labor struggles has occurred under the guise of restoring security.[121] These reactions to social crisis created the conditions of existence for the current material conditions.[122]

The Epicenter of the Crisis

> We are seeing a backlash because we dared to rise up, dared to struggle and dared to put this country on notice about the inequality.
> —Bilal Ali, *Freedom Now!*

> Instead of providing the solution to homelessness—which is housing—Los Angeles and other cities choose to use the police to harass, move, and incarcerate homeless people. . . . Black people by far are the most impacted by homelessness.
> —Deborah Burton, statement at the United Nations' Universal Periodic Review (Geneva, Switzerland), *Freedom Now!*

In the aftermath of Reagan's election as president, there was a pervasive and persistent assault on federal funding for affordable housing. Activists and policy analysts have shown that contemporary mass homelessness emerged as a result. At the same time, city officials passed laws criminalizing homelessness and poverty.[123] In turn, Skid Row in downtown Los Angeles has become an "open-air prison" for people deemed disposable.[124] As Laura Pulido's research demonstrates, the production of this securitized space has been shaped by the "geography of past racial regimes."[125]

Since the late 1970s and early 1980s the Los Angeles city council has promoted the "containment" of homelessness on Skid Row as a way to trap black and poor people in space.[126] Deindustrialized black workers from South LA were forced to migrate to Skid Row as part of their survival strategy to gain food, shelter, and other basic necessities—because there was a concentration of social services in this section of the city. According to the legal scholar Gary Blasi, Skid Row went from being 67 percent white and 21 percent black in the 1970s to majority black by the end of the 1980s.[127] During the 1990s California ranked forty-ninth out of fifty states in terms of providing public housing. Currently Skid Row has the highest concentration of homeless people in the city and the most concentrated poverty in the United States.[128] By analyzing the experiences and political struggles of the poor and disproportionately black low-income residents and homeless people in the first world capital of homelessness, we can gain clarity on the dynamics of racialization, gentrification, criminalization, and capital accumulation during the continuation of what Mike Davis describes as a "cold war on the streets of Downtown."[129]

Since the 1990s Skid Row has undergone gentrification. This development agenda has required the suppression of antigentrification and housing struggles. In an alliance with finance capital, the local state has provided police presence downtown to facilitate the production of new condos and lofts. State repression has been deployed to criminalize resistance to these developments. For example, real estate speculators and developers have transformed single-room occupancy hotels that were rented for about $500 a month into condos and lofts that rent for between $2,000 and $5,000 a month. As housing and land prices rose, state officials, local real estate developers, and journalists have appealed to moral panics about race, crime, and law and order to justify reclaiming this area of the city from its black and poor residents for the gentry moving into the new lofts and condos. In transforming the landscape by constructing art museums, coffee shops, restaurants, dog grooming services, and other amenities for gentrifiers and owners, the city made gentrification a centerpiece of its efforts to compete with other cities in attracting capital. Policing has been central to this urban strategy of capitalist development, and homeless residents and housing activists downtown are persistently subject to arrest as a result.[130]

This criminalization of homelessness, poverty, and dissent in Los Angeles has occurred alongside the rise of mass incarceration in California. These political, economic, ideological, and geographic processes should be understood in their totality. Like mass incarceration, the securitization of the city has attempted to solve social and economic crises.[131] In 2006 Los Angeles city officials launched a strategy of policing the poor they called the "Safer Cities Initiative." With the ideological and political support of the Manhattan Institute and the criminologist George Kelling of Rutgers (who was paid at least a half million dollars in consulting fees), the LAPD unleashed an unprecedented deployment of police power in the less than one square mile of the Central City area, which, as Gilmore and Christina Heatherton argue, has become a laboratory for applying new policing technologies as spatial solutions to social and economic crisis.[132] This political project has required ideological legitimation.

Developed by the Manhattan Institute and implemented at the local scale by Mayor Antonio Villagaroisa and Chief William Bratton, the Safer Cities Initiative represents an update on the revanchist policies that Bratton helped usher in with then New York City mayor Rudy Giuliani in the 1990s. Bratton assumed control of the LAPD in 2002. By 2003 he implemented "broken windows policing" in Skid Row. The broken windows metaphor is revealing, since broken windows are not repaired—they are replaced—much as black, brown, and poor people are literally removed from space.[133] Like the security policies that criminalized dissent during the early Cold War, this policing strategy has a revenge-driven logic.[134] It represents the homeless, poor residents, and housing rights activists as enemies of the local state. It has been part of an ideological and political campaign to legitimate Los Angeles' own version of *policing the crisis*.[135]

Consider, for example, a recent article that appeared in the Manhattan Institute's *City Journal* penned by current LAPD chief Charlie Beck along with Bratton and the coauthor of the so-called broken windows theory Kelling, arguing that the Safer Cities Initiative represents a significant effort "to reduce crime, lawlessness, and disorder." In turn, they assert that the problem they seek to solve has been "lawlessness" rather than "homelessness."[136] Yet such "lawlessness" can be read in an inverse and negative procedure as the dissent of homeless and housing activists challenging systematic human rights abuses in the "revanchist city," which combines vengeful security politics with the elite desire for "taking back" space from aggrieved communities.[137]

Revanchism provides the ideological underpinning for the security turn. Skid Row residents—the homeless, low-income renters, the evicted, the unemployed; in short, the surplus population—have endured increasing authoritarianism because of the revenge-driven policing and security policies downtown.[138] This intensified securitization has included the installation of security cameras to purportedly "curb Skid Row crime," making "the downtown area the most heavily monitored part of the city."[139] In promoting an image of LA as "safe" for gentrifiers, the local state has enacted a strategy of regulating public space. Read in this context, the efforts of the mayor's office to depict the police as protecting the homeless from criminals—when poor and homeless residents actually need protection from police—provides a vivid example of how ideologies of safety and security have hidden the human rights situation in Skid Row.[140]

Drawing on the moral and ethical legacy of the Second Reconstruction, the Los Angeles Community Action Network has organized among black, brown, and poor people downtown to contest securitization and press for their civil, housing, and human rights. For example, in 2009 United Nations Special Rapporteur on adequate housing Raquel Rolnik visited Los Angeles among other U.S. cities to assess the housing crisis, which was cohosted locally by LA CAN. She found that the "subprime mortgage crisis has widened an already large gap between the supply of and demand for affordable housing. The economic crisis which followed has led to increased unemployment and an even greater need for affordable housing."[141] She concluded that gentrification and the foreclosure crisis have been the leading causes of the spike in homelessness. Accordingly, renters and homeowners alike have been affected. Poor people who lost their housing are increasingly forced into homelessness.[142] This increase is also directly related to the promotion of austerity measures and the militarized policing of urban space.[143] Perhaps this is nowhere more evident than downtown LA.[144]

In 2010 Skid Row resident and organizer with LA CAN Deborah Burton traveled to Geneva, Switzerland, to deliver a statement to the United Nations' Universal Periodic Review about the human rights abuses represented by mass homelessness in Los Angeles. She explained that rather than provide housing, Los Angeles city officials "use the police to harass, move, and incarcerate homeless people." "My organization," Burton declares, "LA CAN, works in partnership with dozens of other organizations built and led by impacted residents. We are building power. We will make progress. We can win. But the task is huge and we will need the international communities to join us in pressuring the U.S. government." The words of black working-class women radicals like Burton underscore the importance of the ideological and political struggle for human rights and a social wage.[145] Focusing on the visions promoted by African American women activists—including their critique of state repression and their strategies for responding to the crisis through direct action protest and multiracial alliance building—helps us understand the stakes in their demand for human rights, which Rhonda Williams describes as "a key element of poor women's political movement ideology." Central to this social vision has been the human right to housing. Much like the black freedom struggle has worked to overcome geographic boundaries by "jumping scales" and making their appeals in terms of human rights, so too have public housing residents, low-income renters, single-room occupancy (SRO) tenants, and members of the disproportionately black homeless and marginally housed population claimed the human right to housing to circulate their struggles at different scales.[146]

The right to housing has been ensured by article 25 of the Universal Declaration of Human Rights penned in 1948, yet it is still not enforced.[147] Certainly, criticisms abound of the limits of the human rights framework for challenging the fundamental social relations of racial capitalism, militarism, and imperialism.[148] As the community organizer J. R. Fleming observes, there is a contradiction where the U.S. state will deploy its military to purportedly enforce the doctrine in countries such as Afghanistan and Iraq, while human rights violations persist in domestic spaces such as post-Katrina New Orleans and Skid Row Los Angeles. Under these circumstances he considers the work he is involved in as "human rights enforcement."[149] This intervention underscores the argument that the study of human rights violations should be extended to include gentrification, the destruction of public housing, mass homelessness, militarized policing, and mass incarceration.[150]

The struggle for the human right to housing provides a democratic program to challenge the political economy of the new racial capitalism. In promoting civil and human rights, LA CAN has exposed racism as a central contradiction in the state form. By organizing based on a platform of civil and human rights LA CAN has articulated a social vision that shows how antiracism is in the interest of the working class as a whole.[151] Implementing their "Blues development program" of the abolition of homelessness, the production of public housing, full employment, and an end to the Safer Cities Initiative would require a shift in the urban political economy away from militarism and toward a social budget that would entail radical social transformations.[152]

Through their political campaigns, direct action protests, and community meetings as well as their newspaper *Community Connection* and innovative

Figure 4.
Deborah Burton, Statement at the United Nations' Universal Periodic Review in Geneva, Switzerland, 2010. Photo by National Economic and Social Rights Initiative (www.nesri.org).

use of new media such as blogs, documentary filmmaking, and Facebook, LA CAN documents and challenges the pervasive and persistent violations of human rights experienced by homeless and poor residents. As part of a citywide alliance, the LA Human Right to Housing Collective, they organize themselves to contest the racialization of poverty and homelessness, the criminalization of dissent, and the securitization of Skid Row. By organizing directly with the primarily black and Latino poor at multiple scales—local, regional, national, and international—in a struggle for survival, they have generated antisystemic protest. This organizing demonstrates in practice that the demand for the human right to housing is more than simply reformism.[153] Rather, the efforts of LA CAN and their allies represent a new human rights movement. They are engaged in a struggle for economic justice in a context where neoliberal urbanism protects the interests of the elite.[154]

Housing and human rights organizations across the country and world—including LA CAN, Mayday New Orleans, the Chicago Anti-Eviction Campaign, Picture the Homeless in New York, and Abahlalibase Mjondolo in South Africa—have underscored the importance of the politics of scale in this global social movement against disappearance, displacement, and dispossession.[155] As Clyde Woods argues, their social visions are being used to "build a new society dedicated to replacing trap economics with sustainable communities built on the foundations of social and economic justice."[156] This social movement compels us to reckon with the unfinished business of the Second Reconstruction.[157] The collective memory of these struggles can inform efforts to fire the political imagination and jump scales in the struggle against the securitization of the city. Learning from Los Angeles suggests that the same material conditions that made the region the epicenter of the crisis also make it an epicenter for grassroots challenges to authoritarian populism.[158]

To confront the current crisis we need to listen to artists like Chuck D and grassroots community organizations such as the Los Angeles Community Action Network demanding human rights. The Operation Skid Row music festival provides a particularly compelling example of how artists, activists, and intellectuals articulate alternative solutions to social problems. These blues geographers speak eloquently to the inequalities people endure because of racism, poverty, and homelessness. They suggest another city is not only possible but a burning necessity.[159]

Notes

Many thanks to Paula Chakravartty and Denise Ferreira da Silva for their critiques of and suggestions for this article, to the anonymous *American Quarterly* reviewers for their insightful recommended revisions; to Paula Dragosh for her careful edits; to Gary Blasi, Craig Gilmore, Sarah Haley, Robin D. G. Kelley, George Lipsitz, Ani Mukherji, John Munro, and David Roediger for helping me sharpen the argument; and to Bilal Ali, Eric Ares, Deborah Burton, Becky Dennison, Steve Diaz, General Dogon, Gerardo Gomez, Karl Scott, Joe Thomas, Pete White, and the other members of LA CAN for our discussions about the human right to housing, which have helped me tremendously. Special thanks to Christina Heatherton for our constant conversations about the housing question.

1. Quoted in Steve Diaz, "Operation Freedom and Freedom Now!" *Community Connection*, January–February 2012, http://cangress.wordpress.com/tag/community-connection/.

2. Ernest Hardy, "Public Enemy Puts Spotlight on Skid Row," *Los Angeles Times*, January 17, 2012, http://latimesblogs.latimes.com/music_blog/2012/01/public-enemy-puts-spotlight-on-skid-row-.html.

3. Gary Blasi and the UCLA School of Law Fact Investigation Clinic, *Policing Our Way Out of Homelessness? The First Year of the Safer Cities Initiative on Skid Row* (Los Angeles: UCLA and USC Center for Sustainable Cities, September 24, 2007), http://college.usc.edu/geography/ESPE/publications/policing_homelessness.html; Christina Heatherton, ed., *Downtown Blues: A Skid Row Reader* (Los Angeles: Los Angeles Community Action Network, 2011); Jordan T. Camp and Christina Heatherton, *Freedom Now! The Struggle for the Human Right to Housing in LA and Beyond* (Los Angeles: Freedom Now Books, 2012).

4. Nicholas Dahmann with the Los Angeles Community Action Network, "Los Angeles: I Do Mind Dying, Recent Reflections on Urban Revolution in Skid Row," *Los Angeles Public Interest Law Journal* 2 (2009–10): 210–19.
5. Mike Davis, *A Planet of Slums* (New York: Verso, 2006), 36.
6. Neil Smith, "New Globalism, New Urbanism: Gentrification as Global Urban Strategy," *Antipode* 34.3 (2002): 427–50; Craig Willse, "Neo-liberal Biopolitics and the Invention of Chronic Homelessness," *Economy and Society* 39.2 (2010): 155–56; Ellen Reese, Geoffrey Deverteuil, and Leanne Thach, "'Weak-Center' Gentrification and the Contradictions of Containment: Deconcentrating Poverty in Downtown Los Angeles," *International Journal of Urban and Regional Research* 34.2 (2010): 310–27.
7. Clyde A. Woods, "'Sitting on Top of the World': The Challenges of Blues and Hip Hop Geography," in *Black Geographies and the Politics of Place*, ed. Katherine McKittrick and Clyde Woods (Cambridge, Mass.: South End, 2007), 49.
8. Clyde A. Woods, "Traps, Skid Row, and Katrina," in Heatherton, *Downtown Blues*, 51.
9. Clyde A. Woods, "The Challenges of Blues and Hip Hop Historiography," *Kalfou* 1.1 (2010): 33–34.
10. Stuart Hall, *The Hard Road to Renewal: Thatcherism and the Crisis of the Left* (New York: Verso, 1988), 96.
11. Robin D. G. Kelley, *Race Rebels: Culture, Politics, and the Black Working Class* (New York: New Press, 1994), 207.
12. Clyde A. Woods, "Do You Know What It Means to Miss New Orleans? Katrina, Trap Economics, and the Rebirth of the Blues," *American Quarterly* 57.4 (2005): 1005. On the struggle in language and expressive culture to define material conditions, see Hazel V. Carby, *Cultures in Babylon: Black Britain and African America* (New York: Verso, 1999); Daniel Widener, *Black Arts West: Culture and Struggle in Postwar Los Angeles* (Durham, N.C.: Duke University Press, 2010).
13. George Lipsitz, "The Struggle for Hegemony," *Journal of American History* 75.1 (1988): 146–50.
14. George Lipsitz, *Footsteps in the Dark: The Hidden Histories of Popular Music* (Minneapolis: University of Minnesota Press, 2007), 108.
15. Neil Smith, "Contours of a Spatialized Politics: Homeless Vehicles and the Production of Geographical Scale," *Social Text*, no. 33 (1992): 54–81; Neil Smith and Deborah Cowen, "'Martial Law in the Streets of Toronto': G20 Security and State Violence," *Human Geography* 3.3 (2010): 37–39.
16. Davis, *Planet of Slums*, 36.
17. Clyde A. Woods, "Les Misérables of New Orleans: Trap Economics and the Asset Stripping Blues, Part 1," *American Quarterly* 61.3 (2009): 769–96.
18. Heatherton, *Downtown Blues*.
19. David Harvey, *The New Imperialism* (New York: Oxford University Press, 2003), 137–82. For a trenchant critique of the ideology of "underclass" as a justification for capitalist restructuring and the militarization of space, see Robin D. G. Kelley, *Yo' Mama's DisFunktional! Fighting the Culture Wars in Urban America* (Boston: Beacon, 1997).
20. Stuart Hall, "Gramsci's Relevance for the Study of Race and Ethnicity," *Journal of Communications Inquiry* 10.5 (1986): 24; Laura Pulido, *Black, Brown, Yellow, and Left: Radical Activism in Los Angeles* (Berkeley: University of California Press, 2006).
21. Stuart Hall, "Decoding," in *Culture, Media, Language*, ed. Stuart Hall, Dorothy Hobson, Andrew Lowe, and Paul Willis (1980; New York: Routledge, 1996), 138; Henri Lefebvre, *The Production of Space* (Malden, Mass.: Blackwell, 1991).
22. Edward W. Soja, *Seeking Spatial Justice* (Minneapolis: University of Minnesota Press, 2010); Gaye Theresa Johnson, "Spatial Entitlement: Race, Displacement, and Reclamation in Post-war Los Angeles," in *Black and Brown Los Angeles: A Contemporary Reader*, ed. Josh Kun and Laura Pulido (Los Angeles: University of California Press, forthcoming).
23. Daniel Martinez HoSang, *Racial Propositions: Ballot Initiatives and the Making of Postwar California* (Berkeley: University of California Press, 2010).
24. Robert D. Bullard and Charles Lee, "Introduction: Racism and American Apartheid," in *Residential Apartheid: The American Legacy*, ed. Robert D. Bullard, J. Eugene Grigsby III, and Charles Lee (Los Angeles: Center for Afro-American Studies Publications, 1994), 7.
25. Stuart Hall and Doreen Massey, "Interpreting the Crisis," *Soundings: A Journal of Politics and Culture* 44 (Spring 2010): 57–71.
26. Stuart Hall, "The Neoliberal Revolution," *Soundings: A Journal of Politics and Culture* 48 (Summer 2011): 10.

27. Hall and Massey, "Interpreting the Crisis," 58; Cindi Katz, "Vagabond Capitalism and the Necessity of Social Reproduction," *Antipode* 33.4 (2001): 724; Vijay Prashad, "Second-Hand Dreams," *Social Analysis* 49.2 (2005): 191–98; Doreen Massey, "The Political Struggle Ahead," *Soundings: A Journal of Politics and Culture* 44 (Spring 2010): 6–18.

28. My use of the term *long late twentieth century* draws on Giovanni Arrighi, *The Long Twentieth Century: Money, Power, and the Origins of Our Times* (New York: Verso, 2010), yet has the more limited goal of referring to the current conjuncture. It therefore parallels the efforts to specify the race and class dynamics of the "long early twentieth century," or the period between 1890 and 1945 elaborated in David R. Roediger, *Working toward Whiteness: How America's Immigrants Became White* (Cambridge, Mass.: Basic Books, 2005), 3–34.

29. Hall, *Hard Road to Renewal*, 130.

30. Jordan T. Camp, "'We Know This Place': Neoliberal Racial Regimes and the Katrina Circumstance," *American Quarterly* 61.3 (2009): 693–717. My analytic debt to Cedric Robinson for this conceptualization should be obvious. See Cedric J. Robinson, *Forgeries of Memory and Meaning: Blacks and the Regimes of Race in American Theatre and Film before World War II* (Chapel Hill: University of North Carolina Press, 2007), xii. It also owes a great deal to Stuart Hall et al., *Policing the Crisis: Mugging, the State, and Law and Order* (London: Macmillan, 1978); Mike Davis, *City of Quartz: Excavating the Future in Los Angeles* (1990; New York: Verso, 2006); Kelley, *Race Rebels*; Nikhil Pal Singh, *Black Is a Country: Race and the Unfinished Struggle for Democracy* (Cambridge, Mass.: Harvard University Press, 2004); Ruth Wilson Gilmore, *Golden Gulag: Prisons, Surplus, Crisis, and Opposition in Globalizing California* (Berkeley: University of California Press, 2007); David Harvey, *A Brief History of Neoliberalism* (New York: Oxford University Press, 2005); and David Theo Goldberg, *The Threat of Race: Reflections on Racial Neoliberalism* (Malden, Mass.: Blackwell, 2009).

31. Hall, *Hard Road to Renewal*, 123–60; Neil Smith, *Uneven Development: Nature, Capital, and the Production of Space* (Athens: University of Georgia Press, 2008); and Smith, *The New Urban Frontier: Gentrification and the Revanchist City* (New York: Routledge, 1996), 75–89; Harvey, *Brief History of Neoliberalism*, 87–119; Ruth Wilson Gilmore, "Globalisation and U.S. Prison Growth: From Military Keynesianism to Post-Keynesianism Militarism," *Race & Class* 40.2–3 (October 1998–March 1999): 171–88.

32. Cindi Katz, "Childhood as Spectacle: Relays of Anxiety and the Reconfiguration of the Child," *Cultural Geographies* (2008): 15–17.

33. Hall and Massey, "Interpreting the Crisis," 58.

34. Nikhil Pal Singh, "The Afterlife of Fascism," *South Atlantic Quarterly* 105.1 (2006): 71–93; Avery F. Gordon, "The U.S. Military Prison: The Normalcy of Exceptional Brutality," in *The Violence of Incarceration*, ed. Phil Scraton and Jude McCulloch (New York: Routledge, 2009), 174; Stephen Graham, *Cities under Siege: The New Military Urbanism* (New York: Verso, 2010), 94; Deborah Cowen and Amy Siciliano, "Schooled In/Security: Surplus Subjects, Racialized Masculinity, and Citizenship," in *Accumulating Insecurity: Violence and Dispossession in the Making of Everyday Life*, ed. Shelley Feldman, Charles Geisler, and Gayatri A. Menon (Athens: University of Georgia Press, 2011), 104–21.

35. HoSang, *Racial Propositions*, 20–23.

36. See Widener, *Black Arts West*; Gaye Theresa Johnson, "A Sifting of Centuries: Afro-Chicano Interaction and Popular Musical Culture in California, 1960–2000," in *Decolonial Voices: Chicana and Chicano Cultural Studies in the 21st Century*, ed. Arturo J. Aldama and Naomi H. Quiñonez (Bloomington: Indiana University Press, 2002), 320–23.

37. On racial capitalism, see Cedric J. Robinson, *Black Marxism: The Making of the Black Radical Tradition* (1983; Chapel Hill: University of North Carolina Press, 2000).

38. For a convincing argument that, rather than witnessing neoliberalism's end, we need "neoliberalization" as a category of analysis, see Neil Brenner, Jamie Peck, and Nik Theodore, "After Neoliberalization?" *Globalizations* 7.3 (2010): 327–45.

39. George Lipsitz, "Learning from Los Angeles: Another One Rides the Bus," *American Quarterly* 56.3 (2004): 511–29.

40. Paula Chakravartty and John D. H. Downing, "Media, Technology, and the Global Financial Crisis," *International Journal of Communication* 4 (2010): 693–95. On the ways in which in highly capitalized mass-cultural outlets provide consumers with mediated access to working-class people's lives they have no contact with and memories of places they have no connection to, see George Lipsitz, *Time Passages: Collective Memory and American Popular Culture* (1990; Minneapolis: University of Minnesota Press, 2006), 5.

41. Gary A. Dymski, "Racial Exclusion and the Political Economy of the Subprime Crisis," *Historical Materialism* 17 (2009): 149–79.

42. David Harvey, *The Enigma of Capital and the Crises of Capitalism* (New York: Oxford, 2010), 1.

43. Amaad Rivera, Jeannette Huezo, Christina Kasica, and Dedrick Muhammad, *The Silent Depression: State of the Dream 2009* (Boston: United for a Fair Economy, 2009).

44. David McNally, *Global Slump: The Economics and Politics of Crisis and Resistance* (Oakland, Calif.: PM Press, 2010), 125–26.

45. Amaad Rivera, Brenda Cotto-Escalera, Anisha Desair, and Jeannette Huezo, *Foreclosed: State of the Dream 2008* (Boston: United for a Fair Economy, 2008), v. See also Rakesh Kochhar, Richard Fry, and Paul Taylor, "Wealth Gaps Rise to Record Highs between Whites, Blacks, Hispanics," Pew Research Center, July 26, 2011, http://pewsocialtrends.org/.

46. David Harvey, "The Enigma of Capital and the Crisis This Time" (paper presented at the American Sociological Association Meetings, Atlanta, Georgia, August 16, 2010), http://davidharvey.org/2010/08/the-enigma-of-capital-and-the-crisis-this-time/; Ashok Bardhan and Richard Walker, "California, Pivot of the Great Recession," *Working Paper Series No. 203-210* (Berkeley: Institute for Research on Labor and Employment, University of California, March 2010).

47. Richard Walker, "Golden State Adrift," *New Left Review*, no. 66 (2010): 6–9.

48. David R. Roediger, *How Race Survived U.S. History: From Settlement and Slavery to the Obama Phenomena* (New York: Verso, 2008), 229.

49. National Coalition for the Homeless, *Foreclosure to Homelessness: The Forgotten Victims of the Subprime Crisis (June 2009)*, www.nationalhomeless.org/factsheets/foreclosure.html#fn.

50. George Lipsitz, *How Racism Takes Place* (Philadelphia: Temple University Press, 2011), 20.

51. Mike Davis, *Ecology of Fear: Los Angeles and the Imagination of Disaster* (New York: Metropolitan Books, 1998), 362; Jacob S. Rugh and Douglas S. Massey, "Racial Segregation and the American Foreclosure Crisis," *American Sociological Review* 75.5 (2010): 629.

52. Jordan T. Camp, "Housing Is a Human Right: California's Forty-Years Struggle, an Interview with Daniel Martinez HoSang," in Camp and Heatherton, *Freedom Now*, 94; Pulido, "White Privilege and Urban Development," 561; Graham, *Cities under Siege*.

53. Rugh and Massey, "Racial Segregation and the American Foreclosure Crisis," 634; Lipsitz, *How Racism Takes Place*, 9.

54. Howard Husock, "Housing Goals We Can't Afford," *New York Times*, December 10, 2008, www.nytimes.com.

55. James D. Sidaway, "Subprime Crisis: American Crisis or Human Crisis?" *Environment and Planning D: Society and Space* 26 (2008): 195–98.

56. Smith, *New Urban Frontier*, 211; Jamie Peck, "Liberating the City: Between New York and New Orleans," *Urban Geography* 27.8 (2006): 68.

57. Neil Smith, "Urban Politics, Urban Security" (paper presented at Harvard Graduate School, Cambridge, Mass., September 29, 2010), www.youtube.com/watch?v=xgYvyipO23I; Don Mitchell, *The Right to the City: Social Justice and the Fight for Public Space* (New York: Guilford, 2003), 15–16.

58. Roediger, *How Race Survived U.S. History*, 229.

59. Denise Ferreira da Silva, "No-Bodies: Law, Raciality, and Violence," *Griffith Law Review* 18.2 (2009): 224–27. See also Goldberg, *Threat of Race*, 80–91; Jordan T. Camp and Christina Heatherton, "The Housing Question: An Interview with Mike Davis," in Camp and Heatherton, *Freedom Now*, 85.

60. Hall et al., *Policing the Crisis*. For an analysis of this process in an earlier conjuncture, see Eric Lott, *Love and Theft: Blackface Minstrelsy and the American Working Class* (New York: Oxford University Press, 1993), 137.

61. Jimmie L. Reeves and Richard Campbell, *Cracked Coverage: Television News, the Anti-Cocaine Crusade, and the Reagan Legacy* (Durham, N.C.: Duke University Press, 1994), 86–103.

62. Da Silva, "No-Bodies," 226.

63. James Donald and Stuart Hall, eds., *Politics and Ideology* (Philadelphia: Open University Press, 1986).

64. Hall et al., *Policing the Crisis*, 217; Ruth Wilson Gilmore and Craig Gilmore, "Restating the Obvious," in *Indefensible Space: The Architecture of the National Security State*, ed. Michael Sorkin (New York: Routledge, 2007), 144.

65. Karl Marx, *Capital: A Critique of Political Economy*, trans. Ben Fowkes (New York: Penguin Books, 1976), 640–48; Peter Linebaugh, "Karl Marx, the Theft of the Wood, and Working-Class Composition:

A Contribution to the Current Debate," *Crime and Social Justice* 6 (Fall–Winter 1976): 5; Gilmore, *Golden Gulag*, 77.

66. Mitchell, *Right to the City*, 128–29.
67. Paul Gilroy, *'There Ain't No Black in the Union Jack': The Cultural Politics of Race and Nation* (Chicago: University of Chicago Press, 1991).
68. Smith, "New Globalism, New Urbanism," 433; Gilmore, *Golden Gulag*, 64.
69. Ruth Wilson Gilmore in conversation with Trevor Paglen, "From Military Industrial Complex to Prison Industrial Complex," *Recording Carceral Landscapes*, http://paglen.com/carceral (accessed January 10, 2012).
70. Gilmore, *Golden Gulag*, 79.
71. On "authoritarian populism," see Hall, *Hard Road to Renewal*, 123–60; Reeves and Campbell, *Cracked Coverage*, 73. On the cultural politics of neoliberalism, see Lisa Duggan, *The Twilight of Equality? Neoliberalism, Cultural Politics, and the Attack on Democracy* (Boston: Beacon, 2003).
72. Mike Davis, *Prisoners of the American Dream* (New York: Verso, 1986); Lisa McGirr, *Suburban Warriors: The Origins of the New American Right* (Princeton, N.J.: Princeton University Press, 2001).
73. Hall, *Hard Road to Renewal*.
74. Hall and Massey, "Interpreting the Crisis," 66; Gilmore, *Golden Gulag*.
75. Hall, *Hard Road to Renewal*, 188; HoSang, *Racial Propositions*, 264; Willse, "Invention of Chronic Homelessness," 164.
76. For a generative analysis of the relationship between whiteness and uneven development in the region, see Laura Pulido, "Rethinking Environmental Racism: White Privilege and Urban Development in Southern California," *Annals of the Association of American Geographers* 90.1 (2000): 12–40. On urban security landscapes, see Jeremy Németh, "Security in Public Space: An Empirical Assessment of Three U.S. Cities," *Environment and Planning A* 42 (2010): 2487–507.
77. Cedric J. Robinson, "Race, Capitalism, and Antidemocracy," in *Reading Rodney King: Reading Urban Uprising*, ed. Robert Gooding-Williams (New York: Routledge, 1993), 77.
78. David Wagner and Pete White, "Why the Silence? Homelessness and Race," in Camp and Heatherton, *Freedom Now*, 43–44; Robinson, *Forgeries of Memory and Meaning*, 276.
79. Jodi Melamed, *Represent and Destroy: Rationalizing Violence in the New Racial Capitalism* (Minneapolis: University of Minnesota Press, 2011), 38.
80. Paul Gilroy, "True Humanism? Civilizationism, Securitocracy, and Racial Resignation," *Johannesburg Workshop in Theory and Criticism Salon* 1 (2009), www.jwtc.org.za/the_salon/volume_1.html; and Gilroy, *Darker Than Blue: On the Moral Economies of Black Atlantic Culture* (Cambridge, Mass.: Harvard University Press, 2010), 73, 92, 156.
81. Graham, *Cities under Siege*, 94.
82. Giorgio Agamben, *State of Exception* (Chicago: University of Chicago Press, 2005).
83. Gilmore and Gilmore, "Restating the Obvious," 143; Vijay Prashad, "The New Populism," *Frontline*, November 6–19, 2010, www.frontlineonnet.com/fl2723/stories/20101119272301900.html.
84. Gordon, "U.S. Military Prison," 174; Ashley Dawson and Malini Johar Schueller, eds., *Exceptional State: Contemporary U.S. Culture and the New Imperialism* (Durham, N.C.: Duke University Press, 2007), 16.
85. Gilmore, *Golden Gulag*, 28; Roediger, *How Race Survived U.S. History*, x–xvi, 169–230.
86. Gerald Horne, *Fire This Time* (New York: Da Capo, 1997), 41.
87. Nikhil Pal Singh, "'Learn Your Horn': Jack O'Dell and the Long Civil Rights Movement," introduction to *Climbin' Jacob's Ladder: The Black Freedom Movement Writings of Jack O'Dell*, ed. Nikhil Pal Singh (Berkeley: University of California Press, 2010), 57.
88. Gerald Horne, *A Communist Front? The Civil Rights Congress, 1946–1956* (Rutherford, N.J.: Fairleigh Dickinson University Press, 1988), 333.
89. Martha Biondi, *To Stand and Fight: The Struggle for Civil Rights in Postwar New York City* (Cambridge, Mass.: Harvard University Press, 2003), 175; Shana L. Redmond, *Anthem: Movement Cultures and the Sound of Solidarity in the African Diaspora* (New York: New York University Press, forthcoming).
90. Josh Sides, "'You Understand My Condition': The Civil Rights Congress in the Los Angeles African-American Community, 1946–1952," *Pacific Historical Review* 67.2 (1998): 233–57.
91. Horne, *Fire This Time*, 7–9, 213–14.
92. Christina Heatherton, "Relief and Revolution: Southern California Struggles against Unemployment, 1930–1933," *Rising Tides of Color*, ed. Moon-Ho Jung (Seattle: University of Washington Press, forthcoming).

93. Robin D. G. Kelley, *Hammer and Hoe: Alabama Communists During the Great Depression* (Chapel Hill, N.C.: The University of North Carolina Press, 1990); Michael Denning, *The Cultural Front: The Laboring of American Culture in the Twentieth Century* (New York: Verso, 1996); Penny M. Von Eschen, *Race against Empire: Black Americans and Anticolonialism, 1933–1957* (New York: Cornell University Press, 1997); Singh, *Black Is a Country*; John Munro, "The Anticolonial Front: Cold War Imperialism and the Struggle against Global White Supremacy, 1945–1960" (Ph.D. diss., University of California, Santa Barbara, 2009); Dayo F. Gore, *Radicalism at the Crossroads: African American Women Activists in the Cold War* (New York: New York University Press, 2011); Eric McDuffie, *Sojourning for Freedom: Black Women, American Communism, and the Making of Black Left Feminism* (Durham: Duke University Press, 2011).

94. Horne, *Fire This Time*, 8–9; and Horne, "Civil Rights Congress," in *Encyclopedia of the American Left*, 2nd ed., ed. Mari Jo Buhle, Paul Buhle, and Dan Georgakas (New York: Oxford University Press, 1988), 135.

95. Civil Rights Congress, *We Charge Genocide: The Historic Petition to the United Nations for Relief from a Crime of the United States Government against the Negro People* (1951; New York: International Publishers, 1971); "U.S. Accused in U.N. of Negro Genocide," *New York Times*, December 18, 1951; Biondi, *To Stand and Fight*, 156, 200.

96. William L. Patterson, "'We Charge Genocide!'" *Political Affairs* 30.12 (1951): 43–44; and Patterson, *The Man Who Cried Genocide: An Autobiography* (New York: International Publishers, 1971), 169–208.

97. W. E. B. DuBois, *The Autobiography of W.E.B. Du Bois: A Soliloquy on Viewing My Life from the Last Decade of Its First Century* (New York: International Publishers, 1968), 361–95; Biondi, *To Stand and Fight*, 153; Von Eschen, *Race against Empire*, 187; Angela Y. Davis, *Abolition Democracy: Beyond Empire, Prisons, and Torture* (New York: Seven Stories, 2005), 43–45, 89.

98. Horne, *Fire This Time*, 367n4.

99. Widener, *Black Arts West*, 54.

100. Don Parson, *Making a Better World: Public Housing, the Red Scare, and the Direction of Modern Los Angeles* (Minneapolis: University of Minnesota Press, 2005).

101. Singh, "'Learn Your Horn,'" 21.

102. Horne, *Fire This Time*, 7–8; HoSang, *Racial Propositions*, 81.

103. Ranajit Guha, "The Prose of Counter-Insurgency," in *Selected Subaltern Studies*, ed. Ranajit Guha and Gayatri Chakravorty Spivak (New York: Oxford University Press, 1988), 45–86. See Parson, *Making a Better World*, 198; HoSang, *Racial Propositions*, 68.

104. Horne, *Fire This Time*, 47, 222–23, 249–50.

105. HoSang, *Racial Propositions*, 53.

106. Friedrich Engels, *The Housing Question* (1954; Moscow: Progress Publishers, 1979); Horne, *Fire This Time*, 219.

107. HoSang, *Racial Propositions*, 87.

108. Horne, *Fire This Time*, 219.

109. Quoted in Vincent Harding, introduction to Martin Luther King Jr., *Where Do We Go From Here: Chaos or Community?* (1968; Boston: Beacon, 2010), xi.

110. Quoted in David J. Garrow, *The FBI and Martin Luther King, Jr.: From Solo to Memphis* (New York: Norton, 1981), 214.

111. Harding, introduction, xxi; Von Eschen, *Race against Empire*, 188.

112. On the "blues literary tradition," see Clyde A. Woods, *Development Arrested: The Blues and Plantation Power in the Mississippi Delta* (New York: Verso, 1998), 175.

113. James Baldwin, *No Name in the Street* (New York: Random House, 1972), 196.

114. Antonio Gramsci, *Selections from the Prison Notebooks* (New York: International Publishers, 1971), 276.

115. Davis, *Prisoners of the American Dream*, 160.

116. James Baldwin, *The Price of the Ticket: Collected Nonfiction, 1948–1985* (New York: St. Martin's, 1985), 672.

117. Singh, *Black Is a Country*, 6, 8, 13, 214.

118. Hall, "Decoding," 138.

119. Manning Marable, *Race, Reform, and Rebellion: The Second Reconstruction and Beyond in Black America, 1945–2006* (1984; Jackson: University Press of Mississippi, 2007).

120. Woods, "'Sittin' on Top of the World,'" in McKittrick and Woods, *Black Geographies and the Politics of Place*, 47–48.
121. Richard Walker, "California Rages against the Dying of the Light," *New Left Review*, no. 209 (1995): 43, www.newleftreview.org/I/209/richard-walker-california-rages-against-the-dying-of-the-light.
122. Hall and Massey, "Interpreting the Crisis," 59; Walker, "California Rages against the Dying of the Light," 43.
123. Michael Anderson, Paul Boden, Michael Callahan-Kapoor, boonacheema, Nicholas Dahmann, Becky Dennison, Jennifer Friedenback, Marlene Griffith, Ruth Pleaner, Jeremy Rosen, Briana Winterborn, eds., *Without Housing: Decades of Federal Housing Cutbacks, Massive Homelessness, and Policy Failures* (San Francisco: Western Regional Advocacy Project, 2010).
124. Camp and Heatherton, "Housing Question," 83
125. Pulido, "White Privilege and Urban Development," 561.
126. Gilda Haas and Allan David Heskin, *Community Struggles in Los Angeles* (Los Angeles: School of Architecture and Urban Planning, UCLA, 1981), 13–19; Davis, *City of Quartz*, 232.
127. Christina Heatherton and Yusef Omowale, "Skid Row in Transition: An Interview with Gary Blasi," in Heatherton, *Downtown Blues*, 36.
128. The Labor/Community Strategy Center, *Reconstructing Los Angeles from the Bottom Up* (Los Angeles: Labor/Community Strategy Center, 1993), 31–32; Blasi, *Policing Our Way Out of Homelessness*, 1–9.
129. Davis, *City of Quartz*, 234; Walker, "Golden State Adrift," 5.
130. Wagner and White, "Why the Silence?" in Camp and Heatherton, *Freedom Now*, 45; Smith, "New Globalism, New Urbanism," 442; David Harvey, "The Right to the City," *New Left Review*, no. 53 (2008): 34–35; Daniel Martinez HoSang, "The Economics of the New Brutality," *Colorlines*, December 10, 1999, http://colorlines.com/archives/1999/12/the_economics_of_the_new_brutality.html; Reese, Deverteuil, and Thach, "'Weak-Center' Gentrification," 311; Heatherton and Omowale, "Skid Row in Transition," 38–40.
131. Smith, "New Globalism, New Urbanism," 433; Gilmore, *Golden Gulag*, 130.
132. Ruth Wilson Gilmore and Christina Heatherton, "Fixing Broken Windows without Batons," in Camp and Heatherton, *Freedom Now*, 1. See Gari Blasi and Forrest Stuart, "Has the Safer Cities Initiative in Skid Row Reduced Serious Crime?" (Los Angeles: UCLA Law School, September 15, 2008), *cdn. law.ucla.edu/.../did_safer_cities_reduce_crime_in_skid_row.pdf.*
133. Fred Moten, "The Meaning of 'Broken Windows,'" (talk presented at Eso Won Books, Los Angeles, June 23, 2005); Neil Smith, "Giuliani Time: The Revanchist 1990s," *Social Text*, no. 57 (Winter 1998): 1–20.
134. See Manhattan Institute, "Safe Cities Initiative," www.manhattan-institute.org/html/safe_cities.html.
135. Hall et al., *Policing the Crisis*; Blasi, "Policing Our Way Out of Homelessness," 23; Alex S. Vitale, "The Safer Cities Imitative and the Removal of the Homeless: Reducing Crime or Promoting Gentrification on Los Angeles' Skid Row?" *American Society of Criminology* 9.4 (2010): 867–73.
136. Charlie Beck, William J. Bratton, and George L. Kelling, "Who Will Police the Criminologists? The Dangers of Politicized Social Science," *City Journal* 21.2 (Spring 2011), www.city-journal.org/. On the failures of the "broken windows" metaphor on theoretical and empirical grounds, see Bernard E. Harcourt, *Illusion of Order: The False Promise of Broken Windows Policing* (Cambridge, Mass.: Harvard University Press, 2001); Mitchell, *Right to the City*, 195–222.
137. Guha, "Prose of Counter-Insurgency," 1; Smith, *New Urban Frontier*, 220, 222.
138. Smith, "Giuliani Time," 10.
139. Richard Winton, "LAPD Adds 10 Cameras to Curb Skid Row Crime," *Los Angeles Times*, September 15, 2006, http://articles.latimes.com/2006/sep/15/local/me-cameras15.
140. George Lipsitz, "Learning from Los Angeles: Producing Anarchy in the Name of Order," in Camp and Heatherton, *Freedom Now*, 33–40; HoSang, "Economics of the New Brutality."
141. Raquel Rolnik, *Report of the Special Rapporteur on Adequate Housing as a Component of the Right to an Adequate Standard of Living, and on the Right to Non-discrimination in This Context* (Geneva: Human Rights Council, February 12, 2010), 8.
142. Don Mitchell, "Homelessness, American Style," in Heatherton, *Downtown Blues*, 42.
143. Mazher Ali, Jeannette Huezo, Brian Miller, Wanjiku Mwangi, and Mike Prokosch, *State of the Dream 2011: Austerity for Whom?* (Boston: United for a Fair Economy, 2011).
144. Anderson et al., *Without Housing*, 6, 42.

145. Gore, *Radicalism at the Crossroads*; Katz, "Vagabond Capitalism," 709–28. Deborah Burton, "Statement at the United Nations' Universal Periodic Review, Geneva, Switzerland, 2010."

146. Rhonda Y. Williams, "'We Refuse': Privatization, Housing, and Human Rights," in Camp and Heatherton, *Freedom Now*, 15; Jacqueline Leavitt, "Women under Fire: Public Housing Activism in Los Angeles," *Frontiers* 13.2 (1993): 109–30. On "jumping scales," see Smith, "Contours of a Spatialized Politics," 54–81; Bobby Wilson, "Scale Politics of the Civil Rights Movement" (paper presented at Association of American Geographers, New York, February 2012). On the human rights abuses represented by the disproportionate numbers of black homeless people and their experiences with policing on Skid Row, see Doudou Diène, *Report Submitted by the Special Rapporteur on Contemporary Forms of Racism, Racial Discrimination, Xenophobia, and Related Intolerance* (Geneva, Human Rights Council, April 2009), 20.

147. "Universal Declaration of Human Rights" (Geneva: United Nations Department of Public Information, 1948).

148. See, for example, Randall Williams, *The Divided World: Human Rights and Its Violence* (Minneapolis: University of Minnesota Press, 2010).

149. Jordan T. Camp and Christina Heatherton, "Human Rights Enforcers: An Interview with Willie J.R. Fleming," in Camp and Heatherton, *Freedom Now*, 106.

150. Clyde A. Woods, "Life after Death," *Professional Geographer* 54.1 (2002): 64.

151. Davis, *Prisoners of the American Dream*, 310; Kelley, *Yo' Mama's DisFunktional*, 155.

152. Clyde A. Woods, "Development Drowned and Reborn: The Blues and Bourbon Restorations in Post-Katrina New Orleans," ed. Laura Pulido and Jordan T. Camp (in progress); Davis, *Prisoners of the American Dream*, 311.

153. See, for example, *Community Connection*, September–October 2011, cangress.wordpress.com. See Davis, *Prisoners of the American Dream*, 309; Mitchell, *Right to the City*, 21.

154. Robin D. G. Kelley, "Ground Zero," in Heatherton, *Downtown Blues*, 13, 15.

155. Camp and Heatherton, *Freedom Now!*

156. Woods, "Traps, Skid Row, and Katrina," in Heatherton, *Downtown Blues*, 55.

157. O'Dell, *Climbin' Jacob's Ladder*, 113–16, 263–293.

158. Lipsitz, "Learning from Los Angeles: Another One Rides the Bus," 511–29; Robin D. G. Kelley, *Freedom Dreams: The Black Radical Imagination* (Boston: Beacon, 2002).

159. Daniel Widener, "Another City Is Possible: Interethnic Organizing in Contemporary Los Angeles," *Race/Ethnicity: Multidisciplinary Global Perspectives* 1.2 (2008): 189–219.

Contributors

Radhika Balakrishnan

Radhika Balakrishnan is executive director of the Center for Women's Global Leadership, professor of women's and gender studies at Rutgers University, and has a PhD in economics from Rutgers University. Previously, she was professor of economics and international studies at Marymount Manhattan College. She has worked at the Ford Foundation as a program officer in the Asia Regional Program. She is currently on the board for the Center for Constitutional Rights and the International Association for Feminist Economics. She is coeditor with Diane Elson of *Economic Policy and Human Rights: Holding Governments to Account* (Zed Books, 2011).

Jordan T. Camp

Jordan T. Camp is a visiting scholar in the Institute of American Cultures and the Bunche Center for African American Studies at UCLA. His work appears in *American Quarterly*, *Kalfou*, *Race & Class*, and *In the Wake of Hurricane Katrina*, and he coedited (with Christina Heatherton) *Freedom Now! Struggles for the Human Right to Housing in LA and Beyond*. He is completing his manuscript "Incarcerating the Crisis: Race, Security, Prisons, and the Second Reconstruction" and coediting (with Laura Pulido) Clyde A. Wood's manuscript "Development Drowned and Reborn: The Blues and Bourbon Restorations in Post-Katrina New Orleans."

Paula Chakravartty

Paula Chakravartty is associate professor in the Department of Communication at the University of Massachusetts, Amherst. She has published many essays on technology, the postcolonial state, and inequality, migrant labor, race and caste, and the culture of neoliberal development. She is coauthor of *Media Policy and Globalization* (Edinburgh University Press, 2006) and coeditor of *Global Communication: Toward a Transcultural Political Economy* (Rowman and Littlefield, 2008). She is working on a manuscript on the politics of information and inequality in Brazil and India.

Ofelia Ortiz Cuevas

Ofelia Ortiz Cuevas is a visiting scholar at the Center for Social Theory and Comparative History at UCLA. She is also the research coordinator at the UC Center for New Racial Studies and UC President's Postdoctoral Fellow.

Sophie Ellen Fung

Sophie Ellen Fung graduated from the University of British Columbia (2012) with a BA in geography, specializing in human geography. She has a strong interest in the planning of sustainable communities and the politics of public spaces, and hopes to pursue a career in community planning.

Daniel J. Hammel

Daniel J. Hammel is a professor in the Department of Geography and Planning at the University of Toledo. His research focuses on fundamental changes in the geography of American inner cities—particularly the operation of the housing market and shifts in housing policy in driving nearly four decades of gentrification. He also has written about the mortgage foreclosures, the foreclosure process, and linkages between mortgage lending and foreclosures.

James Heintz

James Heintz is a research professor and associate director at the Political Economy Research Institute of the University of Massachusetts, Amherst. He has published in the areas of employment and labor markets, macroeconomic alternatives, the distributive effects of monetary policy, and development strategies in sub-Saharan African countries. Recent work with Radhika Balakrishnan and Diane Elson has examined the connections between economic policy and social and economic rights.

Bosco Ho

Bosco Ho graduated from the University of British Columbia (2012) with a BA in human geography (honors) and Asian language and culture. His undergraduate studies covered urban, economic, environmental, and political geography. His other interests include cartography, data visualization, and Apple's growing dominance in consumer technology supply chains.

Laura Hyun Yi Kang

Laura Hyun Y Kang teaches in the Department of Women's Studies at UC Irvine, where she is also affiliated with the PhD Program in Culture and

Theory and the Departments of Asian American Studies, English, and Comparative Literature. She is the author of *Compositional Subjects: Enfiguring Asian/American Women* (Duke University Press, 2002). Her new book, *The Traffic in Asian Women*, examines the prolific and shifting visibilities of "Asian women" in select local-international-regional nodes of activism, redress, and global governance.

Zachary Liebowitz

Zachary Liebowitz is in his final year of the BA program in anthropology at the University of British Columbia. His interests focus on the anthropology of architecture and design as they connect postindustrial urbanization with the evolving staples economies of contemporary forestry.

Tayyab Mahmud

Tayyab Mahmud is professor of law at Seattle University. His publications have focused on political economy, colonialism, and legal history. He is working on a book project on extraconstitutional usurpation of power in postcolonial formations.

John D. Márquez

John D. Márquez is assistant professor of African American studies and Latina/o studies at Northwestern University. He has published journal essays that theorize the origins of police brutality and discuss its impact on black and Latino politics, and book chapters that compare the plight of racial "others" in Europe and the United States. His forthcoming book (University of Texas Press) highlights the shared struggle of blacks and Latinos against racial violence in the U.S. south. He has appeared on television programs such as *NBC Nightly News* and in many major newspapers and magazines for his activism against police brutality and gang violence.

Pierson Nettling

Pierson Nettling is working toward an honors degree in human geography at the University of British Columbia. His research interests have focused primarily on deindustrialized cities in America. His work has also been published in the *Nation*.

C. S. Ponder

C. S. Ponder is a doctoral student at the geography department of the University of British Columbia, concentrating in economic and urban geography.

Her research is on the socioeconomic repercussions of the ongoing financial crisis. She holds a master's degree in economic history from Lund University.

Sarita Echavez See

Sarita Echavez See is the author of *The Decolonized Eye: Filipino American Art and Performance* (University of Minnesota Press, 2009). She is at work on a book-length project called "Essays against Accumulation." She teaches Asian American studies at the University of California, Davis.

Shawn Shimpach

Shawn Shimpach teaches film studies and media studies at the University of Massachusetts, Amherst, where he is assistant professor in the Department of Communication and a core faculty member in the Interdepartmental Program in Film Studies. He is author of the book *Television in Transition: The Life and Afterlife of the Narrative Action Hero* (Wiley-Blackwell, 2010).

Denise Ferreira da Silva

Denise Ferreira da Silva is professor and chair in ethics at Queen Mary, University of London. Her writings advance a racial/postcolonial critique of modern thought, which engages critical legal theory, political theory, historical materialism, feminist theory, critical racial and ethnic studies, and postcolonial/ global studies. She is author of *Toward a Global Idea of Race* (University of Minnesota Press, 2007). She is completing two book projects, *The Critique of Racial Violence* and *Human, Race, Rights*. She is a coeditor for the Routledge series Law and the Postcolonial: Ethics, Politics, Economy

Catherine R. Squires

Catherine R. Squires is the Cowles Professor of Journalism, Diversity, and Equality at the University of Minnesota. She is the author of *Dispatches from the Color Line* (State University Press of New York, 2007) and *African Americans and the Media* (Polity, 2009). She has published work on media and identity in many outlets, including *Critical Studies in Media Communication*, and *Critical Rhetorics of Race* (New York University Press, 2011).

Michael J. Watts

Michael J. Watts is Class of 1963 Professor of Geography and Development Studies at the University of California, Berkeley, where he has taught for over thirty years. A Guggenheim Fellow in 2003, he served as director of the Institute of International Studies from 1994 to 2004. His research has addressed food and energy security, rural development, and land reform in Africa, South Asia, and Vietnam. Over the last twenty years he has written extensively on the oil industry in West Africa and the Gulf of Guinea. The author of fourteen books and over two hundred articles, he has received awards and fellowships from such organizations as the Social Science Research Council, the MacArthur Foundation, the National Science Foundation, and the Guggenheim Foundation. His latest book with photographer Ed Kashi is *The Curse of the Black Gold* (powerHouse, 2008). Watts has consulted for a number of development agencies including OXFAM and UNDP, and has provided expert testimony for governmental and other agencies. Watts is chair of the board of trustees of the Social Science Research Council and serves on a number of boards of nonprofit organizations, including the Pacific Institute.

Elvin Wyly

Elvin Wyly is associate professor of geography and chair of the Urban Studies Coordinating Committee at the University of British Columbia. He teaches and publishes on urban social and spatial inequality, public policy, strategic positivism, and radical statistics.

Index